Building Scalable and High-Performance Java™ Web Applications Using J2EE™ Technology

Building Scalable and High-Performance Java™ Web Applications Using J2EE™ Technology

Greg Barish

✦✦ Addison-Wesley

Boston • San Francisco • New York • Toronto • Montreal
London • Munich • Paris • Madrid • Capetown
Sydney • Tokyo • Singapore • Mexico City

Many of the designations used by manufacturers and sellers to distinguish their products are claimed as trademarks. Where those designations appear in this book, and Addison-Wesley was aware of a trademark claim, the designations have been printed with initial capital letters or in all capitals.

The author and publisher have taken care in the preparation of this book, but make no expressed or implied warranty of any kind and assume no responsibility for errors or omissions. No liability is assumed for incidental or consequential damages in connection with or arising out of the use of the information or programs contained herein.

The publisher offers discounts on this book when ordered in quantity for special sales. For more information, please contact:

Pearson Education Corporate Sales Division
201 W. 103rd Street
Indianapolis, IN 46290
(800) 428-5331
corpsales@pearsoned.com

Visit AW on the Web: *www.aw.com/cseng/*

Library of Congress Cataloging-in-Publication Data

Barish, Greg.
  Building scalable and high-performance Java Web applications using J2EE
  technology / Greg Barish.
      p. cm.
  Includes bibliographical references and index.
  ISBN 0-201-72956-3 (alk. paper)
  1. Java (Computer program language) 2. Web sites—Design. I. Title.

  QA76.73.J38 B36 2002
  005.2'762--dc21

                                                    2001056071

Pearson Education, Inc.
Rights and Contracts Department
75 Arlington Street, Suite 300
Boston, MA 02116
Fax: (617) 848-7047

ISBN 0-201-72956-3
Text printed on recycled paper
1 2 3 4 5 6 7 8 9 10—CRW—0504030201
First printing, December 2001

To Seong Rim,
for her love and inspiration

Contents

Preface

When it comes to building Web applications, there are two fundamental problems. One is that there are flat-out too many choices in terms of how to develop them. These days, one can choose from literally hundreds of languages and technologies that claim to make Web application development easier. The other problem is that there is a lack of common knowledge about how to deploy them in a way that yields high performance and scalability—traits essential to anything accessible over the Internet.

Fortunately, there are now some unifying application infrastructures that not only simplify Web application development but also encourage efficient deployment. One of the most popular approaches is proposed by the Java 2 Enterprise Edition (J2EE) specification. The J2EE spec leverages and extends the existing foundation of Java technology so that engineers can build Web applications that encourage high performance and scalability. One of the most compelling features of J2EE is its built-in support for key low-level platform services such as transaction management, naming, and security, each of which normally requires substantial engineering time and expertise.

Although it unifies much of Web application development and deployment, comprehending J2EE is daunting. To understand it, you need to read either the spec itself or a lot of books on each specific J2EE technology (e.g., Servlets, EJBs, and JDBC). The spec itself is dry and not meant to be a practical resource. And the problem with reading books about each technology is that they tend to be overly long—some EJB-only books exceed 1000 pages. Such books also tend to be full of irrelevant details and appendices that you don't need or could have found easily online. Finally, most of them do not address the unspoken parts of Web application design—for example, database design and networking efficiency.

Goals

Building Scalable and High-Performance Java™ Web Applications Using J2EE™ Technology was written to fill the need for an applied summary of how to build high-performance and scalable Web applications using J2EE technology. This called for a delicate balance—introduce a set of new technologies and their relationships and provide enough examples so you can actually see how things work. The objective was not to go too far overboard to produce an overly long book that lacked focus (or one that could cause injury when lifted). Thus, the goal was to produce a concise but practical summary.

We'll cover all the key elements of J2EE—the spec itself, servlets, JSP, EJBs, messaging, JDBC, and more. Along the way, there will be plenty of examples. Many will be presented with deliberate brevity, the idea being that it is better to cut to the chase of how to use a technology rather than to show so many gory details that the readers' eyes start to glaze over. As we already know, there are plenty of books that address such details. When you've decided which parts of J2EE are relevant to you, you might consult those books as a complement to this one.

In addition to being a well-rounded summary, another purpose is to fill in the holes about Web application design that the J2EE specification simply does not address. Although the specification shows how to connect different Java technologies and APIs to build an enterprise application infrastructure, it does not address related issues such as networking and database design. For example, even though the specification describes how HTTP is used to communicate with a J2EE system and how JDBC can be used to communicate to a relational database from a J2EE system, it contains no details about HTTP or relational databases. As any seasoned Web application designer knows, understanding both is critical when designing your system for high performance and scalability.

In summary, this book has the following goals:

- To define and identify the challenges associated with building scalable and high-performance Web applications.
- To provide you with a J2EE technology roadmap for designing Web applications.
- To describe concisely key J2EE technologies, emphasizing details related to high performance and scalability.
- To fill in the gaps of Web application design that the J2EE spec leaves out, such as important details related to HTTP and database design—two of the most common J2EE-related technologies.
- To demonstrate the benefits of various specific J2EE design decisions, illustrating these differences with real performance graphs and charts.

This last item is targeted at making the suggestions in this book more compelling. For example, it is only somewhat comforting to say things like "connection pooling is good," which is the approach that many books take. It is more convincing and clear if real performance charts and graphs back up these claims. This book aims to achieve that goal.

Audience

Building Scalable and High-Performance Java™ Web Applications Using J2EE ™ Technology is written for any engineer or architect who is proficient with Java and wants to build Java-based Web applications for performance and scalability, but does not yet understand how J2EE can be used toward that goal or how all of its underlying technologies work.

This book is also for those who want to see beyond the J2EE spec, in particular, to consider current issues in efficient networking and database design in addition to future issues related to Web services technologies such as XML and SOAP.

Finally, this book is for those already familiar with some parts of J2EE technology (e.g., Java Servlets), but not others (e.g., the Java Message Service).

A Note about Performance Measurements

Throughout this book, there are various performance measurements and comparisons. Although the same general trends apply to nearly every architecture (because the performance trends illustrated are architecture-independent), it may be useful to list the details of the system used for testing.

All tests were conducted on a Dell Latitude running a single 833 MHz Pentium III with 256 KB RAM. The operating system and application software consisted of:

- Windows 2000, Professional Edition
- Apache Web server, version 1.3.14
- Java Runtime Environment and Development Kit, version 1.3
- J2EE SDK and reference implementation, version 1.3 (Beta)
- Apache Jakarta/Tomcat servlet container, version 3.2.1
- Oracle database system, version 8.1.6

The CD-ROM

The CD-ROM that accompanies this book contains most of the source code in this book. This supplement is intended for use on Windows 95/98/NT/2000 machines running Java 1.3, the Cygwin BASH shell and accompanying utilities, and Oracle 8.1.6. For more details about the desired reference system, see the preceding list.

Using the CD-ROM is straightforward: Simply insert the disk into your CD-ROM drive and then use your Web browser to open the index.html file that resides at the top-level directory. From this initial file, you will be able to get to other parts of the included documentation, as well as the source code.

Note that to compile and run some of the source code, first you need to copy the contents of the desired directories to your local hard drive and then compile everything there. More detail about this and the requirements for compilation can be found in the top-level `index.html` file.

Onward!

My hope is that this book acts as an ongoing reference for you as your J2EE application evolves. You will need to continually make choices in terms of how to provide application functionality to your consumers, both individuals and other businesses. You will have to address questions like, "Do I place the business logic in the database or the application server?" and "Should our batch data transfer go through a Web server or a messaging server?" Independent of the details associated with each of these choices, you will want to enable such features in a way that promotes performance and scalability. This book will help you understand the tradeoffs, both general and specific, in Web application design that can help you achieve that goal.

Acknowledgments

The folks at Addison-Wesley did a wonderful job of helping me publish this book. Mary O'Brien, my editor, was an excellent source of creativity, support, encouragement, and understanding right from the start. Mary put up with my rocky schedules and, though I tried my best to disrupt the process more than once, ensured a smooth path for publication. Alicia Carey was a great coordinator and put up with my endless barrage of large-attachment-bearing e-mails. Marilyn Rash deftly led production, despite a very tight schedule. And Joan Flaherty worked tirelessly to ensure that the result was of professional quality, all the while making the process surprisingly enjoyable.

I'd also like to thank the semi-anonymous reviewers of earlier versions of the manuscript that provided constructive feedback. In particular, Scott Miller and Tripp Lilley identified a number of important areas to improve on—their attention to detail made a difference.

I could not have completed this book without the support of a wonderful family: my mom and dad (Tina and Frank), Lisa and Chris, Heather, Max, and now... Jack! Words alone cannot describe how lucky I am to have their love and encouragement.

And finally, there is Seong Rim. She suffered through my unfair schedules and constant complaining, somehow always being able to pick me up and say just the right thing. Without her in my life, I could not imagine wanting to write anything at all.

CHAPTER 1

Scalable and High-Performance Web Applications

The Emergence of Web Applications

In the span of just a few years, the Internet has transformed the way information is both provided and consumed throughout the world. Its hardware and software technologies have made it possible for anyone not only to be an information consumer, but also for nearly anyone to be an information provider. Although the Internet—specifically the World Wide Web (the Web)—has been treated seriously as a platform for information sharing among the mass public for only a short time, many organizations have managed to create useful Web applications that provide significant value to consumers.

These Web applications allow consumers to buy books and compact discs online. They enable businesses to use the Internet for secure data transactions. Workers use Web applications to find jobs; employers use them to find employees; stocks are bought and sold using online applications provided by brokerages; and travelers book flight and hotel reservations using Web applications. The list goes on and on. Obviously, many useful Web applications are available on the public Internet as well as within countless corporate intranets today.

This book describes general techniques for building *high-performance and scalable enterprise Web applications*. Generally speaking, this means building applications that are reasonably and consistently fast and have a strong, gradual tolerance for rising user and request demands. Although we will spend a lot of time considering this topic in general, the core of our discussion will be phrased in terms of a solution built around the Java 2 Enterprise Edition (J2EE) specification. Now, before we dive into the details of building these kinds of applications, it is important to identify and understand the overall problem. More specifically, it is important to define *Web applications* and *scalability*.

Basic Definitions

In this book, *Web application* has a very general definition—client/server software that is connected by Internet technologies to route the data it processes. By "Internet technologies," I mean the collection of hardware and software that comprises the network infrastructure between consumers and providers of information. Web applications can be made accessible *by specific client software or by one or more related Web pages that are logically grouped for a specific productive purpose*. That purpose can be one of any number of things, for example, to buy books, to process stock orders, or to simply exist as content to be read by the consumer.

Notice that our discussion is about Web applications, not just "Web sites." In truth, the difference between the two is essential to understanding one of the key themes of this book. Most nonengineers do not make a distinction between a Web site and a Web application. Regardless of the term, it's the thing that allows them to buy their books online, to make plane reservations, to purchase tickets, and so forth.

If you're an engineer, however, there is a difference. For you, it's likely that when someone talks about, say, the performance of a Web site, you start thinking of back-end details. And so do I. Your mind begins to consider if it's running an Apache or IIS and whether it works using Java servlets, PHP, or CGI-bin Perl scripts. This difference in thinking between engineers and nonengineers could be confusing. Engineers, by habit, tend to associate "Web site" with the server side. However, as we all know, there is more to a Web application than just the server side; there's the network and the client. So, based on just that, a Web site (server) is not the same thing as a Web application (the client, network, and server).

While this book emphasizes server-side solutions, it is also concerned with client-side and networking topics because they have a fundamental impact on how end users perceive Web applications. That is, we will be concerned with the *end-to-end* interaction with a Web site, which simply means from *client to server and back to client*. This is a reasonable focus. After all, most people who use the Web are concerned with its end-to-end behavior. If it takes them a while to buy concert tickets online, it doesn't matter if the problem is caused by a slow modem, an overtaxed server, or network congestion. Whatever the reason(s), the effect is the same—a slow application that's eating up time. As engineers, we are concerned not only that such applications might be slow for one user, but also that the system becomes slower as more users access it.

Now that we have a better fix on the scope of a Web application, let us review its core components. These are the major pieces of any online application and each represents an opportunity—a problem or a challenge, depending on how you look at it. Although you're probably familiar with the components, it doesn't hurt to make sure everyone is on the same page, especially since these terms appear throughout the book. Let's start with the client side.

Figure 1–1
Client, network, and server

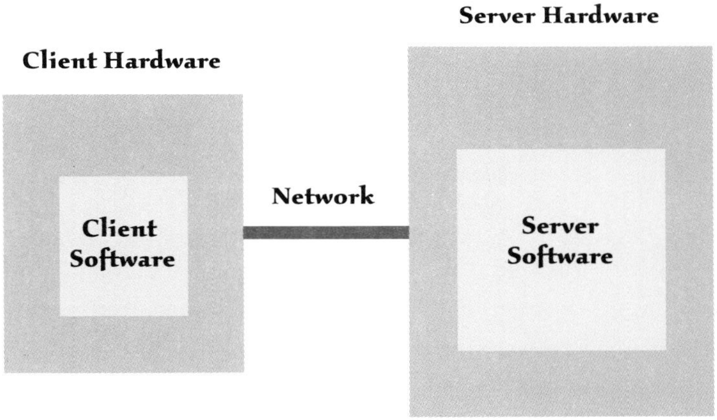

Client Hardware

Server Hardware

**Client
Software**

Network

**Server
Software**

We will say that Web applications are used by consumers via client software (i.e., Web browsers or applications that use the Web to retrieve or process data) running on client hardware (i.e., PCs, PDAs). Application data is provided and processing is handled by producers via server software (i.e., Web server, server-side component software, database) running on server hardware (i.e., high-end multiprocessor systems, clusters, etc.). Connecting the client to the server (from the modem or network port on the client device to the networking equipment on the server side) is the *networking infrastructure*. Figure 1–1 shows the client/server relationship graphically. Notice that the server side is bigger; in general, we assume that the server side has more resources at its disposal.

At this point, it is important to distinguish one piece of server software, the Web server, because it nearly always plays a central role in brokering communication (HTTP traffic) between client and server. In this book, when I refer to the "server side," I am nearly always including the Web server. When it is necessary to distinguish it from the rest of the software on the server side, I will do so explicitly.

The Nature of the Web and Its Challenges

Although Web applications have rapidly made the Internet a productive medium, the nature of the Internet poses many engineering puzzles. Even the most basic of challenges—engineering how a provider can quickly and reliably deliver information to all who want it—is neither simple nor well understood. Like other challenges, this problem's complexity has to do with the nature of the medium. The Internet is different from the information-sharing paradigms of radio, television, and newspapers for several reasons. Perhaps two of the most important reasons are its incredibly wide audience (unpredictable number of customers) and the potential at any time for that wide audience to request information from any given provider (unpredictable work demands).

Unlike in other media, Internet information providers simply do not have the ability to know their audience in advance. Newspapers, for example, know their circulation before they print each edition. They also have the advantage of being able to control their growth, making sure they have enough employees to deliver the paper daily, and have the resources and time to go from deadline on the previous night to delivery on the next morning. Furthermore, newspapers do not have to deal with sudden jumps in circulation. Compared to the Internet, the growth of big newspapers in metropolitan areas seems far more gradual. For example, when the *Washington Post* was founded in 1877, it had a circulation of 10,000. By 1998, that circulation had reached nearly 800,000 for its daily edition and more than that for its Sunday edition.[*] That's an average growth rate of just over 6,500 subscribers per year, or 17 per day.

Deployers of Web applications have a love/hate relationship with their growth rates. In one sense, they would love the gradual growth of 17 new users per day. How nice life would be if you had to worry about scaling at that rate! You could finally go home at 5 P.M., not 9:30 P.M. At the same time, such growth rates are the reason that people are so excited about Web applications—because you can potentially reach the whole world in a matter of seconds. Your growth rate out of the gate could be hundreds of thousands of users. Although this bodes well for the business side of the things, it creates a tremendous challenge in terms of dealing with such demands.

On the Internet, circulation is akin to *page hits*, that is, the number of requests for a given document. Page hits can jump wildly overnight. A favorite example in the Web-caching community is the popularity of the online distribution of the Starr report. As most Americans know, this report was put together by the Office of the Independent Counsel during the Clinton administration. Let us just say that, while it was not flattering by any means, it was eagerly awaited by both the American public and the international press corps.

When the Starr report was released online in the summer of 1998 at government Web sites, tens of thousands of people tried to download it. A representative for Sprint, Inc., one of the Internet's backbone providers, reported a surge in bandwidth demand that ranged between 10 and 20 percent above normal; a representative of AOL reported an "immediate 30 percent spike"; and NetRatings, a Nielsen-like Internet content popularity company, estimated that at one point, more than

---

[*]Source: *http://www.thewashingtonpost.com*.

one in five Web users was requesting the report or news about it. CNET.COM ran a number of stories about the event and its ramifications for Internet scalability in the Fall of 1998.*

The conclusion among network administrators and engineers was universal. There were simply too many requests to be handled at once, and the distribution mechanisms were unable to scale to demand. It was a real test of the scalability of the Internet itself. Not only were the Web servers that provided this information overloaded, but the networking infrastructure connecting consumers to providers became heavily congested and severely inefficient. The effect was much like that of a traffic jam on a freeway.

This phenomenon was unique because it demonstrated the effects of sudden popularity as well as the short-lived nature of that popularity. For example, it is unlikely that you or anyone else remembers the URL(s) where the report was first available. And it is unlikely that you have it bookmarked. Thus, even had those sites been able to accommodate the demands of the time by buying bigger and faster machines, it would likely have been money wasted because the need for those resources dropped dramatically after the public lost interest in the report.

Other media, such as radio and television, are broadcast and do not need to worry about the size of their audience affecting their ability to deliver information. Consider television or radio programs, such as the national and local news. Their programmers know in advance when they are scheduled to broadcast. They have the luxury of being able to prepare ahead of time. Even when live radio or television beckons, the fact that both media are broadcast means that there is only one audience to address. Cable companies and good old TV antennae are already in place to facilitate the transport of that information. If we all watch or listen to the same channel, we all see or hear the same program. This is not the case with Internet audiences, where it is usually impossible to prepare for every request, where every consumer of information requires a unique response, and where there is a continual need for new virtual links (HTTP connections) between consumer and provider to be both created and then destroyed.

Performance and Scalability

Have you ever gone to a Web site, clicked on a link, and really *waited* for a response? Of course you have; we all have. It's annoying and frustrating. Worst are those content-laden sites that are meant to be read like newspapers. You want to jump from link to link, but every time you click, you have to wait *seconds* (not milliseconds) for

*Source: *http://news.cnet.com/news/0-1005-204-332427.html*.

the page and the ads and the embedded applets to download. You almost begin to hate clicking on a link because you know you will have to wait. You've learned to classify this kind of site as *slow*.

Then there are sites that are suspiciously slow. In these cases, you have reason to believe that bazillions of people are trying to connect, and this mass, not the technology, is responsible for the slowness. Say you're ordering a book at a site that has just announced a 50%-off sale. Or suppose tickets for a really hot concert have just gone on sale. When you're able to connect, the site seems unresponsive. When it does respond, it crawls. You guess that the site is buckling under the demand caused by the event. You've learned to classify this kind of site as *not scalable*.

As users, we have learned what poor performance and scalability are because we have experienced them. As engineers, we would like to understand these faults better so that our own users don't experience them. Because that is the focus of this book, let's start our discussion of performance and scalability by defining our terms.

Performance

Performance can be described simply as the raw speed of your application in terms of a single user. How long does a single application-level operation take? How long does it take to search for a book? How long does it take to confirm an online registration once we click Confirm? How long does it take to check out and pay at an online store? Notice that some of these examples describe atomic operations and some don't. When describing performance, we have to be clear if we are talking about one application operation or an entire session.

Consider the user interaction required to buy an airline ticket in Figure 1–2: In this session, there are three application operations, each consisting of a roundtrip between client and server. The operations are listed in Table 1–1 with their code names.

When we are talking about the performance of an operation, such as selection, we are interested in the end-to-end time required to complete that operation. In other words, the clock starts ticking when the user clicks the button and stops ticking when the user sees the information delivered. Why all this focus on end-to-end performance?

Table 1–1: Application Operations

Code Name	User Action	Server Action
Search	Criteria specified	Search based on criteria
Selection	Flight chosen	Confirmation for that flight generated
Confirmation	Flight confirmed	Confirmation processed

Figure 1–2
Application
operations
associated
with buying
an airline
ticket

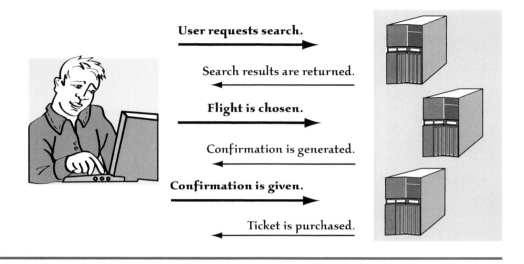

We could, of course, judge performance by measuring the speed of the Web server's response, of the network, of our database retrievals, and so on. But we know that all of these performance marks are irrelevant when compared to the overall time for a logical operation. Although unit performance numbers make us happy or proud (especially if we designed that piece of the application!), end-to-end performance is the one that really counts—this is the metric that either scares users off or wins their loyalty. And thus, this is the one that can spell life or death for your application.

Addressing end-to-end performance means making operations faster for the user. To do that, we can improve the unit performance of some of the components involved in the operation(s). For example, we can improve the performance of the Web server, the database, or the application servers. The exact solution (e.g., better algorithms, more efficient queries, etc.) depends on the unit being tuned. The point is that measuring performance should be a top-down process: Start with the user, move to the components, and then to parts in the components. Look for trends and ask if a single instance of poor performance can be traced to a larger, general problem.

Scalability

Informally, engineers describe the challenge of dealing with large audiences and high demand as a problem of **scalability**. More specifically, we say that a Web application can scale if it continues to be available and functional at consistent speeds as the number of users and requests continues to grow, even to very high numbers. A provider's inability to deliver a document, such as the Starr report, because of server overload was thus a problem of scalability. Note that this definition has nothing to do with performance. As long as a slow application continues to provide consistent performance in the wake of rising demand, it is classified as scalable!

Now, although *scalability* is commonly defined strictly as a measurement of resiliency under ever-increasing user load, nobody expects a single instance of an application server on a single machine to accommodate millions of users. Often people consider how well an application can "scale up" by describing how effective it is to add resources, such as more CPUs, more memory, or more disks. An application is considered to scale up well if it requires additional resources at a low rate. For example, if we need to add 300MB RAM per 10 concurrent users on our system, we are in trouble. As I discuss later, this scale-up attribute is often represented as a cost, for example, a cost per concurrent transaction.

Generally, three techniques can be employed to improve scalability:

- Increase the resources (bigger machines, more disk, more memory).
- Improve the software.
- Increase the resources *and* improve the software.

Although the long-term answer is the third technique, our bias is toward the second. Good design at the beginning of a project is the most cost-effective way to improve scalability. No doubt you will need greater resources to deal with higher demands, but this is never the whole story. Although it can take the purchaser part of the distance, throwing money at the problem cannot ensure scalability. I don't deny the need to spend money at certain points in the process. Rather, I suggest strategic places to spend and strategic opportunities during the design that can give application designers the biggest bang for their buck, thereby reducing their need to purchase more resources than necessary.

The Internet Medium

Six attributes of the Internet as a medium compound the challenge of delivering performance and scalability. The better we understand and appreciate these attributes, the more strategic we can be in meeting the challenge to build Web applications that perform and scale well.

First, as mentioned earlier, there is potentially a *wide audience* for Web application providers to manage—wider than in any other medium. Second, the Web is an *interactive* medium: Consumers not only receive information, they also submit it. Third, the Internet is *dynamic* in the sense that a given user request does not always result in the same server-side response. Fourth, the Internet as a utility is *always on* and providers have no guarantees about when and how often their information will be accessed. Fifth, providing information over the Internet is an *integrated* process that often depends on the coordination of multiple provider subsystems to deliver information. And sixth, providers *lack complete control* in terms of the delivery of information to consumers: There are many networking elements that exist between provider and consumer, most of which are not controlled by the provider.

Some of these attributes may seem obvious; some may not. In either case, thinking about the details and their implications will prepare you for the solutions part of this book.

Wide Audience

I'm not going to beat you over the head with the fact that millions of people use the Internet every day. That is obvious and the increasing numbers are the primary reason that application architects worry about things like scalability in the first place. However, I will inform you of a few things that you may not know—or just may not appreciate, yet.

One is that there is another Internet "audience" to consider, one that is not often addressed. This quieter, hidden, but rapidly growing group of Web clients are better known as "bots." If you are familiar with search engine technology, you already know that search engines use automated softbots to "spider" (recursively traverse) the Web and update search engine indices. This process has been going on since search engines were first deployed; bots are a simple example of one type of *information agent*.

Today's bots are just the tip of the iceberg. More sophisticated information agents are just around the corner that will allow users to monitor multiple sites continuously and automatically. For example, instead of using the Web interactively to watch and participate in online auctions (like those at eBay and Yahoo), users will configure information agents to watch continuously and bid automatically. This is an inevitable and obvious future direction for the Web: People want to do more than sit around watching their monitors all day, manually hunting for information.

Bots and information agents are particularly fond of things like data feeds, which are information sources that continually change and require monitoring. When the Internet was first being commercialized, it was popular to connect real-time data feeds (such as the newswire services) and build access methods to them via Web applications. This trend shows no sign of slowing; in fact, it threatens to become much greater as Web applications gradually become data feeds in themselves.

I've avoided boring, albeit frightening, statistics about the growing number of human Internet users. Instead, I've reminded you that there are and will be new types of application clients, not just those with two eyes. An increasing number of information agents will automate Web querying and a growing trend will be to treat Web applications like data feeds. In short, the Web's audience is definitely growing, not to mention changing, and so are its demands. What's more, this newer audience is persistent and regular, and does not mind testing the 24x7 feature of the Web and its applications!

Interactive

On the Internet, consumers query providers for information. Unlike in other media, information is not distributed at the whim of the provider. Instead, consumers request information via queries, which consist of a series of interactions between the client and server.

In addition to querying, consumer requests can contain submitted information that must be processed. This submission mechanism can be explicit or implicit. Explicit submission is the user's deliberate transmission of information to the provider, such as a completed HTML form. In contrast, implicit submission is the provision of data through the user's Web session. Cookies are a good example of this, in that they consist of data that is chosen by either the provider (e.g., for page tracking) or the consumer (e.g., for personalization).

Regardless of how the information is submitted, the application's processing must often be based on this information. Thus, the Internet is not simply a library where clients request items that exist on shelves; rather, requests involve calculations or processing, sometimes leading to a unique result. Furthermore, the interactive nature of the Web means that a request cannot be fulfilled in advance—instead, the application must respond at the time the request is made, even though substantial processing may be associated with that request.

Dynamic

Web applications present information that depends on data associated with the user or session. As far as the user goes, countless demographic and historical session attributes can make a difference in how an application responds. The response may also depend on things unrelated to the user, such as a temporal variable (e.g., the season or the day or the week) or some other external real-time data (e.g., the current number of houses for sale). In any case, the data being generated by a Web application is often dynamic and a function based on user and/or session information.

The main problem that a dynamic Web application creates for the designer is the inability to use the results of prior work. For example, if you use a Web application to search for a house online, searching with the same criteria one week from the date of the first search may very well return different results. Of course, this is not always the case. If you conduct the same house search 10 minutes after the first one, you will very likely get the same results both times. Obviously, the designer must know when it is safe to reuse results and when it is not.

There is a subtle relationship between interactive and dynamic application behavior. To avoid confusion, keep the following in mind: Interactivity has to do with the Web application executing in response to a user, whereas dynamism has to do with the response being a product of the user, her response, or some temporal or external variable. Thus, dynamic behavior is the more general notion: An application response is the product of a set of variables, some user-specified, some not. Interactivity is simply one means to achieve a dynamic response. Put another way, interactivity describes a cause; dynamism describes an effect.

Always On

This Internet is never supposed to sleep. Banks advertise Web banking 24 hours a day, 7 days a week. This 24x7 mentality is part of what makes the Internet so enticing for users. People naturally assume that, at any time, it exists as an available resource. However nice this feature is for users, it is equally daunting for Web application designers. A good example of what can happen when an application is not available 24x7 is the trouble users had with eBay, the online auctioneer, in late 1999 and 2000.

During various system or software upgrades over that time, eBay suffered intermittent problems that made it unavailable to users. In June of 1999, it was unavailable for 22 hours. Since the purpose of eBay's service is to manage millions of time-limited auctions, its core business was directly affected. Instead of selling to the highest bidder, some sellers were forced to sell to the "only bidder." Users complained, demanding a reduction in fees. The problems made the news, and the company was forced to issue apologies in addition to refunding some fees. This is not to say that eBay is not a scalable service or that the system is always unstable; indeed, eBay is one of the most trafficked sites on the Internet, and except in rare instances, has done a tremendous amount of successful 24x7 processing.

However, this simple example does underscore the importance of 24x7 when it comes to Web applications. Nobody will write news stories about how well you perform 24x7 service, but they will definitely take you to task for glitches when you don't. These problems can affect your whole company, especially if part of its revenue comes via the Web.

Observant readers might argue that failure to provide 24x7 service is not a question of scalability but of *reliability*. True, the inability to provide service because of a system failure is a question of reliability and robustness. From the practical standpoint of the user, however, it does not matter. Whether the application is unavailable because of a power problem with the site's Internet service provider (as was the case in one of eBay's outages) or because the system can't handle a million simultaneous users, the result is the same: The application is unavailable.

Integrated

When consumers request information, providers often refer to multiple local and remote sources to integrate several pieces of information in their responses. For example, if you use the Internet to make an airline reservation, it is common for multiple systems (some of which are not directly connected to the Internet) to be indirectly involved in the processing of your reservation. The "confirmation code" you receive when the reservation is made comes only after all steps of the transaction have been completed successfully.

Integration on the server side is common for most Web applications. To some extent, this is a medium-term problem. The Web is a young technology and most of its important processing still involves some legacy or intermediate proprietary systems. These systems have proved reliable and have seemed scalable. Certainly, they are still part of the loop because organizations believe in their ability to handle workloads, but the question is whether these systems are ready for Internet-level scale.

Consider an airline that migrates its ticketing to the Web. To do so, server-side processing is required to connect to a remote, proprietary invoice database for each request. In the past, hundreds of phone-based human agents had no trouble using such a system to do processing. But it may be the case that, for example, there are some hard limits to the number of concurrent connections to this database. When there were never more than a few hundred agents, these limits were never exposed. However, putting such a system in the server-side mix may turn out to be the bottleneck in a Web application.

Lack of Complete Control

To a provider of information, one of the most frustrating aspects about the Web is the fact that, no matter how much money is thrown at improving application scalability, it does not mean that the application will become scalable. The culprit here is the Internet itself. While its topology of interconnected networks enables information to be delivered from anywhere to anywhere, it delivers very few quality of service (QoS) guarantees. No matter how much time you spend tuning the client and server sides of a Web application, no authority is going to ensure that data will travel from your server to your clients at quality or priority any better than that of a student downloading MP3 files all night. And despite your best efforts, an important client that relies on a sketchy ISP with intermittent outages may deem your application slow or unreliable, though no fault of your own.

In short, the problem is decentralization. For critical Web applications, designers want complete control of the problem, but the reality is that they can almost never have it unless they circumvent the Web. This is another reminder that the solution to scalable Web applications consists of more than writing speedy server-side code. Sure, that can help, but it is by no means the whole picture.

When we talk about the lack of control over the network, we are more precisely referring to the inability to reserve bandwidth and the lack of knowledge or control over the networking elements that make up the path from client to server. Without being able to reserve bandwidth between a server and all its clients, we cannot schedule a big event that will bring in many HTTP requests and be guaranteed that they can get through. Although we can do much to widen the path in certain areas (from the server side to the ISP), we cannot widen it everywhere.

In terms of lack of knowledge about networking elements, we have to consider how clients reach servers. On the Internet, the mechanism for reaching a server from a client involves querying a series of routing tables. Without access or control over those tables, there is no way that designers can ensure high quality of service.

Techniques like Web caching and content distribution allow us to influence QoS somewhat, but they don't provide guarantees. As it turns out, the lack of control over the underlying network represents the biggest question mark in terms of consistent application performance. We simply cannot understand or address the inefficiencies of every path by which a client connects to our application. The best we can do is design and deploy for efficiency and limit our use of the network, and thus limit performance variability, when possible.

Measuring Performance and Scalability

Thus far, I have defined the problem of performance and scalability in the context of Web applications, but I have not said much about their measurement. The measurement of performance and scalability is a weighty subject, and is different from the focus of this book. However, as you apply the various techniques that we cover here to your systems, you will want some simple measurements of the success of your efforts. In this section, we'll cover a few metrics that will tell you if your application is fast and scalable.

Measuring Performance

It's fairly easy to measure performance. We can use the application being tested or we can design an automatic benchmark and observe the original speed of the application against it. Then we can make changes to the software or hardware and determine if the execution time has improved. This is a very simple approach, but by far the most common metric we will use in our study.

It is important that, when measuring performance in this way, we identify the complete path of particular application operation. That is, we have to decompose it into its parts and assign values to each. Let us return to an earlier example, that of buying airline tickets online, and imagine that we're analyzing the performance of the "confirmation" process, which takes 2.8 seconds. Table 1–2 shows one possible set of results.

The way to read this table is to consider that completing the operation in the first (far left) column occurs at some point in time offset by the user's click (shown in the second column) and thus some percentage of time (shown in the third column) of the end-to-end execution. Some of this requires interpretation. For example, "Web server gets request" does not mean that the single act of getting of the request is responsible for over 6 percent of the execution time. It means that 6 percent of the execution time is spent between the initial user's click and the Web server's getting the request; thus, 6 percent was essentially required for one-way network communication. Building these kinds of tables is useful because it allows you to focus your efforts on the bottlenecks that count. For example, in Table 1–2, we can clearly see that the database query is the bottleneck.

To build accurate tables requires two important features. One is that your system be instrumented as much as possible; that is, all components should have logging

Table 1–2: Confirmation Process

Unit Action	Elapsed Time of Action (ms)	End-to-End Time (%)
User clicks	0	N/A
Web server gets request	170	6.07
Servlet gets request	178	0.29
EJB server gets request	1.68	
Database query starts	440	7.68
Database query ends	2250	64.64
EJB server replies	2280	1.07
Servlet replies	2360	2.86
User gets information	2800	15.71

features that allow them to be debugged or benchmarked. Web servers, become familiar with how these systems allow logging to be turned on and off. Make sure that you turn on logging for benchmark testing but turn it off when resuming deployment; if it's on, logging will slow down your application. Also, your code is actually the *least* likely place to be instrumented. Thus, it can be good to place some well-chosen logging statements in your code. For example, if an application server makes three queries (as part of a single transaction) before replying, it would be useful to put logging statements before each query.

The second important requirement is clock synchronization. The components being measured may be on different machines and without synchronizing your clocks, you can mistakenly assess too little or too much blame to an action that is actually much faster than you thought. Exact synchronization of clocks is a bit unrealistic, but as long as you know the clocks' relative drifts, you should be able to compensate in your calculations. Don't overdo synchronization or calibration—for example, being off by less than a hundred milliseconds for an entire operation is not a big deal because it won't be perceptible.

Beyond Benchmarking

In addition to benchmarking, there are other types of performance measurements that are well-suited to certain classes of problems. For example, suppose your Web applications are very CPU bound. To improve performance, you can add multiple processors to your system or process the problem over a cluster of workstations. Both approaches assume that it is possible to either automatically parallelize your computations or leverage explicit parallelization (i.e., thread use) and allocate parallel blocks of instructions to different CPUs/workstations. Whichever solution you choose, you will need to measure its net effect. If you don't, then you're shooting in the dark.

When trying to assess improvement in pure computational performance, we can measure the **speedup** associated with that computation. Speedup is generally defined as:

$$\text{Speedup} = T_{old}/T_{new}$$

where T_{old} is the execution time under the previous computational scenario and T_{new} is the execution time under the new scenario.

The term *scenario* is general because there are two general ways to investigate speedup: at the software level and at the hardware level. At the software level, this means changing the program code: If a program takes 10 seconds to run with the old code and 5 seconds to run with the new code, the speedup is obviously 2. At the hardware level, this means adding processors or cluster nodes. Correspondingly, for multiprocessor or cluster-based systems, the speedup metric is commonly redefined as:

$$\text{Speedup} = T_1/T_p$$

where T_1 is the execution time with one processor and T_p is the execution time when the program is run on p processors.

Ideally, speedup increases linearly, as processors are added to a system. In reality, however, this is never the case. All sorts of issues—processor-to-processor communication cost, program data hazards, and the like—contribute to an overall overhead of computing something on p processors instead of one.

Measuring Scalability

Scalability is almost as easy to measure as performance is. We know that scalability refers to an application's ability to accommodate rising resource demand gracefully, without a noticeable loss in QoS. To measure scalability, it would seem that we need to calculate how well increasing demand is handled. But how exactly do we do this?

Let's consider a simple example. Suppose that we deploy an online banking application. One type of request that clients can make is to view recent bank transactions. Suppose that when a single client connects to the system, it takes a speedy 10 ms of server-side time to process this request. Note that network latency and other client or network issues affecting the delivery of the response will increase the end-to-end response time; for example, maybe end-to-end response time will be 1,000 ms for a single client. But, to keep our example simple, let's consider just server-side time.

Next, suppose that 50 users simultaneously want to view their recent transactions, and that it takes an average of 500 ms of server-side time to process each of these 50 concurrent requests. Obviously, our server-side response time has slowed because of the concurrency of demands. That is to be expected.

Our next question might be: How well does our application scale? To answer this, we need some scalability metrics, such as the following:

- *Throughput*—the rate at which transactions are processed by the system
- *Resource usage*—the usage levels for the various resources involved (CPU, memory, disk, bandwidth)
- *Cost*—the price per transaction

A more detailed discussion of these and other metrics can be found in *Scaling for E-Business: Technologies, Models, Performance, and Capacity Planning* (Menasce and Almeida, 2000). Measuring resource use is fairly easy; measuring throughput and cost requires a bit more explanation.

What is the throughput in both of the cases described, with one user and with 50 users? To calculate this, we can take advantage of something called Little's law, a simple but very useful measure that can be applied very broadly. Consider the simple

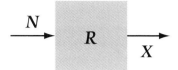

Figure 1–3
Little's law

Throughput = $X = N/R$.

black box shown in Figure 1–3. Little's law says that if this box contains an average of N users, and the average user spends R seconds in that box, then the throughput X of that box is roughly

$$X = N/R.$$

Little's law can be applied to almost any device: a server, a disk, a system, or a Web application. Indeed, any system that employs a notion of input and output and that can be considered a black box is a candidate for this kind of analysis.

Armed with this knowledge, we can now apply it to our example. Specifically, we can calculate application throughput for different numbers of concurrent users. Our N will be transactions, and since R is in seconds, we will measure throughput in terms of transactions per second (tps). At the same time, let's add some data to our banking example. Table 1–3 summarizes what we might observe, along with throughputs calculated using Little's law. Again, keep in mind that this is just an example; I pulled these response times from thin air. Even so, they are not unreasonable.

Based on these numbers, how well does our application scale? It's still hard to say. We can quote numbers, but do they mean anything? Not really. The problem here is that we need a comparison—something to hold up against our mythical application so we can judge how well or how poorly our example scales.

Table 1–3: Sample Application Response and Throughput Times

Concurrent Users	Average Response Time (ms)	Throughput (tps)
1	10	100
50	500	100
100	1200	83.333
150	2200	68.182
200	4000	50

One good comparison is against a "linearly scalable" version of our application, by which I mean an application that continues to do exactly the same amount of work per second no matter how many clients use it. This is not to say the average response time will remain constant—no way. In fact, it will increase, but in a perfectly predictable manner. However, our throughput will remain constant. Linearly scalable applications are perfectly scalable in that their performance degrades at a constant rate directly proportional to their demands.

If our application is indeed linearly scalable, we'll see the numbers shown in Table 1–4. Notice that our performance degrades in a constant manner: The average response time is ten times the number of concurrent users. However, our throughput is constant at 100 tps.

To understand this data better, and how we can use it in a comparison with our original mythical application results, let's view their trends in graph form. Figure 1–4 illustrates average response time as a function of the number of concurrent users; Figure 1–5 shows throughput as a function of the number of users. These graphs also compare our results with results for an idealized system whose response time increases linearly with the number of concurrent users.

Figure 1–4 shows that our application starts to deviate from linear scalability after about 50 concurrent users. With a higher number of concurrent sessions, the line migrates toward an exponential trend. Notice that I'm drawing attention to the nature of the line, not the numbers to which the line corresponds. As we discussed earlier, scalability analysis is not the same as performance analysis; (that is, a slow application is not necessarily unable to scale). While we are interested in the average time per request from a performance standpoint, we are more interested in *performance trends* with higher concurrent demand, or how well an application deals with increased load, when it comes to scalability.

Figure 1–5 shows that a theoretical application should maintain a constant number of transactions per second. This makes sense: Even though our average response

Table 1–4: Linearly Scalable Application Response and Throughput Times

Concurrent Users	Average Response Time (ms)	Throughput (tps)
1	10	100
50	500	100
100	1000	100
150	1500	100
200	2000	100

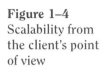

Figure 1–4
Scalability from
the client's point
of view

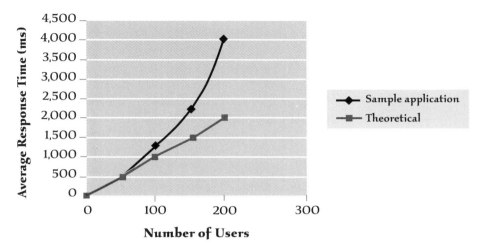

Figure 1–5
Scalability from
the server's
point of view

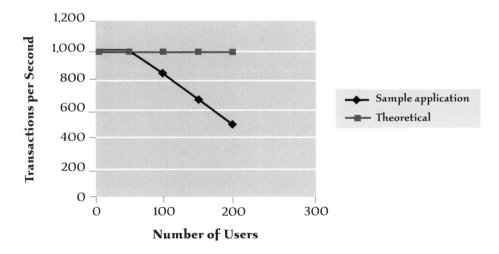

time may increase, the amount of work done per unit time remains the same. (Think of a kitchen faucet: It is reasonable that even though it takes longer to wash 100 dishes than to wash one, the number of dishes per second should remain constant.) Notice that our mythical application becomes less productive after 50 concurrent users. In this sense, it would be better to replicate our application and limit the number of concurrent users to 50 if we want to achieve maximum throughput.

Analyzing response time and throughput trends, as we have done here, is important for gauging the scalability of your system. Figures 1–4 and 1–5 show how to compare an application and its theoretical potential. Figure 1–4 illustrates the efficiency from the client's point of view, where the focus is on latency; Figure 1–5 shows application efficiency from the server's point of view, where the focus is on productivity (work done per time unit).

Throughput and Price/Performance

In measuring throughput, we have ignored the cost of the systems we are analyzing. If a system costing $100 can handle 1,000 transactions per second and a system costing $500,000 can handle 1,200 transactions per second, the latter obviously has better throughput—but it's gained at a much higher cost. The idea of measuring throughput and its relationship to price is something that has been popularized by the Transaction Processing Council (TPC), which has created database benchmarks, better known as the TPC-style benchmarks.

There are three TPC benchmarks: TPC-A, TPC-B, and TPC-C. The most recently developed (as of this writing) is the TPC-C. It measures database transaction processing in terms of how efficiently it supports a mythical ordering system. Specifically, it measures how many "new order" transactions can be handled while the system is busy handling four other types of order-related transactions (payment, status, etc.). While the TPC specification is meant to measure database throughput, you can use the same principle with your systems. After all, Web application transactions are at their core a set of database transactions.

Although it is unlikely that you will benchmark your system against another, you can measure how well your system is improving or lagging over its own evolution. For example, if release 1 of your application requires $100,000 worth of hardware and software and nets 10,000 transaction per second, you can calculate a price/performance index by dividing the price by the performance:

$$100,000/10,000 = $10 \text{ per transaction.}$$

This doesn't mean that it costs $10 to execute a transaction on your system. It is simply a measure of throughput as it relates to the overall cost of the system. Suppose that a year later, release 2 of your application requires $150,000 worth of hardware and handles 40,000 transactions per second. The release 2 price/performance index would be:

$$150,000/40,000 = $3.75 \text{ per transaction.}$$

Obviously, release 2 is more efficient than release 1 by evidence of its lower price/ performance figure.

My interest in price/performance in this section is a reminder of the more general bias throughout this book: *Favor architectural strategies over resources when developing your application.* Once the application is deployed, you can always buy more resources to meet demand. On the other hand, rewriting code, changing designs, or re-architecting your application after deployment comes at a much higher cost. The best solution is obviously good design at the outset for scalability and performance. Not only does this eliminate the need for massive design changes after deployment, but it also typically leads to more cost-efficient resource acquisitions. CPUs, memory, disk, and other resources are purchased less frequently for applications that are inherently fast and scalable. In short, well-designed systems adapt and evolve much better than poorly designed ones do.

Scalability and Performance Hints

Nearly all of the chapters in this book include a section on hints for scalability and performance. The idea is to provide some conclusions or suggestions that have to do with the material presented in the chapter. Since we've just started our journey, there is nothing terribly complicated to conclude. However, we can remind ourselves of a few useful things covered earlier.

Think End-to-End

If nothing else, this chapter should have made clear that scalability and performance are end-to-end challenges. Don't just focus on the server; consider client and network issues as well. Spending all your time optimizing your server and database is not going to help if one part of your solution doesn't scale. You will always be hampered by your weakest link, so spend more time thinking about all of the parts involved in an application session, not just the ones you suspect or the ones you read articles about. Keep an open mind: While many applications face similar dilemmas, not all have the same clients, the same growth rate, or the same 24x7 demands.

Scalability Doesn't Equal Performance

Another thing you should have gotten out of this chapter is that scalability is not the same as performance. The two have different metrics and measure distinct things.

Performance has to do with the raw speed of the application, perhaps in a vacuum where only one user is using it. When we talk about performance, we mean response time—it's as simple as that. Optimizing performance has to do with improving the performance for that one user. If we measure average response time of 100 concurrent users, our performance challenge is to improve the average response time of the same 100 concurrent users.

Scalability, on the other hand, has to do with the ability to accommodate increasing demand. A primary metric for scalability is throughput, which measures transactions or users per second. There is no such thing as infinite scalability—the ability to handle arbitrary demand. Every application has its limits. In fact, for many deployments it is satisfying to achieve just linear scalability, although the optimizer in all of us wants to achieve much better than that. Not unexpectedly, the most successful examples of scalability are those that simply minimize the rate at which new resources are required.

Measure Scalability by Comparison

Scalability is difficult to ensure because its metrics don't allow you to compare it easily to an average (nonlinearly scalable) baseline and make some conclusions. One thing you can do, however, is measure how the scalability of your application evolves. First, define what kind of throughput is reasonable: Create (or buy) an automated stress-testing system that identifies whether your current system achieves that goal for a reasonable number of users. Then, as the application evolves, periodically retest and determine if it's improving relative to past scalability—this is without a doubt something that even your end users will notice.

Another strategy is to measure throughput as the number of users increases and identify important trends. For example, measure the throughput of your applications with 100 concurrent transactions, then with 1,000, and then with 10,000 transactions. Look at how your throughput changes and see how it compares with linear scalability. This comparison will likely give you a better sense for whether your application architecture is inherently scalable.

Summary

In this first chapter, we focused on defining Web applications and the nature of their deployment on the Internet. We also defined and discussed performance and scalability—two important concepts that will remain our focus throughout this book—and described their related metrics.

One very important subtheme of this chapter was the focus on the entire application, not just its parts. Although it may be academically interesting to optimize our bandwidth or CPU use, the end user does not care about such things. Instead, he or she thinks only in terms of time, that is, whether the application is fast. And he or she wants that same response time regardless of how many other users are on the system at the same time. Now that we are focused on the goal of end-to-end performance and scalability, let's move on to talk in more detail about application architectures and the specific challenges that lie ahead.

CHAPTER 2

Web Application Architecture

In a very general sense, this book is about designing efficient Web application architectures. Before we can think about designing an architecture, however, we need to establish some requirements. In this chapter, I propose some very general application requirements, essential to many types of applications. Based on these requirements, we will be able to envision an abstract Web application architecture. Later, we will ground that abstract architecture in something more realistic, in particular to various parts of the Java 2 Enterprise Edition (J2EE) solution. My intention is to gradually define and describe the parts of an application in increasing levels of detail so that we can maintain an end-to-end view throughout our journey.

Although it is tempting, I resist the urge to center this book on a single example, such as online trading, auctions, or portal services. Unfortunately, each of these examples has traits that do not lend themselves to all the performance and scalability challenges we want to cover. For example, an online brokerage application has real-time features, but it is not necessarily a good example of a 24x7 application because its usage varies widely when normal trading hours are over. Portal services, on the other hand, are a better 24x7 example, but they lack the real-time demands of an online brokerage.

For these reasons, I use a prototypical architecture and then relate examples as they become relevant throughout the text. These details are established to set boundaries on solving the problems of scalability and high performance. Although there are many ways to design a Web site, we will focus on the most common current trends while giving a nod to alternative and future paths.

Web Application Terminology

To start, let's introduce a few terms related to Web applications that we will be using throughout our discussion.

As already discussed, a **Web application** is provided by a server and used by a client, and it spans the network distance between those two points. To use an application, clients are required to establish one or more **connections** with the server so that the data to be processed can be routed. In conversing with the server, a client makes a **request** that is typically answered by a server **reply**.

A **transaction** at the Web application level is a request-and-reply dialogue that corresponds to a single logical application behavior. That is, the request made by the client leads to the invocation of application logic on the server side and then eventually a reply to the client. For example, when you use an online application to purchase a book, you click the Buy button. Clicking that button starts a series of activities that refer to the general application notion of "adding a book to your shopping cart." When you are ready to purchase the books selected, clicking a Check Out button corresponds to "adding up your bill." It is important to note that by use of the word *transaction*, I am not equating an application-level and a database-level transaction. The former occurs at a higher level than the latter; in fact, application-level transactions typically consist of a set of database transactions. Despite this, however, application-level transactions and traditional database-level transactions are the same in the sense that a logical higher-level "handle" is used to group a series of related lower-level operations.

Let's distinguish between transactions and isolated requests that require no application logic. For example, if we are browsing a list of books before purchasing, we may be simply accessing static Web pages. Clicking a hyperlink does not require corresponding application logic. While such scenarios are common within any application, we make a distinction between this type of behavior and transactions. Obviously, the difference is that transactions are dynamic, involve more server-side resources, are more likely to affect overall resources or act as a bottleneck, and thus have greater impact on the application's scalability requirements. Serving static Web pages is a less complex problem, although serving many static large objects (such as pictures) is a challenge in its own right. Still, static requests are different from dynamic requests. Unless otherwise specified, we will focus on the latter.

Finally, a **session** is the use of an application by a client over some time period. Sessions are composed of one or more of the transactions we have defined. Thus, just as transactions correspond to a series of application operations, sessions correspond to a series of transactions. However, unlike transactions, this list is not necessarily logically related. For example, we may want to transfer $100 from our bank savings account to make payments on two loans that we have at the bank. On Saturday night, we might log in to our online bank, take care of the first transfer, update our mailing address information, and then log out. On Sunday we might complete the second transfer and log out. Thus, sessions are more about a series of transactions within a well-defined time frame, not necessarily a series of related transactions. For our discussion, sessions are initiated by the user logging on to an application or otherwise opening a connection to the application and then terminated by the user explicitly logging off or by the expiration of a **session lifetime**.

As an example, suppose you need to make plane reservations for three trips later in the year. You access some online travel application at 6 P.M. and spend 15 minutes configuring your options for the first trip. After choosing from several options, you click Submit and receive your confirmation code. Then you do the same thing for the second trip. Realizing that it's 6:30 and time for dinner, you shut down the machine and head out for Chinese food. A few hours later, you come back and realize that you still need to make the third plane reservation. So you go back to the same online travel application and do so. By the time you're finished, you've conducted two sessions; one at 6 P.M. and one a few hours later. During the first session, you conducted at least two transactions (purchasing each ticket).

Application Requirements

Every application has requirements that specify the functionality it must support. Web applications are no different in that they must provide the features necessary to achieve a productive goal. Obviously, business requirements are part of any application, but there are two other classes of requirements worth discussing—data management and interface. We'll look at all three in turn.

Business Logic

The business logic requirements are the most important part of any Web application. These requirements specify which business processes should be captured (in some way) by the application. For example, a banking application is typically required to support the ability to transfer funds and view account history. How these requirements are met—in terms of the user interface—is a separate issue. For example, whether account management is accomplished though a Java applet or a set of HTML pages is irrelevant. Generally speaking, if key business requirements are not met, the application has little value.

Applications obviously vary wildly when it comes to these business requirements. Banking applications have one set of requirements; event-ticketing applications have another. Still, there are some general observations that can be made, regardless of industry and processes.

First, application code that corresponds directly to any normally manual business practice (such as transferring funds from one bank account to another) is typically referred to as **business logic**. Thus, business logic is the set of operations required to provide the advertised service. In its most basic form, this logic is simply a collection of functions, each composed of a sequence of steps with some meaningful purpose, such as the transfer of funds from one account to another.

Second, business logic should be dynamic or customizable. We should be able to replace or modify it without having to rebuild the entire application. In fact, for many applications, dynamic business logic is a requirement. For example, news-filtering applications have filtering criteria and employee benefits management applications have eligibility rules. Having customizable business logic means that the logic itself (or its parameters) might need to be stored in a database.

Data Management

Think of business logic as the pipes of a Web application, and the data associated with the application as the water that flows through them. That is, business logic and application data go hand in hand. For example, a ticket reservation system is meaningless without tickets to reserve, just as a banking application is meaningless without bank customers. While data may not actually be part of the business logic, its existence gives the business logic a purpose and provides evidence of the value of that logic.

Data management has to do with reliable, fair, secure, and efficient access to the data. We want to be able to store lots of data, access it quickly, and relate it to each other. As we will discuss shortly, databases are the primary mechanism used to meet these requirements. They enable the modeling of data (representation) and its persistence (reliability); they support transactions on that data (fairness and order); they provide security; and they are typically fast (efficiency).

Interface

Users of an application will access it via Web browsers, standard telephones, cell phones, or personal digital assistants (PDAs). Typically, all application functionality is accessible from Web browsers, but limited parts of the application can be accessible from the other interfaces as well. We will focus on Web browsers, since nearly every application needs to deal with them, and will give selected attention to the other interface technologies. All the while, our goal will be to avoid situations where we have to develop copies of either application data or functionality. For example, we don't want to discuss how to build a great Web application whose functionality cannot be reused by a different interface such as a wireless or voice-response technology.

Although it's not a major focus of this book, there are ways to optimize your site so that it works better with one browser than with another. Also, different levels of support for browser-dependent technologies, such as JavaScript, Cascading Style Sheets (CSS), and dynamic HTML (DHTML) can have ramifications for server-side scalability. For example, if we can be sure that a certain level of

JavaScript/CSS/DHTML compatibility is supported by all of our clients, we might be able to implement a stylish user interface at a fraction of the normal cost, thereby reducing our server-side data transfer levels.

There are two major browsers at the time of this writing: Microsoft Internet Explorer (IE) and AOL/Netscape Navigator. In mid-1998, the Gartner Group and others studied the browser market and found that IE and Navigator had roughly equal shares of the market. This was a major shift from what was previously Netscape-dominated territory, so it was big news. Since then, Netscape has rapidly lost ground and the company has been purchased by America Online. Nevertheless, despite missing an entire version (Netscape 5), Navigator continues to exist in the form of Netscape 6. The most recent results from `BrowserWatch.com` (although unscientific) indicate that IE has at least 85 percent of the browser market. The rest is made up of Netscape and a collection of more recent browsers, such as Opera.

It is not worthwhile to spend time discussing how to code for one browser over another. There are plenty of books out there on such topics, and it is a landscape that will continue to change. Instead, we'll take a simpler-is-better approach. Since browser differences are likely to persist for years to come, it is better to know how to build Web applications that speak the most common version of the language of Web layout and presentation (i.e., HTML and XML).

Thus, our interface requirements will simply be sufficiency, clarity, optimization for low-bandwidth as much as generically possible, and browser independence.

Web Requirements

Generally speaking, the core requirements of an application can be divided into interface, business logic, and data management. Meeting these basic needs can lead to an application that is:

- *Usable*—can be accessed and operated without error
- *Capable*—emulates real business practices
- *Useful*—operates on real data, achieves some productive or logical purpose

But there is something missing, namely, **accessibility**. Traditional computer applications can be usable, capable, and useful. But they are meant to be installed, used, and managed on one machine, with no sharing of data, limited dynamic application responses, and no user-to-user interaction. Also, every user must purchase the software and install it locally. What makes Web applications truly different is that many limitations of traditional applications are lifted once they are deployed online. User collaboration is possible, applications can be seamlessly and automatically upgraded, client machine requirements are eased, and so on. Of course, all of this is made possible because the application is accessible in a different way—via the network.

It is unclear exactly where the network endpoints are in our picture, but we know that they exist somewhere between the user and the underlying centralized data. Somehow, the client connects to the server side of the application and to the database. The details about which parts of a Web application the network spans is a debate we will get into shortly. For now, though, let's propose some basic network connectivity requirements.

Network Connectivity

Like the Web browser issue, network connectivity is a moving target, albeit one subject to a slower evolution. Designing an application for a single, known connection speed (such as 56 Kbps or LAN speeds) is challenging enough. Designing an application for a range of connection speeds—something that most Web applications have to tackle—is even more challenging because client bandwidth directly influences how much style (HTML or XML) and substance (underlying data) you can pack into an application. If you have to support a range of connection speeds, what is the right amount?

Until recently, home users were stuck with bandwidth that only allowed data to trickle in and out. Even now, the vast majority of Internet home-based clients are confined to bandwidths of between 28.8 and 56 Kbps. However, in recent years, residential consumers have been able to purchase higher bandwidth to the Web in the form of digital subscriber lines (DSL) and cable modems. These alternative connections yield speeds in the hundreds (or thousands) of kilobits per second; for example, many DSL lines can support speeds from 384 Kbps to 1.5 Mbps and higher. In the far future, the majority of Web users will have high-bandwidth access, even those in rural communities. For now, we will assume that most home consumers have access of 56 Kbps. Many of the applications written for this group of users are referred to as **business-to-consumer (B2C)** applications because they involve consumers interacting with businesses.

At the same time, most businesses that need information technology have high bandwidth connections. They can support heavyweight applications that contain lots of applets, images, and animations and seem to download in a split second. While there are many fewer business users of remote Web applications than home users (business users tend to use local software and information sources), businesses also need to use applications provided by other businesses. These applications are often referred to as **business-to-business (B2B)** applications.

With two general connection speeds (low and high) and two general application types (B2C and B2B), what is the best approach? Certainly, you can always support both; how many times have you visited a site that said something like "Click here for the high-bandwidth version!"? You can also generalize—B2C tends to be low-bandwidth and B2B tends to be high-bandwidth. Or you can be futuristic and declare "Everyone will eventually have high bandwidth, so let's not care."

Throughout our discussions, we are going to take the conservative approach and strive for applications that assume low bandwidth, whether the application is B2B or B2C. It won't matter which because our assumptions are that users favor substance over style and that it is better to focus on the performance and scalability for one bandwidth than to juggle support for two very different levels. Yahoo and Google are our prime examples here. These Web-based applications have become successful despite their visual simplicity. Their low-bandwidth approach does not mean that they sacrifice the ability to provide things like pictures or videos or music; just look at some of Yahoo's vertical sites.

In short, we will always be concerned with bandwidth since our client base could comprise anyone from the home consumer to the business user. In choosing to minimize our use of bandwidth, we are assuming that our users will not be offended since the same functionality will be there. Meanwhile, we are helping to achieve our own scalability goals by keeping things simple and conserving server-side bandwidth where possible, so that we can deal with the millions of users that we expect to come knocking.

Abstract Web Application Architecture

Independent of its specifics, an application architecture must be capable of capturing the business logic, data, interface, and network requirements just described. In fact, in describing a prototypical application architecture, it is best to start with a very general design. Then, progressively, we can fill in some of the details, such as where the Web server fits. The important thing here is to not get lost in specifics. Times will change, technology will change, but customer requirements, by and large, will remain constant.

From Client to Server: Thin and Fat Clients

Starting at the 10,000 foot level, Figure 2–1 shows the composition of a very abstract application. We see that the user directly interacts with the interface. Thus, this is where interface requirements should be met. An interface is a proxy to the core business logic of an application, which is composed of the operations that correspond to the business process(es) at hand. As this logic is executed, it typically requires the need to interact with and manage data, specifically, to store and query it.

Figure 2–1
Abstract
application
architecture

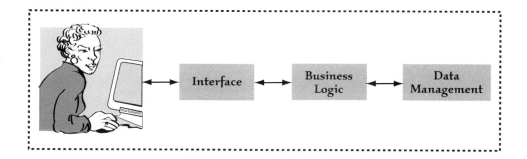

We can now add some more detail. Generally speaking, we know that Web applications consist of a user that interacts with an application over a network. The execution of business logic can be local or remote. In lay terms, this means that the client can be "fat" (local logic) or "thin" (remote logic). In either case, at the very least the interface needs to be near each user and the data needs to be centralized at some server. Figures 2–2 and 2–3 show the difference between a **fat client** and a **thin client**. Notice that the interface always remains on the client side and the data management always remains on the server side.

Finally, Figure 2–4 shows that a hybrid design is possible. In practice, such designs are more common than you might suppose. One example is data validation, such as ensuring that phone numbers look like "123-456-7890." Although it is normally considered a business logic chore, such validation is frequently executed on the client side via technologies like JavaScript.

Persistent Data Management

Before we continue, let's spend a moment to understand some of the data management aspects of our abstract application. The applications we will be concerned with rely heavily on transaction processing using a standard relational database. There are five types of data that these applications typically store:

- *Application data*: This refers to the data that is core to the application domain itself. For example, if we are developing a portal application, it would include the news stories. If we are developing an application for selling some set of products online, it would be the product catalogs.

Figure 2–2
Client/server
application
architecture
(fat client)

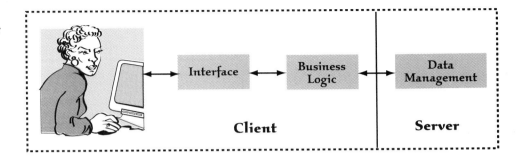

Figure 2–3
Client/server
architecture
(thin client)

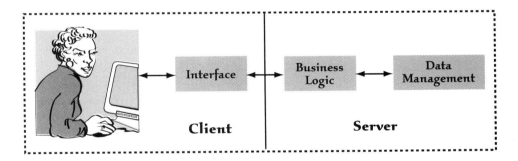

Figure 2–4
Client/server
architecture
(hybrid
design)

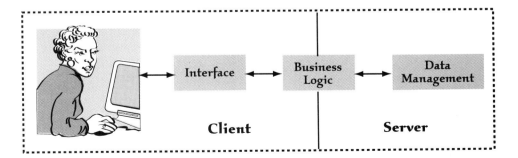

- *Personalization information*: This is data about the users of the application. For example, it might include information about the user name and interests. Data related to personalization can be secure (credit card numbers) and can also be modifiable by the user (i.e., name and address information) or it can be read-only (i.e., history of user purchases).

- *Application metadata*: This is data *about* the application data. For example, the list of product catalog tables in the database might be stored in a table called PRODUCT_CATALOG_TABLES. This information is thus analogous to the data-dictionary type of metadata that most databases have. It exists in the database because it is dynamic, easier to manage (i.e., it is an alternative to the file-system), or needs to be queried.

- *Application logic*: Databases can store code that is accessed and executed via the application components. As we will discuss later, storing code in the database typically yields applications that have better performance.

- *Report data*: Obviously, it is important to generate reports on sales at a product site. Likewise, information about page views and user interest are important. This type of information is gleaned either from automated reports that summarize existing information in the database or via data mining, which aims to identify trends in data. Reporting is necessary but confounding because it steals resources away from the application back end and can thus affect overall performance.

Now that we have some idea of the underlying data and how it is divided, let's return to understanding the client, network, and server pieces discussed earlier.

N-tier Application Architecture

Although Figures 2–2 through 2–4 show different ways to split up the business logic, they all contain three basic components: the client, the server, and the network (which is not shown but is implied by the arrows).

The Client

We want to cover two types of client: the human one and the automated, or software-based, one. Let's start with the human type. The client in this case involves a machine with an operating system and network access. He typically uses a Web browser to access the Web application, although custom interfaces are also possible. This browser speaks the HTTP protocol. One of the unique things about this kind of client is that its sessions with the server do not demand constant servicing; there is plenty of "think time" that allows the server to use its resources for clients requesting service.

The automated client probably runs on a more powerful machine than the human client uses. The automated client may use HTTP or a lower-level or proprietary protocol. This kind of client may also communicate using technologies like messaging, which may not involve the Web server but can certainly involve the rest of the server-side software (application servers and database). An automated client does not need "think time" and could continually pound a server with requests.

The Network

The network between client and server is more commonly known as the Internet. As we all know, the Internet is made up of many machines and subnetworks distributed across the world.

When machines communicate with each other, their packets travel through a variety of hardware and software systems en route to their final destination. For our purposes, most of their messages are communicated using the TCP/IP protocol. IP stands for **Internet Protocol** and TCP stands for **Transmission Control Protocol**. TCP/IP is a connection-oriented protocol that provides quality of service guarantees. Basically, it ensures that bytes can be reliably delivered to parties, even if the underlying network is unreliable.

TCP/IP is our prime concern because the Internet represents an unreliable network, and this protocol has become its default language. However, we should note that there are other transport-layer protocols, most notably the **Unreliable Datagram Protocol (UDP)**. This protocol is not connection-oriented and does not have the same QoS guarantees. However, because it does not have such features, it performs better than TCP. Although UDP is largely unacceptable for Internet applications, it does make sense for certain types of high-performance Intranet applications.

Client-Side Network Elements

There are three parts of the network worth addressing. One is near the client, who is usually not directly connected to the Internet. Most have Internet access through a provider service (called an **internet service provider**, or **ISP**). Before having a request resolved at the original source on the Internet, clients typically access their **browser cache** to see if they already have the desired document. The browser cache is simply the filesystem on the client machine. When a page is requested, if it is not already in the local filesystem, the browser fetches it. The page is rendered and, if the page is cacheable, a copy of it is kept in the local filesystem for future access. This leads to better client performance, since future access requires network roundtrip time. Pages are not cached forever: There are expiration dates and protocols for checking on the updates to a particular Web object. The concept of a browser cache, or any cache, to store remote Web page data locally (the avoiding the cost of contacting the originating server for that content) is known as **Web caching**.

Figure 2–5
Client-side
network
infrastructure

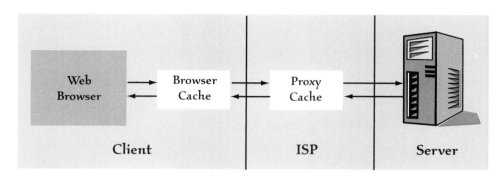

A **proxy cache** is either software or hardware that is designed to cache frequently requested Web pages so that an ISP does not have to repeatedly fetch the same pages for its clients. When client A fetches Web page X for the first time, the proxy cache requests the page from the original server and stores a copy of the page in its cache (assuming the page is cacheable; more about that later) as well as providing a copy to client A. When client B requests page X, the proxy cache can simply fetch the page from storage without accessing the network again. This leads to better client performance, and what's more, the effect can be shared among clients. Figure 2–5 shows the relationship between the client Web browser and the intermediate client-side caches. Later, we will discuss more about Web caching and how you can design an application to leverage client-side browser and proxy caches.

Server-Side Network Elements

The second part of the network that interests us is the server side. Like the client, the server side has an ISP; however, the ISP choice here is one we can control. It is important, when designing an application, that you know the bandwidth limits and the backbone network access available to your provider.

Another important aspect of the server-side part of the network is the way incoming connections are distributed to server resources. Local **load balancers** provide both simple and sophisticated techniques for sharing the workload among multiple machines. Requests can be routed based on Web server availability or on the nature of the request. For example, image requests can be routed one way and static page requests can be routed another. A typical-load balancing hardware device is the Cisco Local Director.

The balanced load is often distributed among **Web server farms**. Each farm consists of a set of Web servers designed to access the same kind of content. Each Web server typically resides on a separate machine, a redundancy that increases Web site reliability.

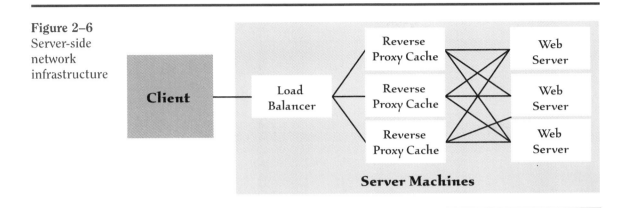

Figure 2–6
Server-side
network
infrastructure

Finally, a **reverse proxy cache** can be set up on the server side to reduce the demand on the server by providing quick access to frequently accessed objects. A reverse proxy cache works just like the proxy cache on the client side: It stores frequently requested objects. It is useful on the server side because it allows frequently accessed content to be cached even though clients may not share an ISP. Figure 2–6 shows one type of deployment strategy that involves a load balancer, a reverse proxy cache, and a Web server farm.

Between Client-Side and Server-Side

The third part of the network is the unpredictable mesh of routers and switches that separate client and server. We cannot control this mesh any more than we can control the client-side of the network. However, like the client side, intermediate caches are strewn along this path. They do not exist specifically to help you or your clients; rather, they are trying to provide a general cost-effective service by reducing congestion for heavily demanded resources. However, if you know how intermediate caches work and how the HTTP protocol works, you can at least inform the network of the nature of your data. With enough information, the intermediate network elements can help you by significantly reducing load on your site for static Web pages and the like.

In general terms, the communication between client and server sides consists of the client ISP, capable of T1 and T3 speeds, forwarding requests through its backbone **network service provider (NSP)**, which speaks in terms of OC-1 and OC-3 speeds. These NSPs provide access to **network access points (NAPs)**, which are public exchange facilities where ISPs can reach each other through a process known as ISP-peering. NAPs are distributed across the world; collectively, they represent the points where the Internet backbone is "stitched" together. Communication at NAPs occurs at very high speeds—for example, OC-12 (622 Mbps)—and in a point-to-point manner.

To get a feel for the connection between client and server, see Listing 2–1, output from `traceroute`, a diagnostic network tool that tracks a packet from client to server. This packet goes from Carnegie Mellon University to Yahoo.

Listing 2–1: `traceroute` output describing the route from CMU to Yahoo

```
 1 CAMPUS-VLAN4.GW.CMU.NET (128.2.4.1) 1.744 ms 1.052 ms 0.992 ms
 2 RTRBONE-FA4-0-0.GW.CMU.NET (128.2.0.2) 37.317 ms 54.990 ms 75.095 ms
 3 nss5.psc.net (198.32.224.254) 2.747 ms 1.874 ms 1.557 ms
 4 12.124.235.73 (12.124.235.73) 11.408 ms 22.782 ms 21.471 ms
 5 gbr1-p100.wswdc.ip.att.net (12.123.9.42) 17.880 ms 21.404 ms 23.662 ms
 6 gbr4-p00.wswdc.ip.att.net (12.122.1.222) 13.569 ms 10.793 ms 11.525 ms
 7 ggr1-p370.wswdc.ip.att.net (12.123.9.53) 11.814 ms 10.948 ms 10.540 ms
 8 ibr01-p5-0.stng01.exodus.net (216.32.173.185) 12.872 ms 20.572 ms
   20.885 ms
 9 dcr02-g9-0.stng01.exodus.net (216.33.96.145) 29.428 ms 10.619 ms
   10.550 ms
10 csr21-ve240.stng01.exodus.net (216.33.98.2) 10.998 ms 32.657 ms
   19.938 ms
11 216.35.210.122 (216.35.210.122) 11.231 ms 20.915 ms 32.128 ms
12 www7.dcx.yahoo.com (64.58.76.176) 36.600 ms 10.768 ms 12.029 ms
```

We see that CMU is connected to Yahoo through the backbone providers AT&T and Exodus Communications.

In recent years, there has also been focus on one approach to optimizing the area between client and server. **Content distribution** has emerged from the Web-caching community as a way for providers to replicate their content through providers that act as reverse proxy caches. Content distributors such as Akamai strategically replicate their hosted content so that client access is very fast and does not involve the originating server. Content distribution is often a solution for bandwidth-heavy objects, such as images, which quickly clog up server-side bandwidth even though they don't require server-side application logic.

The Server

The server-side application architecture is both the most complex and the most interesting. While you can tune your application to some extent by understanding and playing to the features of the client and network pieces of the application, your efforts will have a much larger effect on the server side. This is also where the greatest scalability and performance challenges lie. Figure 2–7 shows the major pieces of this part of the architecture. Moving from left to right, the **request processor** is usually the first component an incoming application request reaches.

One example of a request processor is a Web server. The Web server has two roles: to resolve requests it can handle and reroute those it cannot. For static Web pages, the Web server can resolve requests locally by accessing the filesystem to get the

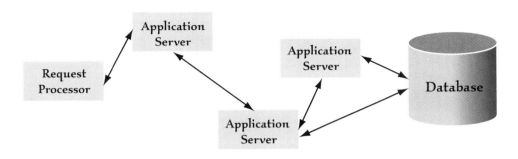

Figure 2–7
Server-side
organization

desired page. As a request router, the Web server determines the kind of request and dispatches it to the proper handler, which in this book, typically means a Java servlet engine or **servlet container**. The servlet container invokes the proper servlet instance, that is, a method on a Java class. The servlet takes care of unpacking request arguments and will likely play a role in constructing the HTML reply. In the middle, it may do many things, such as contact an application server or the database for query processing.

The job of the request processor is to identify the nature of the request and route it to an instance of functionality that can execute the desired business logic. This mechanism is generally referred to as an **application server**. For example, an application server is typically used to locate an instance of an application logic. This logic could be in the form of a Java class implemented as an **Enterprise JavaBeans (EJB)** or a **CORBA object**. These technologies, EJB and CORBA, are middleware technologies that make application logic robust, scalable, and interoperable by the application server (which manages them).

In a well-designed system, this is all done behind the scenes. The application logic is coded independently of the application server. They are obviously two distinct things: One provides access and the other provides business functionality. The trick is to give the application server the ability to automatically manage the deployment of business logic in a way that gives maximum flexibility to the server mechanism while remaining invisible to the underlying code. Later in this book, we will see how EJB containers and EJBs themselves enable engineers to build real application servers.

To resolve an application request in terms of existing application data, the data must be accessed from its persistent storage, which is typically a **database**. At a minimum, the database stores information about the state of the application, including users, orders, profiles—anything that is part of the application data. However, in addition to data about the application state, the database can store a good deal of business logic. It does so in the form of stored procedures, triggers, and database constraints.

The data in the database is organized according to a data model, a logical specification for how the data is to be stored. Physically, data is associated with tables. Table data (as well as other structures) is written to disk, just like data in the filesystem.

At this point, it is good to remind ourselves that there are other clients to the application server and the database. These can be messaging or legacy systems that communicate using technologies such as electronic data interchange (EDI). These clients are typically other businesses, not individual users, and they often interact with server-side software in batch mode.

Tier–Based Designs

The many layers through which a client request has to pass before it is resolved are called **tiers**. Each tier is associated with one or more types of logic: presentation, business, or data access. Two-tier applications typically consist of combined presentation and data layers—for example, a client applet that directly accesses a server-side database. A three-tier application takes this one step further: A thinner client contacts a servlet or CGI program, which then contacts a database. Presentation and data are more clearly separated, and the server side distinguishes business logic from data access logic. An *n-tier* application consists of three or more levels of request progression, including the database. One example is a client who contacts a servlet that contacts a set of application servers, each of which can access the database. Many of today's Web application systems are *n*-tier.

You might wonder, Are *n*-tier designs really desirable? What's the payoff? Intuitively, it seems that client/server connectivity becomes more complicated. The communication path now consists of *client-to-server1-to-server2-to-. . .-serverN-to-database*. This seems like a route that requires more hops, which means more latencies and more chances for error or crashes. That can't be good, can it? YES, if it's done right.

Increased Modularization and Component Reusability

Having multiple tiers means dividing the work and routing the parts of the problem at hand to independent modules. But what if we didn't do this? What if everything were handled in a single server-side program?

For example, suppose you need to build a server-side module that enables Web users to order books. In writing the module, you need to make sure that the following events occur when a Web user presses Confirm on his order:

- Receipt of the interactive client request
- Credit card check
- Creation of a work order

- Updating of the customer's profile
- Updating of the book inventory
- Generation of the interactive client response

You could bundle all of these operations in the Confirm-and-Pay-for-a-Book module. But suppose two months later application requirements change and you need to handle DVD orders. Guess what? You need to create a new module; call it the Confirm-and-Pay-for-a-DVD module. And here are its necessary operations:

- Receipt of the interactive client request
- Credit card check
- Creation of a work order
- Updating of the customer's profile
- Updating of the DVD inventory
- Generation of the interactive client response

It looks familiar, doesn't it? Too bad you can't reuse the functionality in the book module. Maybe you can create a more generic module called Confirm-and-Pay-for-a-Product.

Now suppose you are asked to support a mechanism for the bulk ordering of products. For example, suppose a reseller communicates its orders to you nightly and you need to process those orders. In this case, you just can't reuse your generic product module because the request type is fundamentally different. Once again, you need to create a new module, which must include the following operations:

- Receipt of batch requests
- For each request:
  - Credit card check
  - Creation of a work order
  - Updating of the customer's profile
  - Updating of the product inventory
- Generation of a batch summary response

You should have the idea by now. We have been unable to reuse the independent operations involved in coarse modules or components. Just as in programming, poor modularization allows little reuse. Instead, you get code bloat, replication of functionality, and potentially inconsistent application behavior.

What's worse is the scalability angle to all of this. By failing to reuse functionality and replicating it among coarser modules, you unnecessarily eat up memory on your server machines. Instead, if you break these modules into finer-grained components, you will be able to not only reuse functionality but also more efficiently iron out performance bottlenecks.

Better Distributed Processing and Task Parallelism

With increased modularization come more options. Assuming that we have the technology (such as Java RMI or CORBA) to connect the modules, it is possible to deploy each of the smaller modules on different machines. For example, we could have all of the credit card checking done on one host and all of the database updating on another host. This is an attractive solution because it allows us to distribute the processing load to different machines.

In some cases, modularization leads to significantly better performance because one operation is independent of all other operations. Consider the updating of the customer profile operation in our earlier example. Updating a profile conceptually returns no useful information. It is just a necessary procedure. Updating product inventory, which follows profile updating, need not wait for it to be completed. Theoretically, it could execute in parallel with the profile updating process.

By being able to farm out the processing of the independent modules to different machines, we can increase parallelism during execution, and better parallelism translates into better performance. Of course, to effectively parallelize these tasks, we have to build communication solutions that are asynchronous, that is, that do not require an immediate response. Still, once we learn to do that, we can make a real difference in application performance by increasing the level of task parallelism.

More Efficient Service Replication

Along with the luxury of being able to deploy components across multiple machines, we have the opportunity to tackle scalability and performance challenges with a finer level of control. That is, we can target our solutions and potentially address a very specific system problem. A common problem in any application system is that one or more subtasks in a larger task are slow and become bottlenecks.

Let's go back to the book-ordering example. Suppose that credit card checking takes 3 seconds per request, and that we need to process 100 book orders at once. Assume for now that we have only one copy of our application service running on our server machine, and assume that this service is single-threaded. This means that:

- The fastest credit check will take at least 3 seconds.
- The slowest credit check will take at least $(100 \cdot 3) = 300$ seconds (5 minutes).
- The average credit check will take at least $(50 \cdot 3) = 150$ seconds (2.5 minutes).

This is unacceptable. Perhaps we can replicate the service 100 times and service all 100 clients at once. Then the fastest, slowest, and average times will all be at least 3 seconds.

For the sake of example, suppose that each copy of the large Confirm-and-Pay-for-a-Product module requires 5 Mb (the code requires much less, but the code to have it function as an application service might very well require that much). Replicating the larger module 100 times—even if we have enough hardware to support it—means that we need 500 Mb of memory just to deal with 100 clients that want to use this one piece of functionality simultaneously!

In contrast, suppose that the credit-check operation itself requires only 1 Mb of that 5 Mb. By splitting the Confirm-and-Pay-for-a-Product module into smaller independently distributed components, and making things like credit checking into distinct components, we can limit our replication to those parts that need it. For example, we can replicate the credit-check operation 100 times, requiring only 100 Mb, not 500 Mb, of space.

Clearly, the space-efficiency advantage to finer-grained business logic processing makes *n*-tier deployment attractive. If there are bottlenecks in the application, we can identify the components responsible and replicate them as necessary (much like increasing the number of lanes on a freeway). If our components are more fine grained, the cost of this replication (in terms of memory) is less and thus our application will be able to scale better.

Multithreaded Application Servers

If you have experience with application servers, you're probably wondering why I'm talking so much about replicating code. Actually, the reason goes back to an earlier assumption I made—that our application servers are single-threaded. Now, let's assume that we can build multithreaded application servers.

First, think about why we want to do this. As you probably know, threads are lightweight processes—mechanisms for execution that share an address space. By "mechanisms for execution," I mean that they are scheduled by the operating system and can use the CPU (when their turn comes up) to execute program code. In their most simple form, threads consist of a program counter, registers, and a stack. Generally speaking, threads maintain bookkeeping information about their state of execution, sharing other common program resources with other threads.

Thread-scheduling policies vary, but by far the most common is round-robin, in which one thread at a time has access to the CPU. Later, we'll talk about upcoming processors that are specifically designed to run multiple threads efficiently in a truly parallel manner.

Since multiple program threads share an address space, it is possible to have them access a common block of code in that address space. This means that multiple threads can execute the same instructions (regardless of what other threads are doing). Taking this one step further, threads can be managed by yet other threads and used as "workers" to service incoming requests. The idea is that when multiple

Figure 2–8
A multi-
threaded
application
server

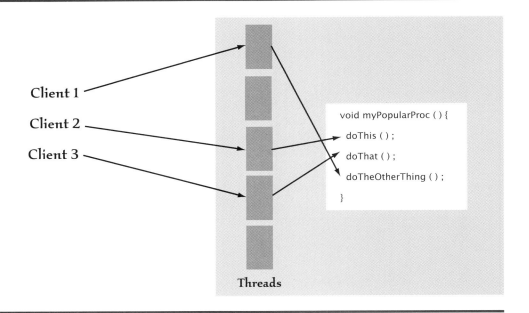

clients want to access the same piece of code, they can be assigned to an available thread and have that thread execute the code they want.

Figure 2–8 shows three concurrent requests to a program that has five threads. All three requests want to execute the same block of code called myPopularProc(). As the figure shows, each one of these threads can execute this code at the same time (since the CPU runs one thread at a time, this is not quite true, but it's very close depending on the function). In fact, each thread is currently executing a different line of code, as the figure shows. Thus, threads do not have to wait in line to execute the same piece of code. They can be interleaved so that the execution is very nearly parallel.

All of this means that we don't need to replicate code; we just need to make our programs multithreaded and assign threads to individual client connections as they arrive. This is exactly what most application servers do today. They separate the logic from its access mechanism and, instead of replicating code, they assign threads to service requests. Later on, we'll see that EJB containers do the same thing.

One note of caution here: I have quietly avoided the main problem associated with writing multithreaded code; namely, synchronization. If some portion of code must be executed serially, we need to identify that part and make sure that access to it is synchronized. Fortunately, Java makes this very easy, by allowing us to synchronize at the function level or create synchronized blocks as necessary. As long as we know what we are doing, Java gives us the tools to make sure that it is done safely. For an in-depth discussion of synchronization and writing highly concurrent code, see *Concurrent Programming in Java: Design Principles and Patterns* (Lea, 1999).

The Challenge of Efficient Middleware

Everything is not all roses in the land of *n*-tier applications. Though we have increased our ability to reuse components and our potential for parallel execution, and produced an environment that can be fine-tuned for scalability, there are costs we have so far ignored.

Certainly, an obvious cost is the increased complexity of development: engineers need to know how to build and deploy *n*-tier applications. A second cost is the greater thought required: Application designers have to spend longer thinking about which parts of an application should be independent and which should be bundled. These are not really scalability or performance issues—they just require more design time.

One issue that does have efficiency implications is increased communication among application components. Think about it: Now that we have split up our business logic into finer-grained, more independent component services, more interapplication communication is required to process each application task. For example, communication is no longer limited to clients talking to servers. Now, servers are talking to each other. Granted, much of their communication occurs at high-bandwidth LAN-like speeds (or exists as interprocess communication among services on one machine). But extra work is still necessary and the associated costs must be considered overhead.

As we discussed earlier, the technology that ties together our fine-grained component services so that they can contact each other easily, regardless of whether they exist on different machines, is called middleware. EJB and CORBA are middleware technologies that use techniques such as Java Remote Method Invocation (RMI), Internet Inter-ORB Protocol (IIOP), and remote procedure call (RPC) to achieve the goals of connecting objects or programs, even across network boundaries. Thus, they allow programs to communicate as if they were making a local function call—except that the call travels beyond the boundaries of the process address space.

Since this communication happens frequently, it is important to understand its costs and to optimize its usage where possible. It is also important to choose the most efficient middleware technology—synchronous or asynchronous. As we will see, these two approaches have very different performance implications. Finally, we can of course reduce our middleware demands by bundling functionality and having fewer components. But taken to an extreme, this puts us right back at square one and the problem of an unwieldy application service! Clearly, the solution is to identify a middle ground that allows functionality to be modularized ("componentized") and distributed as needed.

Scalability and Performance Hints

Based on our discussion about general Web application architecture, thin and fat clients, multithreading, and component granularity, let's now consider some relevant scalability and performance hints.

Don't Always Starve Thin Clients

For maximum portability, you may think it is wise to take the thin-client approach when designing your application. After all, this allows you not only to reach out to clients with limited resources (i.e., memory and CPU) but also to avoid developing a Java client (which may be slow to download) or designing some other kind of custom client. Even better, putting all of the application logic on the server side can give you the most flexibility as far as extending your application architecture to wireless or very low bandwidth deployments.

However, embracing the thin-client approach too tightly has important implications. First of all, think about what you're sacrificing. You have, say, 100,000 clients that access your Web application and do so with fully packed, powerful desktop computers. Having them interact with your application through a very thin interface wastes the opportunity to really do some distributed processing—that is, to put some of the computational work on the client side. Instead, clients sit idle, just passing network packets back and forth. Of more concern is that all of the computational burden is on the server side. If the computational requirements for your application are high, accommodating sudden bunches of concurrent clients can lead to serious CPU contention.

There may be a compromise here, one that at least leans less heavily on the server. Consider the common application need for client data validation. Things like phone numbers and e-mail addresses need to be matched against a template to see if they conform to the right general "picture." Or numeric fields need to be checked to see that they contain numeric data, that their lengths are respected, and so on. For these tasks, it's not unreasonable to use something like JavaScript or to put some thought into the HTML you're generating so the client does the work. Admittedly, this may be a small amount of computation to push onto the client, but for sites with many forms or many clients the cycles saved can add up. Never underestimate the leverage of 100,000 remote machines doing your processing for you. Also keep in mind that things like client-side data validation not only save server-side CPU; they also cause fewer request/reply HTTP dialogues between client and server, thus allowing the Web server or request processor to handle the rest of its workload.

Still, there are problems with putting things even as minor as data validation on the client side. One is that you might be replicating business logic. For example, if you use the same application architecture to process batch transactions other than through your interactive Web site, all of a sudden you'll need to code the data validation logic in two places (batch transactions will never execute your JavaScript data validation logic). Now what?

There's no one answer that fits all situations. It depends on your application, your client base, and your mode of client interaction. The main message here is not to blindly design your application with the "thinnest of clients" mindset, but to think carefully about the following issues when deciding how much (if any) business logic to put on the client side:

- Does your application consist of many forms with data fields that need validation?
- Are there some calculations you can do on the client side (e.g., totaling an order)?
- Are interactive Web application users your only type of client?
- Do your data validation rules remain static for the most part?
- How costly is it to replicate certain parts of the business logic? Is the gain in performance worth that cost?

If the answer to any of these questions is yes, you should think about fattening up your clients a bit. Again, this doesn't mean putting all of your logic there, just certain small parts of it.

Use or Build Multithreaded Application Servers

As we discussed, the main advantage of using multithreaded application servers is that multiple clients can concurrently access a single copy of program code. This is obviously more scalable than spawning a separate process for every incoming client request, which is what happens with CGI-bin program execution. Because server-side application programs are invoked by multiple clients at once, using a thread to service their requests allows you to add the minimum of overhead (one thread) per request.

Some application technologies, such as EJBs, provide this kind of infrastructure for free. As we'll see in later chapters, EJBs allow you to focus on writing the business logic while they handle the thread management for you. All clients have to do is locate the EJB they want and make their requests. EJB containers manage the concurrency demands. Some types of CORBA deployment (depending on the vendor and infrastructure included) can provide similar support.

If you're writing multithreaded application servers (or if your needs exceed the functionality of EJBs), keep in mind these general points:

- *Make sure you write thread-safe code*. The Java `synchronized` keyword provides a very easy way to identify blocks of code that are not thread-safe. If you're using any of the Java Collections classes or any other Java data structure that you did not write, make sure that you understand its thread safety issues, if any.

- *Instead of spawning one thread per request, consider pooling threads*. If you have 1,000 clients per minute, is it worthwhile to spawn 1,000 threads? Can your machine handle the memory demands (1000 • *thread_overhead*), not to mention the context-switching needs? Not likely. Using n threads does not mean you'll enjoy n degrees of parallelism. Remember, you still have only one CPU (or at least fewer CPUs than threads). There will be a point of diminishing returns, based on the computational demands of your application. It's wise to *pool* threads and use a single dispatcher to assign work to pool members. This enables concurrent request processing while providing an upper bound on number of threads in use.

- *Take care when using external resources, such as a database*. Remember, just because you write thread-safe code does not mean that external resources, such as databases, will be protected in all cases. These resources will maintain state and, if you access them concurrently, all kinds of unexpected behavior might occur. It is often wise to wrap access to an external resource (especially one that requires serial access) in a separate Java class and make sure the access methods are synchronized.

Find the Right Granularity

Earlier we talked about the advantages of breaking application logic into self-contained objects or components. The idea was that by modularizing this functionality better, we could have more control over the distribution and replication of our functionality because modularization improves reusability and allows us to iron out bottlenecks more precisely. However, there is a tradeoff: The finer the granularity of components, the more overhead required to tie them all together—especially if they are distributed.

From this, you can glean the following lessons:

- Design your systems in an object-oriented way.
- Make your functions as "functional" as possible (no side effects).
- Use procedures judiciously.
- Write modular code.

Code that consists of small, tight modules can be separated easily in distinct containers (not necessarily the same as J2EE containers) and deployed as needed across a distributed network of machines.

Before you get into the business of distributing your objects, it is often wise to start with a very coarse level of granularity, then deploy your application and see what testing reveals. Through good testing, you'll be able to spot the bottlenecks in an application's execution and break them up by isolating the modules at the root of the problem and either distributing them across different machines, replicating them, or both.

If you break up your objects too much, you may incur the overhead of remote communication and marshalling for no good reason. In fact, this was one of the problems of an earlier incarnation of the EJB spec (i.e., the problems of fine-grained entity beans). The principle of "doing it only if you need to" really applies here. Coarse granularity followed by an evolution of selected granularity modifications frequently leads to the best of both worlds. By making sure that you follow the listed points, you'll give yourself the most flexibility in coupling and decoupling your application internals.

Summary

In this chapter, we've talked a lot about abstract application architecture and only grounded ourselves here and there. As abstract as we're being, it is all relevant not only to J2EE application designs but to other distributed object technologies (e.g., CORBA) as well.

We started our discussion by describing the three basic parts of any application—the client, the network, and the server. We then broke up the server into its two distinct parts—business or application logic and persistent data—and discussed where to put the business logic. As it turns out, a good case can be made for sprinkling a little of it on the client side and dumping as much of it as possible in the database.

As we will see, the J2EE specification doesn't force you into anything, but it does strongly suggest that you keep your application logic at the EJB level. As a default choice, this makes reasonable sense and avoids the problems of replicating code and possibly causing inconsistent behavior. However, when optimizing performance and scalability, you may find that, just as selectively denormalizing data models can be useful, selectively replicating logic has its advantages, despite the maintenance costs and the inconsistency involved.

Finally, we discussed the merits of tier-based design and why some Web applications have *n*-tier architectures. The basic message is that multiple tiers allow deployment flexibility—we can replicate and distribute functionality as appropriate. Also, we saw the tradeoffs associated with different levels of component granularities and suggested a conservative approach to granularizing your deployments that takes into account these tradeoffs.

As we move on to more specific aspects of Web application design, particularly J2EE, we will see how these techniques are implicitly promoted by the specification as well as the practical forms they take.

CHAPTER 3

The J2EE Specification

Sun Microsystem's Java 2 Platform, Enterprise Edition (J2EE) specification is the proposed Java-based solution to the problem of building *n*-tier applications. J2EE focuses on defining client- and server-side technologies that make these applications not only easier to build but also easier to integrate. The J2EE spec encompasses all kinds of client/server types and interactions: It deals with Web clients, Web-based information servers, pure application servers, applets, and both synchronous and asynchronous solutions.

Although J2EE specifies many complex and powerful technologies, it is still just a specification. It requires vendors to actually develop what it proposes. Several have: BEA offers its WebLogic suite of products and IBM offers WebSphere, just to name the two most well-known. Sun has also released a reference implementation, which is a very useful and cost-effective way to get started with J2EE. Vendors differ on some important details, as we'll see later, but they must all implement the specification correctly or they won't be certified.

In this chapter, I provide a brief overview of J2EE and highlight the key component- and platform-level technologies it defines.

Overview of the Specification

The J2EE specification (version 1.3) describes a set of technologies designed to address the presentation, business logic, and persistent storage needs of *n*-tier applications. Generally speaking, a J2EE environment consists of several types of *components* that communicate with each other and a persistent storage device (a database). There are four categories of components:

- *Java applets*, which typically execute in a Web browser on a client machine
- *Java applications*, which execute on a local or remote client machine

- *Java servlets, JavaServer Pages (JSPs)*, filters, and Web event listeners, which execute on a server machine
- *Enterprise JavaBeans (EJBs)*, which are application objects that execute on a server machine

Each of these component categories is associated with a specific type of J2EE *container*:

- *Applet containers,* which host applet components
- *Application containers,* which host application components
- *Web containers,* which host servlets and JSPs
- *EJB containers,* which host EJBs

Containers manage their components. Component developers can assume that the containers exist and manage the components per a specified *contract* (agreement). In plain terms, this means that components must obey certain interface guidelines and that containers rely on interface-guaranteed functionality in the course of their management duties.

From the component perspective, a container is used to access the rest of the J2EE services. Thus, the container acts as the layer (or API) that makes the rest of the system visible to the component being contained. Through this layer, components can access other components or resources, such as an external database.

Each container type is targeted toward a particular style of deployment:

- Applet containers are the most limited. They simply act as proxies to the other types of container. Applets run in a Web browser and can contact Web containers in order to access the underlying business logic.

- Application containers run as standalone programs and can access Web containers, EJB containers, or the database.

- Web containers receive requests and format replies for Web clients. They enable a J2EE system to be accessed via HTTP.

- EJB containers represent the heart of the J2EE architecture: They manage the underlying business logic of the application. This is where operations like order processing occur or new accounts are created. EJBs are constructed based on the language of your business. They consist of a number of built-in features to enable reliability, availability, security, scalability, and robustness.

Figure 3–1 shows the general relationships of the different types of containers. The purpose of each of four J2EE containers is to permit access to underlying J2EE services (local or remote) through a set of common APIs. These APIs allow the containers to do things such as conduct transactions, manage security, and pool resources. The APIs and their basic purposes are listed in Table 3–1. Figure 3–2, a more detailed version of Figure 3–1, indicates where the various APIs and services fit into the different J2EE containers.

There is considerable opportunity for J2EE containers to interoperate with technologies that live outside a J2EE environment. For example, a Web container can use the HTTP, HTTPS, or IIOP protocols for communicating with other objects and systems. Table 3–2 summarizes the basic interoperability capabilities of the four types of containers.

There are many details of the J2EE spec that we could cover at this point. Rather than discuss all of them, we will focus on those that will play a role later in our discussions about scalability and performance.

Figure 3–1
Relationships among J2EE containers

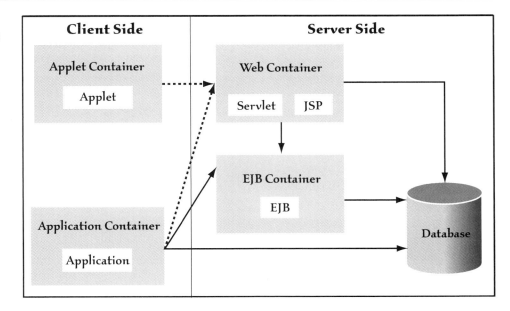

Table 3–1: J2EE Services and APIs

Service	*Purpose*
HTTP	Message-based Web communication
HTTPS	Message-based secure Web communication protocol
RMI-IIOP	RMI accessibility for CORBA objects
Java Database Connectivity	Database management
Java Naming and Directory Interface	Resource identification and state management
Java Message Service	Asynchronous messaging between containers
Java Interface Definition Language	Access to CORBA objects outside of a J2EE deployment
JavaMail	Notification via e-mail
JavaBeans Application Framework	(*Required by Java Mail*)
Java Transaction API	Transaction management
Java API for XML Parsing	Parsing XML
Java Connectors	Container access to Enterprise Information Systems
Java Authentication and Authorization	Security within J2EE containers

Figure 3–2
APIs
supported
by J2EE
containers

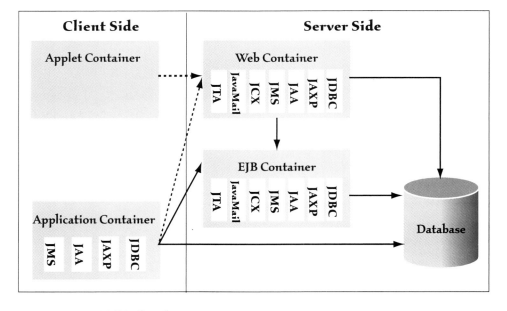

Table 3–2: J2EE Container Interoperability

Container Type	Inbound Protocols	Outbound Protocols
Application		HTTP, SSL, IIOP, JRMP
Applet		HTTP, SSL, IIOP, JRMP
Web	HTTP, SSL	HTTP, SSL, IIOP, JRMP
EJB	EJB, IIOP, SSL	HTTP, SSL, IIOP, JRMP

Deployment Issues

In this book, we will not be covering things like how to run a certain implementation of the J2EE or the exact details of variations of J2EE across vendors. In fact, we'll generally ignore detailed deployment issues, because they tend to be highly vendor specific and relate more to J2EE operation than architecture and design. Nevertheless, it is useful at this point to say a few things about how a J2EE application is packaged and deployed. Later, when I refer to something as being a deployment issue, it is often related to one or more of the aspects that I'm going to cover here.

Packaging

In terms of packaging, a J2EE application is stored in a file with an .ear extension (hereafter called an EAR file). An EAR file is the same as a .jar (JAR) file, except that it refers to an enterprise Java application archive, not just to a Java application archive. Another important type of file is the Web application archive, or .war (WAR) file, which archives files related to servlets and their JSP pages.

An EAR file can contain one or more of the following:

- JAR files for each EJB component
- JAR files for each application client (if any)
- WAR files for each servlet and set of related JSPs

The EJB and application client JARs contain the relevant .class files, any related files, and something called a deployment descriptor (more about this in a moment). The WAR files contain servlet .class files, static Web resources such as GIF files, a set of related files (i.e., utility Java classes), and a deployment descriptor file.

Figure 3–3
J2EE service
packaging and
deployment

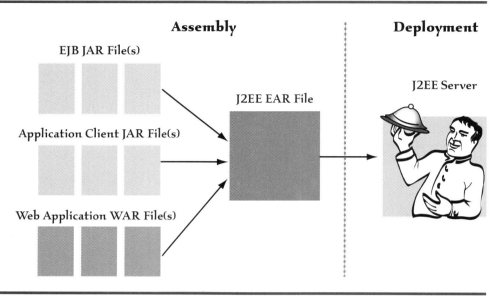

To get a feel for what an EJB JAR file looks like, consider a JAR file for a sample EJB called **BenefitSession** (this EJB will appear in a later example). Here are its contents:

```
BenefitSession/
     EjbBenefitSessionbean.class
     EjbBenefitSessionRemote.class
     EjbBenefitSessionHome.class

META-INF/
     ejb-jar.xml
```

The relationship between what is assembled and what is deployed is shown in Figure 3–3. As you can see, WAR and JAR files are the guts of a J2EE application EAR file, which is deployed as a J2EE server.

Deployment Descriptor Files

A deployment descriptor file is simply an XML file that typically contains structural, assembly, and runtime information about J2EE components. A J2EE application consists of a deployment descriptor for the application as a whole and specific deployment descriptor files for each component as necessary. The information in a descriptor file has to do with the component assembly (e.g., the names of EJB interface classes), security information (e.g., definitions and applications of roles), and other runtime dependencies and information.

Part of a sample EJB deployment descriptor file is shown here. This snippet indicates something about the structure of the object (i.e., its attributes and relationships) and its resource dependencies (i.e., database information):

```
<persistence-type>Container</persistence-type>

<cmp-field><field-name>first_name</field-name></cmp-field>
<cmp-field><field-name>last_name</field-name></cmp-field>
<cmp-field><field-name>hire_date</field-name></cmp-field>

<resource-ref>
    <res-ref-name>employee</res-ref-name>
    <res-type>javax.sql.DataSource</res-type>
    <res-auth>Container</res-auth>
</resource-ref>
```

Without going into the details of what a deployment descriptor is made of, we can observe that it is simply an XML file that contains metadata about the EJB or the application component being deployed. As an XML file, the deployment descriptor helps to ensure the portability of deployment—independent of the deployment platform, the same set of properties can be used. The XML file is, after all, just a text file that is independent of the operating system and CPU. If you are new to XML, you may find it helpful to skip ahead to the first part of Chapter 12.

To illustrate how deployment descriptors can contain information about security roles and privileges, consider the following example.

Listing 3–1: Sample deployment descriptor

```
<ejb-jar>
      ...
<enterprise-beans>
    ...
    <entity>
        <ejb-name>MyBean</ejb-name>
        <ejb-class>MyEntityBean.class</ejb-class>
        ...
        <security-role-ref>
            <role-name>entity-admin</role-name>
            <role-link>administrator</role-link>
        </security-role-ref>
        ...
    </entity>
    ...
```

```
</enterprise-beans>
...
<assembly-descriptor>
    <security-role>
        <description>The Admin Role</description>
        <role-name>administrator</role-name>
    </security-role>
</assembly-descriptor>
...
</ejb-jar>
```

Notice that new security roles can be both defined and linked, as well as applied to various application components such as EJBs.

The entire XML DTD for J2EE deployment descriptors can be found at http://java.sun.com/dtd/application_1_3.dtd. Taken almost directly from the J2EE specification, Figure 3–4 is a graphical summary of this DTD, which may help you visualize how a J2EE application breaks down and organizes its assembly and deployment information.

As the figure shows, a deployment descriptor contains information about all types of application information, including its modules. Note that this DTD is relevant for the entire application (i.e., the EAR file). Individual elements of the application, such as the EJB JAR file and the WAR file, have their own deployment discriptor DTDs.

Again, we won't consider the detailed modifications of the deployment descriptor file for each component. Books devoted to specific J2EE technologies like JMS

Figure 3–4   J2EE deployment descriptor XML DTD

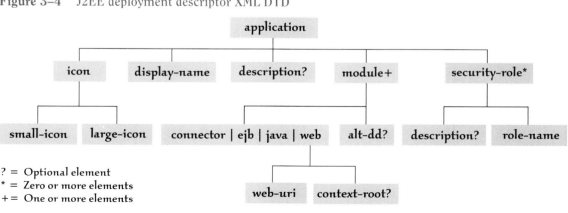

and EJBs already offer such information. They are often the best resource because there are so many possible deployment descriptor settings, many of which are independent. The J2EE vendor documentation is also a good source; it will provide the most comprehensive information about deployments. Finally, continual comments about deployment descriptor settings would be tedious and a distraction. We are occasionally interested in what *kind* of information is stored in a file for a given component—not so much in how it is actually specified.

Platform Technologies and Services

One of the benefits of building your application on top of the J2EE infrastructure is that doing so allows you to inherit key technologies that facilitate scalable deployment. In this section, we visit some of the key platform technologies and services J2EE infrastructures provide. These technologies are related to simplifying and empowering distributed application components to coordinate and communicate. Providing this type of transparency in a distributed system allows application designers to focus on the business logic of their applications, rather than waste their time tuning the replication and distribution of components that implement that logic.

Component Communication via RMI–IIOP

A large part of J2EE centers around the idea of making sure that business logic is accessible from many types of clients and from other middleware standards, particularly the **Common Object Request Broker Architecture (CORBA)**. CORBA and the Internet Inter-ORB Protocol (IIOP) specify how distributed objects can be deployed and can communicate across network boundaries.

CORBA has its own huge specification, which consists of many core services (e.g., naming) and the Interface Definition Language (IDL). IDL is a platform-neutral language for specifying services. Its compilers generate "stub" and "skeleton" code in languages such as C++ and COBOL, which allow the functionality in those languages to be deployed as accessible (i.e., CORBA objects). Using the generated stub/skeleton code, objects can communicate with each other (more about this in Chapter 8).

An **object request broker (ORB)** is the mechanism by which objects locate and bind to each other. IIOP is simply a protocol for CORBA objects to communicate over a network. If you're somewhat familiar with RMI (Remote Method Invocation) and EJB, but new to CORBA, you're perhaps beginning to sense a similarity.

Figure 3–5
Integrating
Java and C++
CORBA
objects

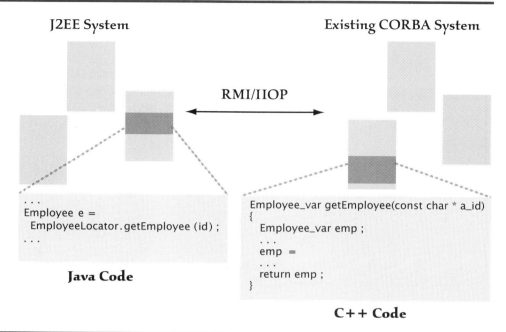

In the Java 2 Standard Edition (J2SE) version 1.3, RMI was fused with IIOP to create RMI-IIOP. Although it uses IIOP as its means of communication, RMI-IIOP retains an RMI-style API. This enables IIOP-style communication without forcing Java developers to learn yet another API.

For a J2EE system, RMI-IIOP is the primary method of communication across tiers. In addition, it essentially allows Java developers to construct CORBA services without having to learn IDL. In the old days, you had to buy a CORBA product produced by companies such as Visigenic or IONA. Now J2SE comes with a fully functional CORBA ORB and support for stub code generation through its RMI compiler.

What all this means for the application system architect is that Java developers can easily access existing CORBA application systems and vice versa. Thus, it allows legacy functionality to be incorporated easily in a J2EE deployment.* Figure 3–5 shows Java objects communicating with remote CORBA objects over RMI-IIOP, and Figure 3–6 shows how IIOP works. Notice that it's simply a layer through which objects associated with different ORBs can be coupled.

---

*An important restriction, which we don't address in detail here, has to do with legacy CORBA objects, which must be deployed by vendors who support the recent Objects-by-Value extension of the CORBA specification. More about this at http://cgi.omg.org/cgi-bin/doc?formal/99-10-07.

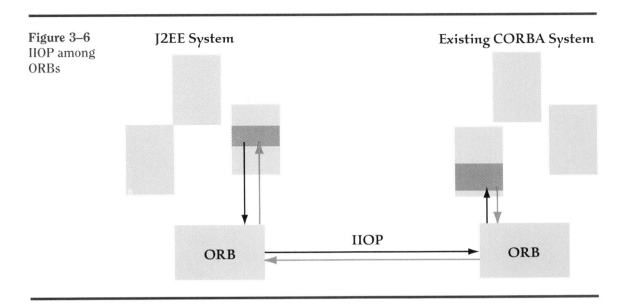

Figure 3–6
IIOP among
ORBs

J2EE System

Existing CORBA System

IIOP

ORB

ORB

Figures 3–5 and 3–6 show a J2EE system talking to an existing CORBA System. I do this to show why you would connect CORBA objects written in two languages—in this case, something new (a J2EE application system written using Java)—to something that already exists (a CORBA application system written in, say, C++ or Smalltalk and deployed using a different ORB vendor). In reality, however, these are two CORBA systems. J2EE and RMI-IIOP allow Java programmers to represent their services as CORBA objects, without the additional work of coding an IDL file, and so on.

The main message here is that in addition to allowing you to use RMI to communicate easily with existing Java-based RMI objects, RMI-IIOP allows you to extend object sets to include CORBA objects. Since RMI-IIOP is the language spoken between components in J2EE containers, it's important to be aware of what it is, and how it generally works.

Transaction Management Using the Java Transaction API

A J2EE **transaction** enables a series of operations, perhaps distributed, to be executed in an orderly way that guards against errors with any one of them. It also protects the integrity of these operations across program boundaries.

For example, suppose your server-side application system is an automatic conference organizer that allows one-touch registration. A user enters her name, address, conference options (i.e., tutorials she wants to enroll in), and travel options. She provides a credit card account number and the system does the rest. The conference organizer, in turn, does the following:

- Register participant for conference
- Register participant for hotel
- Register participant for rental car
- Debit user's credit card for the total amount

Each operation may be handled by a different application server. There's no telling what can happen with any one operation; for example, the hotel registration may fail or return an error. If there are errors, we certainly don't want to continue the series of operations and we want to undo actions that occurred in earlier operations. This is just the kind of thing transactions are good at.

With transactions, there are two important terms to remember: **commit** and **rollback**. When one operation is completed, it is still not finalized. Instead, all such operations wait until the last one has completed. At that point, the transaction can explicitly issue a commit operation, which finalizes all of them. If an error or failure occurred during the execution of any of these operations, a rollback can be issued to signal to the other operations that finalization will never occur and that uncommitted actions should be undone.

The Java Transaction API (JTA) supports transaction management among various J2EE containers. The operations that take place during a transaction are typically JDBC or JMS related, although the J2EE spec also supports external adapters that conform to the XA transaction standard. Note that the `javax.transaction` package specifies a very general form of transactions that has nothing directly to do with using JDBC or JMS in isolation—it merely ties together operations for a logical operation, including those (e.g., database updates) that involve external resources.

The J2EE platform offers transaction services because of the complexity and possibility of errors when developers code their own transaction logic, especially between tiers. In fact, a single client interaction might cause many components in many tiers to be invoked and create confusion about who starts the transaction and who is responsible for committing or rolling back that transaction. By offering transaction services at the platform level, J2EE allows a collection of distributed components to easily coordinate execution common to a single, logical client operation.

Transactions and Web Components

When designing Web components, such as Java servlets, you can always get a handle to the current transaction. This is guaranteed by the specification and is a responsibility of the platform. In particular, the spec states that Web components can obtain access to a transaction that implements the `javax.transaction.UserTransaction` interface. Web components are allowed this access via the JNDI API, which we discuss in more detail shortly.

Transactions in Web components don't span client sessions. More specifically, for servlets, they are started in the servlet's `service()` method and must be completed (committed or rolled back) before this method returns. If not, the Web component is in an error state.

Web components can consist of multiple threads, but transaction resource objects should not be shared by threads. This means that threads should not use associate transaction resources with common memory addresses. Thus, resource objects should not be stored in static variables or in instance variables.

Since servlets often interact with EJBs, which interact with the database, it is important to know how a transaction propagates. The specification declares that when a Web component contacts an EJB, the platform must be responsible for propagating that transaction to the EJB's context.

Transactions and EJBs

Transaction management gets a bit more complicated when it comes to EJBs, partially because J2EE assumes that the bulk of application logic resides in EJBs. It's also because management of persistent data in the application is abstracted by EJBs, specifically in the form of entity beans. In contrast, session and message-driven beans (the other two types of EJBs) represent session logic, not data.

It's useless to speak about the details of EJBs and transactions here, since we haven't discussed EJBs in detail. For now, the important things to remember about EJBs and transactions are:

- For some types of bean (session and message-driven beans), transaction management may be handled by the bean itself; that is, the developer writes the logic to start, commit, and possibly roll back a transaction.

- Session and message-driven beans can be configured so that transaction management is automatic—by the container. In fact, details about their transaction management (e.g., does a transaction get passed from one bean to another when the first calls the second?) can be defined per method.

- In contrast to session and message-driven beans, entity beans can't manage transactions explicitly. Everything is handled by the container, regardless of whether that bean interacts with the database (bean-managed persistence) or the container does (container-managed persistence).

Many of these details, especially the types of EJBs that can be developed, are covered in Chapter 8.

JNDI for Resource Location

Although J2EE supposes a distributed application system, it's often necessary to maintain a common state among the system's components. For example, resources, names, or addresses may be common among components (i.e., location independent). Access and management of this state are provided by the Java Name and Directory Interface (JNDI).

For those familiar with directory services, JNDI is the means with which to access such services as LDAP. For most other J2EE developers, JNDI is simply an easy way to manage resources shared by tiers.

From a component standpoint, JNDI gives location-independent access to a common application state, or **context**. The J2EE specification also views the JNDI context as a mechanism for making application components dynamic. Instead of altering the source code for a component, it bases a conditional part of component execution on the values obtained by access to the context. Then, at runtime, when the component accesses its context, such variable settings (i.e., variable values or rules) are resolved. This can be done on a deployment basis. That is, the deployer can set the proper value in the deployment descriptor, and the component can obtain that value via the JNDI. All of this occurs without recompilation.

For example, suppose we wanted to customize the multiple to use as the basis for salary raises. If we assume that this value is deployment specific or otherwise dynamic, then our application component needs to read this value from the JNDI and act appropriately.

The following snippet of application code does just that for a mythical function called `calculateNewSalary()`. The method shown requires the prior salary value as a parameter and uses the value of `raiseMultiple` to determine the new salary.

```
public double calculateNewSalary(double a_origSalary) {

  /* Obtain handle to our naming context. */
  Context initCtx = new InitialContext();
  Context localCtx = (Context)initCtx.lookup("java:comp/env");

  /* Look up the salary multiple */
  double raiseMultiple = ((Double)
    localCtx.lookup("raise_multiple")).doubleValue();

  /* Raise salary per the multiple */
  return raiseMultiple * a_origSalary;

}
```

Thus, we first initialize the context and locate the desired node within the context tree structure. Once found, we read one leaf of that directory tree—`raise_multiple`—for its value. Thus, for example, a 10 percent raise means that this value is 1.10. We then use that value as the basis for calculating the new salary.

In the deployment descriptor, `raise_multiple` might be stored as follows:

```
...
    <env-entry>
          <env-entry-name>raise_multiple</env-entry-name>
          <env-entry-type>java.lang.Double</env-entry-type>
          <env-entry-value>1.10</env-entry-value>
    </env-entry>
...
```

Another use of the JNDI is to provide access to various shared J2EE resources, such as the following:

- Databases
- Message queues
- EJBs
- Transactions
- Mail servers
- URLs

Using the JNDI to locate these objects provides a simple and consistent interface for obtaining access to a common resource.

As an example of how these other objects can be fetched from the context via the JNDI, consider how a well-known Java Message Service (JMS) message queue is located. Although its name is known (i.e., the queue was registered to JNDI under that name), its location is not. This is the value of the JNDI: Instead of forcing every application component to know where every resource is physically located, J2EE provides a logical handle to that distributed resource. This makes coding application components simpler and allows the component to be relocated without having to recode or recompile the application components that use that resource.

The following code is an example of how to obtain a handle to a well-known message queue using the JNDI, the following code might suffice:

```
/* Obtain handle to our naming context. */
Context initCtx = new InitialContext();
Context localCtx = (Context)initCtx.lookup("java:comp/env");
```

```
/* Look up the message queue we want */
Queue myQueue = (Queue)localCtx.lookup("jms/MyQueue");
```

Just as the `raise_multiple` value was defined in the deployment descriptor, so too is the information corresponding to the JMS `MyQueue` object. Notice that in both cases, the resource type and description can be included in the descriptor entry, thus making the environment self-describing.

```
<resource-env-ref>
      <description>
            My message queue
      </description>
      <resource-env-ref-name>jms/MyQueue</resource-env-ref-name>
      <resource-env-ref-type>javax.jms.Queue</resource-env-ref-type>
</resource-env-ref>
```

J2EE and Your Architecture

At this point, you may be wondering, do I need to use all of J2EE? If not, how much of its technology should I use? The answer is, *as much as you want*.

To be sure, most Java development efforts already use popular parts of the J2EE architecture, such as servlets, JSPs, and EJBs. JDBC has already become a popular mechanism for integrating databases into Java applications. More recently, JMS is gaining converts as people (re)discover the joys of asynchronous communication. However, one of the nice things about the J2EE model is that you don't have to embrace all of it to use some of it. For example, you don't have to use EJBs; you can simply use servlets and JSPs. Or, you can use servlets and EJBs, but not JSPs. With the exception of the platform technologies, which tie everything together, the component technology you use depends on your needs.

When you do use J2EE, however, it means choosing a vendor. Again, the J2EE is merely a specification. Unless you are planning to implement it yourself, you should settle on a vendor that is not only J2EE compliant but offers an implementation that suits your needs. For example, as we will discuss in Chapter 8, vendors differ on how they implement container-managed persistence (automatic data management) for EJB entity beans. This is the kind of detail you should know before choosing a vendor.

Finally, regardless of your path, if you're interested in building highly scalable Web applications, you should strongly consider an *n*-tier approach. In building those tiers, you may find that part or all of the J2EE specification fits your needs and plans.

Summary

In this chapter, we learned that the J2EE specification describes how *n*-tier applications can be built and deployed. Although these applications are often thought of as Web applications, they don't need to be. In fact, Web integration is only one facet of the specification.

J2EE is a set of application components, containers to manage those components, and integration or platform "glue" to tie everything together in a secure, location-independent manner. Component management is enforced via interface contracts. Simply put, a container has guarantees that the component has certain methods (i.e., lifecycle methods), so that it can be managed as necessary.

We covered the key services provided by the J2EE platform and gave special attention to transactions and resource management. From the component perspective, the container provides APIs that not only allow access to these technologies, but also enable other J2EE functionality—such as Java Mail—to be easily accessed.

It's unlikely that you will use every J2EE feature in a single application. For example, your application may be such that messaging services, such as that provided by JMS, do not make sense. Still, I strongly suggest that if you plan on deploying any application system for the Web, you consider J2EE. It is portable and is integrated with a number of Web/non-Web, asynchronous/synchronous technologies that give a great flexibility and freedom to the architect designing an application solution. For our purposes, J2EE provides a great example of how some scalability and performance techniques (e.g., caching and redundancy) have crept into a practical and enterprise-level application system.

CHAPTER

4

Scalability and Performance Techniques

Throughout this book, we'll discuss techniques for addressing scalability and performance in all phases of an application. Our discussion will range from the HTTP protocol to J2EE technologies, such as EJBs and Java servlets, to relational databases. Although some techniques will be relevant to only one type of technology, a few general scalability and performance strategies will permeate most, if not all, of them.

Many of these techniques were originally developed for the then-revolutionary distributed systems designed a couple of decades ago. However, they continue to be relevant today and will likely remain so for years to come. They include:

- Caching/replication
- Parallelism
- Redundancy
- Asynchrony
- Resource pooling

We'll discuss why each is generally useful and provide real examples that demonstrate its benefits.

Caching and Replication

A **cache** is a structure that contains a copy of information that originates at some source. Generally speaking, a cache consists of a table of key/value pairs. For each pair, a key represents a question and the corresponding value represents an answer.

Table 4–1: Sample California City/County Cache

City	County
Pleasanton	Alameda
Santa Clara	Santa Clara
Livermore	Alameda
Palo Alto	Santa Clara
Marina del Rey	Los Angeles
Garden Grove	Orange

For example, to look up the California county that contains the city of Marina del Rey, we ask a question—What county is Marina del Rey located in?—and obtain an answer—Los Angeles. Table 4–1 shows this information in a sample cache of cities and counties.

The keys and values in a cache can be more complex objects and are not limited to strings; the only requirement is that the key object support some sort of equality test so that we can successfully test its membership when we query the cache.

Caches typically hold much less information than that in the originating source. For example, there may be thousands (or hundreds of thousands) of city/county pairs, even though only a fraction of them are contained in the cache. There are a variety of techniques to determine what information should be retained in the cache and what should be eliminated or "flushed."

Generally speaking, when information not in the cache is requested, the system fetches it from its original source, returns it to the requestor, and adds it to the cache. Of course, a cache has limited size and eventually it must be decided which information to flush. Obviously, it's desirable to keep those pieces of information that will be the most frequently queried because that will provide the best system speedup. Keep in mind, however, that I just said "*will be* the most frequently queried." Since there's no way to predict the future with 100 percent accuracy, part of the challenge in designing a caching system is identifying a good **cache flush policy**.

One example of such a policy is *least recently used* (LRU), which keeps only the most recently queried information. For example, consider the sample city cache and assume that it can store only six key/value pairs, as shown. Also, assume that the table shows the order of information access—thus, Garden Grove was the last city queried. Now, if the county for San Ramon is queried, the system fetches the answer (Alameda) from the originating source and replaces the least-recently-used pair—Pleasanton / Alameda—from the cache.

Table 4–2: City/County Cache with Access Counts

City	County	Accessed
Pleasanton	Alameda	100
Santa Clara	Santa Clara	1
Livermore	Alameda	1
Palo Alto	Santa Clara	1
Marina del Rey	Los Angeles	1
Garden Grove	Orange	1

Although there are many cases where LRU ends up being the best or close-enough-to-the-best policy, this is not always the case. For example, suppose that we also keep track of how many times information is accessed. Our table might be amended as shown in Table 4–2.

As you can see, even though Pleasanton was queried 100 times, it wasn't the object of the last five queries. Then, when San Ramon was queried, LRU forced out Pleasanton because it hadn't been requested recently. Since the cost of accessing information from its originating source can be very high, it can be better in the long term if things like access counts are taken into consideration.

Using caches to duplicate information can improve performance if the cache is more physically proximate, naturally quicker to access, or both. The speed of light guarantees that a more proximate structure is always quicker to contact than a remote source. That's just a rule of physics, and there is no getting around it. Network optimizations aside, if I'm in San Francisco and I have to access my e-mail, it's going to take longer if the e-mail database is in New York than if it's in San Francisco.

On your computer, a CPU maintains a cache so that a memory request doesn't need to travel along the system bus to the actual static RAM chips. Similarly, Web browsers maintain a cache so that they don't have to send a request over a network and withstand network latencies for a reply from the originating source. Figure 4–1 illustrates this similarity. In both cases, the reasoning is the same: It's physically faster to query a more proximate source.

There's another compelling reason for caching: better access time. If the access time of a cache is quicker than that for the same information on the originating source, the cache may be more efficient, even if it's more remote. You see this all the time on the Web. Suppose there's a great Web site hosted in your city but its server is slow or the network infrastructure connecting it to an Internet backbone is lightweight. A content distributor like Akamai or a publicly available cache like Google may

Figure 4–1
Caching to
reduce
latencies
caused by
distance

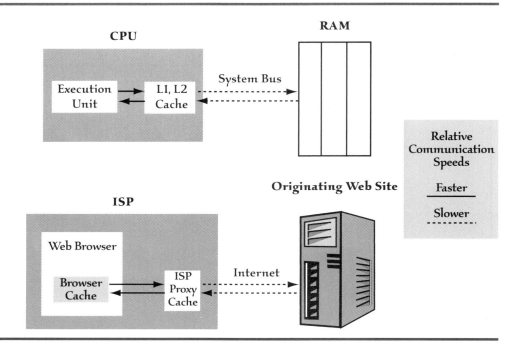

have a copy of that information that, although remotely located (perhaps it's even more remote than the original source), is still quicker to access because the servers are snappier and the bandwidth for clients is higher.

Then there's what I call the cut-to-the-chase aspect of querying that makes a cache quicker to access. Suppose I want to find out the vice president of an employee's division. I have the employee ID, but to get the VP information I need to query an EMPLOYEE table to find the department ID for that employee, query a DEPARTMENT table to find the division ID for that department, and finally query a DIVISION table to find the division information I want. In contrast, a cache can simply map employee IDs to department VP information, as shown in Figure 4–2. The effect is the same: Caches can provide faster access than the original source.

In summary, there's a tradeoff in the caching benefit equation, which can be shown as

$$\Delta \text{Time (per object)} = (RT_{orig} - RT_{cache}) + (ACC_{orig} - ACC_{cache})$$
$$RT = \text{Roundtrip time}$$
$$ACC = \text{Access time.}$$

Figure 4–2   Caching to reduce access time

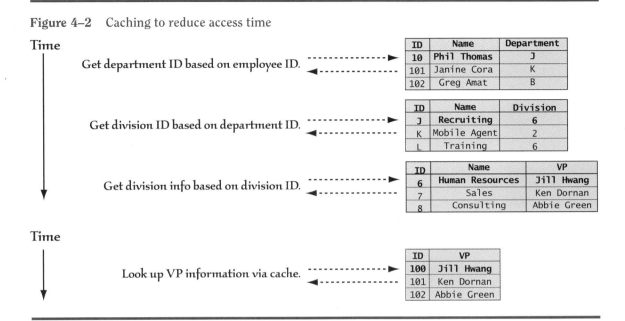

Thus, response time is a function of cache proximity as well as cache efficiency, both relative to the originating source.

As the equation indicates, that's just the performance benefit. Caching can also provide scalability benefits because it reduces demand for server resources in the forms of less bandwidth, fewer CPUs, and fewer connections to manage. By copying information to a more local or more efficient source, we delegate the rising resource demands in an effort to provide consistent performance. Generally speaking, then, caching improves both performance and scalability.

Caching is not without its problems. The most obvious among them is guaranteeing data consistency: ensuring that the cache contains the same information as the server contains and that multiple caches are kept in sync. For example, if your application maintains a main memory cache of session data (such as user information) normally stored in a database, it's important that any changes to the data be reflected in both. It's even worse if you have multiple caches and/or multiple databases; then you need to make sure that the data is consistent across all sources.

Clearly, this can get tricky. Suppose you have a banking application that keeps track of checking and savings accounts. For improved performance, the application caches account data in memory as accounts are accessed. So, while Joe Smith (an account holder) is logged in, his checking balance of $100 and savings balance of $0 are kept in a memory cache.

Let's say that this is a write-through cache, meaning that it forwards all updates to the database as they're made. Now, what will happen if—at the same time that Joe is online—the bank processes a check he's written for $50? Check processing has nothing do with the online application (or so it would seem), so some sort of check-processing software updates the database with Joe's new balance. Of course, if Joe uses his online session to transfer money from checking to savings, there can be a serious problem because the cache is unaware of the changes made directly to the database.

This isn't as unlikely as you might think. Valuable data often has many interfaces and problems like this can occur unless these interfaces share a process for interacting with the database. The extent of the damage in this example may depend on the write-through nature of the cache. Are two SQL UPDATE statements taking place, blindly ignoring the current database values and trusting the cache alone? If not, where's the logic that ensures that Joe won't have a negative balance? In any case, either Joe will get an error or the bank will give him some money back! Obviously, neither of these is a satisfactory solution.

The consistency problem gets even worse as we try to make our application more scalable. Say an organization provides scalable access to its information by deploying its application across several servers and uses load balancing to distribute the load among Web servers and application hosts. (Figure 4–3 shows this deployment.) Now, suppose that the application uses a memory cache to retain account information; however, as Figure 4–4 shows, since the application is distributed there are multiple caches.

Even if the organization has somehow ensured that the cached information will be consistent with the database, how do they ensure consistency among caches? If two users share volatile data—load-balanced and directed to an available server—we can encounter this type of inconsistency between caches. Figure 4–4 shows that the first entry for each of the two host-based caches is different. To prevent this, some additional consistency mechanism must be built in or added to the system.

In short, caching solves some problems but creates others. Inconsistency is merely one of several risks. Another is the security or ethical issue of caching: Should Web proxies be allowed to cache content (is that legal?)? Should you cache usernames and passwords in memory? Probably not, unless you can guarantee their protection. The same may be true of very personal data, such as medical

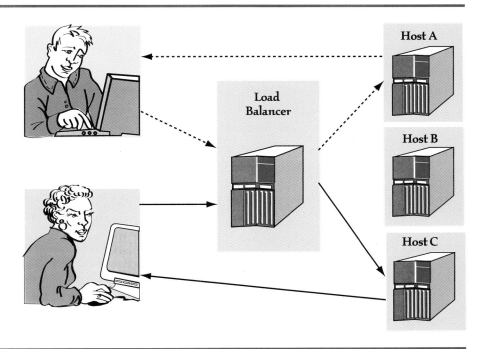

Figure 4–3
Load balancing for
scalability

records. Back to Web caching, what happens when intermediate caches don't obey your HTTP cache directives? Are you liable?

Still another problem is cache reliability. What happens when caches without write-through policies crash? To illustrate, let's take a look at the Oracle high-performance database management system (DBMS).

Oracle uses multiple processes (or multiple threads, depending on platform and database version) not only to cache query results but also to implement what might be called a "delayed write-through" policy regarding data updates. It avoids writing updates immediately to disk because disk I/O is slow and because permanent updates to data files shouldn't be made until the corresponding transaction is committed. However, Oracle still must ensure that system failure doesn't cause transactions to be lost. To solve this problem, it logs transactions so that if the server fails all committed transactions are saved, even those in memory awaiting update on disk.

Figure 4–4
Cache
consistency

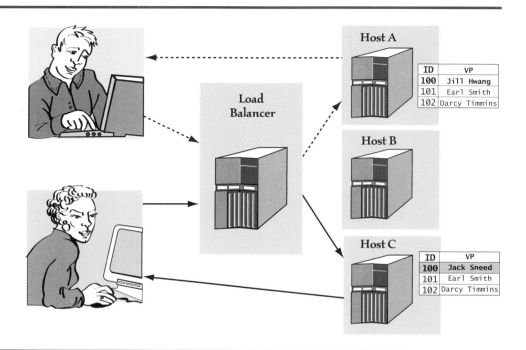

Parallelism

Conceptually, parallelism is the notion of doing more than one task at once. Many parallel machines exist and have been used for research and for processing scientific data sets, but it's probably safe to say that the majority of Web applications don't run on parallel infrastructures. Nevertheless, many can benefit from parallelism on several levels. The key challenge is to understand what aspects of a particular application demand parallelism and what the options are. We'll visit techniques for increasing parallelism later in this book, but first let's define the types of parallelism that exist.

First, there are two parts of any application where parallelism can be extracted —in hardware and in software—and each offers a variety of ways to exploit it. At the hardware level, there are architectures that, by design, are parallel. The major ones relevant today are

- *Massively parallel processors (MPP)*, which consist of processing nodes that *don't* share data (i.e., shared-nothing) but compute by routing data between nodes.

- *Symmetric multiprocessing (SMP) machines*, which consist of multiple processors that *do* share the same data. Basically, any processor is free to use any data.
- *Clustered computing systems*, which consist of multiple computers that typically don't share the same data but route it between computers over a network.

The trend that emerges from the list is the growing distance between processor nodes. More distant nodes mean higher latencies, but closer nodes mean increased cost and complexity. For example, programming for MPP architectures is expensive and not something just any developer can do well. MPP architectures are likely nonexistent for Web applications (although some technologies, such as those for video streaming, may use them); however, many applications do run on SMP machines and clusters.

In addition to these basic architectures, there's the notion of on-chip parallelism, which has to do with the ability to extract parallelism from a set of instructions or concurrent processes or threads. Most CPUs today do an excellent job of exploiting instruction-level parallelism (ILP), using techniques such as multiple issue, pipelining, and speculative execution to intelligently schedule and predict low-level machine instructions.

However, as processors have become more powerful, ILP techniques have actually leveled off. For example, the deeply pipelined processors of today can schedule many instructions at once. The problem is, which ones? Studies show that branches typically occur once every five machine instructions. Branch prediction and speculative execution can be employed, but they become less relevant as the size of the pipeline increases. For example, if a deeply pipelined processor allows many concurrent instructions, CPUs are forced to engage in highly speculative behavior, making predictions based on predictions of predictions of ... and so on. You get the idea: the deeper you go in a pipeline, the less valuable its contents become.

Newer architectures promote the trading of deeper pipelines for multiple pipelines and the increased use of *multithreading*. This trend is a direct response to the limits of ILP as the size of processor pipelines increase. The increased use of multiple threads gives rise to a new category of parallelism—thread-level parallelism (TLP). Note that the emergence of TLP does not spell the death of ILP. Instead, it is widely envisioned that hybrid processor designs, reaping the benefits from both ILP and TLP, will yield the best performance. Finding the optimal tradeoff between ILP and TLP will likely remain an important issue in processor architecture research for years to come.

You may wonder: Why did multithreading emerge and why has it become a popular means for achieving parallelism? In fact, there has always been the need for parallelism in computing. Computer architecture research and scientific programming have generated interest in parallel architectures since the 1960s. As you probably know, a great many mathematical operations and problems naturally lend themselves to parallel computation. Matrix multiplication is a good example; it is one of many complex operations that consist of a natural set of independent internal subproblems that can be computed in parallel.

However, parallelism for mass-market, consumer-oriented software (which typically consists of less scientific computations) is a relatively new phenomenon. There are two major reasons for this. One has to do with the recent increase in computer networking. Prior to the rise of the Internet, most consumers bought shrink-wrapped software that operated on only local data (i.e., data on disk). Of course, most applications today (in fact, all Web applications) involve a network. Increased network use yields applications that tend to be I/O-bound, and can thus significantly benefit from increased parallelism.

Another reason has to do with the phenomenon of Web applications and the need for concurrent request processing. Instead of traditional (local) applications that execute only on the machine owned by the client, more recent (Web) applications contain logic that executes on a remote server. This remote server often needs to handle hundreds, if not thousands, of simultaneous requests. Since each request is independent, there is great interest in parallelizing as much of this request processing as possible.

Advances in programming languages have also made threads more attractive. The Java phenomenon is probably the primary example. Only recently, programmers who could write threaded code were few and far between. Java changed all that by making threads accessible, easy to manage, and relatively safe. The result: more threaded software, which demands more TLP.

When you use Java threads for parallelism, you should carefully assess their value against the cost of the overhead involved. This isn't to say that Java threads are expensive—they aren't. It can be more expensive not to create them. However, it's important to understand *when* to use them—specifically, the conditions in which they tend to improve efficiency.

Let's see how two threads compare to one for two very different tasks. The first task will be a CPU-bound activity. Suppose an application server needs to increment multiple counters 10,000,000 times each. Is it faster to increment them by proceeding sequentially, incrementing each counter 10,000,000 times, or by proceeding in parallel? Of course, there may be hundreds of concurrent transactions that a given application server processes—as you'll see, however, the effects of parallel versus sequential approaches becomes clear in the early going.

Figure 4–5
Sequential
versus
concurrent
counting
(CPU-bound
activity)

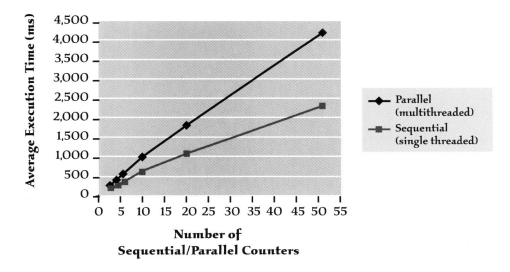

To answer our counting question, we can write two Java programs, one that counts sequentially and one that counts in parallel. The results are shown in Figure 4–5. Clearly, sequential counting is more efficient.

Now consider the task of fetching a page over the network. Suppose we need to fetch a set of 200 K Web pages. Is it faster to fetch one page at a time or fetch in parallel? Again, we can write two Java programs: one that fetches each copy sequentially and one that performs all fetches in parallel using threads. The results are shown in Figure 4–6. In short, parallel fetching is more efficient. Thus, a simple rule of thumb is to use threads when

- *Your processing is at least somewhat I/O bound.* For a single processor, multiple threads don't yield extra parallelism if you're entirely CPU bound (and you may adversely affect performance).
- *You have multiple processors or an architecture that encourages TLP.*

Especially for Web applications, it's *rare* that all processing is CPU bound. After all, some of the time will be spent accessing remote functionality, remote databases, and the like. Thus, threads often make sense. However, if your application does engage in serious computation, don't overdo it—or avoid writing multithreaded

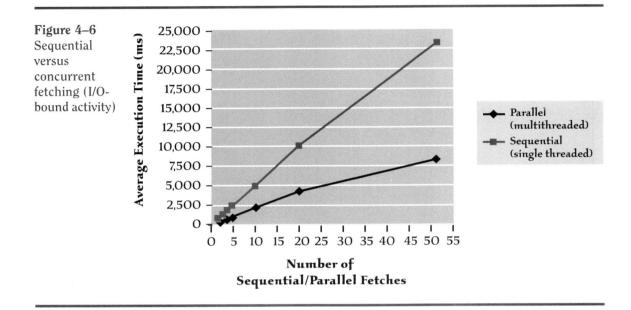

Figure 4–6
Sequential
versus
concurrent
fetching (I/O-
bound activity)

code altogether. The overhead may very well not be worth it. Also, if you have the flexibility of choosing which processes (i.e., application servers) to run on which machine, try to mix I/O- and CPU-bound processes so that you get better efficiency.

Redundancy

Redundancy typically refers to the duplication of hardware or software so that more resources are available for execution. For example, it's possible to have redundant Web servers or redundant disk drives, such as RAID. With either, the redundancy not only increases the ability of a system to scale, it also increases reliability—if one of several Web servers crashes, a Web site remains accessible.

Note that redundancy, as used here, is not the same as replication. The former refers to the duplication of *resources*, the latter refers to the duplication of *data*.

There can be a performance benefit to redundancy, depending on the resource involved. Consider a Web server farm. By replicating the number of Web servers, we can effectively increase the parallelism of request processing. We can achieve near-linear speedups for environments that normally have very busy Web servers, which is why server farms are such a popular scalability solution.

The only real drawbacks to redundancy are its deployment cost and the data consistency challenge. Cost increases not only for the duplicate resources but for the added hardware/software to employ them. Redundant Web servers, for example, require not only more machines to run them but a load balancer or redirector to control workload distribution. Dealing with this extra cost is simply a matter of money: Either you have it or you don't. While throwing money at a Web application is generally not the best way to improve scalability, this is one case where it literally pays off.

Data consistency can be a more complex issue. As we discussed previously in greater detail in the section on caching, maintaining consistency requires careful planning and synchronization techniques. This can be such an arduous and vexing problem that, in some cases, it demonstrates how the costs of redundancy can outweigh its gains.

To see how, let's return to our example of caching user account information, this time with redundant write-through caches. Initially, the caches were used to reduce the time to access the database—accessing a cache located in the same address space is faster than communicating with another process (the database server). However, as Figure 4–4 showed, if we have redundant caches on different machines, we have to update cache B whenever cache A is updated (in addition to eventually updating the database).

In short, the round-trip time we saved by not having to access the database server is erased by the round-trip time required for redundant cache synchronization. And, as the number of redundant caches increases, the problem obviously gets worse. Essentially, when we create a redundant cache we cause the access time to balloon, transforming simple updates into completed transactions.

The trick with redundancy is knowing when its costs outweigh its benefits. In almost all cases where redundancy is successful, the hardware or software is stateless. This is why redundant Web serving works so well: HTTP is by nature stateless, and thus Web servers don't need to cache anything and can be reproduced at will. Incidentally, Web serving here refers to resolving static pages, not application request. As we'll see in later chapters, certain application technologies can cause this stateless deployment strategy to become stateful and thus limit the redundancy of certain application components.

Remember, *redundancy* refers to "providing additional independent instances" of hardware or software, whereas *replication/caching* refers to data "copying." This distinction is important and underscores how replication affects redundancy. For example, in revisiting the data consistency issue previously discussed, we see that it isn't the redundancy that causes problems so much as it's the replication of data.

Asynchrony

Dictionaries define the word *synchronous* to mean "happening at the same time." For software and hardware systems, *asynchronous* has a different (but related) meaning: "happening independently of one another."

We frequently encounter instances of synchrony throughout computer science. For example, clocks are said to be synchronous if they keep the same time (more specifically, if neither moves ahead of the other). Communication is said to be synchronous if one process makes a request of another and waits for a reply. In this sense, the exchange is considered synchronous because events happen in a dependent manner—a reply always follows a request. Similarly, code execution is synchronous: The next instruction comes after the previous one terminates. In each of these cases, synchrony is necessary to ensure reasonable activity; for example, if code really did execute out of order, we would get unpredictable results.[*]

Synchronous communication is a part of almost all distributed computing systems. Web applications, being distributed, are inherently synchronous when the user is involved. When you use your Web browser to download a Web page, the download is a synchronous process: An HTTP request is issued and an HTTP response follows shortly thereafter. In most server-side application systems, servers contact each other synchronously (for example, using RMI, CORBA, or COM) as well as the database. All of this makes sense given that queries must be answered for the application to continue.

However, while synchronous behavior may be necessary in certain scenarios, it's *never desirable* from a performance or scalability standpoint because it effectively serializes execution. Synchronous communication means that a requestor is idle while its reply is being constructed. A called function or an instruction must complete before execution proceeds.

In many situations, asynchronous methods may be applicable and can dramatically improve parallelism and thus performance. For example, suppose you develop a Web application that broadcasts live pitch-by-pitch baseball coverage in which the user downloads some graphical client that shows the play by play. Under a synchronous model, the deploying Web site would have to keep track of all clients and contact them individually—waiting for their replies—whenever a pitch was thrown. But this seems inefficient. Since client replies don't really mean anything, why waste server-side time waiting for them? If it were possible to asynchronously communicate or broadcast this information to the clients, server-side performance would improve substantially. For example, the server could write the updated data to some

---

[*]Although modern CPUs actually support out-of-order execution, committal of results remains in order.

public data source that clients could access at will. Since there would be no value in their replies (other than that they got the message), the server wouldn't need to wait for them to receive the data.

Asynchrony doesn't apply only to communication between remote pieces of functionality. If single-threaded synchronous execution is recast as multithreaded, asynchronous execution within a given program can yield important efficiency benefits. Consider a Web application that downloads a set of URLs, and inserts their contents into a database *db*.

A simple way to accomplish this task would involve the following pseudo-code:

for each url *u* in the list of URLs to be downloaded
    page ← FETCH-PAGE(*u*)
    DATABASE-INSERT(*db, page*)

This means that, after the first download, each successive download occurs only after the DATABASE-INSERT of the previous one. It seems like a waste. We know that fetching the page is an I/O-bound activity, while database insertion is generally CPU-bound. It would seem optimal to request the next page be downloaded *while* the database insertion of the previous one is taking place. Thus, both activities would be occurring in parallel. Now, the only thing one needs to do is identify a way for data (i.e., the downloaded page) to be passed between them.

For this type of parallel, asynchronous solution, we might create two threads—one for downloading and one for database insertion. In doing so, suppose that the threads are able to communicate over a common thread-safe queue *q*. Given these assumptions, consider sample pseudo-code related to the first thread, which is in charge of downloading the content:

for each url *u* in the list of URLs to be downloaded
    page ← FETCH-PAGE(*u*)
    ENQUEUE(*q, page*)
ENQUEUE(*q*, End-Of-Stream)

Next, consider sample pseudo-code related to the second thread, which is in charge of inserting the extracted information *i* into a database *d* as it becomes available:

object ← DEQUEUE(*q*)
while *object* ≠ End-Of-Stream
DATABASE-INSERT(*db, object*)
object ← DEQUEUE(*q*)

Thus, by allowing multiple threads to communicate asynchronously via a global data structure, we increase overall processing parallelism.

In this example, idle CPU cycles were put to more efficient use at the expense of a slightly more complex implementation. When applicable, asynchronous designs such as this perform well and are easier to scale because of the more efficient use of resources. The main challenge is in implementation—writing correct multithreaded code and ensuring serialization (when necessary) for certain important operations on shared data structures. Later in Chapter 9, we'll also discuss how technologies like the Java Message Service (JMS) make distributed asynchronous solutions very easy.

Resource Pooling

Popular Web applications have to deal with hundreds or thousands of requests in parallel, many of which rely on application and database resources. The overhead of providing access to these resources can balloon quickly as parallelism demands rise. Consider highly concurrent database access. Each client that wants to use the database will require a database connection. Each connection requires the overhead of memory to store its state and also the overhead to create and initialize it. When you're talking about hundreds or thousands of database clients, this overhead can become unmanageable.

One very common technique to reduce overhead is resource pooling—in this case, pooling database connections. The idea here is that it's cheaper to create a fixed pool of connections that are shared among many clients than to create one connection per client. By cheaper, we're talking about the cost of memory and the cost of thread initialization. Does resource pooling actually work and provide these benefits? Let's see.

Suppose we have some number r of concurrent application server requests and that each request makes five JDBC calls. We're interested in the throughput of requests as their number increases. Our example has two types of application server: one that uses a connection for each of the five queries made per request and one that borrows from a connection pool whenever it makes a JDBC query. For the sake of simplicity, our pool is small—say 10 connections.

The code for our example is shown in Listings 4–1 through 4–5 that follow. The five important classes are: the client test (`PoolTest.java`), our connection pool (`ConnPool.java`), the shared connection (`SharedConnection.java`), the JDBC query executor (`RequestRunnable.java`), and finally the barrier for test synchronization (`Barrier.java`). Because this isn't a book about Java or synchronization, we'll skip an exhaustive discussion of the code. Instead, we'll simply describe the overall flow and identify selected interesting parts. Here's the general flow:

- `PoolTest.java` takes in client input on the number of concurrent accesses to simulate (i.e., `java PoolTest 100`) and creates the proper number of threads.
- `Barrier.Java` makes sure that we start all of the threads at once—this may seem a bit unfair if we don't make sure all threads are initialized before starting the test.
- `RequestRunnable.java` simulates each client request and deploys it as a thread.
- Each `RequestRunnable` performs five JDBC queries when it runs.
- To access the database, All `RequestRunnable` instances draw from the same connection pool (`ConnPool`), which was initialized in `PoolTest.java`.
- `RequestRunnable` objects "loan out" a `SharedConnection` object (they don't own it) and return it when they're done with each query.

Listing 4–1: Class `PoolTest.java`

```
 1 import java.sql.*;
 2
 3 /* Connection pool test client */
 4
 5 public class PoolTest
 6 {
 7   public static void main(String[] args) throws Exception
 8   {
 9     /* Register JDBC driver - Oracle used for example */
10     Class.forName("oracle.jdbc.driver.OracleDriver");
11
12     /* Identify number of concurrent threads for test */
13     int numThreads = args.length > 0 ?
14       Integer.parseInt(args[0]) : 1;
15
16     /* Initialize connection pool */
17     ConnPool p = new ConnPool(10);
18
19     /* Initialize and setup thread barrier for test */
20     Barrier b = new Barrier(numThreads);
21     for (int i=0; i<numThreads; i++)
22       (new Thread(new RequestRunnable(i, p, b))).start();
23
24     /* Let all threads attempt to execute at once */
25     b.release();
26   }
27 }
```

Listing 4–2: Class `RequestRunnable.java`

```
 1 import java.sql.*;
 2
 3 /* Simulates a single request that requires 5 JDBC queries */
 4
 5 public class RequestRunnable
 6   implements Runnable
 7 {
 8   private ConnPool m_pool;
 9   private Barrier m_barrier;
10   private int m_id;
11
12   public RequestRunnable(int a_id, ConnPool a_pool, Barrier a_barrier)
13   {
14     m_id = a_id;
15     m_barrier = a_barrier;
16     m_pool = a_pool;
17   }
18
19   public void run()
20   {
21     m_barrier.enter();
22
23     /* Run 5 queries */
24
25     PreparedStatement ops;
26     ResultSet rset;
27
28     for (int i=0; i<5; i++)
29     {
30       try {
31         Connection oconn = m_pool.loanConn();
32         ops = oconn.prepareStatement(
33           "SELECT count(*) FROM EMPLOYEE");
34         rset = ops.executeQuery();
35         m_pool.returnConn(oconn);
36       }
37       catch (Exception e) {
38         System.err.println("ERROR during querying.");
39         System.exit(1);
40       }
41     }
42   }
43 }
```

Listing 4–3: Class ConnPool.java

```
1  import java.sql.*;
2
3  /* A very simple connection pool class */
4
5  public class ConnPool
6  {
7    private SharedConnection[] m_list;
8
9    public ConnPool(int num) {
10     m_list = new SharedConnection[num];
11     try {
12       for (int i=0; i<num; i++) {
13         m_list[i] = new SharedConnection(
14           DriverManager.getConnection(
15             "jdbc:oracle:thin:@mydb"))
16       }
17     }
18     catch (Exception e) {
19        System.err.println("Error when allocating connections.");
20        System.exit(1);
21     }
22
23   }
24
25   /* Distribute a connection if/when we have one */
26
27   public synchronized Connection loanConn() {
28     Connection conn = null;
29
30     while (true) {
31       for (int i=0; i<m_list.length; i++) {
32         if (!m_list[i].inUse()) {
33           m_list[i].markBusy();
34           conn = m_list[i].getConn();
35           break;
36         }
37       }
38       if (conn !=null)
39         break;
40       try {
41         wait();
42       }
43       catch (Exception e) {
44         System.err.println("Error when waiting for a connection.");
45         System.exit(1);
46       }
47     }
48
49     return conn;
50   }
```

```
51
52    /* Gather a connection back */
53
54    public synchronized void returnConn(Connection a_conn) {
55      for (int i=0; i<m_list.length; i++) {
56        if (m_list[i].getConn() == a_conn) {
57          m_list[i].markAvailable();
58          notify();
59        }
60      }
61    }
62  }
```

Listing 4–4: Class SharedConnection.java

```
1 import java.sql.*;
2
3 /* Same as a normal database connection except that it is shared */
4
5 public class SharedConnection
6 {
7    private Connection m_conn;
8    private boolean m_inUse;
9
10   public SharedConnection(Connection a_conn)
11   {
12     m_conn = a_conn;
13     markAvailable();
14   }
15
16   public Connection getConn() { return m_conn; }
17
18   /* Keeps track of shared status */
19   public synchronized void markAvailable() { m_inUse = false; }
20   public synchronized void markBusy() { m_inUse = true; }
21   public synchronized boolean inUse() { return m_inUse; }
22 }
```

Listing 4–5: Class Barrier.java

```
1 /* A very simple barrier class */
2
3 public class Barrier
4 {
5    /* Local class for synchronization bookkeeping */
6
7    private class Marker {
8      private boolean m_locked = true;
```

```
 9     public synchronized void setDone() {
10       m_locked = false; notify();
11     }
12     public synchronized void waitDone() {
13       if (m_locked) try { wait(); } catch(Exception e) { }
14     }
15   }
16
17   int m_num;
18   Marker m_marker;
19
20   public Barrier(int a_num) {
21     m_marker = new Marker();
22     m_num = a_num;
23   }
24
25   /* Add a thread to the barrier holding tank */
26
27   public synchronized void enter() {
28     m_num--;
29     try {
30       if (m_num == 0)
31         m_marker.setDone();
32       wait();
33     }
34     catch (Exception e) {
35       System.err.println("Error when entering barrier.");
36       System.exit(1);
37     }
38   }
39
40
41   /* Notify all listeners */
42
43   public void release() {
44     m_marker.waitDone();
45     synchronized (this) {
46       notifyAll();
47     }
48   }
49
50 }
```

Executing the code demonstrates the effect of connection pooling. Figure 4–7 shows how long it takes under both approaches (connection pool and no connection pool) to process various numbers of concurrent client requests.

Figure 4–7
Pooling

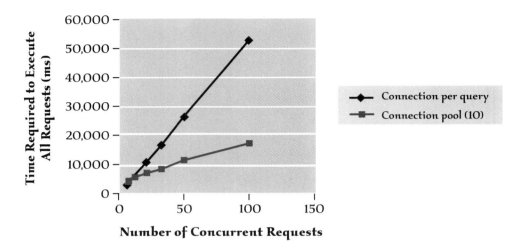

Summary

In this chapter, we have focused on some of the most important general techniques for ensuring scalability and performance in Web applications. In fact, these techniques and concepts also apply to distributed systems in general, of which the Internet is but one. No matter how the Internet evolves in terms of specific new technologies (e.g., Web services), its continued existence as a distributed system ensures that the material covered here will continue to be relevant.

To recap, here are some of the key points of this chapter:

- *Caching* and *data replication* involve copying data for the sake of improving performance. Such techniques work because they reduce the latency between the requestor and the data (i.e., data locality is increased), they summarize the translation of request to response (fewer operations in between), or both. Although both caching and replication are useful techniques, the issue of data consistency sometimes makes their implementation difficult.

- *Parallelism* increases the amount of work done at one time. In an environment where processing power and bandwidth are unlimited, parallel execution can dramatically improve performance. In most practical environments, however, local resources are limited and it is simply not feasible to parallelize everything. Doing so could exhaust resources or create a situation where a great deal of time is spent context switching and communicating among multiple threads or processes. Nevertheless, there is a middle ground here. Understanding where your application is I/O-bound and where it is CPU-bound enables you to identify the best opportunities for parallel execution and to design accordingly.

- *Redundancy* enables better application scalability. As the number of concurrent requests rises, redundant software or hardware architectures allow those requests to be attended to without noticeable degradation of service. Well-designed redundant systems make very high scalability achievable by making it easy for operations staff to deploy new machines or new software instances to meet increased demand. One important key to a successful architecture for redundancy is the effectiveness related to balancing the request or processing load.

- *Asynchrony* encourages parallel execution; thus, it can be considered complementary to such architectures. Typically, asynchronous solutions decouple the execution of one component from the execution of another. Instead of having a consumer wait for the producer to finish producing everything, effective asynchronous solutions allow the producer to stream results to the consumer and to have the latter start executing (in parallel) as soon as possible.

- *Resource pooling* bounds the overhead required to serve concurrent demand to specific resources, such as a database. By pooling objects such as connections or threads, the cost to create each instance is bounded by the maximum size of the pool. This allows concurrent execution without skyrocketing overhead costs. However, the obvious challenge is to size the pool correctly (or to grow it effectively) and to reduce the synchronization overhead required to manage the pool (i.e., issue and reclaim resource instances).

Effective use of all the techniques can lead to very efficient systems. The key is to understand the demands on your application, and then to choose your battles accordingly during the design phase. Fortunately, as we saw in Chapter 3 and as we will see in greater detail in future chapters, J2EE embraces these techniques and makes them available to application deployments as part of an underlying platform. By understanding how such features are offered by J2EE and how they can be leveraged, you can build applications that are generally scalable and encourage high performance.

HTTP Client/Server Communication

The language of the Web is the Hypertext Transfer Protocol (HTTP). HTTP is an application-level protocol that forms the basis of all directives we issue from our browsers (as well as many other standalone applications and software agents). You may believe or have heard that certain aspects of HTTP are inefficient. As it turns out, HTTP (especially its more recent versions) has evolved to become a very fast protocol, thanks to careful analysis of its weaknesses by the Web infrastructure community. Still, although HTTP can be used efficiently, just setting up and starting a Web server doesn't guarantee that you'll be using its optimizing features.

Since HTTP is the basis for most of the network communication we're interested in, it's definitely worthwhile to understand it better and also understand just how efficient (or inefficient) it can be. In particular, it's useful to know which aspects of the protocol to be concerned about and what options you, as a Web application engineer or architect, have for producing high-performance and scalable communication.

We'll explore HTTP in this chapter, but, as with other chapters in the book, we're going to resist getting lost in all of the gory details and instead focus mostly on HTTP's efficiency.

To start, let's quickly review what HTTP is and look at the major scenarios under which communication via this protocol makes sense.

The HTTP Protocol

HTTP is a request/reply protocol that is the basis for most communication on the Internet. It has evolved into a de facto standard of network-independent communication, much like Java is a language for platform-independent computing. Through HTTP, two programs can communicate without having to worry about the complexities of the lower-level network protocols and the physical infrastructure that connects them.

HTTP is a message-based protocol in the sense that communication between client and server consists of readable text (i.e., plain text). Instead of directives being phrased in ones and zeroes (bits), as in binary protocols (such as Java RMI and CORBA IIOP), HTTP requests and replies look like brief, readable notes. Here's a sample request to fetch the Web page at `http//www.example.com/index.html`:

```
GET /index.html HTTP/1.1
Host: www.example.com
```

Here's a sample reply:

```
HTTP/1.1 200
Date: Sun, 01 Jul 2001 12:00:01 GMT
Content-Type: text/html

<HTML>
      <HEAD></HEAD>
      <BODY>
            Hello World!
      </BODY>
</HTML>
```

The obvious disadvantage of a message-based protocol versus a binary one is increased message size. Since the individual letters must be sent over the wire as ones and zeroes, the resulting message is longer. For example, it takes $3 \cdot 8$ bits/byte = 24 bits to say GET; in a binary protocol, it would require far fewer. However, notice the key advantage of a message-based protocol—it's easy to see what's happening, so it's easier to debug. As it turns out, the readability and debug-capability of a message-based protocol is one of the common justifications for another recently proposed B2B protocol, Simple Object Access Protocol (SOAP), which is winning converts from established, more cryptic protocols like Electronic Data Interchange (EDI).

Now that we've seen an example of how HTTP works, let's step back and describe the general model of its request/reply behavior. In the most general form of HTTP, a client sends a request to the server composed of

- A request method
- A Universal Resource Identifier (URI)
- The protocol version
- A MIME-like message, consisting of request modifiers, client information, and, potentially, a body component

The server responds with

- A status line
- The protocol version and a success or error code
- A MIME-like message, consisting of server information, some meta-information, and, potentially, a body component

MIME (Multipurpose Internet Mail Extension) was originally based on RFC 822. Later, RFCs 2045, 2046, 2047, 2048, and 2049 extended and formalized it. Generally speaking, the MIME RFCs describe how text messages and message bodies are formatted—for example, these RFCs describe how everything from simple text messages to richer media, like audio and video, are transmitted using a message-based protocol.

Keep in mind that HTTP is an application-level protocol. According to the OSI model of network programming, that means it exists above session-level protocols like TCP, so its deployment is an option. That's right—there's nothing that prevents it from being deployed over a non-TCP session-level protocol such as ATM AAL-5. Nevertheless, since we're talking about Web applications in this book, it's best to assume the model where HTTP is deployed over TCP/IP.

There are currently two versions of HTTP in existence: 1.0 and 1.1. The latter was developed in 1997 and includes some important changes that affect overall network bandwidth consumption and caching. It became an Internet Engineering Task Force (IETF) draft standard in 1999, and it will eventually become the dominant version. Complete descriptions of both versions can be found in two Internet RFCs: HTTP 1.0 in RFC 1945 and HTTP 1.1 in RFC 2616. Instead of trying to deal with both versions at once, we'll limit our discussion to HTTP 1.1 and only refer to HTTP 1.0 for comparison or to discuss backward compatibility.

Deployment Paradigms

When considering Web applications, there are two basic deployment paradigms to consider—those that involve Web browsers as application clients and those that don't.

Applications with Browser Clients

Most interactive Web applications assume that a Web browser interface will be used to view and navigate their content. A browser has two primary jobs: to communicate with a Web server based on user directives and to render the content it receives from that server in response. Here we're interested in the efficiency of browser-to-server communication, not in its rendering details.

With regard to this efficiency, it is important to note the version of HTTP that your client browsers speak. Today most browsers, including current versions of Microsoft Internet Explorer, speak HTTP 1.1. A few older browsers, such as Netscape 4.75, speak HTTP 1.0. Depending on the nature of your client base and the platforms they use, you may not be able to assume that everyone speaks HTTP 1.1. Thus, it is important to develop a profile of your clients and their connectivity technologies.

Knowing what version of HTTP is supported by the client browsers of your application, as well as what versions are relevant to any additional intermediate network hardware such as routers and switches, is important in understanding whether optimizations associated with a particular protocol version will have an impact on scalability or performance. Right now, things are pretty simple because HTTP 1.1 has been adopted widely. But, if a new version of HTTP is developed, it will be important to understand which parts of your architecture are affected and how. Nevertheless, to keep things simple in this chapter, our discussion will focus on HTTP 1.1.

Applications with Nonbrowser Clients

Web servers don't always have Web browsers as clients. This can be true if your application involves a special client that retrieves information from a Web server or if you have multiple clients for your data (Web browsers, other software agents, etc.) and you want to consolidate your data serving. If that's the case, you may be concerned about data transfer rates. Again, the question arises: Why a message-based protocol instead of a binary protocol?

Since HTTP is deployed on top of TCP/IP, you may be tempted to think that its overhead is too costly for such scenarios. Depending on the application, you may be right. Certainly, there's no need to shovel data between client and server using HTTP just for the fun of it. For example, if the communication doesn't have to be synchronous (i.e., it's not interactive), a synchronous approach like HTTP can often yield worse performance. Also, TCP provides guaranteed delivery; yet there are many application design scenarios where such guarantees aren't really necessary.

For other kinds of deployment, the primary clients aren't browsers—instead, they're wireless PDAs, integrated voice response (IVR) systems, or even software agents running on remote machines. Just like Web browsers, these types of client want to provide access to data (often the same data that's delivered to Web browser clients). However, given their limited resources or specific nature, you might be tempted to use an alternative (possibly binary) protocol. Again, this may turn out to work best. We can't dissect every possible protocol and every possible client/server relationship, so it's difficult to evaluate.

Still, the performance difference between a non-HTTP protocol and HTTP may be less than you think. This is particularly true given how the most recent version of HTTP 1.1 works in terms of its support for caching and persistent connections. Keep in mind that, if you *don't* use something like HTTP, you may need to develop not only a custom protocol but also a *custom server* to process requests. For HTTP serving, both free and commercial products already exist that have proven to be efficient and scalable. However, if you choose to use your own protocol for your application needs, the request processing will then be in your hands and you'll have to develop a novel solution from the ground up.

Before you go down that path, it may be wise to reconsider what you're giving up. In fact, as we'll discuss in greater detail later in the chapter, there are at least three major scalability/performance reasons for using HTTP 1.1 as the basis for communication between Web servers and nonbrowser clients. Here they are now, in a nutshell:

- *Connection management*: The Web server already provides a fast and scalable way to give access to the data objects you want to make public. It takes care of issuing connections to clients (i.e., assigning a thread to an incoming request), persisting them when directed, and tearing them down when done (or returning them to a thread pool). Thus, it handles basic network connection management (and then some). Instead of spending your time reinventing the wheel—and possibly having the result compete with the Web server for resources, locks, and the like—it's typically better to let the Web server own the job of connection management and find a way to integrate your back-end software so that the server directs application requests to it ASAP.

- *Intermediate network support*: Network communication on the Internet is centered around HTTP. Correspondingly, many intermediate network elements (i.e., routers) have a great deal of built-in HTTP-based caching support. Although a proprietary protocol might traverse the same network path as an HTTP request, it can't benefit from reusing cached HTTP data.

- *Concurrent request processing*: The majority of Web servers already support parallel request processing (derived from either pipelined requests or concurrent sessions). Increasingly, they're handling massive numbers of concurrent connections with highly multithreaded deployments and so enjoy significant parallelism without significant overhead.

HTTP Efficiency

If you're an application programmer, you may be tempted to skip this discussion. After all, application designers won't be changing or extending the protocol (although extensions are considered by the IETF. Furthermore, since Web browsers are the primary generators of HTTP requests and Web servers are the primary handlers of these requests, it may not seem worthwhile to understand HTTP details because there's no opportunity to directly interact with it.

As it turns out, this is simply not the case. For one thing, as the deployer of an application you have the ability to choose your Web server and how to deploy it (e.g., Web server farms). You also have the ability to configure certain parameters of deployment. Understanding the implications of the knobs and dials made available to you by the server configuration files (e.g., the `http.conf` file for Apache Web servers) can help you deploy your server better.

During the initial stages of Web application design, it can be very useful to understand how HTTP works and the efficiency features it offers. Armed with this knowledge, you'll be able to:

- Architect your application in a way that encourages caching.
- Identify key settings of an HTTP server that affect scalability and performance.
- Understand important efficiency-related parameters of a typical HTTP API, such as that provided by Java.

Such knowledge encourages good design from the outset of a project, instead of being shoved in once testing and benchmarking begin.

Finally, understanding the key efficiency features of HTTP may cause you to rethink your strategy for Internet communication that does not involve a Web browser (e.g., such as that related to batch and B2B-style processing). Despite its earlier reputation (or your intuition) about its inherent overhead, the HTTP protocol has matured into an efficient means for communicating among systems linked by the Internet. Its built-in optimizations related to caching, connection management, and security are often convincing reasons to abandon more cryptic, proprietary protocols that might have seemed more efficient.

HTTP Details

The HTTP 1.1 protocol as specified by RFC 2616 includes information about the following:

- Overall protocol semantics
- Supported methods (e.g., GET and POST)
- Connection management (i.e., persistent connections)

- Caching support
- Security
- Request/reply status codes (e.g., HTTP 200), header fields, protocol parameters, and so on
- Content negotiation and other miscellaneous topics

In our discussion, we'll be primarily concerned with the HTTP aspects that have the most impact in terms of scalability and performance for Web applications—the request methods (GET and POST), caching, and connection management. But first we'll start out with a review of how the protocol works.

Semantics

As we saw earlier, when HTTP is deployed on TCP/IP its requests and replies are delivered over TCP channels that are established by the client and the server. Since TCP (Transmission Control Protocol)—not UDP (Universal Datagram Protocol)—is employed, delivery of packets is guaranteed. While beneficial in some respects, this guarantee has performance implications as well. To understand why, consider a typical HTTP connection scenario in which a client requests a simple HTML page from a Web server at http://www.example.com:

```
<HTML>
       <HEAD></HEAD>
       <BODY>
              Hello world
       </BODY>
</HTML>
```

Figure 5–1 shows how this request is fulfilled. Notice that the following steps occur:

- The client requests a TCP connection to the server.
- The server agrees to the connection and acknowledges that to the client.
- The client sends an HTTP request on the open channel.
- The server receives the request and responds to it (in our example, with the HTML file above).

These steps show that two client/server TCP roundtrips are required: one full trip for the initial connection establishment, a half trip for the client HTTP request,

Figure 5–1
Normal communications required for Web page fetch

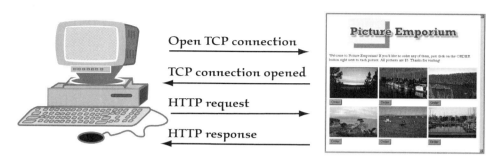

and a half trip for the beginning part of the returned data (the file). The entire transfer process can be summarized by

$$(2 \cdot RT) + T_c$$

RT = Roundtrip time between client/server
T_c = Time to transfer the actual bytes of content

If we consider a more typical HTML file, we may be dealing with a page that contains JavaScript, Java applets, and /or images. Transferring applets and images for a page requires separate HTTP connections, and this means that a given URL may represent many HTTP request/replies—and even more TCP request/replies. If the network latencies between client and server are high, or if the bandwidth between them is narrow, the client sees a slow application. If you want a reminder of this, fire up a 56K dial-up connection, navigate to your favorite advertising-driven commercial site, and watch and wait while all of the image-based advertisements download.

Obviously, there's another, darker, side to application sessions that require a high number of HTTP connections: They can exhaust servers, particularly their available socket descriptors. Also, if the data being passed along these connections is sizable, the resulting bandwidth demand quickly rises. The sad part of this is that many of these connections are established simply to perform what are in fact redundant retrievals. At the same time, a greater number of Web applications packed with graphical and animated content (e.g., Flash animations) are starting to appear. Both trends lead to more HTTP connections, raising the scalability bar for servers in terms of connection and bandwidth management.

We know that, from the presentation (GUI) perspective, there are ways to reduce the number of HTTP connections. For example, we can design pages that use fewer images, reuse objects, use style sheets, and employ dynamic HTML techniques for things like menus and other navigation structures. On the server side, we can deal with excessive connections with an HTTP 1.1 feature called persistent connections. We'll talk more about these later in the chapter as well as other server-side alternatives (caching, content distribution, load balancing, etc.) that can be employed.

Application architects should always take the implications of their interfaces seriously. The number of HTTP connections demanded by a Web interface makes scalability and performance more problematic during deployment as the client base grows. Lots of images, dynamic pages, and unproductive HTML forms can result in many more requests—and thus greater scalability challenges—than might otherwise be necessary.

HTTP Requests

Although there are nine possible HTTP request methods specified by RFC 2616, the ones of most interest to us are the two that you're probably already familiar with: GET and POST. Most people know them as the methods that allow an HTTP client to look up some information on the server.

Once a TCP connection has been established between client and server, the client can issue an HTTP request, such as GET or POST, and receive an HTTP reply. In HTTP 1.1, multiple HTTP requests can be made on the same connection.

HTTP requests and replies contain a **header** and a **body**. The header is a series of name/value pairs—the metadata of the communication. The body contains the application-level content, such as an HTML file. For a better feel for the request/reply dialogue between client and server, I'll describe something similar to our city example (from Chapter 4) and discuss it in more detail.

Suppose a user wants to retrieve `http://www.example.com/cities.html`. As shown in Figure 5–2, this page lists all of the cities in the world, with their corresponding countries and populations (quite a big list!). When the user types the URL into the Web browser's location field, the browser establishes a connection to the server and issues an HTTP request to retrieve the information. Since the user typed the location into the browser location field, this request will be an invocation of the HTTP GET method.

The GET Method

The HTTP GET method is used to retrieve the specified URI from the Web server. In our example, the browser might make the following request in order to resolve `http://www.example.com/cities.html` from `www.example.com`:

```
GET /cities.html HTTP/1.1
Host: www.example.com
```

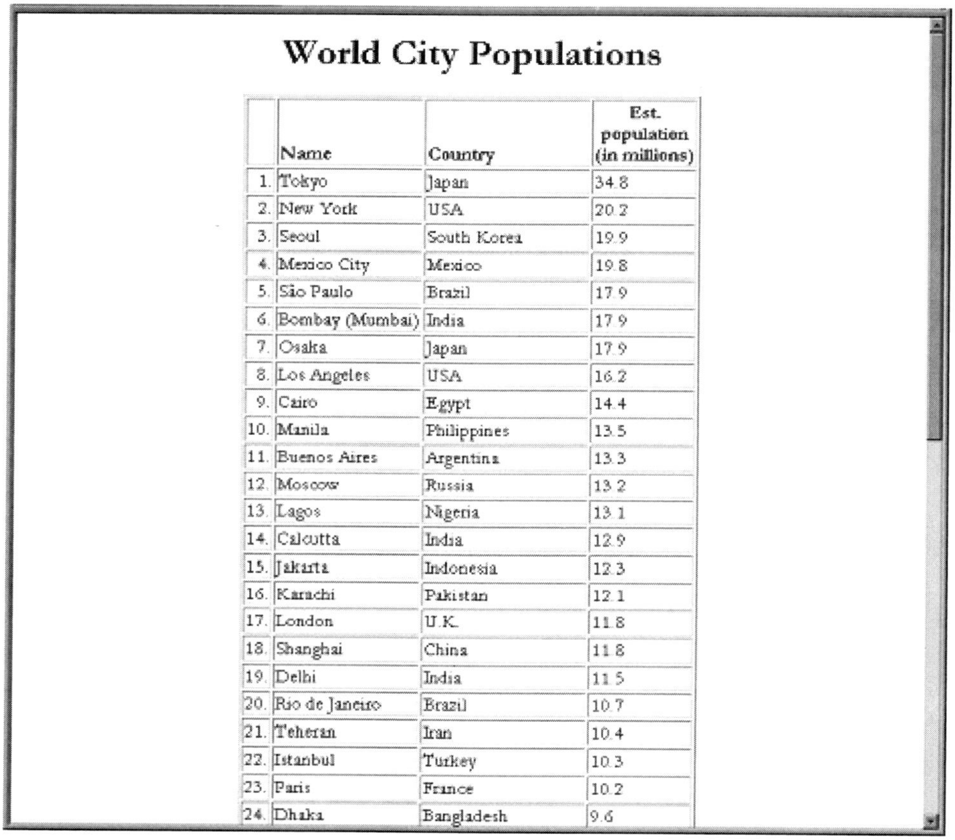

World City Populations

	Name	Country	Est. population (in millions)
1.	Tokyo	Japan	34.8
2.	New York	USA	20.2
3.	Seoul	South Korea	19.9
4.	Mexico City	Mexico	19.8
5.	São Paulo	Brazil	17.9
6.	Bombay (Mumbai)	India	17.9
7.	Osaka	Japan	17.9
8.	Los Angeles	USA	16.2
9.	Cairo	Egypt	14.4
10.	Manila	Philippines	13.5
11.	Buenos Aires	Argentina	13.3
12.	Moscow	Russia	13.2
13.	Lagos	Nigeria	13.1
14.	Calcutta	India	12.9
15.	Jakarta	Indonesia	12.3
16.	Karachi	Pakistan	12.1
17.	London	U.K.	11.8
18.	Shanghai	China	11.8
19.	Delhi	India	11.5
20.	Rio de Janeiro	Brazil	10.7
21.	Teheran	Iran	10.4
22.	Istanbul	Turkey	10.3
23.	Paris	France	10.2
24.	Dhaka	Bangladesh	9.6

Figure 5–2 Web page listing city populations

This is the actual content of the message being transferred from client to server. A corresponding reply from the server might contain

```
HTTP/1.1 200
Date: Sun, 01 Jul 2001 19:54:02 GMT
Content-Type: text/html

<HTML>
        <HEAD>World City Populations</HEAD>
        <BODY>
                <H1>World City Populations</H1>
```

```
            ... (rest of the web page HTML)...

        </BODY>
</HTML>
```

The semantics of a GET request are such that clients can assume that no side effects occur when such a request is processed. Thus, GET is a "safe" HTTP method in this sense and has important implications as far as the caching model of HTTP is concerned. It's also distinct from the other popular way to process application requests—POST. More about HTTP POST shortly, but for now let's preface this discussion with this simple message: If you've been lumping POST and GET together and using either arbitrarily, *think again*. Even though they appear similar to many Web programmers writing applications to fetch data from remote Web sites, they contain very different assumptions in terms of their potential impact on server-side resources.

Caching Static GET Requests

One of the interesting things about the GET method is that it can be considered *conditional* if the HTTP request also contains one of these optional header fields:

- If-Modified-Since
- If-Unmodified-Since
- If-Match
- If-None-Match
- If-Range

These fields express certain conditions about the object being requested. Based on how the conditions evaluate, a local copy of the object may be sufficient and the original won't have to be retransferred. Thus, a *cached version* of the object can be used. This is an important aspect of the GET method because it directly affects overall server-side application load, available network bandwidth, and network latency involved in server replies. If an intermediary between the client and the server caches the server's responses, it can use these fields to update its caches only when necessary.

To understand how the header fields are used, let's consider an example—the commonly used If-Modified-Since field. Suppose a user requests the static page verylongpage.html from www.example.com. We'll assume that the client machine is located at a residence, and to keep things simple for now, that there are no intermediary proxy servers involved in the network transfers. When the client attempts to retrieve the page for the first time, the following happens:

- The client browser requests the information from the original server via an unconditional GET request.
- The originating Web server resolves the request and returns the document to the user's browser.

Since the GET had no conditions associated with it, when the same client requests this document, the same costly process takes place. Thus, the example.com Web servers not only have to serve everyone who wants the verylongpage.html file, but they have to serve the same clients who make multiple requests for it!

However, if the browser sets the If-Modified-Since request header when communicating with the originating server, a needless data transfer can be avoided. For example, during step 2 it can amend the GET request by indicating the date that the currently cached object was last transferred:

```
GET /cities.html HTTP/1.1
If-Modified-Since: Mon, 3 Apr 2001 18:00:00 GMT
```

If the originating server determines that the requested object has been modified since this date, it sends the object to the client, just as if it had been requested for the first time. If the requested object hasn't been modified, the originating server can return an HTTP 304 message, indicating that the cached object is still up-to-date, and thus avoid a redundant data transfer:

```
HTTP/1.1 304 OK
```

Subsequently, the browser can use its cached copy to resolve the request, which is what the most recent versions of the Netscape and Microsoft browsers do today.

The other conditional GET header fields act in a similar or predictable fashion. For example, If-Unmodified-Since works in reverse of If-Modified-Since: If the document requested has been modified since the time specified, the specified operation (GET in our case) *shouldn't* be performed. Obviously, this is of much less use than If-Modified-Since from the GET perspective, and it actually makes more sense when it comes to HTTP update requests (perform the requested update only if the document *hasn't* changed since this time).

If-Match and If-None-Match are similar to If-Modified-Since and If-Unmodified-Since and will be discussed in detail later in this chapter. The main point is that the GET request can be augmented with these parameters to leverage intermediate caches.

We should note the part that proxy servers (both client-side and server-side) play in brokering client/server communication. In general, they can extend the client-side caching model so that multiple users can benefit from the same local cache. In this way, the proxies act as intermediate caches and obey caching logic just as a browser might (because they're shared, RFC 2616 does make some important distinctions about how they handle certain cache directives).

Content distribution networks also play a role in reducing the latencies associated with the transfer of static content by replicating and distributing relatively static and bandwidth-hungry content (such as images). While such replication obviously benefits the client because it reduces latencies and improves the perception of server availability, it also greatly benefits the server because dramatically fewer connections and server-side bandwidth are required.

Caching Dynamic GET Requests

As we've seen, the GET method requests that the Web server return the information specified. Often this is simply a static page, in which case it's always an exact copy of the page stored on the server. Sometimes the specified URI is a so-called "data-producing process" (i.e., a CGI program), in which case the *information produced by this process* is returned. In such a scenario, it's also possible to pass parameters from the client to the server. The primary mechanism for this is the HTML FORM element, which enables client input to be sent to the server. Based on the URI requested (the process) and the client-side parameters, a custom HTTP reply (Web page) is generated.

To understand this more clearly, let's return to our earlier example of a Web page that lists the cities of the world. We'll extend it to include an initial page that displays a list box containing the major cities and their countries. On this page, shown in Figure 5–3, the user chooses a particular city from the list box. A server-side CGI-bin program called `cityquery.cgi` processes this request to return dynamic results. When the user clicks the Submit button, the following GET request is sent to the server:

```
GET /cityquery.cgi?city=Paris%2C+France HTTP/1.1
```

Thus, we see that the request that the client made is a combination of the FORM target and the data associated with the list box selection. We can also see that there's some encoding and reformatting of the data when the request is made. The main point here, however, is that a dynamic page can be generated through a GET request.

Figure 5–3
Querying a
specific city

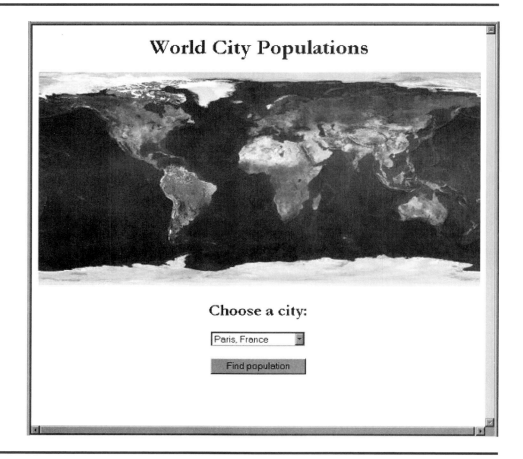

You probably already know how GET requests are constructed from HTML forms and how parameters are encoded. But did you realize that the responses to GET requests with parameters *can be cached*? In fact, they can, and this has obvious important performance implications. As long as the server properly indicates it as cacheable, a dynamically generated GET response can be delivered faster to the requestor, without incurring additional server load. This support is built in to HTTP 1.1. As an application designer, all you need to do is make sure that the HTTP responses include the proper header information to indicate to the client and the intermediate network elements that the data can be cached.

The way to do this is with the `Expires` HTTP header field. For example, a server can return a result that includes the following information:

```
HTTP/1.1 200 OK
<... other header fields ...>
Expires: Fri, 1 Jan 2010 00:00:00 GMT

<HTML>
        <HEAD></HEAD>
        <BODY>
                <... data ...>
        </BODY>
</HTML>
```

which indicates that the response is valid until Friday, January 1, 2010. If the user bookmarks this page and returns to it, he'll get the cached copy. Or he can type the same URL into the browser location bar (this works for IE 5.5 and Netscape 4.x on Windows). It's only if he clicks on the browser Reload button that he'll get a refreshed copy.

There's a very important difference between `Last-Modified` and `Expires` for caching Web content. With the `Last-Modified` approach, the browser always checks with the server to see if a new copy of the requested document has been generated. If there are networking problems at the client site, `Last-Modified` won't work (it won't be able to contact the server) and the user will notice the hanging. However, with the `Expires` approach the cached copy of the document is reused, independent of network availability. There's a very important consequence to this: Once a document has an `Expires` tag associated with it, there's no requirement that the client refetch it until that `Expires` date is reached. This means that, even if we make an important change to the document, we have no right to request that the client refetch it—we're stuck with our original date.

We've seen how the HTTP `GET` method can be used to fetch static and dynamically generated content from the server. We've also seen that careful use of additional optional header fields can prevent redundant data transfers and use information already in a cache. Later, we'll see that HTTP 1.1 caching model is even more complex than we've discussed thus far and contains additional mechanisms to encourage caching of information at several levels. Before we get into that topic, let's look at the second most popular way Web clients interface with servers.

The POST Method

If you're not familiar with the HTTP standard, you might be surprised to learn that `POST` isn't just a more sophisticated form of `GET`. It's convenient to think of it this way, since most developers who have a basic understanding of `GET` and `POST` know that GET has limitations, such as the size of the URL, whereas POST seems like a more general mechanism for passing name/value information when requesting an object.

As it turns out, the HTTP standard views the POST request as the way to create the requested entity on the server, as a subordinate of the request URI. Upon a POST request, the server can simply respond with an acknowledgment (HTTP 200 or 204) and provide no other data. Or it can indicate that the entity has been created (HTTP 201) and provide information corresponding to this creation. "Information corresponding to this creation" is what makes POST appear to us like GET.

That POST is a mutable operation on the server is a key reason why it's less efficient than GET for certain types of dynamic content. As stated in the HTTP 1.1 specification, the HTTP methods PUT, DELETE, and POST *must* cause a cache to invalidate its entry.

In our cities example, an HTML form that performs a POST when the user selects a country from which to view a list of cities has no chance of having that response cached by any intermediate cache, including the client agent itself. Just from the standpoint of what is cacheable, then, POST is less efficient (on average) than GET as means for processing things like HTML forms.

HTTP 1.1 Caching

As we discussed, some static and dynamic GET responses can be cached. Careful compliance of the Expires header field on an HTTP GET response and use of the If-Modified-Since header field on an HTTP GET request can affect performance and scalability.

While the Expires, If-Modified-Since, and Last-Modified headers apply to both HTTP 1.0 and 1.1, version 1.1 actually goes much further in terms of cache control with several important header field additions.

Before diving into the details, let's step back a moment and review the roles client and server play, at least from the standpoint of caching. Although caching mechanisms can be employed by the client or the server, in many cases both need to take an active role for the process to be effective.

Generally speaking, the server can indicate the following information about the content in its response:

- Dates associated with content expiration
- Tags for ensuring cache consistency
- Whether or not the response should explicitly be cached
- What type of cache (private or shared) should cache the response

In contrast, clients can request the entire contents of a resource:

- Conditionally, if the content is more recent than the date indicated by the client
- Conditionally, if the content tag is different from the one indicated by the client
- Unconditionally, ignoring any server-based caching suggestions

Date-Based Validation

We saw how dates are used in the `Expires` and `Last-Modified` header fields. Browsers and intermediate caches use these dates to know when to refresh cached information. This style of validation is known as date-based because dates are the basis for object freshness determination.

HTTP 1.1 has a simple and obvious date-based validation model that causes a document to be refetched if its *age* exceeds its *freshness lifetime*. The `Expires` tag is one variable that affects the value of this lifetime. A few other important HTTP response fields can do so as well. One is the `Date` response header field. This is required by HTTP 1.1 and indicates the date on which the document was generated. It can be used to calculate the document's age. However, an `Age` header field can also be generated by the server. This field actually takes priority over calculated age, for good reason.

The HTTP 1.1 expiration model assumes that other intermediate caches can be in the path of client/server communication; it allows them (if HTTP 1.1 compliant) to augment the `Age` header to better represent the document age, taking into account things like cache-to-server response time. Thus, intermediate caches set the `Age` value based on estimations of network latency to make it as accurate as possible. There's also a `Max-Age` field, which indicates at what age a document becomes stale.

The overall age calculation algorithm can be summarized as follows:

- The *apparent age* of the document is the maximum of either zero or the document `Date` header value minus the server response time.

- The *corrected received age* is the maximum of either the *apparent age* or the `Age` header field value. Intermediate caches not HTTP 1.1 compliant won't forward this `Age` value.

- The *response delay* is the local time difference between the client request and receipt of the response from the network (server or intermediate cache).

- The *corrected initial age* is the *corrected received age* added to the *response delay*.

- The *resident time* is the difference between the *response time* and the current time.

- The *current age* of the document is the sum of the *corrected initial age* and the *resident time*.

Once the current age of the document is determined, it can be compared to the value of the Max-Age field. If there's no Max-Age field, the Expires field is used—note that accurate use of Expires requires that client and server have their clocks synchronized. Finally, if no Expires field is present and no other caching control information is included, the document will be refetched in response to any duplicate queries that follow.

As you can tell, the purpose of the Age and Max-Age fields is to improve the accuracy of document freshness determination. Simply doing the math to get the age of the document based on local clocks, without taking into account response times, isn't very precise. Unlike HTTP 1.0, which doesn't consider intermediate caches, HTTP 1.1 is a more sophisticated, intermediate-cache-aware expiration model.

Tag-Based Validation

Date-based validation can sometimes be problematic. One of its assumptions is that client and server clocks will be synchronized, but, if the client (or some intermediary) has an incorrect clock there is not much a server can do about it. Similarly, if the server clock is incorrect for some reason, that may lead to problems for clients. What can also be troubling about date-based validation is its "genie-out-of-the-bottle" aspect. For example, once a server has replied to an HTTP GET with a response that includes an Expires field set to some time in the future, it can't expect clients to check back, even if it realizes later that the content will indeed change.

As an alternative to date-based validation, HTTP 1.1 supports tag-based validation. The idea is that servers can construct responses with one or more tags that summarize a response. These tags are commonly referred to as opaque because they have no meaning to the client, only to the server. When requests are made for previously viewed content, clients and intermediaries can determine whether their cached response is stale by comparing its entity tag to the entity tag of the currently served response. To associate a response with a tag, the server amends it with the ETag header field.

For example, when requesting http://www.example.com/foo.html, a server would include

```
ETag: "0-90-3ad8c299"
```

A client or intermediate cache could then associate the URL with this tag so that, when future requests were issued (from the same or another client), the intermediate cache could check with the server to see if the cached copy was still valid. In doing so, the client or intermediate would construct a GET request and include the header field If-Match or If-None-Match.

The `If-Match` field tells the server to construct a full response if the tag(s) it lists are the same as those on the server-side resource. The client can thus amend its request to have the following HTTP field:

```
If-Match: "0-90-3ad8c299"
```

From the standpoint of caching, `If-Match` isn't as relevant as `If-None-Match`, which allows the client to conditionally request the resource. With `If-None-Match`, the client can request that the resource be re-sent by the server if any of the listed tags fail to match those on the server side.

To continue with our example, if the client issues

```
GET /foo.html HTTP/1.1
Host: www.example.com
If-None-Match: "0-90-3ad8c299"
```

the server will return the entire content only if `If-None-Match` fails to match the corresponding server-side tag. In this sense, `If-None-Match` is used very similarly to `If-Modified-Since`. Both make an HTTP GET conditional, but one is based on dates whereas the other is based on tags.

Cache-Control Headers

The HTTP 1.1 `Cache-Control` header field can be very useful because it offers more control over what can be cached as well as which party (client or intermediate system) performs the caching. In general, the presence of this header field serves as evidence that the HTTP standard has begun to recognize the existence of the internetwork between client and server, and the important role intermediate network elements can play in terms of overall communication efficiency.

`Cache-Control` specifies that the response be classified as

- `public`: Client or intermediary (shared) cache can attempt to cache the response.
- `private`: Only client can cache the response.
- `no-cache`: Client and intermediary cache(s) should not cache the response.
- `no-store`: Intermediate caches (private and shared) can't store document text for security reasons.
- `max-age`: Maximum age of the document (used with calculated age).
- `s-maxage`: Overrides `max-age`, but only for a shared cache.
- `must-revalidate`: Requires clients to always revalidate their cached copy.

- proxy-revalidate: Same as must-validate, but applies only to intermediate shared proxy caches.

As an example, we can limit the caching of foo.html from example.com to client caches and set Cache-Control as follows:

```
HTTP/1.1 200 OK
Cache-Control: private
```

This prevents intermediate caches from storing the response, but allows the client's private cache to do so. This is a reasonable way to encourage both security and performance. Notice that I say "encourage"—in no way do these techniques enforce security. Unless encrypted, documents that pass through intermediaries are always subject to RFC violations and possible tracking or rebroadcast.

There are a number of other parameters to the Cache-Control field that have to do with requests, but since these are actually important for security or in relation to the implementation of an intermediary cache, we won't address them here. If you're interested, Section 14.9 of RFC 2616 makes for interesting reading.

Connection Management

Earlier, we discussed the semantics of HTTP. Recall that a single HTTP connection using TCP can require two roundtrips: one to establish the connection and one to transfer the content. The designers of HTTP 1.0 and 1.1 realized early on that this was going to be a problem. As the popularity of the Web grew and Web pages and sites became more complex, with lots of graphics, it became clear that the number of HTTP connections generated at any one time was going to raise major scalability and bandwidth issues.

What's more, there seemed to be a lot of waste in the process of transferring Web objects composed of even a single page. For example, when a user connected to a single logical Web page, such as http://www.cnn.com, separate HTTP connections were required for downloading the page, each image, and any applets. Given that a user had already established a connection with cnn.com, couldn't there be some batch-style transfer?

To remedy this situation, protocol designers came up with the notion of *persistent connections*. The initial idea was to leverage the TCP connection already established with a server to transfer other objects associated with the site or page. To understand how this feature improves performance, consider what happens when a user has to download any Web page that includes several embedded objects (e.g., images or graphics), such as the one shown in Figure 5–4. Suppose that, in addition to the basic HTML for this page, there are some 50 images embedded within.

Figure 5–4
A Web page with several embedded images

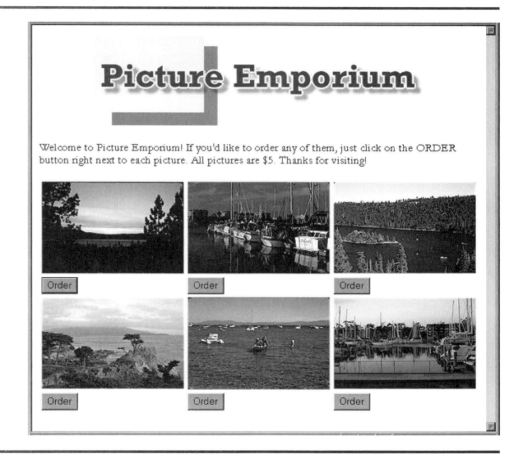

Without persistent connections, Web browsers would use one HTTP connection to fetch the HTML page and then one for each image, leading to a rough total of

$$\text{transfer time} = (2 \bullet (50 + 1) \bullet RT) + T_c$$
$$= 102 \bullet RT + T_c$$

With persistent connections, this could be reduced to

$$\text{transfer time} = (2 \bullet RT) + (50 \bullet RT) + T_c$$
$$= 52 \bullet RT + T_c$$

The practical effect of this difference is noticeable. Let's assume that the total content required to transfer this page (including images) is about 75 K, that it takes 100 ms to transfer the content, and that it takes 15 ms to send a packet between our client and the sample Web site (the RTT is thus 30 ms). This means that the total transfer time for both scenarios will be

- $102 \cdot 15 + 100 = 1630$ ms without persistent connections
- $52 \cdot 15 + 100 = 880$ ms with persistent connections

By using persistent connections, we've reduced the transfer rate about 50 percent. Convincing, isn't it? In addition to better end-to-end transfer times, there are a number of other advantages to persistent connections, among them:

- *Less CPU and memory demand* of routers and servers (fewer TCP connections).
- *Less bandwidth required* to transfer a set of related objects (i.e., a Web page plus its images).
- *Better network congestion control*— as more time is given to an established TCP connection, the built-in congestion control features of TCP have more time to improve overall network throughput.

Support for persistent connections actually started in HTTP 1.0 with use of the `Keep-Alive` header. By constructing an HTTP request that included `Keep-Alive`, HTTP 1.0 clients could request that the connection be persistent. However, it was discovered that the `Keep-Alive` approach led to undesirable effects when proxy servers existed on the client/server path.

HTTP 1.1 doesn't use the `Keep-Alive` approach. Instead, its exchanges assume that all connections are kept persistent unless the server or client explicitly indicates otherwise. For example, a server can close a connection by including the following in its response header:

```
Connection: close
```

Persistent connections also require the server to notify the client of the message length. They can do so by including either a `Transfer-Encoding` or a `Content-Length` header to indicate the size of the content being delivered. `Transfer-Encoding` represents a special self-describing method for encoding the data being transferred; `Content-Length` simply indicates the length of the entire message. Both let the client know when a logical object has been completely transferred.

Note that HTTP 1.1 and 1.0 clients differ on how they use these header fields. For example, suppose that a server includes the following in its transfer:

```
Transfer-Encoding: chunked
Content-Length: 8192
```

Many HTTP 1.0 clients don't understand the `Transfer-Encoding` field and instead use the `Content-Length` field. However, HTTP 1.1 clients are required to ignore `Content-Length` and use `Transfer-Encoding`. If only the `Content-Length` field is returned (i.e., by an HTTP 1.1 server), HTTP 1.1 clients use that information.

The reason that HTTP 1.1 supports `Transfer-Encoding` is that it's not always possible to determine content size in advance. This is typically true with dynamic content. Instead of committing to a specified length at the beginning of the transfer, the units of data being transferred can be self-describing. With the "chunked" style of `Transfer-Encoding`, the client receives a series of chunks (each with a self-describing size) and knows that it has read everything when the size of the current chunk is less than zero.

Persistent connections provide another important feature: *request pipelining*. This allows a client to transfer a series of requests over an HTTP connection instead of waiting for each response to arrive before distributing the next request. Obviously, this is useful for pages that refer to additional objects, such as images. When the page is read, the client can identify a list of images to be transferred and pipeline its requests for them to the server. In effect, this asynchronous style of request/reply improves the overall parallelism of the transfer process.

Scalability and Performance Hints

With a survey of HTTP and its efficiency features under our belts, it's now time to consider specific strategies that encourage scalability and high performance for any Web application.

Use GET and POST Judiciously

An application designer has the ability to determine how data queries and updates are processed. As we've discussed, its best to require POST requests only when there are going to be side effects of the communication—that is, data will be updated on the server. If not, you are strongly encouraged to code your HTML input forms for GET requests because of GET's tight integration with the HTTP 1.1 caching model.

A good default strategy is

- Use GET requests for queries or views of your data.
- Use POST requests for updates to your data.

Keep in mind that things like updating session tracking data can be considered "updates," even though they may have no bearing on core application purpose or behavior. Thus, you'll find it difficult to track detailed client behavior if you don't force all session requests to be implemented as POSTs. I'm not saying that tracking client browsing behavior is important or even ethical. Nevertheless, it does happen on the Web, many times for well-intentioned reasons. Ask yourself which is more important—to track your clients' browsing behavior (which they might object to) or conserve resources and improve your overall scalability. Unless tracking your clients' every move is fundamental to your application, you might want to loosen up a bit and reward your clients with a quicker application.

Consider HTTP for Nonbrowser Clients

As we discussed, HTTP might seem inefficient because it's message based and inherently leads to bulkier communication between client and server. For nonbrowser clients, you may be tempted to use another protocol. In truth, however, HTTP support for caching and persistent connections buys a lot of performance improvement. What's more, a different or custom protocol may involve using a less efficient server. Web servers have become highly efficient request processors, so it may be in your interest to have your nonbrowser clients use HTTP because of its built-in performance and scalability features.

This isn't to say that all nonbrowser clients should use HTTP. In particular, those client/server relationships that are very different from the browser/Web-server relationship might consider an alternative. I'm talking primarily about asynchronous processing models, such as those used in messaging or broadcast paradigms. The synchronous nature of HTTP data transfers may result in worse performance for normally asynchronous scenarios, even with some of the features described throughout this chapter.

Promote HTTP Response Caching

In deploying your site, you'll rarely (if ever) have any direct control over whether or how clients cache your content. You won't know what browser they're using or what kind of intermediate caching systems exist between you and them. How, then, should you annotate the content you serve? Should you use the Last-Modified or the Expires field? Maybe the ETag field instead?

As usual, it depends on the particulars of your deployment. However, I highly suggest that you

- Assume the potential for some caching between you and the client.
- Attempt to support both HTTP 1.0 and 1.1 caching models. To do that, you should construct your responses so that they contain valid values for the Expires or the Last-Modified field, the ETag field, and the Cache-Control field.

One tricky issue is choosing the Expires or the Last-Modified field. It can be argued that Last-Modified is safer than Expires because it limits the server's commitment to the consistency scheme. It places the burden on the client to validate the content, and the nature of conditional GET requests is such that the overhead for this validation is insignificant (compared to the content, which may be substantial).

True, this approach requires an HTTP request and response and is therefore not as scalability friendly as the Expires approach. However, it provides a safe way to encourage caching by both HTTP 1.0 and 1.1 clients. In contrast, the Expires approach suffers from the genie-out-of-the-bottle syndrome: Once you release an object with Expires, you have to wait the specified time before assuming that clients will update their copy. Such a risk may be too costly depending on the nature of your application.

Of course, there are clear advantages to Expires. First of all, it eliminates the need to make even a conditional request on a resource. A smart client or an intermediary can use an Expires tag set to a future date to avoid the need to have the server validate its content.

Expires is really the only option for dynamic content. Recall that it's possible for clients and intermediaries to cache GET responses—even if they're dynamically generated (from CGI scripts, servlets, etc.). However, if that dynamically generated content contains only a Last-Modified field, HTTP clients might need to generate an If-Modified-Since request to check and validate its consistency. This seems to indicate that the server needs to *regenerate* the content and *then* compare the dates. But, as stated in RFC 2616, HTTP 1.1 avoids this problem by explicitly stating (in section 13.9) that clients shouldn't assume that cached URIs containing a "?" are fresh unless the originating server has explicitly indicated an expiration date.

It should be mentioned that there are smart ways to use Expires. Realize that, if you simply change the name of the resource that has an Expires tag, it won't be in the client or intermediary cache and will thus have to be downloaded. So, if you serve a page named foo.html that contains a dynamic image called image.gif, you simply need to change the name of image.gif to image1.gif. *But be very careful here*. Remember that the foo.html static page may itself be cached and that your updates to it to include a pointer to image1.gif may not be seen immediately. In this sense, it can be smarter to use a Last-Modified approach on the foo.html page but an Expires approach on the image.

As far as entity tags are concerned, using the ETag validation method is encouraged because HTTP 1.1 clients will choose it over the If-Modified-Since approach. Since clock synchronization may be an issue between client and server, ETag is a cheaper and more accurate way to ensure consistency. Unfortunately, its scope is limited to HTTP 1.1 clients. Also, it has the same problem that If-Modified-Since has when it comes to dynamic content that's expensive to generate.

`Cache-Control` directives may be in order if the content delivered is personalized. Since there may be many intermediate caching systems between client and server, an explicit `Cache-Control` directive is the best way for a server to specify whether and how responses should be cached. For example, if an HTTP `GET`-based dynamic response is personalized and you want to limit who caches it, you can set the `Cache-Control` to `Private`.

Support Persistent Connections

The pipelining and reduced TCP connections encouraged by persistent connections have been shown to make a difference.

One of the more important quantifications of improvement was documented by Nielsen and colleagues (1997). They found that using persistent connections with pipelining significantly improves performance over HTTP 1.0. Interestingly, an HTTP 1.1 transfer without pipelining or persistent connections requires fewer packets than an equivalent HTTP 1.0 transfer, but proved to be slower! So, while HTTP 1.1 is more bandwidth friendly than HTTP 1.0 in general, it's only the use of persistent connections and pipelining that allows it to perform faster.[*]

In order to support both HTTP 1.0 and 1.1 clients, it's wise to use both the `Transfer-Encoding` and the `Content-Length` header. It's a few bytes of extra overhead, but it buys you HTTP 1.0 compatibility. Your HTTP 1.1 clients will ignore `Content-Length` anyway (per the RFC).

Summary

The network is one of the three basic parts of any client/server application. Since our focus here is on Web applications, that usually means understanding HTTP over TCP/IP. One of the more interesting things about the HTTP part of the Web application equation is that it's not an API like JDBC that you program with. Instead, it's something that you *use*—it's the basis of communication between your application and its browser clients (and potentially its nonbrowser clients as well). Knowing how to use it can have dramatic effects on performance and scalability.

We saw that there are significant differences between HTTP 1.0 and 1.1. It's still important to understand and support both and even more important to know what your client base uses. In terms of differences, HTTP 1.1 has some important new efficiency features, such as persistent connections and sophisticated cache control, that address the performance and scalability concerns with HTTP 1.0. We spent a

---

[*]It should be noted that Nielsen and colleagues tuned the buffering behavior of both client and server and avoided the effects of the TCP Nagle algorithm (from the client) by turning that option off during socket communication.

considerable amount of time addressing some of the important HTTP cache-related header fields and how to use them.

Finally, we learned that the two most popular HTTP requests—GET and POST—have important assumptions and implications that many engineers simply don't know or take for granted. GET requests, in particular, are encouraged for read-only data, and by nature they can leverage some key caching features (especially in terms of HTTP 1.1 communication). POST requests, meanwhile, are associated with data updates. While they can't leverage GET's caching features, they should be used when client requests (such as database updates) can cause application side effects.

6

Request Processing

For *n*-tier Web applications, the request processor plays a key role in the client/ server exchange. It acts as the intermediary between the two and thus has a major influence on performance and scalability. No matter how well designed and well oiled the server side of the equation is, a slow or less-than-scalable client request handler will reflect poorly on the whole application.

During the writing of this book, it was announced that an interesting database containing information about American immigration was soon to be made available to the public via the Web. It would contain detailed records of foreign immigrants who arrived at Ellis Island, New York, in the early 1900s.

The museum at Ellis Island attracts tens of thousands of visitors each year, many of whom are interested in tracing their historical roots. Given such public interest in the place, news that immigration records were to be made available over the Web spread quickly. To make the situation more interesting, a number of well-known organizations were advertising the site. A commentator for a major network radio station, unaffiliated with the site, described and advertised it the day before it was launched. Given all the attention and my own interest—my ancestors had come through Ellis Island—I was curious to see how well the site would hold up to what I expected to be a lot of initial attention.

Because it was in fact a ".org" site, it was unlikely that big money was being thrown at making it highly scalable. I didn't expect much, but I hoped it would do better than earlier launches of similar "hot spot" sites. Also, I figured that there were now a number of turnkey Web application systems available, most of them providing for reasonable efficiency and scalability. In short, I thought that maybe a do-it-yourself, out-of-the-box approach would not prove to be that bad.

Unfortunately, this didn't turn out to be the case. I tried logging on to the site on April 17, the day I heard it advertised on the radio. It was there, with nice graphics, but it contained a very brief notice that it wasn't going to launch until April 18. Since the notice was pretty terse, my first thoughts were that either they tried to launch it on April 17 and it buckled under the demand or they already had a number of public inquiries about when it would launch. Anyway, I waited until the morning of April 18 and logged on. At 9 A.M. PST, I attempted to connect—alas, I was greeted instead with an HTTP 503 error (service unavailable).

I kept trying to connect over the next few minutes, but kept getting the same response. As a techie, I immediately guessed that the site was being hammered with requests. Suppose the problem had occurred on a day other than the launch day. Would the problem have been just as clear? Most likely not. You might have wondered: Is the site down? Their database? The network? Is your ISP slow?

But let's assume for a moment that the problem was purely one of a Web server that couldn't handle enough incoming connections (it ran out of memory, file descriptors, etc.). This can be a problem for many Web sites that suddenly become popular. Now let's consider the irony of such a situation. Although the application may have been broken up into tiers (Web server and application system at a minimum) to make it more scalable, the failure of one tier, which contained no core application logic, ended up disrupting everything.

Unfortunately, this is the case for many overtaxed Web applications. No matter how sleek or efficient the back-end system may be, a Web server unable to handle its connections is all it takes for a site to be terribly slow, unable to scale, or just plain unusable. Incidentally, a few hours later I was still unable to access the Ellis Island site (but at least I received a friendlier message).

By the way, the purpose of this example is not to criticize one particular Web site or the Web server software they used. Obviously, this same scenario plays out frequently and is experienced by many online users. Instead, the purpose is twofold:

- To underscore the importance of request processing—specifically, its important middleman role in the overall client/server exchange
- To show how the inefficiency of only one small task can easily misrepresent an otherwise efficient application system

That said, this chapter is about request processing, which, though it involves the execution of code not related to core application logic, nevertheless plays a major role in Web application execution. The inefficiencies associated with request processing can be responsible for a slow application, one that's unable to scale, or both.

The General Problem

As you probably know, client/server relationships aren't limited to the end user and the Web server but in fact exist throughout many parts of any *n*-tier application architecture. For example, the Web server itself may also be a client to various other server-side application components, like CORBA or EJB objects, and these components, in turn, may be clients to each other (i.e., EJB session beans communicating with entity beans). Still others may be clients to a database server.

In short, all of these interactions require request processing. We'll touch on the important details of each scenario as we go along in later chapters. However, as they all have so many things in common, it's useful to step back and examine the problem from a very general perspective.

To reduce confusion, I'm going to make things simple here and just refer to *clients* and *servers*. Obviously, there are some interactions that scream out "client and server"; however, there are others that aren't so obvious.

As an example of the latter, consider applications that monitor information feeds, such as applets or screen savers (like the old PointCast ones), and consume information pushed out at periodic intervals. In fact, they're not necessarily making requests. Such applications are typically called "consumers"; those providing the information are referred to as "producers." Still, just like clients getting replies from servers, both are getting data they're interested in. It's just that the mode and duration of the request are different.

Our general goal, then, is to understand what makes a good request-processing strategy. That is, we want to understand what types of question and answer techniques allow client/server communication to be as fast and scalable as possible. Let's start by breaking down the general problem into its underlying subproblems and look at each one in a bit more detail.

Specific Challenges

To really focus on the pieces of the request-processing puzzle, we need to look first at the deceptively simple and pretty picture and then zoom in on the ugly details. Let's consider an example where a client requests and receives data from a server. We won't assume anything about client/server proximity. In fact, we'll consider the worst case—that they're not in the same address space (like threads in a common program) and communicate over a network.

For this example, consider a client that makes a simple request of a server: *Return all of the pizza restaurants in Chicago*. Figure 6–1 represents the "pretty picture" view of this request. In contrast, Figure 6–2 illustrates the ugly details.

From Figure 6–2, we see that the following requirements need to be met for the communication to be successful:

- *Connection management*: Clients need to be able to establish connections to servers, and servers need to be able to distribute and manage client connections.

Figure 6–1
The pretty picture of request processing

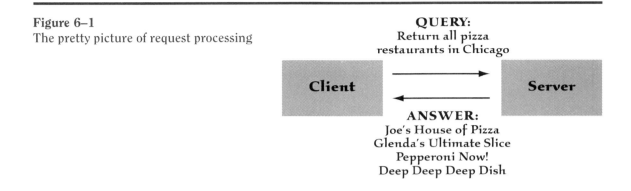

- *Data marshalling*: Requests and replies need to be converted to a suitable form for transmission over a network.
- *Request servicing*: In a client/server communication, the primary job of the server is to service requests. This process can be CPU intensive or I/O intensive, the latter when the server needs to access an external resource such as another component or the database system.

Just to remind you: Throughout our discussion of request processing, we'll be interested primarily in issues with important scalability and performance implications. Other issues, such as identifying a server that can service a client request or dealing with communication or processing errors, are unquestionably important and should be part of any general discussion. However, they have few (if any) associated scalability and performance concerns, so we won't discuss them in any detail here.

Figure 6–2
The ugly details of
request processing

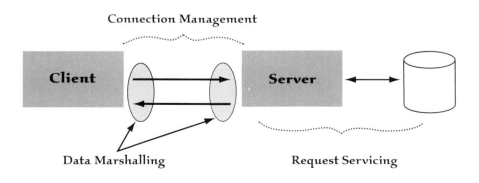

Connection Management

Perhaps chief among the requirements of any request processor is that it efficiently manage connections and scale in terms of concurrent client requests. The inability to handle large numbers of concurrent connections can result in a scenario similar to that of the Ellis Island Web site, which we saw earlier in this chapter.

Meanwhile, the failure to efficiently provide new connections or to manage those that already exist can make the overall application seem sluggish. For example, if a client has to continually wait a noticeable amount of time for a connection to be issued by a Web server, every interaction he has with the application will seem slow. He won't blame the server but the application itself.

There are two aspects of connection management to address. One is the availability of connections as a resource. When one client wants to connect to a server, *connections must be available*. Likewise, when thousands or tens of thousands of connection requests come in at once, *connections must be available*. Unlike other request-processing issues, the failure to perform connection management not only affects scalability, but directly affects the ability of transactions (some of which are critical) to proceed and can easily anger existing users and scare off potential new ones.

Consider what happens if connections are unavailable for a stock-trading system. A user places an order, clicks Submit, and then gets back an error message similar to the HTTP 503 message I described earlier: No connections available. What is the user to think? Have you lost her order? Has it been submitted? Should she call customer support? One thing is for sure: You've just given her a good reason to abandon your application for good.

In this example, having insufficient connections not only revealed the inability of the application to scale but also exposed embarrassing application behavior and confused the user. If the application were just slow, that would be one thing—it would at least be functional. But to have it respond with an "out of connections" error is cause for serious concern—it can cost you serious business.

Another connection management issue has to do with the efficient use of connections once they're established. For example, when we discussed the HTTP protocol in Chapter 5, we saw that downloading a single logical Web page can result in hundreds of TCP connections because of the extensive dialogue required per HTTP connection. We also saw how persistent connections can alleviate this problem and result in more efficient use of file descriptors, lower bandwidth demands, and lower resulting latencies. But under what circumstances are persistent connections most important? How long does *persistent* mean? More generally, how long should connections between client and server be maintained?

Data Marshalling

Another request-processing issue relates to how the request processor and client speak to each other over the wire (network hardware) that connects them. In particular, there's the problem of deconstructing the client request so that it can be sent over the connection infrastructure and then reconstructing it in terms of the objects the server-side handler can understand. Obviously, when it comes to hardware-level network communication between the client and the server, only ones and zeroes—no higher level data structures—are allowed.

The process of unpacking client requests and then converting them into objects for transmission to back-end application servers (or to the database itself) is referred to as **marshalling**. Those who have used RMI or are familiar with middleware solutions like CORBA will recognize the term, since it's typically used in those domains to describe the transposing of language-level data structures to those suitable for network transmission.

To be more precise, however, marshalling data is said to involve the transfer of data across application boundaries, most of the time over a network. Since network latency is one of the biggest factors in performance, and since the size of the data being transferred plays a direct role in this latency, our interest is in reducing the amount of data being marshalled and/or the complexity of marshalling.

Another factor is the cost of **serialization**, which is the process of converting complex objects into ones and zeroes. Obviously, it has to be done in order to send the data over the network. Also, upon receipt of the zeroes and ones, the callee reinterprets them into the types sent by the caller. This is true in most RPC implementations as well as in Java RMI.

As it turns out, however, Java serialization is actually less efficient than other forms of remote communication. One reason is that it also attempts to support polymorphism. Specifically, RMI allows the caller to send over arguments that may be defined only on the caller's side. Thus, RMI requires more class metadata to be sent per call so that the server can adequately reconstruct the object received. Also, because of the way Java deals with system memory, there's excessive data copying under RMI's hood and thus a decrease in performance.

In short, the process of data marshalling, especially in Java, and particularly in RMI, is a costly phase of request processing that should be considered when constructing remote method signatures.

Request Servicing

Request servicing isn't another way to say "request processing." The latter is concerned with all of the issues involved when a client wants to obtain an answer from a server. The former is merely one part of this process: the details of how a server, once it receives the request, arrives at an answer.

The request servicing can involve (a) performing some computation, (b) querying some local or external resource, or (c) both. Generally, I'll refer to (a) as CPU bound (lots of computation required) and to (b) as I/O bound (lots of time waiting for the external query to be answered). We're interested in reducing the amount of time it takes to accomplish both. Not only do we want them to be fast so that clients get their responses ASAP, but we also want to reduce the contention for resources that can be caused by slow request servicing.

This last point might not be obvious, so let's discuss it briefly. When a server agrees to answer a request from a client, it allocates resources to the answering process. For example, with multithreaded application servers it allocates a worker thread for executing server code. It also allocates things like file descriptors and memory to that connection and the session or transaction associated with it. In fact, the memory demands may not be known until runtime since object creation within a server-side method may be conditional or variable.

In the simplest case, when state is not maintained between client and server, server-side resources are returned after a response is sent to the client. These freed resources can then be used for new incoming connections. By the way, notice that things get worse when servers aren't stateless: Many of the resources involved won't be returned until after the logical session or transaction completes. Regardless of server state, request servicing should be as fast as possible to ensure that resource pools are adequately stocked.

CPU-Bound Servicing

When the process of servicing a request is CPU bound, the server is spending the bulk of its time performing calculations that will produce the client's answer. This is the simpler of the two request-servicing scenarios: If servicing requires lots of computation, the obvious challenge is making that computation more efficient.

There are two general subchallenges of more efficient computation:

- Making your algorithms more efficient
- Making your Java code more efficient

The two may be related, but they don't have to be. Making your algorithms more efficient can involve things like tuning loops and identifying sources of parallelism. Making your Java code more efficient involves understanding how Java works and knowing which platform classes/approaches are more efficient than others.

There's not enough room in this book to tackle either subchallenge in great detail; plus, it would cause us to lose our focus. Fortunately, a number of excellent resources are already out there. For algorithmic efficiency, try *Introduction to Algorithms* (Cormen et al., 2001). This is a modern favorite in computer science circles for data structures and algorithms, and you won't regret its purchase. For optimizing Java code, try *Java*™ *Performance Tuning* (Shirazi, 2000) and *Java*™ *Performance and Scalability, Volume 1: Server-Side Programming Techniques* (Bulka, 2000).

I/O-Bound Servicing

To say that request servicing is I/O bound means that it spends the bulk of its time "waiting" on data (or, more generally, on an answer) that's not local. It can refer to many cases, including those where the server is

- Issuing its own request to a second server
- Reading or modifying shared data that requires synchronized access
- Accessing data on disk
- Accessing data from a database system
- Accessing data from some other kind of external cache (beyond application boundaries)

Notice that I consider serialization of data access to be an I/O-bound process. In reality, depending on how an operating system implements this serialization, it can be either CPU or I/O bound. For example, the Java Virtual Machine (JVM) allows synchronized access to be implemented via `wait()` and `notify()` mechanisms. Typically, when multiple threads want access to the same synchronized object, one thread waits until another's exclusive access is over. Then one of the waiting threads is notified that it can now have exclusive access.

Under this scheme, however, the waiting thread doesn't pummel the CPU with polling activity; that is, it does not engage in "busy-waiting." Instead, the JVM simply reschedules that thread when it has been notified. Thus, for threads in the state of waiting there exists I/O-style blocking behavior very similar to what happens when a program is waiting for a reply from a remote server.

Except for those involving synchronized access to a common data structure, many I/O-bound dilemmas can be addressed by caching. For example, instead of querying a remote data provider, the answer can be retained locally (as described in our definition of caching in Chapter 4). The issue then becomes choosing a good caching policy and deciding what parts of the data (including intermediate data) to cache. Another issue has to do with placing the cache. Is there only one application component interested in the cached data? If not, is it better to have multiple independent caches or to have a single, unified cache? We'll get into that question in a bit more detail in a moment.

Incidentally, keep in mind that resource references themselves can be cached. Connections to databases, references to EJBs, and file handles are all costly to establish and can potentially be reused. We've already discussed resource pooling as a way to address this issue. Another way is to create a global resource cache or context, much like what JNDI provides. (Or, we can just use JNDI properly!)

Data Locality in Caching Environments

Interestingly, solutions to some request processing problems create new problems. Such is the case with the kind of caching we've been discussing. To understand how, consider load balancing, one popular solution for connection management in Web servers today, and its effect on data locality.

The basic idea of load balancing is to spread the work around in terms of incoming requests. As requests arrive, they're farmed out to handlers (servers) using some distribution policy (such as round-robin). This helps reduce the load on any one server, but it creates a new problem if the application maintains state or establishes local caches. Specifically, by effectively spreading the application over multiple machines, load balancing suddenly makes cache consistency an issue for all mutable data. It also creates a new challenge: How can cached information be shared between request processors? That is, how can the caching by one server be leveraged by another?

To illustrate, let's look at a farm of Web or application servers managed by a collection of load-balancing hardware and software for a human resources application. With this application, administrators can change employee addresses, phone numbers, titles, and the like.

To make the application faster, we can design it so that employee data is cached on the local machine that services a given request. For example, if a client calls up information on "Jane Hill," the application caches all of that employee's information so that future requests for it will be faster. When the user modifies some part of that data (say, Jane Hill's address), the cache is updated and so is the database.

Now consider how that method of write-through caching affects our server farm. Unless we change the architecture, replicating our application across multiple machines will cause multiple independent caches to be created. And now, suddenly, we're forced to make sure that these independent caches are consistent.

Related to this is the new challenge I referred to: sharing cached data. Generally speaking, we're interested in how work done by one server (to look up the data) can be leveraged by the other servers. Of course, we don't have to share data between caches—if it's read-only, nothing forces us to do this. However, consider the inefficiency involved: We're effectively wasting our aggregate memory by replicating data. Also, we're looking up data repeatedly, even though it has already been looked up once.

Dealing with this challenge as well as the consistency issue makes things increasingly complex. We'll certainly have to do a lot of thinking during the design stages to make the system both correct and efficient. And, if we don't design our system correctly, the problem of managing distributed cached data will turn out to be bigger than that of dealing with the normal disk latencies associated with retrieving this data in the first place.

Request–Processing Modes

It's tempting to think of request processing as something only a Web server does. In fact, there are infinite request-processing scenarios—any client can, conceivably, make a request of any other server or subsystem. For all of these scenarios, there are in fact only two *modes* of request processing: **synchronous** and **asynchronous**. We now turn our attention to understanding the pros and cons of both.

Synchronous Communication

Synchronous request processing involves a mode of communication in which the client contacts a server and waits for a reply. Typically, the reply will contain meaningful information in the sense that the value contained in the reply is important to the client. For example, when users click on a Web page link, the Web browser makes an HTTP request of the Web server that contains the associated document. The corresponding HTTP response is required by the client to render the corresponding Web page.

The main advantage of synchronous communication is that, when things are working well, a request is answered with a timely response. There's almost no guesswork involved, and the results are known right away. I say "almost no guesswork" because sometimes a client contacts a server and waits for long periods before getting a reply (or never gets one) and has to decide when to time-out. This is one of the disadvantages of synchronous communication, but it affects asynchronous forms as well, so it's an unavoidable reality. Outside of this situation, there's *no* guesswork: The client can be sure that the server processed its request because . . . it got a reply!

Many times synchronous communication is mandatory or at least desirable. It's mandatory if the application semantics require an immediate reply. For example, if the user of an online mail application sees that he has new mail in his virtual mailbox and asks to see it, it's not reasonable to say "Come back later for your new mail." Synchronous communication is also typically necessary for tasks that require order, such as distributed transactions. Consider a bank application comprising several components, distributed across a network of machines. When a request to transfer funds between one account and another arrives, we typically need to be sure that the funds have been successfully withdrawn from the source account before we attempt to deposit them in the destination account. Thus, the second operation is dependent on a confirmation of the first.

In fact, most programming languages (including Java) force engineers into this way of thinking because the default coding style involves declaring a list of sequential instructions. This is just a by-product of von Neumann computing, where an instruction counter (physical or logical) drives execution. As it turns out, there are alternative-programming models that don't pigeon-hole engineers into this style of coding (a dataflow model comes to mind).

There are several examples of synchronous communication related to building Web applications. In addition to the dialogue between browser and server, there's the notion of a remote procedure call (RPC), which can occur in many forms. The most common is the straight-no-chaser RPC available on many operating systems as a linkable library. RPC has a long history and represents the first logical, abstract approach to remote function execution, one that doesn't force the coder to worry about the low-level socket details associated with the underlying network communication.

There are also distributed object technologies based on RPCs. Java RMI, CORBA, and DCOM are perhaps the best known. Of the three, CORBA is the most generic, for two reasons. One, its protocol (IIOP) is open and thus nonproprietary. Two, it allows communication not only between disparate systems but between different programming languages. It's possible, for example, to use CORBA as a means of communication between a C++ client and a Java-based server. As we discussed in Chapter 3, RMI-IIOP is the Java solution to this problem; it attempts to combine the advantages of RMI (simplicity) and IIOP (interoperability).

Asynchronous Communication

Although a key advantage of synchronous communication is that a requestor receives a reply as part of the process, this feature can actually be viewed as a major disadvantage. Not only can there be a long latency involved in a reply (which may lead to confusion or time-out), but any time spent waiting for a reply is less efficient than not waiting for it. Also, in many cases a reply is either not needed or not needed immediately. The mode of communication in which a request receives a reply at some later time (or receives no reply at all) is referred to as asynchronous.

It helps to visualize the difference between synchronous and asynchronous communication to understand why waiting for a reply can be considered a disadvantage. Suppose that company A and company B have established a partnership where B resells some of A's products. They develop a B2B-style notification system where A uses software to automatically refigure and determine prices on its products (it can do this monthly, for example) and notifies B about such changes.

Figure 6–3 shows how A and B might accomplish their goals by communicating synchronously. It assumes that each computation takes one second and disregards any network latency.

We see that company A needs 1 second to calculate the price of a hammer and then stalls for 1 second while communicating the price to B. This is because B requires 1 second to update that price in its own database. After receiving a reply from B that it has updated the hammer price, A determines the new price on

Figure 6–3
Synchronous price update
processing

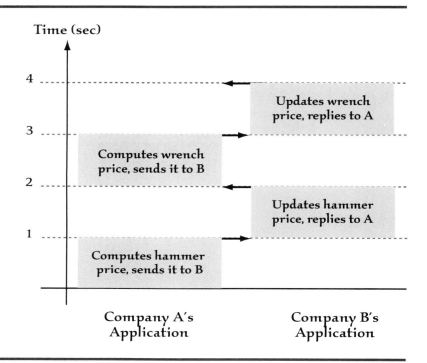

a wrench, which again requires 1 second. Notice that there is an arrow at the top of the figure—this lets A know that its request was fulfilled. The total time to process these price updates is at least 4 seconds because the communication is synchronous and so A needs to receive a reply from B.

Figure 6–4 shows how the same process might occur asynchronously. Since company A doesn't require any reply from B (perhaps later it will want to know that B received the price changes, but this isn't immediately necessary), it can calculate the price of a hammer, communicate it to some queue that B can access—without waiting for a reply. Instead, it can go on to calculate the price for the wrench. On its own time, B will eventually visit the queue and process the information A has left for it there. Instead of wasting a cycle waiting for B to do its work, A moves right along to the next task, which makes it 50 percent more productive in this example! It completes its work in 2 seconds instead of 4. Notice that B isn't slowed down because A was waiting on its first update. It's only active for 2 seconds as well, not the original 3.

Performance improvement from asynchronous communication varies, of course, because it depends on the network latency, the time B requires to do its work,

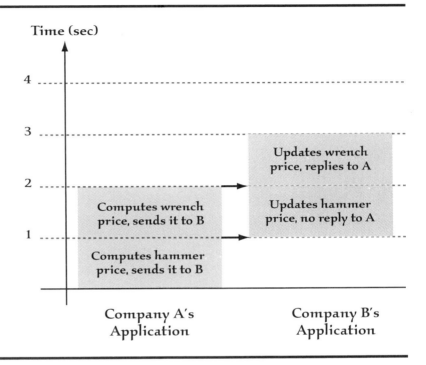

Figure 6–4
Asynchronous price update
processing

and the amount of work A has to complete. It also has a lot to do with the application itself and its business requirements. For example, why can't A simply do all of its work first and then send all of the updated product prices to B at once? Also, is it really necessary for B to commit the change to its database before acknowledging A? Can't it simply hold the data in some temporary memory, respond to A, and then commit the data at some later time?

There are many ways to construct asynchronous communication solutions, but all of them use some sort of queuing approach. This is fundamental to asynchrony: If the consumer is unavailable, the producer needs some way to log his request so that he can continue with another activity. The queue represents this logical log file.

For example, Figure 6–4 shows organization A using software to communicate requests at some future time to a queue that's accessible by software run by organization B. Without a queue, there's no place to temporarily store requests while they await processing. Thus, behavior has to be synchronous or the data will be lost.

Messaging Systems

Probably the most popular form of asynchronous communication today is the one associated with messaging systems. Not to be confused with e-mail, messaging allows applications from different organizations or companies to integrate easily and efficiently. Most of these systems are based on an asynchronous communication model.

In addition, messaging systems provide a consistent interface that doesn't force either side to learn new proprietary APIs or change existing ones. There's no need for two companies to worry about what language their application(s) are written in and on what operating systems they're deployed. Just like HTTP and the JVM, messaging systems implicitly define a region of platform independence so that, instead of worrying about the ugly details of software integration between disparate machines and programming languages, companies can focus on the more interesting and pressing business problems related to the data they exchange.

Messaging systems are so named because they rephrase client/server communication between systems in the form of text messages. As in the HTTP protocol, normalizing communication between the two parties in this way is necessary to achieve platform independence. And like HTTP, there's a nice side effect to messaging: It's far easier to debug than a binary, possibly proprietary, protocol. This makes it a more attractive approach to application integration than more cryptic methods such as Electronic Data Interchange (EDI).

What's more, message-based integration schemes are perfectly positioned to work on top of HTTP, since this protocol is itself message-based. This allows them to

- Leverage the network optimizations of HTTP (such as persistent connections)
- Leverage security features (such as SSL)
- Avoid many of the firewall issues that can hamper non-HTTP approaches

One distinction between normal synchronous communication and asynchronous messaging is that the former is associated with the client/server model, whereas the latter is typically associated with the *peer-to-peer* model. In client/server systems, one party requests information and one party provides it. In peer-to-peer systems, both parties produce and consume information.

Still as I said earlier, the difference between these two approaches is smaller than it sounds. Even under a messaging scheme, there's going to be a provider and a consumer. The difference is that the consumer doesn't have to request the information in order to get it; rather, the information is *subscribed* to so that it can be received if and when it's *published* by the provider.

Scalability and Performance Tradeoffs

Now that we've clarified the two basic forms of communication between systems, how do we decide which is the best one to use?

Although each has some performance and scalability tradeoffs, the most important factor obviously has to do with the business requirements of a given situation. Certainly, interactive Web applications need to operate in a mostly synchronous manner. They have many processes (transferring money, purchasing a product, etc.) where synchronous communication is simply mandatory because a user needs to be assured that the operation just requested has been performed. However, there may be opportunities to solve problems asynchronously as well. Let's look at some of these tradeoffs in the context of the challenges we outlined earlier.

Connection Management

Synchronous communication brings with it a difficult connection management issue. Interactive Web applications must be able to maintain a large number of available connections at all times to service high demand and to handle longer usage times per connection. For example, the HTTP 1.1 persistent connections feature improves performance for a series of HTTP exchanges, but it also frees connections at a lower rate than nonpersistent connections.

In contrast, asynchronous communication has to worry only about providing enough connections to ensure highly available queuing. These connections are typically short-lived and don't sit idle during periods of client think time, as a persistent connection might.

Caching and Data Locality

Synchronous communication has much stricter requirements for efficient memory management than does asynchronous communication. This has to do with the difference in processing between the two. Synchronous clients, by definition, must wait for an answer. Good caching schemes can translate into shorter average latencies; bad caching schemes (or none at all) obviously can result in the opposite. Shorter latencies mean better request processing performance and thus better throughput.

Although caching can also improve the efficiency of asynchonrous communication models, it is not always a necessary feature. For example, many asynchronous solutions involve large "pushes" of data (i.e., batch loads) that—with or without caching—take hours (not milliseconds) to complete. While businesses generally strive to build efficient systems, waiting 3 hours for the consumption of data instead of the 2 that a caching solution might yield may not be a major problem. The point at which a delay becomes unacceptable depends on the nature of the application.

Some asynchronous applications may in fact require good consumer caching. Consider a stock market information system that works using a broadcast paradigm. Suppose that a client receives stock quotes from an information producer and must flash the ticker symbols on the user screen along with some other data (such as the name of the company). Caching this "other data" is going to be very important in this scenario or else the lag time between when the message is produced and when it's consumed and processed will be too great to be useful (i.e., the report of a price drop or rise will arrive too late for the user to do anything about it). In such cases, data is changing fast and client/listener processing needs to be as quick as possible.

In short, caching and data locality are usually more critical for synchronous systems because the client can't make progress until he receives a reply. However, they can also be critical for some highly dynamic asynchronous scenarios. One thing is for sure: Good caching improves the performance of both approaches as long as the complexity in implementing it isn't unreasonable.

Data Marshalling

Here's a case where synchronous systems are often more efficient, for two reasons. First, a messaging intermediary represents yet another layer in the communication between two parties, which potentially means

- Another level of reconstructing and deconstructing serialized forms into an intermediate data structure
- Possibly another level of request comprehension (so that the right consumer can be contacted)

In addition, the actual application data may need to be converted to another format. This is very common in messaging systems, many of which support transformation rule building so that deployers can easily customize just how data is to be translated between producer and consumer.

Consider the transfer of records that consist of several codes that indicate employee history information. These codes may mean something to the producer but mean nothing to the consumer, who has his own codes. The producer's codes may need to be translated to make sense in the consumer's application or data model.

In contrast, synchronous systems usually have fewer data transformations and don't have to worry about this intermediate hop in the request-processing network flow. Still, keep in mind that the client is waiting in the synchronous case, so the lack of efficient data marshalling has a greater impact here than it does in the asynchronous case.

Request Processing and J2EE

Various parts of J2EE system design relate to request processing. Some are synchronous, some are asynchronous, and some provide options for both modes. In this section, we'll describe how these parts are used and which modes of processing they support.

Web Serving

For most Web applications, a standalone Web server is essential. However, although J2EE supports the notion of a "Web container" (which is responsible for Java servlets and JSP generation), there's little mention of the role of a Web server. The specification merely acknowledges that HTTP requests are handled by Web containers and routed to the application objects (the Enterprise JavaBeans) or to the database. Although Sun supports the Java Web Server, it is not necessary for a J2EE deployment. As long as a vendor's Web containers handle and route HTTP requests, that vendor's implementation of J2EE has met the requirements of the spec. In fact, this is one of the nicer aspects of the spec in that it provides flexibility in terms of how tightly the Web server and servlet container are coupled.

Another probable reason why the J2EE spec does not address Web serving specifically is because existing systems, such as Apache Server and Microsoft Internet Information Server (IIS), are well-established and do a very good job of efficient request handling. These systems have focused on optimizing the serving of static documents and provided several options that allow clients to reach server-side application programs and databases.

Although it doesn't address static Web page processing, the J2EE spec does include support for HTTP processing at the application level. That is, as shown in Chapter 3, the Web container handles HTTP requests. In practice, however, these requests are only for a subset of all application requests. Most Web applications are composed of both static pages and forms that are processed by the server-side application system. Thus, HTTP support by the Web container really addresses the latter, not the former, need.

Synchronous Processing with Java Servlets and JavaServer Pages

J2EE envisions synchronous request processing as handled by Java servlets and JavaServer Pages (JSPs). The idea is that client applications connect to servlets directly (or are routed there by the Web server) and provide a Java interface to the rest of the application system. Servlets are typically responsible for unmarshalling the structures in the HTTP request and repackaging them as Java objects, which are then sent either to the database or to application-level objects such as EJBs. Thus, they act as true request processors, that is, as the intermediary between the client and the application system.

Servlets represent an alternative to Web server API extensions as well as to request processing by Common Gateway Interface (CGI) programs such as those written in Perl or C. Unlike CGI programs, which are usually implemented as processes created for each request made, servlets are Java classes that execute by associating a pooled thread with an incoming client request and then using that thread to execute the corresponding class methods. Normal CGI programs are inherently inefficient in that execution time is spent on forking a process, repetitive initialization of expensive data structures (such as database connections), and exhaustion of memory when processing many concurrent requests.

In contrast, the use of threads and the idea of thread pooling in the Java servlet specification encourage fast, scalable, and resource-efficient servlet execution. Servlet threads share the same address space (and can span multiple machines for better reliability) and can share/pool expensive data structures to be used between invocations and by concurrent invocations.

JSPs are an alternative to coding HTML pages and allow a page designer to interact directly with servlets. They clearly separate the visual representation of data from the business logic that computes it. Motivated by the fact that generating HTML had become a bulky, unwieldy part of the servlet development process, JSPs make the HTML and servlet code smaller and more focused. However, they have nothing to do with the servlet execution model but are simply a development methodology. Servlets, with or without JSP front-ends, are still mechanisms for synchronous request processing.

Asynchronous Processing with the Java Message Service

If servlets form the backbone of synchronous request processing in J2EE, the Java Message Service (JMS) does the same for asynchronous request processing. Unlike servlets, messaging technology was not introduced by Java effort. As middleware solutions, they have been around for a while, traditionally associated with the need to handle enterprise application integration—that is, to easily and reliably connect applications from different organizations (i.e., companies). However, in the past two years or so, messaging has undergone a rebirth, at least in terms of the Java and Web application community.

Messaging solutions such as JMS are seeing increased support by other application-level components. For example, the J2EE specification describes how EJBs can be designed to integrate with JMS (i.e., message-driven beans). This makes sense: Even though messaging clients and servlet clients are typically very different (one is

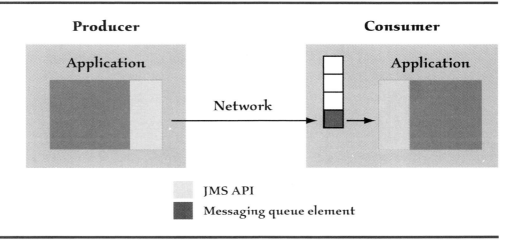

Figure 6–5
JMS
messaging
architecture

a company; the other, a single user), they both want access to the same business logic. Under the J2EE model, that logic is associated with EJBs, so it makes sense to enable them to handle both synchronous and asynchronous requests.

JMS acts as a thin API layer that exists on both the producer and the consumer sides of the communication. As shown in Figure 6–5, the producer uses the API to communicate with a messaging system that conforms to the JMS while a consumer uses the JMS to access the transmitted messages. JMS thus acts like JDBC. Instead of abstracting database access, however, it abstracts messaging behavior. As long as it conforms to the JMS, a messaging solution from any vendor can be integrated into your application scheme.

Scalability and Performance Hints

Although we have been discussing request processing paradigms and design trade-offs at a fairly abstract level, we can nevertheless identify some practical suggestions in terms of overall Web application design.

Build Asynchronous Solutions

As we've seen, asynchronous communication is inherently faster than synchronous communication. The bottom line is that parallelism is better exploited under an asynchronous model—at the cost of complexity or flexibility if the return value (if any) has any meaning.

In Chapter 9, I'll discuss the Java Message Service—the primary J2EE technology for building asynchronous solutions. However, before you can even begin to consider how to use JMS, you must be able to identify asynchronous opportunities. Toward that end, let's consider one common task that system designers often (mistakenly) assume can only be handled synchronously.

Generating Highly Dynamic Web Pages

Highly dynamic Web pages are those where the data changes (or may change) frequently. They're all over the place and include

- "Live" sports scores or sports event statistics (e.g., baseball box scores, like those provided by the Yahoo or ESPN Web sites)
- Current weather conditions
- Flight status for a particular airline or airport
- Newswire stories
- Concert/event seating availability

The problem is that readers of these pages know they change frequently and tend to request them more often (to get the latest information). This means that request-processing demands rise. Another unfortunate thing is that data that's looked up or computed isn't shared between clients, which causes a lot of repetition resulting in a significant waste of server-side resources.

However, there's an asynchronous way to approach this problem. Notice that our Web page delivery is *reactive* (and synchronous)—when a client wants an updated page version, we have to generate a new copy (even if it contains the same data). However, suppose that we instead have a *proactive* application server that periodically generates a static page, called, say, `http://www.example.com/current_results.html`.

Instead of dynamically fulfilling client requests on a demand basis, we can change our strategy and have all clients access a single static page. Rather than dynamically generate HTML per request, we can generate dynamic HTML only when the data changes. This is an approach that, by itself, scales beautifully.

Admittedly, this solution will not be acceptable in some situations where a response has to be the freshest possible or in cases where the data generated is user/request specific (i.e., personalized data such as stock portfolios). Even in this latter case, a simple change in your page design can result in significant performance benefits. Consider a Web page for an airline that lists the status of all flights. Instead of designing the page so that users enter a number and get back a flight status, it may be possible to get away with publishing a single list showing the status of all flights and letting the user locate the one she wants.

In short, highly dynamic Web page generation can be made efficient by pregenerating a single static page. This removes a tremendous burden on the application as the number of concurrent users rises. If you stand back and look at the whole solution, you'll see that it's effectively asynchronous at the application level: A message (the data results) is periodically pushed out to the filesystem, and the client simply gets the latest copy of it.

Stream Data between Threads

As we discussed earlier, the main advantage of asynchronous request processing is that it can make the producing application more efficient by enabling it to continue with its computation as soon as possible. Moreover, such asynchronous paradigms aren't limited to the interaction between two distributed components but can be relevant for applications with multiple threads. Just as was the case with two applications, thread-based situations involve one thread producing the data and the other thread consuming it.

When opportunities for interapplication parallelism are identified, there are a few ways to address them. Sure, we can use JMS between threads if we want. But many people view that solution as overkill. First, if we don't already have JMS-compliant messaging software, we have to purchase it. Second, and of more concern: The overhead (e.g., marshalling costs) to achieve this asynchrony alone is fairly pricey, especially when we are talking about communication within a single process.

An alternative to all this is to simply write our own Queue class, which allows one thread to stream objects to a consumer asynchronously. This is conceptually similar to what JMS allows (although JMS allows many more configurations and different messaging paradigms).

It turns out that implementing something like this is very simple. Listing 6–1 shows how to develop a Queue class that allows one or more writers to insert Java objects into a common queue and one or more readers to consume them. The guts of the queue are a circular buffer (where the objects are stored until retrieval by the consumer) and the proper synchronization to make sure that writers block when the queue is full and readers block when there's nothing to read.

Listing 6–1: A Simple Queue for Communication between Threads

```
1 /**
2  *
3  * A Queue is a data structure that allows a producer thread to
4  * communicate with a consumer thread asynchronously.  It is
5  * also possible to have multiple producers and/or multiple
```

```
 6   * consumers write and read from this same queue.
 7   *
 8   */
 9  public class Queue
10  {
11    protected Object[] m_buf;
12
13    protected int m_max;
14    protected int m_size;
15    protected int m_rSpot;
16    protected int m_wSpot;
17    protected int m_rBlocked;
18    protected int m_wBlocked;
19
20    public Queue(int a_size)
21    {
22      m_buf = new Object[a_size];
23      m_max = a_size;
24
25      m_size = 0;
26      m_rSpot = 0;
27      m_wSpot = 0;
28
29      m_rBlocked = 0;
30      m_wBlocked = 0;
31    }
32
33    public synchronized void putObject(Object a_obj)
34    {
35      if (m_size >= m_max-1)
36      {
37        m_wBlocked++;
38
39        do {
40          try { wait(); } catch (Exception e) { }
41        } while (m_size >= m_max-1);
42
43        m_wBlocked--;
44      }
45
46      m_buf[m_wSpot] = a_obj;
47      m_wSpot = (m_wSpot+1) % m_max;
48      m_size++;
49
50      if (m_rBlocked>0)
51        notify();
52    }
53
54    public synchronized Object getObject()
55    {
```

```
56      if (m_size == 0)
57      {
58        m_rBlocked++;
59
60        do {
61          try { wait(); } catch (Exception e) { }
62        } while (m_size==0);
63
64        m_rBlocked--;
65      }
66
67      while (m_buf[m_rSpot]==null)
68        m_rSpot = (m_rSpot+1) % m_max;
69
70      Object obj = m_buf[m_rSpot];
71      m_buf[m_rSpot]=null;
72
73      m_rSpot = (m_rSpot+1) % m_max;
74      m_size-;
75
76      if (m_wBlocked>0)
77        notify();
78
79      return obj;
80    }
81 }
```

Without going into great detail, notice the following:

- The code is really a data structure meant to be simultaneously accessed by two threads.
- The constructor, shown in lines 20 through 31, initializes the Queue internal data structures, including the circular buffer, which has a variable size determined by Queue's creator.
- The putObject() method, shown in lines 33 through 52, allows a producer to write objects into the buffer. As lines 50 and 51 show, the next waiting Queue reader (if any) is awakened to consume this object.
- The getObject() method, shown in lines 54 through 83, allows a consumer to fetch objects from the buffer. As lines 78 and 79 show, the next blocked writer (blocked because the queue buffer was exhausted) is awakened as necessary.
- The data structure is thread safe; because the putObject() and getObject() methods are synchronized, there is no chance of a reader deciding that no new objects are available at the same time that a producer appends a new object to the buffer.

Using a `Queue` class similar to this one in your own multithreaded code is pretty straightforward. For example, consider this simple program:

```
public class QueueMain
{
  public static void main(String[] args)
  {
    /* Create a queue with a buffer big enough to hold 1000 objects */
    Queue queue = new Queue(1000);

    /* Create producer and consumer threads */
    QueueProducer pro = new QueueProducer(queue);
    QueueConsumer con = new QueueConsumer(queue);

    /* Start them up! */
    con.start();
    pro.start();
  }
}
```

This program uses a producer thread to write objects into the queue:

```
public class QueueProducer
  extends Thread
{
  protected Queue m_queue;

  public QueueProducer(Queue a_queue)
  {
    m_queue = a_queue;
  }

  public void run()
  {
    /* Put 100 objects */
    for (int i=0; i<10; i++)
      m_queue.putObject(new String("some-string-"+i));

    /* Put an end-of-stream marker */
    m_queue.putObject("_DONE_");
  }
}
```

Correpondingly, a consumer thread reads these objects:

```
public class QueueConsumer
  extends Thread
```

```
{
  protected Queue m_queue;

  public QueueConsumer(Queue a_queue)
  {
    m_queue = a_queue;
  }

  public void run()
  {
    String cur;

    /* Read objects from the queue until we get the EOS marker */

    do {
      cur = (String)m_queue.getObject();
      System.out.println("Read: <"+cur+">");
    } while (!cur.equals("_DONE_"));

    System.out.println("Done reading from queue.");
  }
}
```

The QueueMain program creates a queue and producer and consumer threads that communicate over it. It then starts both threads. The consumer reads the data when it's available and blocks otherwise. When the producer inserts a special token (the string "_DONE_" in this case) into the queue, the consumer exits.

Running QueueMain thus results in

```
% java QueueMain
Read: <some-string-0>
Read: <some-string-1>
Read: <some-string-2>
Read: <some-string-3>
Read: <some-string-4>
Read: <some-string-5>
Read: <some-string-6>
Read: <some-string-7>
Read: <some-string-8>
Read: <some-string-9>
Read: <_DONE_>
Done reading from queue.
```

This simple example shows that you can still achieve an asynchronous solution within a single multithreaded component (i.e., the same address space) without the overhead of something like JMS.

Our solution works best when the number of CPU-bound threads is roughly equal to the number of CPUs on your system. This allows maximum parallelism. If this isn't the case, you may want to think twice about this approach. For example, if two threads will be competing for a single CPU, there may not be much benefit in parallelizing the overall computation.

Develop Efficient Remote Interfaces

There are many situations where improving the design of a remote interface can reduce request-processing overhead. One example is eliminating the overhead caused by successive remote request processing. Let's look at an example.

Suppose we're developing a two-part application to process student course registration requests. One part is an applet that runs on the client machine and serves as the user interface. This applet sends requests over RMI to the second part, a remote application server. A student uses the applet to select courses and then presses a button to confirm her choices.

One way to code the remote application is to expose a method for adding a course, for example:

```
public void addCourse(int a_studentId, int a_courseId);
```

If this is the only way to add courses, the client applet needs to have code somewhere that looks roughly like this:

```
public class RegistrationApplet extends Applet {
  ...
  protected int m_studentId;
  protected int[] m_courses;
  ...
  public void processEnrollment()
  {
    ...
    RegistrationManager serverApp = (RegistrationManager)Naming.lookup(
        "//remotehost/RegistrationManager");
    ...
    for (int i=0; i<m_courses.length; i++) {
      serverApp.addCourse(m_studentId, m_courses[i]);
    }
    ...
  }
  ...
}
```

Notice that addCourse() is called for each course. That is, the price of the overhead of remote communication is paid *n* times, where *n* is the number of courses that the student takes.

Although this is a simple example, it's easy to see the waste here. It would be much more efficient if we had a different remote method available:

```
public void addCourses(int a_studentId, int[] a_courseIds);
```

and had a client that looked like this:

```
public class RegistrationApplet extends Applet {
  ...
  protected int m_studentId;
  protected int[] m_courses;
  ...
  public void processEnrollment()
  {
    ...
    serverApp.addCourses(m_studentId, m_courses);
    ...
  }
  ...
}
```

which results in significantly less communication overhead! What we've learned here is this: *It can be more efficient to develop remote methods that permit bulk processing* (that is, they take lists of objects that need to be processed).

Here's another example in the same domain. Suppose our applet allows students to find out who is teaching a particular class. Also suppose that the following remote methods exist:

```
/* Given a course name like "Art 101", returns its course ID */
public int getCourseId(String a_courseName);

/* Gets the instructor ID for the given course ID */
public int getInstructorId(int a_courseId);

/* Gets the instructor full name for the given instructor ID */
public String getInstructorName(int a_instructorId);
```

This means that the client applet needs to contain code that "chases around" a lot of data—something like the following.

```
public class RegistrationApplet extends Applet {
  ...
  public String identifyInstructor(String a_courseName)
  {
    ...
    RegistrationManager serverApp = (RegistrationManager)Naming.lookup(
        "//remotehost/RegistrationManager");
    ...

    /* Remote request #1 */
    int courseId = serverApp.getCourseId(a_courseName);

    /* Remote request #2 */
    int instructorId = serverApp.getInstructorId(courseId);

    /* Remote request #3 */
    String instructorName = serverApp.getInstructorName(instructorId);

    ...
    return instructorName;
  }
  ...
}
```

Again, we see an efficiency problem. The client is forced to chase around the remote data. This causes a lot of remote requests and thus an inefficient application. It would have been better to have a remote method like

```
/* Given a course name like "Art 101", returns its instructor */
public String getInstructorName(String a_courseName);
```

which would have resulted in a client like

```
public class RegistrationApplet extends Applet {
  ...
  public String identifyInstructor(String a_courseName)
  {
    ...
    RegistrationManager serverApp = (RegistrationManager)Naming.lookup(
        "//remotehost/RegistrationManager");
    ...

    /* Remote request #1 */
    String instructorName = serverApp.getInstructorName(a_courseName);

    ...
```

```
      return instructorName;
   }
   ...
}
```

This requires only one remote method invocation and thus allows us to reduce our communication costs approximately by a third. What this example teaches us is that *it can be more efficient to design methods that encapsulate a meaningful sequence of data manipulations* so that the client doesn't have to do it manually and at great expense.

Neither of the tips presented here is difficult to grasp. The basic challenge is to look at what your clients want to do remotely and then offer them interfaces to do it.

Of course, the problem with taking this approach to an extreme is that you end up with a lot of server-side methods that are overly specific and not reused. This isn't necessarily bad, mind you—I'm all for reusability and interface simplicity. However, if developing a few efficiency methods here and there significantly improves performance and scalability, it may not be a bad option. Remember, clients don't care how much reusability you were able to achieve. They just want fast applications.

So in short, my advice is to selectively write efficiency methods. By packaging data in bulk and by encapsulating a series of remote operations into one, you can improve the performance of your clients as well as the overall scalability of your system.

Summary

In this chapter, we looked at the general concept of request processing as well as some of its key challenges and issues. We also identified some surprisingly specific solutions to the challenges.

It's fair to say that request processing is all about managing connections, efficiently associating a connection with an existing session, and marshalling data between client and back-end application objects. Request processors are on the front line of server-side processing. Regardless of how efficient the application system or the database system is, request processing itself needs to be scalable. Load balancing and multithreading can be important techniques that improve both scalability and performance.

We also discussed the tradeoffs between synchronous ans asynchronous solutions. Although the former are often more natural or necessary for various scenarios, the latter are often more efficient because they increase the opportunity for parallel execution. Because of this, it is often worthwhile to consider novel asynchronous solutions when developing Web applications. The frequent generation of highly dynamic Web pages is one example we discussed.

Finally, we hinted a number of times about the coupling of request processing and application logic. J2EE suggests that the two be decoupled—and this is indeed a wise choice. Partitioning the two activities allows you to separate the problems of application availability and application scalability. So, for example, although you may be tempted to code application logic in servlets, there's a strong end-to-end argument for consolidating this logic in either EJBs or the database itself.

Session Management with Java Servlets

Having discussed request processing in general, it's now time to look at specifics. Our first case will be the most popular one: handling HTTP requests for interactive sessions. As you know, what typically happens here is that an interactive client (i.e., a user with a Web browser) communicates with a Web server, asking it to process its HTTP request. The Web server responds as appropriate. The communication is synchronous, and a logical "session" often involves more than one roundtrip, either because users have temporarily navigated somewhere else or, more likely, because the application simply presents its logical operations over a series of Web pages (i.e., the notion of a shopping cart).

In general, there are two ways to handle incoming HTTP requests. One is to deliver a *static response*—specifically to attempt to locate and return the object identified in the request as if it were a file located on the server side. Static objects include predefined HTML pages and JPEG or GIF images. These requests are the kind that Web servers are designed to serve quickly and that don't require communication with any server-side application system.

The other way to handle a request is to deliver a *dynamic response*. In this case, the request is forwarded to an application system where the resulting reply is generated dynamically (i.e., data is generated through server-side program execution). Dynamic responses are necessary when the requested data is constantly changing and/or is a function of the request parameters.

Generating Dynamic Responses

Three Web server techniques can be used to generate dynamic responses:

- Write a CGI program.
- Extend the Web server through its API.

- Redirect Web server requests to a separate application system, usually through a prebuilt redirection module or script.

For the last option, I use the term *separate* because this option usually implies that the application system technology exists beyond the process boundary of the Web server and is treated by it as a black box. One example is Java servlets, the main topic of this chapter. Before we explain what servlets are, however, we need to justify their use in comparison to these other alternatives.

Common Gateway Interface

Common Gateway Interface (CGI) programs reside on the server machine and are executed when a request for them is made. The Web server passes along the context of the request, so it's possible to query this metadata and respond accordingly. CGI is almost always the slowest and least scalable approach because a separate process (an instance of a program) is forked for each CGI invocation. Not only is forking on demand inherently slow and burdensome, but highly concurrent CGI request processing quickly exhausts server memory and CPU resources.

FastCGI is a related alternative to CGI that persists a process (instead of forking it each time). However, its fundamental flaw is that it too associates server-side functionality with a process, not a thread. As a result, handling concurrent requests still requires multiple processes and thus scalability remains less than optimal.

Extending the Web Server through Its API

Another option for generating dynamic content is to write an extension for a Web server by hand, using an API such as NSAPI (for Netscape Web servers) or ISAPI (for Microsoft Internet Information Server). Typically this means writing the extension in the language of the Web server, which is usually C/C++.

Web server API extensions can perform well, but they're platform and Web-server specific. Thus, they're not portable and are painful to maintain. Plus, they require that you reinvent—by hand—a lot of the technology for session management that already exists elsewhere.

Arguably, extending the Web server yourself may lead to better performance and scalability if you come up with a better solution than what already exists or if your solution somehow better fits your application needs. However, such cases are rare and require significant time and resources. And what are you left with? Probably a solution that only marginally improves performance and scalability. It's good to remind ourselves that successfully fighting the performance and scalability war requires picking our battles carefully, and this isn't one I recommend picking unless testing or deployment benchmarks strongly indicate otherwise.

Redirecting the Web Server Request

The final option for generating dynamic content involves using an alternative Web server extension, such as a custom module or adapter. In this case, the Web server knows nothing about how the module or adapter works—it just forwards certain requests as they arrive. Actually, CGI is often implemented in Web servers in this very way. For example, Apache contains a *mod_cgi* module that handles all CGI requests. However, since CGI tends to be packaged with the Web server itself, its implementation as a distinct module is not so obvious.

To ensure that requests are forwarded properly, there must be some way to let the Web server know where to reroute the incoming request, and the details of this are obviously Web-server specific. For example, with Apache, configuration files are modified to let the Web server know which types of request will be handled by which modules. With Microsoft Internet Information Server (IIS), there are two popular options. One requires that developers write Active Server Pages (ASP) scripts that can reroute requests to separate application handles. The other requires building an ISAPI extension that redirects the request. In any case, nearly all Web servers have the ability to reroute requests—they just differ on where and how this redirection is specified.

Incidentally, keep in mind that rerouting a request means the whole request. Recall that an HTTP request, such as

```
GET /portfolio/show_portfolio?userid=9302&view=full HTTP/1.1
Host: www.example.com
```

is simply asking for some object named /portfolio/show_portfolio with parameters of 9302 and full. It's up to the request handler to cast these parameters appropriately, to translate the request into the proper set of server-side function calls, and finally to coordinate a single response.

Redirection to a Script Processor

Now that we know it is possible to reroute requests, the next question is, *where should they be rerouted?* One option is do something similar to CGI—reroute the request directly to a specific application program. This is the case with Perl and Tcl, where the corresponding interpreter is launched to process the requested script. With Apache Web servers, for example, redirection to Perl can be accomplished by the *mod_perl* module. A similar *mod_tcl* extension also exists.

The problem with redirecting a request to any old script-processing module is that most have no infrastructure for scalability. That is, they're fine for executing a single request, but they tend to get bogged down handling multiple concurrent requests. One reason for this is that the application program runs in the same process space as the Web server. Not decoupling the Web server from the application reduces opportunities for parallelism and can result in excessive memory demands.

Another problem is interoperability. While it may be suitable to handle a request in Perl or Tcl, it becomes a problem when communicating with any part of your application system not written in these languages (such as Java). Not that it can't be done: Certainly you can use sockets to communicate between Java and another interpreted language. However, such solutions aren't always available and you may have to develop your own protocols to integrate disparate application systems.

Redirection to Java Servlets

An alternative option is to redirect the request to a more scalable, Java-based application request dispatcher or handler. The role of the dispatcher is to ensure scalable, highly concurrent execution of requests. It doesn't execute requested functions—it just schedules them, typically by assigning a thread (usually from a thread pool) to deal with each one. As we discussed in Chapter 2 when defining application servers, multithreaded servers are generally more scalable than their alternatives in terms of both memory and CPU. Also, using a Java-based dispatcher makes integration with any Java-based application system, such as that defined by J2EE, much easier.

Java servlets are the J2EE solution to the problem of implementing a scalable system for generating dynamic HTTP responses. They're mainly attractive because of their built-in scalability features, their tight integration with Web server request-processing, and because they enable Java-based session management.

Using Servlets

We will review the basic steps for building a servlet and discuss various options developers have in its design and deployment. We'll also introduce JavaServer Pages (JSP) and look at how they aid the development and maintenance process and their general impact on performance. Later, we describe the integration of servlets with Enterprise JavaBeans and discuss why servlets are better for session management than for core application logic.

Servlets and Servlet Containers

Java servlets are simply Java classes that process HTTP requests programmatically for the purpose of interacting with a back-end application system, generating dynamic content, or both. They're seamlessly integrated into the Web server request-handling logic so that the Web server automatically forwards servlet requests to a **servlet container** (i.e., servlet engine). Servlet containers run a Java Virtual Machine (JVM) so that Java request-processing code can be executed. Alternatively, a servlet container like Apache's Tomcat server can be communicated with directly over

HTTP. In either case, when a container receives a request it assigns a thread to handle it (i.e., it calls the proper method on the servlet class).

Figure 7–1 illustrates the various ways in which client requests can be processed by servlets using a servlet container. As shown, a request can be made directly to the container. When this occurs, the container (which includes a JVM) executes the servlet request and replies to the client. A second way, also shown, is one wherein a client request can be sent to a Web server, which redirects it to the servlet container. Thus, the Web server acts as a broker during communication. In the second method, there are two options: Either the servlet container can run as its own process (the middle part of the figure) or it can run in the same address space with the Web server (the bottom part of the figure), as is the case with the Java Web Server.

In this chapter, we assume the out-of-process servlet container model. There are two reasons that this model is preferred. First, the out-of-process approach is obviously more flexible than the in-process approach because it allows the Web server to be load-balanced independently of the container. Thus, the container can be migrated to different hosts or the Web server can be part of a larger farm that does more than handle servlet requests. In short, the decoupling of server and container enables more scalability options at the expense of communication between the two processes.

A second reason for choosing the out-of-process approach over the in-process approach, where the client is directly connecting to the servlet container, is that the Web server is already very good at delivering static pages and is a very robust general request handler. This is an opinion shared even by container architects, such as

Figure 7–1
Servlet
container
integration
options

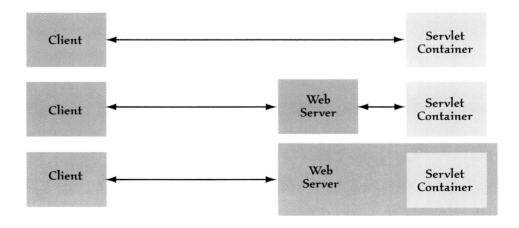

those involved in the Apache Tomcat project.* In short, the cost of an extra interme- diate hop (the Web server) is not as much as the cost of losing an already highly tuned, flexible request processor that can simply redirect the request to the servlet container when necessary.

Interacting with a Servlet

To illustrate better the role of servlets in an application, and the way the user interacts with them, let's consider a very simple example. Suppose that part of our application requires collecting membership information so that user profiles can be stored and user IDs and passwords can be assigned. We can use an HTML form to collect this information, as shown in Figure 7–2. When the form is sub- mitted, we want the information to be stored in a database and a dynamic, per- sonalized response to be generated, such as that shown in Figure 7–3. Suppose, for the sake of example, that the Web page shown in Figure 7–2 is actually based on the notion of an HTML form and communicates its input to the Web server via an HTTP POST request.

To handle the processing in a servlet, we need to develop a Java class and imple- ment a specific method (`doPost()`) that will be automatically called by the servlet container. The code for this method will insert the membership data into a database and compose a response to the user. The container provides the necessary handles to request input and output, so extracting HTTP request data and issuing an HTTP response is a simple matter of calling a few methods on objects passed into the pro- cessing method as parameters.

Web Server and Servlet Container Integration

As we discussed previously, out-of-process servlet processing (e.g., script or CGI- based Web request processing) is typically enabled in Web servers through a special module or adapter that redirects specified URLs or URL ranges to the servlet con- tainer. This redirection requires that the module contact the container using a cus- tom protocol over TCP/IP sockets. In turn, the container calls the proper method on the proper Java class (as identified by the HTTP request).

As an example, let's consider how to integrate the Apache Server with the Jakarta Tomcat servlet container. Apache has a module-centric style of processing that associates certain URLs with various modules. Correspondingly, Tomcat pro- vides a precompiled binary module (a library) and associated configuration files. The two are linked by a special protocol communicated between the Web server module and the container (also called a "worker" in Tomcat-speak).

---

*For details, see the Tomcat 3.2.1 installation note at `doc/tomcat-apache-howto.html`.

Figure 7–2
Sample
membership
application

Membership Application

To obtain a membership, fill out the following information and click SUBMIT.

First name: Jane
Last name: Doe

Street: 100 Main St
City: Anycity
State: CA
Zip: 90000

Phone: 800-555-1212

SUBMIT

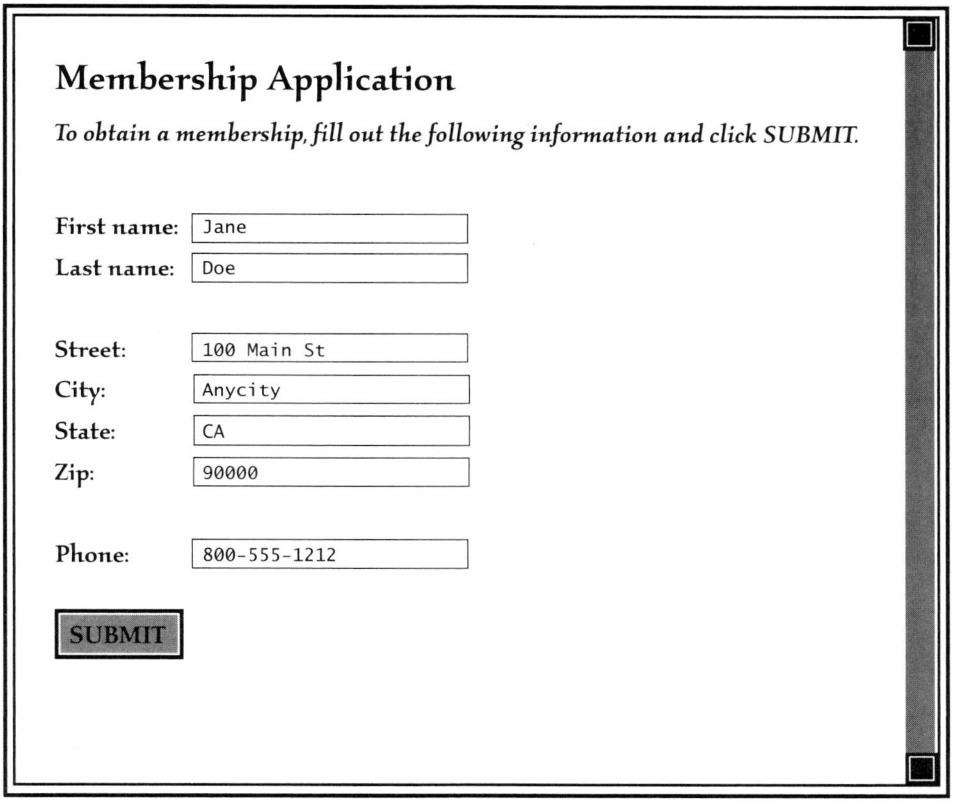

Conceptually, the integration between Apache and Tomcat resembles Figure 7–4. As shown, the Web server uses a separate module (*mod_jk* in this case) to communicate with the servlet container using the Apache JServ Protocol (ASP).* In turn, the container assigns the request to a thread executing the proper servlet class method (based on the HTTP request). To achieve the integration between server and container as Figure 7–4 suggests, we minimally need to

- Modify the Apache configuration files so that they're aware of the servlet container module (and can thus route the proper URLs to it).
- Edit the Tomcat configuration files to define servlet properties (e.g., where Java is located, where Tomcat is installed in the filesystem).

*It's now also possible to connect Tomcat to Apache via JNI, eliminating the need for TCP/IP.

Figure 7–3
Results from
membership
processing

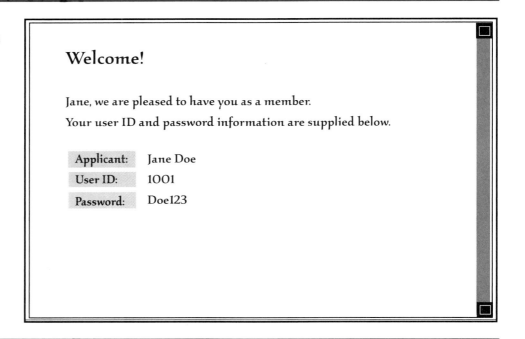

Welcome!

Jane, we are pleased to have you as a member.

Your user ID and password information are supplied below.

Applicant:	Jane Doe
User ID:	1001
Password:	Doe123

Figure 7–4
Apache/Tomcat
integration

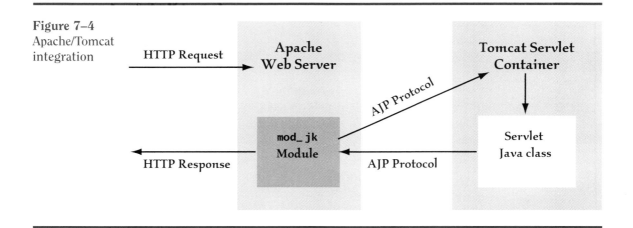

Our focus here isn't on Apache and Tomcat configuration, so I don't go into details about configuration file modifications. I refer you to the documentation. After we modify these files, we're ready to start developing and deploying servlets.

Developing Servlets

The development process for a servlet is straightforward:

1. Design the Web interface to the servlet—usually an HTML page that invokes servlet functionality. For example, have an HTML form request that the servlet process its contents upon clicking the Submit button.
2. Code and compile the servlet, making sure that the servlet class is designed to handle the HTTP requests of interest (such as POST or GET).

Let's see how this process works in terms of developing and deploying our example.

Designing the Servlet Interface

There's nothing magical or complicated about the HTML that leads to the invocation of the servlet. If you've written Web pages that invoke CGI functionality, Web pages that invoke servlets will look pretty much the same. Listing 7–1 shows the key parts of the required HTML code for our membership-processing example.

Listing 7–1: HTML Code for the Web Page in Figure 7–2.

```
<!DOCTYPE HTML PUBLIC "-//W3C//DTD HTML 4.0 Transitional//EN">
<HTML>
<HEAD>
<TITLE>Membership Application</TITLE>
</HEAD>
<BODY>
...
<FORM method=POST
action=http://www.example.com/servlets/ProcessMembership>
<TR>
<TD>First name:</TD>
<TD><INPUT type=text name=first_name></INPUT></TD>
</TR>
...
<INPUT value="Apply" type=submit></INPUT>
</FORM>
</BODY>
</HTML>
```

The only really interesting part of this code is the `action` attribute of the `FORM` element, which specifies that the form be processed by the `ProcessMembership` servlet. What this means is that a Java class, `ProcessMembership.class`, will be invoked by the servlet container. Thus, the servlet container must be configured to identify the location of `ProcessMembership` in the filesystem and the Web server must be configured so that requests to the `servlets` directory will be referred to the servlet container (e.g., Tomcat). Both of these issues are related to configuration files, so we'll avoid them here.

Coding the Servlet

Servlets in Java are generic and not explicitly tied to HTTP processing. Instead, a superclass—the Java abstract `GenericServlet` class—is extended by the abstract `HttpServlet` class. `GenericServlet` defines the `init()` and `service()` methods, among others, which are semantically necessary for any type of servlet. The `HttpServlet` class overrides some of these methods and defines HTTP-specific methods, shown in Table 7–1.

Servlet programmers implement their servlet classes simply by extending the `HttpServlet` class and overriding the desired methods. Listing 7–2 shows the code for our sample membership-processing servlet. Notice that this servlet is nothing more than a regular Java class that extends the `HttpServlet` class and overrides the `init()`,

Table 7–1: Commonly Overridden `HttpServlet` Methods

Method	*Purpose*
`void init()`	Convenience method used during servlet instantiation. Any session-independent data structures (such as a cache or database connection pool) can be initialized here.
`void doGet(HttpServletRequest a_req, HttpServletResponse a_resp)`	Processes HTTP GET requests. The details of the request are in `a_req` and the output stream for formatting the response is in `a_resp`.
`void doPost(HttpServletRequest a_req, HttpServletResponse a_resp)`	Processes HTTP POST requests. The details of the request are in `a_req` and the output stream for formatting the response is in `a_resp`.
`void destroy()`	Convenience method used during servlet destruction. Any session-independent data structures can be cleaned up here (connections closed, etc.).

doGet(), and doPost() methods shown in Table 7–1. The overridden init() method is commonly the place to initialize data structures; doGet() and doPost() override HTTP requests of the same name.

Listing 7–2: Sample Servlet for Membership Processing

```
1  import java.io.*;
2  import java.text.*;
3  import java.util.*;
4  import javax.servlet.*;
5  import javax.servlet.http.*;
6
7  /**
8   * EXAMPLE SERVLET: processing a membership application.
9   */
10
11 public class ProcessMembership extends HttpServlet
12 {
13   private class UserLogin
14   {
15     public String username;
16     public String password;
17   }
18
19   /**
20    * Initialize instance-specific data structures.
21    */
22   public void init() { }
23
24   /**
25    * Handle HTTP GET requests: these should be disallowed.
26    */
27   public void doGet(HttpServletRequest a_request,
28     HttpServletResponse a_response)
29       throws IOException, ServletException
30   {
31     /* Respond with a very rudimentary error message */
32
33     a_response.setContentType("text/html");
34     a_response.getWriter().println("ERROR: Only POST requests are
           allowed");
35   }
36
37
38   /**
39    * Insert new member in the database.
40    */
41   public UserLogin addMember(String a_first, String a_last, String
         a_street,
```

```
42      String a_city, String a_state, String a_zip)
43   {
44      /* Generate user login information */
45      UserLogin userLogin = new UserLogin();
46
47      userLogin.username = (a_first+a_last).toLowerCase();
48      userLogin.password = userLogin.username+"123";
49
50      /**
51       * Insert member into database, most likely using JDBC.
52       * Since we have not discussed JDBC yet (and since it's a detail
           here),
53       * no code for this is shown...
54       *
55       * ---- JDBC code goes here ----
56       *
57       */
58
59      return userLogin;
60   }
61
62   /**
63    * Handle HTTP POST requests
64    */
65   public void doPost(HttpServletRequest a_request,
66      HttpServletResponse a_response)
67         throws IOException, ServletException
68   {
69      /* Extract form parameters (membership input data) from
            request */
70      String firstName = a_request.getParameter("first_name");
71      String lastName = a_request.getParameter("last_name");
72      String street = a_request.getParameter("street");
73      String city = a_request.getParameter("city");
74      String state = a_request.getParameter("state");
75      String zip = a_request.getParameter("zip");
76
77      /* Store new member into database, obtain login information */
78      UserLogin userLogin =
79         addMember(firstName, lastName, street, city, state, zip);
80
81      /* Construct a response, include new user ID and password */
82      PrintWriter outWriter = a_response.getWriter();
83      a_response.setContentType("text/html");
84
85      /* Write out the actual HTML */
86      outWriter.println("<HTML>");
87      outWriter.println("<H1>Welcome!</H1>");
88      outWriter.println(firstName+", we are pleased to have you");
89      outWriter.println("as a member.<BR> Your user ID and password");
90      outWriter.println("are supplied below.<P>");
91      outWriter.println("<TABLE>");
```

```
 92      outWriter.println("<TR><TD bgcolor=#CCCCFF>");
 93      outWriter.println("<B>APPLICANT:</B><TD>"+firstName+"
            "+lastName);
 94      outWriter.println("</TR><TR><TD bgcolor=#FFCCCC>");
 95      outWriter.println("<B>USERNAME:</B><TD>"+userLogin.username);
 96      outWriter.println("</TR><TR><TD bgcolor=#FFCCCC>");
 97      outWriter.println("<B>PASSWORD:</B><TD>"+userLogin.password);
 98      outWriter.println("</TR><TR><TD>");
 99      outWriter.println("</HTML>");
100    }
101 }
```

A few things are worth noting about this implementation code. First, the logic is pretty lightweight and, as shown by line 55, no real database integration exists. The user isn't inserted into a database, and the username and password are generated based on the input (so name clashes are possible). Since our immediate goal is to demonstrate how to write servlets, not how to write full-blown, airtight applications, the code is as simple as possible.

A second, more important observation is that the code is actually a combination of **presentation logic**, **session management**, and core **application logic**—all in the same file. The HTML generated by lines 86 through 99 represents the presentation logic. The extraction of request parameters in lines 70 through 75 of the doPost() method is related to session management—nothing about our presentation or core logic requires doPost(); rather, it's a necessary part of coding a servlet. The core application logic is created by simply extending the servlet class. The addMember() method, shown in lines 38 through 60, is a peer of doPost()—even though it has nothing to do with request processing.

This mixing of the three types of logic isn't pretty; *and that is exactly the point.* While the code shows that you can get the job done by combining everything in the servlet class itself, this makes for poor software engineering. There's no way to really reuse the application logic to add a member, even though this seems like potentially useful code. Also, if we want another interface for adding members, we'll likely replicate code—always a dangerous practice.

It's also a troublesome scenario when considering how multiple developers work on such applications. For example, a user interface designer, who focuses on look and feel, may know a lot about color combinations and usability but know nothing about servlets and their maintenance.

A member of the operations staff, responsible for scaling the application deployment, couldn't care less about the look and feel or even what the application does. He's simply interested in making access to servlets fast and scalable, but he's forced to reckon with presentation and application logic when all he really wants is to insert session management code.

Finally, there's the core application logic programmer, who builds useful application code and doesn't care how it's deployed. She just wants to make it as functional and reusable as possible. She also wants to make sure that application logic executed via multiple interfaces is consistent, which allows her to ensure common functionality and to consolidate performance optimizations in a single place.

Servlets are best used as mechanisms for executing session management logic because they're great at managing connectivity between a Web-based interactive user and the application. However, they're not necessarily well suited to presentation and core application logic. For the former, it's recommended that you use JavaServer Pages (JSPs). For the latter, Enterprise JavaBeans are suggested. We'll discuss both more later on. For now, let's focus on the process of servlet execution.

Servlet Execution

Now that we've seen how to develop a servlet, and we can imagine how it's invoked, we can discuss some of the details of what goes on behind the scenes. For performance and scalability reasons, it's of particular interest to know how the servlet container works.

Servlet Containers

First, let's consider the term **container** versus an older term used to describe this entity: **engine**. When you think of a container, you think of a host—a mechanism for *storing a resource* such as a servlet. In contrast, an engine connotes a mechanism for processing, which is not at all what happens. *Container* is a better, more accurate term to be sure, since the real execution has to do with the code written by the servlet programmer. Interestingly, this shift in terminology fits well into a discussion we'll have later about the role of servlets in the overall application architecture, but for now let's return to understanding what containers are all about.

At the minimum, a servlet container is an intermediary/facilitator between the Web server and servlet. It's responsible for

- Creating a servlet instance
- Calling the servlet `init()` method
- Calling the servlet `service()` method whenever a request is made
- Calling the servlet `destroy()` method before the servlet is terminated
- Destroying the servlet instance

Like a Web server, a servlet container is a continually running process. It takes care of creating a servlet instance when needed and using threads to execute the code in it. Specifically, when a request comes in for a servlet, the container does the following:

- Maps the request to identify the servlet class being requested.
- Marshals input and output data by constructing Java objects corresponding to the request (HttpRequest) and reply (HttpResponse) descriptors; it's through these descriptors that servlet developers can interrogate things like request parameters and produce dynamic output.
- Sets up the environment associated with the request; the Java classes HttpSession and ServletContext represent **request-level state**, and **application-level state**, respectively.
- Creates an instance of the servlet class if one doesn't already exist.
- Creates a thread and executes the corresponding servlet method(s).

If multiple requests arrive for a servlet at the same time, threads are created for each one of them; however, the same servlet object instance is used. Using threads to execute the servlet instance code is efficient because it eliminates the need to continually recreate and destroy the servlet instance (which may have an expensive initialization section). The obvious minor drawback is that it requires programmers to write thread-safe code.

When a servlet instance hasn't been requested for a while, it may be destroyed by the servlet container. However, the lifetime of servlet instance is a servlet container configuration parameter and can be adjusted as needed. Furthermore, the servlet container can be designated to create instances of various servlets upon startup—before the servlets are requested by clients.

Servlets and Multithreading

By default, a servlet container can service concurrent requests by associating each one with a thread and executing the servlet service() method for it. This is generally considered a feature because it increases parallelism during application processing. Since Web applications are primarily I/O bound (waiting for requests from the client or for output from an external resource such as a database), this concurrency is often realized during execution, resulting in more efficient applications. Also, using threads—as opposed to processes—for each request is generally more scalable. As we've discussed a few times already, memory and CPU resources can be shared more efficiently by deploying multithreaded servers instead of multiple processes.

Although parallel request processing is efficient, there are certain cases where a developer needs to serialize request execution. The most common instances involve third-party data structures that are not thread-safe. Incoming requests that use these data structures should do so one at a time. For such cases, there are two options for serialization:

- Explicit synchronization of methods or use of the `synchronized` keyword to designate serialized execution within an instance
- Implementation of the servlet under the `SingleThreadModel` to ensure that only one thread at a time is executing the `service()` call (and its descendants, such as `doGet()`) of a particular instance

The first option is well understood by most Java programmers. By synchronizing the `doPost()` or `doGet()` method, for example, you ensure that only one thread is executing these methods *for that instance* at a given time.

Consider the very simple example in Listing 7–3, which echoes the ID of the user who invokes it.

Listing 7–3: Example of Unsafe Membership Processing (Requires Serialization)

```
/**
 * Process new member - not thread safe.
 * Adds new member to the system.
 **/
public class ProcessMembershipUnsafe extends HttpServlet
{
    private int m_nextUserId;

    ...
    ...

    /**
     * Initialize instance-specific data structures.
     **/
    public void init()
    {
        m_nextUserId = 0;
    }

    ...
    ...

    /**
     * Insert new member in the database.
     **/
    public UserLogin addMember(String a_first, String a_last,
        String a_street, String a_city, String a_state, String a_zip)
    {
```

```
m_nextUserId++;

/**
 * Simulate inserting a member into database.
 * To grossly demonstrate a synchronization issue, we sleep
 * for 5 seconds when inserting the first user.  Though contrived
 * here, unpredictable orderings of request completions are
 * common, especially when reliant on external sources (like a
 * database).
 **/
if (m_nextUserId == 1) {
   try {
      Thread.sleep(5000);
   }
   catch (Exception e) {
   }
}

/**
 * At this point, all processing using m_nextUserId when
 * the first member is created is particularly unsafe because
 * addMember may have been called during the sleep time above.
 **/

/* Generate user login information */
UserLogin userLogin = new UserLogin();

userLogin.username = m_nextUserId;
userLogin.password = userLogin.username+"123";

return userLogin;
}
```

To underline the concurrency problem, the code sleeps for 5 seconds when processing the first user ID. Thus, if the first and second users are submitted at roughly the same time, the second user will finish before the first and—more alarmingly—any processing done on her behalf that involves m_nextUserId (such as creation of UserLogin) will be incorrect. The implication is that if requests don't take a deterministic time (nearly always the case when relying on an external resource such as a database), their order of completion won't be predictable. Thus, state maintained in the context of a call isn't guaranteed to be consistent.

To solve this synchronization problem, you can use the synchronized keyword on a code block or method. For example, we can change addMember() to

```
public synchronized UserLogin addMember(String a_first, String a_last,
String a_street, String a_city, String a_state, String a_zip)
```

Many developers *believe* that the same effect can be achieved by having the servlet implement the `SingleThreadModel` class. So, instead of synchronizing the `addMember()` method, it would seem that we should do the following:

```
public class ProcessMembershipSafe extends HttpServlet
    implements SingleThreadModel
```

However, I emphasize "believe" because the `SingleThreadModel` design has created a lot of confusion. It sounds like one thread will be associated with an instance, but in fact the specification notes that *multiple instances can be active within a container* and guarantees only that only one thread will be allowed to execute the service method *of a particular instance at a time*. The details are important here, so it's worthwhile to quote the spec directly (SRV 2.2.1 of the Java Servlet Specification 2.3):

> The use of the `SingleThreadModel` interface guarantees that only one thread at a time will execute in a given servlet instance's service method. It is important to note that this guarantee only applies to each servlet instance, since the container may choose to pool such objects. Objects that are accessible to more than one servlet instance at a time, such as instances of `HttpSession`, may be available at any particular time to multiple servlets, including those that implement `SingleThreadModel`.

To confuse things further, elsewhere the spec indicates that although all non-`SingleThreadModel` servlets have only one instance in a given servlet container, instances of `SingleThreadModel` servlets may be pooled! Thus, the only real benefit of this model would appear to be implicit, instance-specific isolation.

From my point of view, although `SingleThreadModel` *appears* to make request serialization easier, it's probably more confusing and can lead to unexpected execution results. Also, its actual implementation depends on the container vendor. Given the specification guarantee that there will be only one instance of non-`SingleThreadModel` servlets, synchronization of methods or code blocks using the Java `synchronized` keyword is far easier and more natural. There are two other very good reasons to use this method rather than `SingleThreadModel`:

- Serialization is more explicit, which is better programming practice.
- Performance tends to be better because the periods of serialization will be minimal (i.e., only when it's needed).

Servlets and Session Management

Earlier I suggested that servlets are best used as interactive session managers. To understand this a little better, we need to discuss session management in more detail.

Simply put, session management is the idea of associating a series of activities with a distinct end user. For example, if we're deploying an online bookstore, a session might be composed of the following activities:

1. User logs in.
2. User searches for mystery books.
3. User investigates a new book by Philip Margolin.
4. User purchases the book.
5. User searches for new Java books.
6. User logs out.

Thus, a session is a series of activities that may contain zero or more transactions or, more to the point, a session is the logical use of an application by a client. However, the HTTP protocol is stateless, so it's not trivial to associate the preceding operations with the same logical session. The client or the server needs some way to link them.

Session Identification

The most common way to identify a session—independent of servlets—is to have the client remind the server of the session in which it's participating. Incidentally, most applications assume that a user can participate in only one session at a time. Thus, identifying the user and identifying the session are often viewed as equivalent. The question now is, what options exist for "reminding" the server of the user or session? It turns out that there are a few.

HTTP User Authentication

One way to identify a session involves using the built-in user authentication features of HTTP. For example, when a user logs in to an application, the protocol reminds the server that future actions are being generated by a known user. Identifying a user is thus automatically enabled by the protocol.

While it's possible to use authentication information as a means for managing sessions, this is largely viewed as a poor choice: Authentication is meant not for session management but for access control. Plus, there's still the problem of assigning unique session identifiers and maintaining very long-lived sessions. Standard HTTP user authentication isn't a good solution for either problem. However, it does have the built-in feature of security, preventing sessions from being "spoofed" (concocted manually by a nefarious user).

Hidden Form Fields

A second method of session identification is to include hidden form fields throughout Web pages application. Thus, user form submissions will contain an additional unseen field that identifies the user. For example, an HTML page with a FORM element can contain the following hidden input field:

```
<!DOCTYPE HTML PUBLIC "-//W3C//DTD HTML 4.0 Transitional//EN">
<HTML>
<HEAD>
<TITLE>Membership Application</TITLE>
</HEAD>
<BODY>
...
<FORM method=POST
action=http://www.example.com/servlets/ProcessMembership>
...
<INPUT name="sessionID" type=hidden
value=9203></INPUT>
</FORM>
</BODY>
</HTML>
```

While including hidden inputs is relatively easy to do, it has its disadvantages:

- It doesn't handle long-lived or interrupted sessions well.
- It restricts navigation: Users must click Submit for each screen.
- It's not secure: The session ID is visible and can be spoofed.

To explain better the limitation suggested by the first and second bulleted points, consider the case where the user uses a single browser window to interact with the application. When he first logs in, a unique session ID is generated (such as 9203, as in the example above) and this ID is encoded as a hidden field on every form generated. When the user clicks Submit, the ID is also sent to the server, reminding it of the session. The server uses it to associate state (such as an in-progress shopping cart) with the user.

However, suppose that, in the middle of a session, the user types a new URL (not related to the application) in the browser location bar. When he returns to the application (either by bookmark or by typing in a well-known application URL), the session ID can't be resent to the application server because the user has contacted the server other than via a FORM (which resends the session ID). Thus, the ID is no longer available and the session will have to be restarted. In short, session state is fragile when usage is interrupted or navigation is nonstandard.

Rewritten URLs

A third way to remind the server of the current session involves generating URLs that are rewritten to associate the request with the user. For example, once we know that Jane Doe has logged on, all future URLs involved in the application include Jane Doe's name or user ID on their argument list. In this way, all processing of requests includes a parameter indicating the requestor.

For example, the HTML code for processing a membership would look something like this:

```
<!DOCTYPE HTML PUBLIC "-//W3C//DTD HTML 4.0 Transitional//EN">
<HTML>
<HEAD>
<TITLE>Membership Application</TITLE>
</HEAD>
<BODY>
...
<FORM method=POST
action=http://www.example.com/servlets/ProcessMembership?sid=9203>
...
</FORM>
</BODY>
</HTML>
```

Rewriting URLs is obviously very similar to using hidden form fields. Correspondingly, it shares the same advantages and disadvantages.

HTTP Persistent Cookies

The final and most popular means for session tracking is to use HTTP persistent **cookies**. Cookies are simply name/value pairs that exist on the client side of the application. Each one is associated with a particular host and essentially acts as an identifier for a user. When the user connects to a host through his Web browser, the cookies associated with that host are sent to the site's Web server. Thus, they tell the Web server some details about the connecting client. For example, a cookie might indicate the user ID or the catalog ID of a product. A given Web site is allowed to have multiple cookies associated with a client if desired.

Cookies are generally a better solution than HTTP user authentication, hidden form fields, and rewritten URLs because they're more robust for session management. Since a cookie is stored in a file on the client's local disk, interrupted sessions and alternative navigation don't affect the server's ability to query it. Unless the user physically removes a cookie (or declines to receive it), the cookie will continue to be available and thus can continue to be used for session identification.

Example: Implementing Session Management with Cookies

The Java servlet API allows you to manage cookies directly. For example, you can set a cookie value—and thus associate a name with a value—and attempt to have it stored on the client side. Later, when a client connects to your site, you can read the value associated with that cookie to identify the user or to discover other session-based information.

Listing 7–4 shows a servlet that reads the session ID from an incoming request. If no session ID exists, one is created. It can then be used as a key for looking up other information (username, shopping basket information, etc.) in the database or local, server-side caches.

Listing 7–4: Reading a Session ID from an Incoming Request

```
 1 import java.io.*;
 2 import java.text.*;
 3 import java.util.*;
 4 import javax.servlet.*;
 5 import javax.servlet.http.*;
 6
 7 /**
 8  * Session tracking with cookies
 9  */
10
11 public class SessionIdentifier extends HttpServlet
12 {
13   public void doGet(HttpServletRequest a_request,
14     HttpServletResponse a_response)
15       throws IOException, ServletException
16   {
17     /* Initialize the session ID */
18     String sid = null;
19
20     /* Check current cookies to see if session ID is set */
21     Cookie[] cookies = a_request.getCookies();
22     if (cookies != null) {
23       for (int i=0; i<cookies.length; i++) {
24         if (cookies[i].getName().equals("sid")) {
25           sid = cookies[i].getValue();
```

```
26            break;
27          }
28        }
29
30        /* Generate new session ID */
31        if (sid == null) {
32          sid = genNextSessionId();
33          a_response.addCookie(new Cookie(sid, sid));
34        }
35
36        /**
37         * Rest of the processing can be done based on session ID
38         *
39         * ....
40         *
41         */
42    }
43 }
```

The most important parts of the listing are

- Lines 23 through 27, which check for the value of the cookie named sid
- Line 33, which sets the cookie if it was unset, using the session ID generated from line 32

Now, although it's possible to use persistent cookies very easily, as shown above, there's actually a more general way to manage sessions: with a special servlet API for session tracking.

The Servlet Session-Tracking API

The Java servlet session-tracking API provides a transparent way for the server-side developer to easily manage session data. It's closely related to URL rewriting and particularly to cookies. Generally, the basic idea of this API is that it provides a layer of indirection in session management. Instead of worrying about exactly how session data is managed (by cookies, by URL rewriting, etc.), the server-side engineer simply uses an API that can query or store named attributes. Like cookies, each attribute is essentially a name/value pair: The name is the name of the attribute; the value is associated with the attribute's value.

As I mentioned earlier, the beauty is in the indirection this API provides. Using some method (for example, URL-rewriting or cookies), it ensures that all requests from a given client session are associated with the same unique ID. Thus, the server can easily associate incoming requests with existing server-side state without having to worry about the details of how this association is accomplished.

The following snippet of servlet code uses the session-tracking API to add a new attribute to the current session:

```
public void doGet(HttpServletRequest a_request,
  HttpServletResponse a_response)
    throws IOException, ServletException
{
  ...
  /* Get the session object */
  HttpSession session = a_request.getSession();

  /* Obtain the session ID */
  String sid = session.getId();

  /* Add a name/value pair to the current session state */
  session.setAttribute("name", "Joe Smith");
  ...
}
```

In summary, the main advantage of using the session-tracking API rather than something like persistent cookies directly is that it's a logical way to manage session information. The server side doesn't need to know how sessions are being maintained but just that they are and that attributes can be queried and managed using the provided API. Using cookies explicitly, however, is a more physical approach and ties the server-side engineer to a particular session management implementation.

Deploying Servlets

Once you develop a servlet, you need to decide how to make it available. Recall that servlets execute within a container and that each container has an associated JVM. For many deployments, having one servlet container will be enough. However, to promote scalability, most servlet systems give you the opportunity to distribute servlets across a set of machines for improved load balancing and fault tolerance—key attributes that encourage scalability.

Session Management with Multiple Containers

Distributing servlet containers across multiple machines is a common way to improve the scalability of your servlet deployment. For the most part, it's an effective strategy—until you again get to the sticky issue of session management. Although distributing containers allows you to handle high numbers of concurrent requests, it complicates how state is maintained between those requests.

The problem here is that, if requests are arbitrarily distributed to different machines running different containers (and thus different JVMs), how can sessions be managed? There's no guarantee that each request from a given client will always be routed to the same container (and thus the same JVM, where the session information is stored).

There are two common solutions to this problem: deterministic load balancing and leveraging the ability for servlet containers to migrate (and/or persist) state.

Deterministic Load Balancing

When you route incoming requests to multiple machines, you need some mechanism for distributing the load. Typically, this is the job of the load balancer. There are hardware and software load-balancing solutions, but both commonly offer features that ensure that a client will be routed to the same physical server every time.

One hardware example is the Cisco LocalDirector, which supports a "Cookie Sticky" feature. This feature makes sure that clients will be redirected by the LocalDirector to the same physical machine (as long as the machine is available) and thus the same JVM. When cookies are issued to clients, the response is snooped by the LocalDirector so that it can make a note of the cookie and the machine with which it's associated.

Figure 7–5 shows how this works by highlighting six key links in a simple example. Consider link 1, where an incoming request is received by the load balancer. Because no cookie is currently set, the load balancer can route the request to any of its target machines as it sees fit. Using some algorithm (round-robin, for example), it then farms out the request, which by chance goes to machine A, as link 2 shows. In the context of servlet execution, a session cookie is set. Next, the client reply is communicated back to the client, passing through the load balancer, as shown by link 3. The load balancer makes a note of the cookie and the machine that returned the response. It then continues to return the HTTP response to the client, as shown in link 4, where the client stores the cookie on his local machine. When the client connects to the application system again, as shown in link 5, the cookie is automatically re-sent. However, this time the load balancer identifies that a cookie exists and routes that request to the machine associated with that cookie, as shown in link 6.

A software analog to this is the Apache Web server, which can be set up so that it intelligently redirects clients to a secondary server, typically by altering the Web server configuration files so that the *mod_rewrite* module load-balances requests to a logical host name to a set of physical hosts. The result is similar to that achieved by the LocalDirector, although the hardware solution tends to be more robust and scalable.

Figure 7–5
Maintaining
session state in
hardware load
balancing

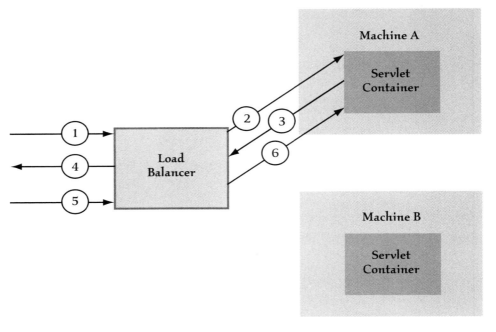

Automatic Session Migration and/or Persistence

Routing server invocations for a common client session to a fixed server may ensure that session state can be recovered per invocation, but it does have some disadvantages. First, there's the issue of failover—suppose the fixed server crashes (along with the state). Nearly all load-balancing solutions have some plan for failover, but of course none of them can really ensure that all state is restored because the load-balancers don't know anything about "servlets" or "JVMs"—they only know about network connections.

A second disadvantage is cost and configuration. Using a load balancer potentially requires more money and definitely more time configuring your deployment. Admittedly, this is a trivial concern when deploying a costly Web site to begin with, but I mention it here for completeness.

An alternative approach for managing state with multiple containers is to make use of any session migration features that your J2EE vendor provides. One example is the session persistence feature offered by BEA's WebLogic Server (J2EE) as part of its clustering facility. With WebLogic, you can configure your sessions to be persistent; the location of persistence can range from memory to the filesystem to a JDBC data source.

Obviously, saving state to a filesystem or database solves the failover problem. Even if the entire site crashes, data persisted to the database should be recoverable when the site is restored. Of course, it's worthwhile to understand how session persistence occurs with your J2EE vendor. In particular, is it synchronous or asynchronous with servlet execution?

WebLogic also supports a mechanism for HTTP in-memory session replication. This mechanism isn't as robust as more persistent storage, like a filesystem or database, but its performance can be better. Also, if complete site failures are rare and your session data is not mission critical, this solution may be fine for your needs.

In addition to session persistence, another supported feature is automatic session migration. Using some of the same infrastructure for replication and persistence, products like WebLogic allow client requests to be received by any machine in a defined cluster and then have the state always accessible, whether or not the current target machine is the same as the machine used for a previous session invocation. Of course, it's not free—on-demand network communication of state between cluster participants may be required —but at least it's possible.

The network communication required by automatic session migration is one disadvantage of this cost-friendly approach to distributed servlet containers. Another is serialization. Systems like WebLogic that allow you to persist and migrate sessions require that session objects be serializable, and serialization can be costly at runtime and can make servlet development more burdensome. However, if session persistence is a priority, it may be worthwhile.

Developing Servlets with JavaServer Pages

JavaServer Pages (JSP), like Microsoft Active Server Pages (ASP), are a way to combine HTML and server-side function calls so that Web application development can more easily separate presentation logic from core application logic. Generally speaking, JSP isn't so much a technology to optimize servlets as it is a methodology for application development. We'll address JSP-like technology briefly in this chapter, since so many developers use it and because its performance impact has long been debated.

Sample JSP Page

The best way to get started with JSP is to look at example code, compare it to the Web page it's associated with, and fill in the blanks. We need evidence of programmatic logic in our page, so we'll use a Web page that welcomes all visitors, declaring which number visitor they are. It's shown in Figure 7–6, welcoming the first visitor. When the tenth visitor arrives, a special response is given, as shown in Figure 7–7. Our simple example thus involves a page that is dynamically generated. Listing 7–5 shows the JSP, stored in a file named hits.jsp, required to pull this off.

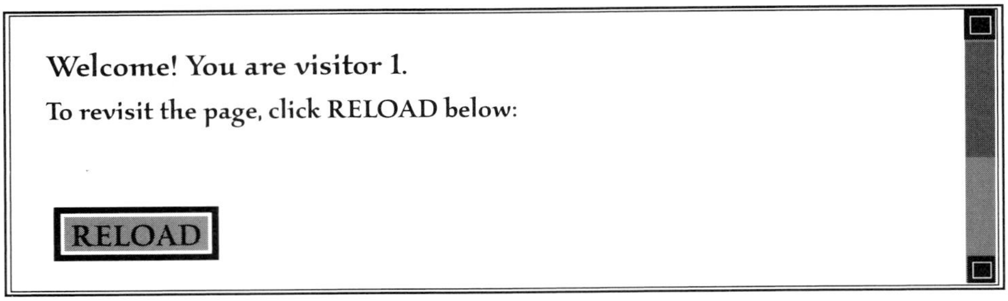

Figure 7–6
What the first
visitor sees

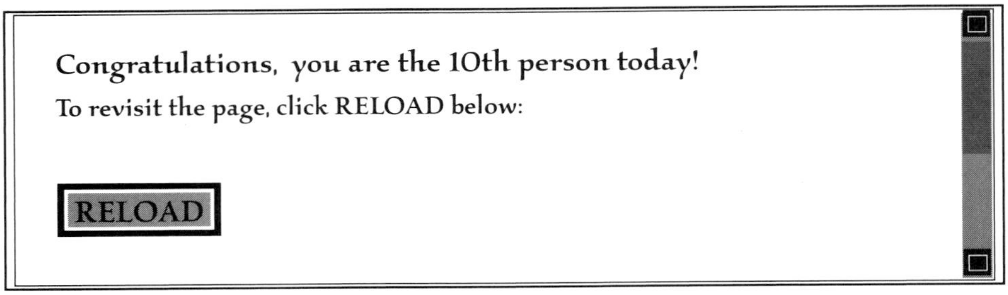

Welcome! You are visitor 1.
To revisit the page, click RELOAD below:

RELOAD

Figure 7–7
What the
tenth visitor
sees

Congratulations, you are the 10th person today!
To revisit the page, click RELOAD below:

RELOAD

Listing 7–5: Sample JSP for Counting Page Hits

```
1  <%@ page import = "hits.HitsBean" %>
2  <jsp:useBean id="hits" class="hits.HitsBean" scope="session"/>
3  <jsp:setProperty name="hits" property="*"/>
4  <!DOCTYPE HTML PUBLIC "-//W3C//DTD HTML 4.0 Transitional//EN">
5  <HTML>
6     <HEAD>
7           <TITLE>Hit Counter</TITLE>
8     </HEAD>
9     <BODY>
10          <% if (hits.incrHits() == 10) { %>
11               <B>Congratulations, you are the 10th person today!</B>
12          <% } else  { %>
13               Welcome! You are visitor #
14               <%= hits.getHits() %>
15          <% } %>
16
```

```
17              <P>To revisit the page, click RELOAD below:
18              <FORM method=get>
19                  <INPUT type=submit value="RELOAD">
20              </FORM>
21      </BODY>
22 </HTML>
```

The Structure of a JSP Page

From Listing 7–5, it's obvious that a JSP is really nothing more than a regular HTML page with special hooks that allow you to embed server-side function calls and raw Java logic. More generally, JSPs are text documents that consist of two types of text: **static page data** (or "template data" per the JSP spec), consisting of the native presentation language (such as HTML, XML, or WML), and **dynamic page data**, consisting of different JSP scripting elements. These elements can be directives, scriptlets, expressions, or declarations.

JSP **directives** (such as those shown in lines 1 through 3) are instructions for JSP processing. They mean nothing to Java itself, just to JSP technology and integration. For example, the directive in line 1 tells the JSP processor what Java class to load, and the JSP element in line 2 refers to which server-side bean to create and use.

JSP **scriptlets**, such as those shown in lines 10, 12, and 15, represent actual Java code that typically has some bearing on which parts of the static page data are returned to the client. For example, lines 10 through 15 show how simple conditional logic (expressed in Java) can control which static page data is shown.

JSP **expressions**, such as that shown in line 14, are replaced with values resulting from Java execution. For example, processing line 14 results in a value that is then displayed on the page itself. Notice the difference between JSP scriptlets and expressions: The former look like <% ...> while the latter look like <%= ...>.

There's one thing not shown in Listing 7–5: JSP **declarations**. These are simply blocks of a JSP where objects and/or methods are declared and implemented. One example is this block:

```
<%!
   private String myString;

   public int subtract(int a_x, int a_y) {
      return a_x - a_y;
   }
%>
```

The JSP parts of a document are typically associated with one or more Java objects. For example, the JSP code for counting visitors works with this simple Java class in Listing 7–6.

Listing 7–6: Application Logic for Counting Page Hits

```java
package hits;
import java.util.*;

public class HitsBean {

  private int m_hits;

  public HitsBean() {
     resetHits();
  }

  public int incrHits() {
     return ++m_hits;
  }

  public void resetHits() {
     m_hits = 0;
  }

  public int getHits() {
     return m_hits;
  }

  public void setCounter(String counter) {
     m_hits = Integer.parseInt(counter);
  }
}
```

Right off the bat, you should notice that the separation between presentation logic and core logic is well defined. A JSP author only needs to know the specification of the core back-end Java class (HitsBean in the example). Likewise, the class implementer doesn't need to worry about the HTML associated with a particular deployment, but simply focuses on writing a functional class. This means that the resulting Java class isn't tied to any assumed mode of presentation; thus, the common problem of application logic intermingled with presentation logic is avoided.

How JSP Works

If a JSP page isn't just plain HTML and contains expressions that need to be compiled, how does it work at runtime? When a user requests a JSP page, a check is first made to see whether the code on the page needs to be compiled (i.e., was it previously compiled and is that compilation up to date?). If compiling is required, it's done at request time along with any remaining JSP translation (processing directives, etc.). The result of compilation is a new servlet—one that the developer doesn't edit directly—which

Figure 7–8
JSP life-cycle
flowchart

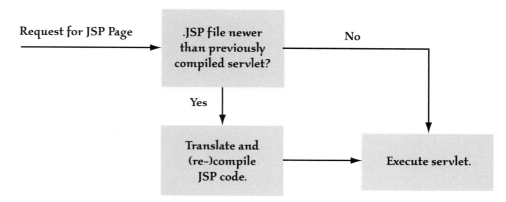

combines the presentation logic of the JSP file and the references to other Java objects (such as HitsBean, shown earlier). This is the servlet that's actually executed at runtime. The entire process is shown in Figure 7–8.

There's good news and bad news about the execution flow shown in Figure 7–8. The good news is that servlet compilation is automatic. If a JSP page is changed, the next request to it will trigger recompilation. Of course, the bad news is that some errors made to the page can be identified only at runtime! More bad news is that the first request to a JSP needing recompilation obviously will trigger recompilation, making this request (along with ones concurrent to it) slower. However, when you're dealing with a Web site that has thousands of clients, this may not be that big a deal.

You might wonder what this generated servlet code actually looks like. It's not pretty (in terms of code spacing and comments); in fact, its content can be downright cryptic. However, it's useful to look at a snippet of it here so that you can be convinced that nothing out of the ordinary is happening. Listing 7–7 is some of the generated code for the JSP example we've been using throughout this chapter. It was generated by Apache Jakarta/Tomcat 3.2.1.

Listing 7–7: Example of Generated Servlet Code

```
1 public class _0002fjsp__0002fhits_0002fhits_0002ejsphits_jsp_3
2   extends HttpJspBase {
3
4     // begin [file="C:\\jsp\\hits\\hits.jsp";from=(2,0);to=(2,62)]
5     // end
6
7     static {
```

```
 8          }
 9          public _0002fjsp_0002fhits_0002fhits_0002ejsphits_jsp_3( ) {
10          }
11
12          private static boolean _jspx_inited = false;
13
14          public final void _jspx_init() throws JasperException {
15          }
16
17          public void _jspService(HttpServletRequest request,
18            HttpServletResponse  response)
19              throws IOException, ServletException {
20
21              JspFactory _jspxFactory = null;
22              PageContext pageContext = null;
23              HttpSession session = null;
24              ServletContext application = null;
25              ServletConfig config = null;
26              JspWriter out = null;
27              Object page = this;
28              String  _value = null;
29              try {
30
31                  if (_jspx_inited == false) {
32                      _jspx_init();
33                      _jspx_inited = true;
34                  }
35                  _jspxFactory = JspFactory.getDefaultFactory();
36                  response.setContentType("text/html;charset=8859_1");
37                  pageContext = _jspxFactory.getPageContext(this, request,
38                   response, "", true, 8192, true);
39
40                  application = pageContext.getServletContext();
41                  config = pageContext.getServletConfig();
42                  session = pageContext.getSession();
43                  out = pageContext.getOut();
44
45                  // HTML
46                  // begin
                     [file="C:\\jsp\\hits\\hits.jsp;from=(0,36);to=(2,0)]
47                      out.write("\r\n\r\n");
48                  // end
49                  // begin
                     [file="C:\\jsp\\hits\\hits.jsp";from=(2,0);to=(2,62)]
50                  ...
51                  ...
52                  // begin
                     [file="C:\\jsp\\hits\\hits.jsp";from=(8,2);to=(8,32)]
53                      if (hits.incrHits() == 10) {
54                  // end
```

```
55              // HTML
56              // begin
                [file="C:\\jsp\\hits\\hits.jsp";from=(8,34);to=(12,0)]
57                  out.write("\r\n\r\n<B>Congratulations, you are the "+
58                    "10th person today!</B>\r\n\r\n");
59              // end
60              // begin [file="C:\\jsp\\hits\\hits.jsp"
61              //    ;from=(12,2);to=(12,13)]
62                  } else  {
63              // end
64              // HTML
65              // begin [file="C:\\jsp\\hits\\hits.jsp";
66              //    from=(12,15);to=(16,0)]
67                  out.write("\r\n\r\nWelcome! You are visitor
                    #\r\n\r\n");
68              // end
69              // begin
                [file="C:\\jsp\\hits\\hits.jsp";from=(16,3);to=(16,19)]
70                  out.print( hits.getHits() );
71              // end
72              // HTML
73              // begin
                [file="C:\\jsp\\hits\\hits.jsp";from=(16,21);to=(17,0)]
74                  out.write("\r\n");
75              // end
76              // end
77              // begin
                [file="C:\\jsp\\hits\\hits.jsp";from=(17,2);to=(17,5)]
78                  }
79              // end
80              ...
81              ...
82 }
```

Here are the main things to note:

- *Line 1*: The name of the class is dynamically generated and based (at least for Jakarta) on the revision level of the original JSP file.
- *Line 2*: HttpServlet isn't what's extended; HttpJspBase is.
- *Lines 4 and 5* (and throughout the code): At least for Jakarta, notes are made as to which parts of the JSP file are spliced into the generated servlet Java file.
- *Lines 21 through 43*: A number of special variables are introduced that are actually accessible to developers writing a JSP page. For example, a JSP page can reference the application or session objects. (How to use these variables is a fairly detailed topic and beyond the scope of this introductory discussion.)

- *Lines 53 through 78*: The JSP scriptlets and HTML are spliced in; the placement isn't surprising, and we can now see how our Java code in the JSP file makes a real difference during servlet execution.

JSP Directives

Since we already know how to code the static part of any JSP page (i.e., the HTML, XML, or WML we want), the only thing we need to learn is the set of JSP scripting elements available and how they work. As mentioned, these elements are directives, scriptlets, expressions, or declarations. Assuming that we know Java already, the only real mystery is the JSP directives themselves.

Directives are specified in a JSP page using the following syntax, where a directive type is expressed along with its attributes:

```
<%@ directive attribute="value" %>
```

For example, line 1 of the `hits.jsp` file shown in Listing 7–5 uses the `page` directive with one attribute named `import`.

The JSP spec defines three types of directive:

- `page` communicates page properties to the servlet container.
- `taglib` provides a means for abstracting functionality in a JSP page.
- `include` includes other files directly in the current JSP.

`taglib` and `include` aren't of interest to us—they merely make JSP development easier. However, there are a few attributes of `page` that can have an effect on performance, so we'll address them here.

As of JSP 1.2, the `page` directive supports 12 possible attributes, summarized in Table 7–2. Two are of particular interest as they can have a direct impact on servlet performance:

- `isThreadSafe` obviously controls concurrent access to the page (i.e., the servlet). Although the default value is true, you should ensure that your code really is thread safe. The value of this attribute obviously affects the degree of parallelism the resulting servlet enjoys during execution.
- `buffer` indicates the size of the response buffer. A smaller size (or none) gets the first part of the content to the client quicker. If the value is `none`, the content is sent to the underlying Java `PrintWriter` object of the servlet's `ServletResponse` object. `buffer` is related to the `autoFlush` attribute: if `autoFlush` is set to false and a buffer overflow occurs, an exception is thrown.

Table 7–2: JSP Page Directive Attributes

Attribute	Purpose
language	The name of the scripting language that interprets the declarations, expressions, and scriptlets in the JSP page. The default value is java.
extends	The name of the superclass of the generated servlet. The default value is javax.servlet. http. HttpServlet.
import	List of classes that the resulting servlet should import. The default value is java.lang.*, javax.servlet.*, javax.servlet.jsp.*, javax.servlet.http.*.
session	Denotes whether the page participates in a session (true) or not (false). If the value is true, the JSP has access to the variable session to interrogate session data. The default value is true.
buffer	The size of the buffer, in kilobytes, or none, no buffering. The default value is 8K.
autoFlush	Whether buffer should be flushed when full (true) or an exception should be thrown (false). The default value is true.
isThreadSafe	Specifies whether the scripting elements in the JSP can be run by concurrent clients. The default value is true.
info	Defines an arbitrary string incorporated into the generated page.
errorPage	URL of the error page to issue to the client if an error occurs during JSP translation (i.e., any Java Throwable object propagates from the code).
isErrorPage	Specifies whether the current JSP page is the target URL for another JSP errorPage value.
contentType	Relates to the MIME type of the page.
pageEncoding	Relates to the character-encoding properties of the page.

What Is JSP Really?

As I said before, JSP is really just a development methodology. There's nothing you can do with it that you can't do with a servlet. The main difference is that JSP can help you separate presentation logic from business logic so that, instead of generating HTML from a servlet, you can keep it in a JSP file. This can make development much more efficient, especially once you embrace the integration of JSP, HTML, and Java classes. And, as we discussed, JSP is arguably a cleaner way to develop servlets.

It makes sense to have the presentation and pretty-print code in a static, HTML-like file while the core functionality remains in a reusable Java class. It also helps enforce good coding style for your Java classes: You can focus on making them functional and minimal—two good programming traits—without littering them with HTML generation code that's specific to a single application need.

Scalability and Performance Hints

In this chapter, we've focused on the essentials for building and using servlets and paid some attention to their general efficiency features. In this section, we explore some specific architectural suggestions targeted at optimizing scalability and performance.

Use Fine-Grained Serialization

For maximum concurrency, make sure your servlet code is thread safe. However, as we discussed earlier, sometimes this just isn't feasible. In such situations, you have three options, presented in order of their granularity:

- Implement the `SingleThreadModel` interface.
- `Synchronize` methods as necessary.
- `Synchronize` code blocks as necessary.

Implementing the `SingleThreadModel` interface is the most coarse-grained approach of the three, and as discussed earlier, it's confusing and ultimately never necessary. The second approach, synchronizing methods, works fine for member methods of the servlet class, but you should be as selective as possible. As is normal in good Java programming, extract and make methods only those parts of the code that really require synchronization.

The final and preferred approach is to synchronize code blocks as necessary, which limits runtime serial execution to parts of the code where it's absolutely necessary. This is the most fine-grained approach of the three listed. Since it's recommended that the bulk of your servlet focus be on session management—not application logic—it's unlikely that you'll need to do that much synchronization.

Use Hardware-Based Load Balancing

You have a few options when deciding how to balance servlet load:

- Use hardware-style load balancing (with something like the Cisco LocalDirector).
- Use software-style load balancing (with something like the Apache Web server).
- Ignore load-balancing hardware/software and rely on session migration (often provided by servlet or J2EE vendors).

The last option may be the easiest to set up because, as a servlet deployer, you don't have to worry about integrating other hardware or software into your design. However, the serialization and potential synchronization requirements of persistence/replication can make migration slow, particularly if you have a large number of machines running servlet containers (i.e., a large servlet cluster).

The second-to-last option is fine, but may be slightly slower and less robust than the first option. Using software-style load balancing may require that you restart the software every time a new machine is added. Worse, since the software can crash, it may be a service availability risk. From a performance standpoint, an extra Web server represents another software hop and thus slightly increases client/server latencies.

A hardware-based load balancer tends to be the quickest and most reliable way to distribute servlet load. It's also often the easiest to administer—many of these devices allow you to plug in new servers without shutting down the load balancer (and thus sacrificing its existing session state information). Hardware load balancing is probably the most expensive choice, but it's the one I recommend for the best scalability.

Use Servlets for Session Management, not Business Logic

It's very tempting to write all of your application code in a servlet. Since you're developing in a server-side Java environment, it seems quite attractive to handle the request directly, interact with the database via JDBC, and return the result to the client. However, there are at least two major reasons why this strategy isn't recommended:

- *Implementing all of your business logic in servlets limits you in terms of application interface flexibility.* There are more clients than just interactive Web heads. You might eventually need to develop a B2B messaging-style interface to your application. Do you really want to replicate all of your business logic? I don't think so. As we'll discuss in later chapters, it's generally better to stick business logic either in business object technologies, like Enterprise JavaBeans (EJBs), or in the database itself (via stored procedures).

- *Servlet scalability can't be fine-tuned.* If all your application logic exists in servlets, how will you scale its different parts? Keep in mind that some functions and objects will be exercised more frequently than others and that the finer grained your application objects are, the more control you have over their scalability. However, if all your business objects are in a servlet, there's no way to scale them independently. You're forced to replicate the entire servlet (i.e., more instances) or add another machine and servlet container. Neither approach is a terribly efficient way to scale, especially the latter. As we'll see in

Chapter 8, EJBs address this problem by associating independent threads (from existing thread pools) with requested business objects. Thus, they can provide "targeted scalability," replicating only those objects that are bottlenecks.

The recommendation here is to use servlets for session management tasks because they're very good at serving as the application entry point and as coordinators of session state. However, once they have a request and locate the proper state (if any) for that session, have them hand off processing to a business object technology, like EJBs, which offers better application interface flexibility and can scale in a more fine-grained manner.

Think Twice about JSP

I think I've made my point: JSP and similar technologies aren't necessary when developing servlets. They're primarily a tool for development managers. JSPs have a few downsides in terms of execution, most notably in that recompilation at run-time might be necessary because coding errors may not be revealed until then. Furthermore, depending on your vendor the code generated may not be performance optimal.

In general, JSPs are an indirect way to write a servlet. Although they probably won't lead to significant performance or scalability problems, they do pose a few risks and obviously won't improve servlet performance (unless you're a very bad servlet coder). Also, if you eventually agree that servlets are best left for the task of session management, your servlet development will become considerably less complex. This makes it a bit easier for you to write your own HTML generation code (there's less chance that you'll embed application logic between HTML generation logic), and it's not that hard to isolate it in well-named procedures or functions. It's not fun, but it isn't rocket science, and as a general rule "direct" programming is more attractive than "indirect" programming because it gives us more control and makes things easier.

However, if you decide to use JSP, make sure that you set the `isThreadSafe` and `buffer` attributes of the JSP `page` directive appropriately. If possible, set the buffer value to `none`, as in

```
<%@ page buffer="none" %>
```

This will allow output to be streamed to the client as it's produced.

Summary

In this chapter, we surveyed the general landscape of Java servlet technology, covering the basics related to

- Understanding and using servlets
- Developing servlets
- Deploying servlets
- Managing sessions with servlets
- Using servlet-related technologies, such as JSP

We concluded that servlets provide an efficient, Java-based infrastructure for processing HTTP requests from interactive clients, particularly users with Web browsers. They're very good at mapping requests to session data and at forwarding requests to business object technologies like CORBA and EJBs. Focusing on session management—and not core business logic—can help make your application more flexible in its interfaces and more scalable in its execution. Finally, we concluded that JSP is an attractive technology as a development tool, but it's not necessary for servlets and may even adversely affect performance, depending on the scenario.

Now that we have the user request in our hand, let's discuss how to route it to the part of our application that contains the actual business logic. That means looking at EJBs in some detail.

CHAPTER

8

Building Application Servers with Enterprise JavaBeans

The Need for Application Servers

Gone are the days when an application was a single piece of software. Now, applications are broken up into many pieces sprinkled throughout a collection of machines. The distributed pockets of functionality are then combined in some way to represent a single application to each network client, the end user. There are good design reasons for distributed, multitier applications: They allow automatic evolution (i.e., the server side can change whenever necessary), and they encourage modular and logical design.

There are good performance and scalability reasons for them as well. Well-focused components can be deployed as needed, distributed and replicated strategically, so that resource use can be optimized for the most demanding aspects of an application. When implemented correctly, such solutions allow deployers to easily scale their applications by purchasing additional hardware as needed. There's no need to re-engineer the application for the extra hardware, so adapting to increased load is simple. In general, application logic deployed as distributed objects represents an important tradeoff: better availability and scalability for the complexity of managing a distributed system and the overhead of network communication between objects.

Application servers are perhaps the most indispensable part of this scheme, particularly for thin client (i.e., HTML-based) deployments. Along with the databases on which they rely, application servers represent the essential component of the server side. As described earlier, the role of an application server is to provide interfaces for and execute code associated with core application logic. While some of the topics we've discussed thus far (such as HTTP and servlets) are examples of connectivity technologies, application servers are the first example we've seen of a technology made to host the application logic itself.

Application Logic and Where to Deploy It

Application logic is often called "business logic" because it relates to the core business goals of an application. For example, an application server might contain logic to calculate the total value of a user's electronic shopping cart. Or it might provide automatic membership approval for a credit card. Other kinds of application logic are more subtle or indirectly executed. For example, an application server may contain logic that determines a list of books or CDs that best fit a user profile. These items might then be displayed on the side of an application screen to entice the user during her session.

Recall that, at a bare minimum, a Web application consists of a client and a server separated by a network. It's no surprise, then, that these are our main choices for where to deploy business logic. So-called "fat client" solutions, such as Java applet–based applications, can package the logic inside the client itself. This is often a good choice if your application is heavily CPU bound, works with many local files and resources, or requires some kind of local security. Since Java applets can be rebuilt when necessary, there's no loss of control over the application.

However, fat clients are generally unpopular because most Web applications are actually I/O bound, either reading and writing data to a remote database or sitting idle waiting for user requests. Fat clients can also require long downloading times, making the application seem bulky. Also, although Java itself is portable, not everyone has it—let alone the latest version—so the assumption that applets will run anywhere doesn't always hold up. Furthermore, packaging logic in an applet typically means that some sort of host application (like a browser) is required to launch Java for logic execution.

This means that such designs are less flexible and less amenable to more general application integration needs, making the logic available only to the interactive end user. For example, B2B-style integrated applications connected via a fat client may not be possible—the client is always remotely accessing business logic and can't interact with an applet or anything other than a remote resource over a network. In short, fat clients have their place in Web-based applications, but they tend to be the exception for now.

Instead, most Web applications rely on a thin client approach. In contrast to fat clients, thin clients position logic squarely on the server side, in either the application server or the database. Making the logic available on the server side as a generic set of functionality accessible through multiple interfaces makes it usable not only by interactive Web clients but also by other integrating applications and technologies. One of the nicest things about server-side application logic is that clients can pick and choose the functionality they want without being forced to deal with application baggage they don't need.

There are some disadvantages to server-side application logic. The primary one is that resources such as CPU and memory can quickly become exhausted. With server-side application logic, a provider is effectively supplying computing power to the hundreds, thousands, and perhaps millions of clients that use its application. Thus, it faces the very scalability and performance challenges that are the subject of this book. To scale effectively and perform consistently, a server-side application must be strategically partitioned into components and distributed across multiple application or database servers.

An interesting debate involves determining *where* to place the application logic. In particular, should it be encoded in an application server or directly in the database? As we'll see, modern databases have the capability to integrate with and execute powerful procedural languages (such as Oracle's PL/SQL or even Java), enabling execution even within the same address space of the database server itself. The lure of encoding application logic in the database is that logic requiring many database calls will, by and large, execute faster—no extra overhead is required to transfer intermediate data streams back and forth between the database and application server. However, this also means that anyone who wants access to application logic needs to contact the database to execute it. Certainly, this makes little sense for applications that rarely or never need persistent storage or for those that don't have the database-specific interfaces necessary for access.

Enterprise JavaBeans: The J2EE Solution

The J2EE solution for serving application logic is **Enterprise JavaBeans (EJBs)**. As described earlier, a J2EE Web application can comprise up to four distinct types of container: an application client container, an applet container, a Web container, and an EJB container. EJB containers and the objects they manage are our focus here. An EJB container consists of one or more EJBs that contain the core business logic for an application.

Unlike Java servlets, which are fundamentally associated with J2EE Web containers, EJBs represent a more flexible and presentation-neutral location for business logic. They can be contacted directly by servlets, by applet containers, or by the Java Message Service (JMS). In contrast, servlets are primarily meant for HTML-based, thin client session management and for delivering queries and results to the application in a format tailored for an interactive user (i.e., in HTML). By offloading the Web-based session management and presentation issues to servlets and technologies like JSP, an EJB can focus on the scalable processing of business logic—not only for HTML-based interactive users but also for enterprise application integration systems that request batch processing or some other noninteractive form of application access.

EJBs contain built-in support for many lower-level technologies that enhance the scalability of a server-side application, specifically:

- *Object persistence*: EJBs can be automatically integrated with persistent storage to make applications robust and distributable. As we'll discuss later, they give developers two choices: to assume responsibility for defining the details of object persistence, or to leave the entire task to the container.

- *Transaction management*: Code written by developers for transaction management is often inconsistent and sometimes leads to suboptimal performance. Crafting code to coordinate transactions between distributed objects is often difficult and error-prone. One way to avoid the pitfalls of manually specifying transaction management is to provide a platform-level service that automates the process. The J2EE specification for EJBs enables built-in support for distributed transaction management. Taking advantage of this feature allows developers to write simpler, more focused, error-free EJBs without worrying about when and how to manage transactions in a distributed environment.

- *Location transparency*: No matter where EJB clients are on the network, it is easy and efficient to find an EJB and remotely execute its functions. Such easily distributed and relocatable application functionality is instrumental in achieving good scalability.

Beyond these explicit or "obvious" EJB features, the specification provides others that are more implicit or "concealed" (but just as important, if not more so). These features have important scalability and performance implications. We'll get to those later in this chapter, but for now let's stick with the basics and embark on a journey to understand how EJBs work and how they're developed.

How EJBs Work

Under the J2EE model, EJBs are distributed objects managed by containers. The real work is done by individual bean instances. The container provides surrogates (EJB objects) that interact with these instances, on behalf of the client. It's responsible for the creation and destruction of beans as necessary—in other words, for the **lifecycle** of its bean instances. The relationship between clients, the EJB container, and bean instances is shown in Figure 8–1.

As the figure shows, a client communicates with an `EJBObject`, provided by the EJB countainer. There are actually two types of EJB object interface; we will discuss these both shortly. The `EJBObject` acts as a middleman in the communication

Figure 8–1
Interaction of EJB clients,
containers, and bean
instances

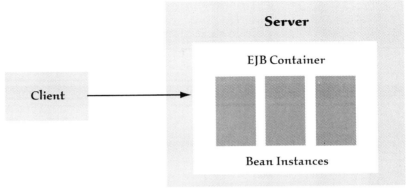

between client and bean. Its assignment to a bean instance is coordinated by the container.

There are actually two kinds of EJBObject involved in client/EJB communication. To understand them, we need to get a little more specific about how EJBs are used. Independent of the application, client interaction with EJBs consists of the following steps:

1. A handle to an EJBObject is acquired by the client.
2. Business methods of that object are called by the client as needed.
3. After use, the client relinquishes the handle to the EJBObject.

Two types of EJBObject interfaces are required here: a **home** interface for steps 1 and 3, and a **local** or **remote** interface for step 2. The purpose of the home interface is to provide factory-like services (i.e., creation and destruction methods) for the EJB requested. For one type of EJB, the home interface also provides a means to "find" certain bean instances. The purpose of the local or remote interface is to provide a clean API to the application logic (i.e., business methods) encapsulated by the bean. The difference between the local and remote interfaces may already be obvious: The former is meant to be accessed by clients located on the same host as the bean, whereas the latter is meant to be accessed by clients not located on the same host.

Treating them as black boxes of functionality, containers manage beans by calling **life-cycle methods** on individual bean instances. These are callback-like methods related to bean creation, destruction, activation, and passivation. In general, when a bean is moved into a particular state by a container, one or more of these methods are called. Let's define and discuss each method type:

- *Creation*: Bean instances need to be created when there is client demand but no available instance exists. Thus, the container must instantiate a new instance.
- *Destruction*: Bean instances can be periodically garbage-collected or destroyed.
- *Activation*: Bean instances may be members of an instance pool that the container can draw from when a new client request arrives. This has obvious performance implications, as it's cheaper to assign a request to a member of an instance pool than to create a new instance and assign the request to it.
- *Passivation*: Just as activation is a "lite" form of instance creation, passivation is a "lite" form of instance destruction. Instead of being destroyed after use, a bean instance can be returned to the pool of instances. This means that it can be reactivated on demand.

Now that we understand a little about what containers and EJBs do and how they work together, let's turn our attention to the different EJB types and when each is applicable.

Types of EJB

There are three basic bean types supported by the current EJB 2.0 specification:

- *Session beans* are associated with a specific business action, particularly one requested during an interactive session. For example, the logic for totaling up an order might be encoded in a session bean. As their name implies, session beans are the primary application interface for synchronous, interactive sessions.
- *Entity beans* are associated with an application object that requires persistent storage. For example, order and customer objects themselves could each be represented using entity beans. Session beans and message-driven beans typically interact with entity beans during execution when persistent data needs to be managed.
- *Message-driven beans* are associated with a specific business action, particularly one that's necessary for application integration or periodic batch processing. For example, all in-store orders might be batch-processed after each business day through a message-driven bean. Currently, message-driven beans are accessible only via the JMS.

Figure 8–2 General role of EJB types and possible interbean relationships

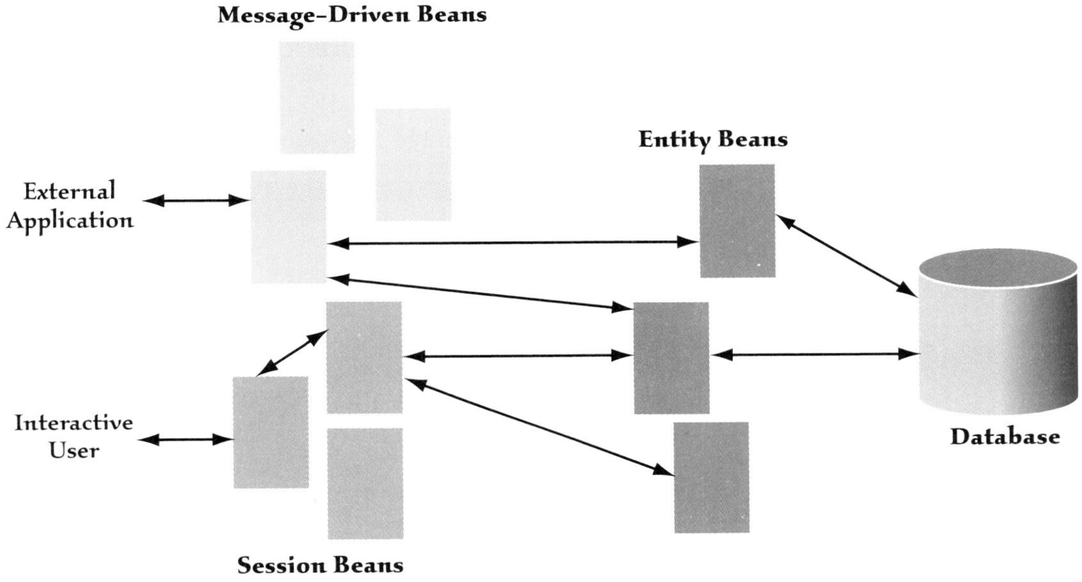

Figure 8–2 shows the general relationship between the different EJB types. Notice that some clients invoke the application via session beans, some via message beans. Regardless, these "interfacing" beans then interact with each other and possibly with a set of entity beans that represent persistent data.

A large application implemented with EJBs usually involves several EJB types. To understand how application data and functionality requirements map into these types, let's consider an example.

Sample Application

Throughout this chapter, we'll discuss EJBs in the context of a simple employer benefits-processing system. The goal is a system that allows members to iteratively choose benefits. In addition, an alternative interface enables enrollments to be processed in batch mode. Our sample application has the following requirements:

- Members can select and deselect benefits.
- The current benefit listing for any member can be obtained.
- Batch enrollment of member benefit elections is possible.

Notice how these features can be neatly mapped into the EJB types I introduced earlier. Iterative member enrollment is the main business task, so it can be handled by a session bean—let's call it `BenefitEnroller`. Batch enrollment is a business task, but this kind of bulk, offline processing is better suited for a message-driven bean—we'll call it `BatchBenefitEnroller`. Finally, the key objects involved—*members, benefits*, and *member benefits*—need to be persisted and are thus well suited to entity beans—so we'll call them `Member`, `Benefit`, and `MemberBenefits`, accordingly.

The ease of mapping our application requirements into EJB types is no accident. The types made available by the specification encompass the ability to execute core business logic and to manage persistent application data, and nearly every application demand can fall into one of these two categories. From this perspective, message-driven beans can be viewed as more of an optimization than anything else. Certainly, we can get by with just session and entity beans, but, since cross-company integrated and batch processing tasks are so prevalent in the business world, message-driven beans are a natural extension that results in better integration and more efficient processing.

EJB Design

Now let's explore the details of each EJB type. We'll first look at how beans are designed and then focus on examples of their implementation. Based on their purpose and capabilities, we'll see that our rough mapping of requirements to beans is in fact reasonable.

Session Beans

Session beans correspond to business tasks primarily related to interactive sessions. When an end user or client wants to execute some action, such as appending to an order, he routes his request to a session bean. It's sometimes helpful to think of a session bean roughly as the device through which a logical connection to an application is established between client and server.

Session EJBs come in two flavors: stateful and stateless. As the name implies, **stateful session beans** maintain state during communication with a client. More specifically, they retain the values of their instance variables between client requests. This state disappears when the client and bean session ends (i.e., the client terminates it). Obviously, since the bean is maintaining state between client requests, it's important that the client continue to converse with the same bean. Theoretically, there should be as many stateful session beans as there are concurrent sessions, since each session will have a client that needs its own state to be managed. According to the J2EE spec, stateful session beans may be periodically written to persistent storage.

Stateless session beans *don't* maintain state between requests and therefore can be used to process requests from any client. Since they're not associated with any one client, the number of stateless session beans does not necessarily have to equal the number of concurrent sessions. Sessions frequently consist of inactivity, so it's possible for only a few stateless session beans to be required to handle application requests for many clients. They're thus inherently more scalable—from the bean perspective—than stateful session beans.

From my description, stateless session beans seem like an obvious win-win situation. Pooling beans instead of issuing one per client interaction seems an obvious way to improve scalability and conserve resources. However, keep in mind that sessions often require state management. For example, online retail applications usually need virtual shopping carts. The state must be stored somewhere: at the client (i.e., via cookies), in rewritten URLs, in server-side memory, or in the database. There's just no getting around that. Designing an efficient solution for state management is one of the challenges facing an application architect. We'll discuss some options at the end of this chapter.

Entity Beans

Entity beans correspond to application objects that are meant to be persistent. By *persistent*, I mean that they contain potentially valuable information across sessions. Thus, unlike stateful session bean instance variables, which only make sense for a single session (such as a shopping cart), entity beans are associated with state that exists across sessions and perhaps is shared between them. For example, historical purchasing information for a particular customer is relevant not only for one session but for every future session.

It may be more convenient to think of entity beans as similar to tables or relations in a relational database. Like relations, they're named objects that consist of one or more attributes. Like foreign key attributes in relations, they can contain attributes that relate them to other entity objects. As is the case with the relational database model, they use primary keys to enforce entity* integrity. That is, instances of the same entity bean can be distinguished from one another, just as primary keys enable rows to be distinguished in a relation.

---

*This use of the word *entity* is slightly different from its use in the phrase *Entity bean*. Entity integrity—ensuring that each tuple is unique—is typically provided in relational database systems by primary keys. Entity beans simply refer to object-oriented representations of data.

Client Interaction

There are a few other important properties of entity beans. One is that they differ from session beans in how they interact with their clients. Recall that session beans may be stateful or stateless and that this choice directly impacts whether a session bean is shared by multiple clients. With entity beans, things are different: They can be shared by multiple clients. Think of a specific instance of a bean as a row in a database table. Just as multiple queries might access the same row concurrently, multiple clients may access the same entity bean concurrently.

Entity Bean Relationships

Another important entity bean property is the notion that entity beans can relate to each other. Again, the relational data model analogy is relevant here. Just as tables in a relational data model have relationships to other tables, so do entity beans. What's more, the relationship—that is, the cardinality—can be just as flexible as that found in relational data models, for example, one-to-many. Consider our benefits management example. We can develop a `Member` entity bean that can be associated with one or more `MemberBenefit` entity beans.

In fact, entity bean relationships can be any of the following:

- *One-to-one*: Each instance of bean type X is related to, at most, one instance of bean type Y. Consider members and employees: Member records are always associated with (at most) one employee.

- *One-to-many*: Each instance of bean type X may be related to one or more instances of bean type Y. Consider the member and member benefits example described above.

- *Many-to-many*: Many instances of bean type X may be related to a single instance of bean type Y, and many instances of bean type Y may be related to a single instance of bean type X. Consider the real relationship between members and benefits: Many members can choose the same benefit and, conversely, many benefits can be chosen by a single member. In the data modeling world, many-to-many relationships are often normalized using cross-reference tables. By designing a `MemberBenefit` entity bean, we have effectively achieved this.

At the database level, integrity between the entities is enforced through foreign keys. For example, in the one-to-many relationship between members and their benefit elections, the `MEMBER_BENEFITS` table may have a column for `MEMBER_ID` that exists as a foreign key to the `ID` column of the `MEMBER` table. At the bean level, integrity enforcement depends on how bean persistence is managed.

Methods of Bean Persistence

When you define an entity bean, you specify that its persistence will be container managed or bean managed. Simply put, **container-managed persistence (CMP)** means that your J2EE vendor figures out how to persist your entity bean whereas **bean-managed persistence** (**BMP**) means that you must explicitly code this mapping.

The obvious reason that BMP exists is that a J2EE implementation can't know everything—it can't know where an existing database is or what the corresponding table names might be. As it turns out, many people use the following rule of thumb: If you already have a database with tables representing deliberate analogues of the entity EJBs you create, use BMP for those beans. If you just need to persist something that isn't part of a preexisting data model, use CMP. I should warn you that this is a very simplistic way of thinking: The debate is actually more complicated for those serious about optimizing bean persistence. Nevertheless, for light persistence needs or for the casual application designer, it can be a reasonable approach.

Container-Managed Persistence

The main advantages to CMP are simplicity and portability. You don't have to write any SQL that describes how your objects are mapped onto relational tables. All you have to do is provide a few methods that meet the requirements of your bean contract and specify some key information in the deployment descriptor. J2EE does the rest. Thus, your beans consist of much less Java code.

Since you're defaulting persistence to the container, you don't have to worry about dragging your database around to every deployment locale. For example, if you develop a J2EE application composed of only session beans and CMP entity beans, you don't need to buy a database wherever you wish to deploy it. The responsibility for ensuring persistence lies with the J2EE vendor.

CMP's method and mechanism for persistence vary between vendors. The EJB spec says nothing about how persistence should be achieved, it just conceptually recognizes the need for it. That means that CMP could be implemented by writing serializable Java objects to the filesystem or by tight integration with a high-performance database. If you choose CMP and you have a complex object/data model or if you store and update a lot of data, it's well worth your while to understand the details of your vendor's CMP implementation.

The EJB 2.0 spec has made some important changes to CMP. One has to do with the introduction of the so-called "local model" of CMP, which allows entity beans to interact more easily and optimally than in the model defined by EJB 1.1.

Since entity beans have relationships with other entity beans, there's a considerable likelihood that they'll be chatting it up quite a bit. Just as navigating a relational data model can result in many queries to the database, navigating through entity

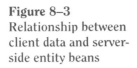

Figure 8–3
Relationship between
client data and server-
side entity beans

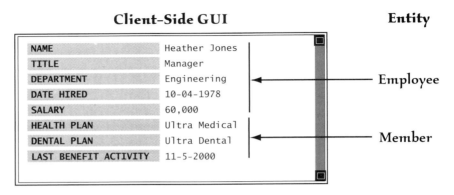

EJB objects can result in substantial cross-object communication. EJBs are actually distributed objects, which means that substantial marshalling and network communication may be necessary.

EJB 2.0 addresses this by offering a **local model** for use by entity beans that tend to act as stepping-stones to other data. The best way to understand this is with an example. Suppose that, in our benefits processing system, application clients need to query member information. Part of this information might be statistics (name of health plan, name of dental plan, etc.); another part might be employee information (name, date hired, etc.). From the end-user point of view, however, this information is combined into one visual record. We can imagine this relationship as that shown in Figure 8–3.

It might seem natural to implement such an application with at least two entity beans—one for members and one for employees—and maintain a one-to-one relationship between the two. A client request for an employee record contacts the Member entity bean, which contacts an Employee entity bean and returns the resulting compounded information to the client. This relationship is shown in Figure 8–4.

However, since application clients *never* directly access employee objects (they do so only indirectly through the Member entity bean), having the Employee entity bean maintain a remote interface is a waste. In other words, we know that this bean will only be contacted by other server-side entity beans, yet the same marshalling cost continues to be applied. The EJB 2.0 solution for this dilemma is to develop the Employee bean with a local interface, making it a local object. Incorporating local objects into your application design offers two basic advantages:

■ *More efficient argument marshalling*: Communication with local objects enables parameters to be passed by *reference*, not by *value*—as they would be over the network in a normal call to an entity bean.

Figure 8–4
Requesting
member and
employee
information
from EJBs

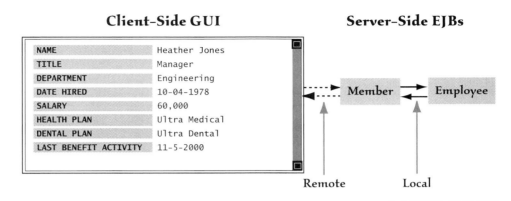

- *More flexibility in terms of security enforcement*: Under EJB 2.0, calls to local objects can be classified as "unchecked"; thus, the deployer can avoid unnecessarily secure communication between objects.

A second important CMP feature found in EJB 2.0 is **container-managed relationships**. In this model, a developer can specify relationships between entity beans and be sure that the relationships are enforced properly. This is a referential integrity issue.

In our member/benefits example, suppose a request is made to delete a member from the system. The relational database answer to this request is to prevent the deletion until all child records (i.e., benefit elections) are deleted or to support a cascading-delete model, wherein deleting the student record implies deleting all transcript entries as well. In the EJB 2.0 spec, CMP now supports better enforcement of referential integrity and offers powerful automation features like cascading deletes in entity bean relationships.

Finally, CMP includes **dependent objects**, which you can think of as extensions to entity beans. Dependent objects allow complex CMP fields to be represented in a separate class. For example, each benefit entry might include the attributes benefitID, benefitName, and benefitRestriction. Each benefitRestriction may actually be complex (i.e., composed of several subfields, such as max_age, min_age, min_seniority, etc.) and could thus be represented as a single dependent object. The key to dependent objects is that they're not the same as local EJB objects that expose only local interfaces. They're simply a way of breaking up a more complex object into distinct parts. Local objects are a way of simplifying and optimizing communication with truly distinct objects but ones that the client never interacts with directly.

Bean-Managed Persistence

Although it's more complex to implement, BMP generally provides greater flexibility and potentially better performance than CMP. Depending on your application architecture, it may even be a necessity. As mentioned above, if you need to connect your entity beans to a database not supported by your J2EE vendor's CMP implementation, or if you need to do things like persist an application entity across multiple tables in the underlying database, you really have no choice but to use BMP for those beans. In doing so, you code—via JDBC and SQL—just how the object is mapped onto a table.

It's true, BMP does result in more time-consuming and complex development responsibilities. Engineers must code methods that describe how bean instances are loaded, stored, and located, which means that they must be familiar with the underlying database and how to achieve their goals via JDBC and SQL. Not only that, but continued integration with the underlying data model must be maintained. When the data model changes, BMP entity beans must be reevaluated to ensure that the code they contain is consistent with the data model modifications. The code maintenance demands I'm hinting at here can probably be most appreciated by those who have struggled with keeping code bases in sync with continuously evolving data models.

Nevertheless, many people are quick to point out the flexibility of BMP. Complex data relationships can be more easily resolved because the developer has explicit control. Thus, if it's necessary to store an object across multiple tables or, conversely, to query an object by joining multiple tables, this can easily be done with BMP. Also, consider the flexibility of the data source. With BMP, we can use any mechanism for persistence storage, even legacy or nonstandard storage systems. In contrast, CMP limits us to the options for persistence provided by the J2EE vendor.

In terms of performance, BMP *may* be more desirable. I emphasize "may" because it really depends on the developer and the application. Since the developer is writing the database integration code, she is obviously in the driver's seat in terms of how it's optimized. The effectiveness and efficiency of persistent storage thus depends on how well data source integration—in particular, JDBC and SQL query optimization—is understood. It also depends on whether or not performance-enhancing mechanisms like caches exist in the development environment.

CMP already handles much of this optimization using its own buffering and caching scheme. Theoretically, depending on the application, a developer could write a more optimal caching mechanism and thus exceed CMP's benefits, but this may translate into a lot of extra programmer hours that, despite its optimality, lead to just a small performance improvement.

We'll revisit this discussion at the end of the chapter. For now, however, let's get back on track with our description of the EJB types. Our next focus is message-driven beans, a new type provided by the EJB 2.0 specification.

Message-Driven Beans

Message-driven beans are similar to session beans in that they're associated with a business task. However, they're not meant for interactive sessions. Thus, there's no reason to maintain state across invocations of a session, making them sound very much like stateless session beans. In addition, like stateless session beans, they can be used by multiple clients and thus are more scalable than stateful session beans.

Message-driven beans are unique in at least one important way: the method of invocation. Unlike with session and entity beans, clients don't contact message-driven beans by binding to and calling a remote Java method. Instead, message-driven beans rely on an asynchronous listener style of communication. Clients send messages via the JMS that are forwarded to message-driven beans, resulting in the automatic execution of an onMessage() bean function. This asynchrony stands in contrast to the synchronous style of communication involved in session and entity bean communication and is generally more efficient.

EJB Implementation

When developing an EJB, part of the job involves coding the actual business logic. This is no different than coding any regular Java class that you would use in a local application. You'll have public and private methods that are directly related to the application purpose of your bean, but depending on the type of bean you're developing, you may have some additional coding responsibilities.

Session and entity beans require code that enables remote clients to access a subset of your bean functionality. This code is known as the **remote interface**. They also require that you code life-cycle methods that have to do with how the bean is managed automatically by the EJB container. These methods are part of what is known as the **home interface**. For entity beans, the home interface also provides functionality for clients to locate the instance they want. For message-driven beans, you won't need remote interfaces but you will need home interfaces.

Let's examine the implementation of each of these beans, focusing on how the business logic (i.e., the actual bean code) as well as the factory and proxy objects (i.e., the home and remote interface code) are developed. We'll do this in the context of our benefits processing system example.

Session Beans

When developing a session bean, you need to write code for each of the following classes/interfaces:

- *The remote interface*: methods exposed to remote clients
- *The home interface*: methods related to the bean life cycle

- *The bean class*: methods related to the actual business logic, some public and others private (similar to a regular Java class)

For our example, we'll examine the code for a stateful session bean. We need to maintain state so that a member can progressively elect benefits and then confirm his complete enrollment. Although we'll be looking specifically at developing a stateful session bean, coding a stateless session bean is very similar. The minor differences are better illustrated in books specifically about EJBs.

Session Bean Life Cycle

Before discussing how to code a session bean, we need to describe its life cycle and the need for callback methods. Recall that EJB containers are responsible for bean instance management. That is, they take care of creating, destroying, activating, and passivating bean instances as necessary; with entity beans, they may even handle persistence. To do this properly requires some agreement with the bean developer as containers can't always blindly manage beans. This agreement between a bean and its container, also called a **contract**, can be described by a state diagram that illustrates which methods lead to which bean states. As a developer, you need to know this because you can initialize, alter, or destroy business logic data structures as appropriate to the state transition.

When a container wants to do some kind of bean management, it calls the proper method on the bean class. If the developer has chosen to implement something in response to a callback, then the code provided is executed. However, even if the developer doesn't intend for any action to occur, he must still declare the method—it's just that the implementation can be empty. The key point here is that for all bean types the automatic container management requires bean developers to implement callback methods. These will be called by the container as necessary during bean state transitions.

Consider the state diagram for a stateless session bean shown in Figure 8–5. The nodes or blocks indicate the current state of the bean. The edges indicate the bean class implementation methods called by the container during the transition to that state. When a container transitions a bean, part of the process involves calling the methods on the bean implementation class in the order specified.

For example, when a stateless session bean is created (through the `create()` method on one of the bean's interfaces, as we'll see shortly), the bean implementation functions `setSessionContext()` and `ejbCreate()` are called, in that order. These methods must be declared in the bean instance class by the developer, even if their implementation is empty. Alternatively, depending on the method, other instance-specific resources can be initialized. This all makes sense: When a bean is

Figure 8–5
Stateless session bean life cycle

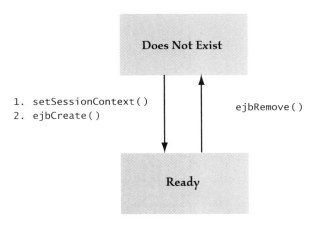

created, it moves from a state of "Does not exist" to "Ready," and various callback methods are executed to allow the developer to respond to such events.

Once these two methods have been called, the bean is considered in the "Ready" state and will remain that way until it's destroyed (by the client or container). However, before the bean returns to the "Does Not Exist" state, we're guaranteed that the ejbRemove() method will be called by the container, allowing us to do any necessary cleanup. Still, we're talking about stateless session beans here, so this shouldn't be an issue unless the bean maintains references to some session-independent resource (like a database connection).

Now, let's look at the state diagram for the stateful session bean, shown in Figure 8–6. We can see that it's similar to the stateless bean diagram, except for an additional state, "Passive," and additional bean methods that are called upon entering that state (passivity) and upon leaving it (re-activity).

The stateful session bean state transition diagram is a good example of why callback methods can be useful for scalability and performance. For example, when passivity is initiated by the container, expensive resources can be unlocked or returned to a shared pool. Specifically, since the ejbPassivate() method is called upon container-initiated passivation, a developer can do things like release locks or connections it currently has. Then, when the bean instance is reactivated, these resources can be regained by properly coding the ejbActivate() method.

In general, understanding the contract between container and bean through a state transition diagram helps developers understand what their responsibilities are and gives them the opportunity to manage or optimize an application-specific resource unknown to the container.

Figure 8–6
Stateful session
bean life cycle

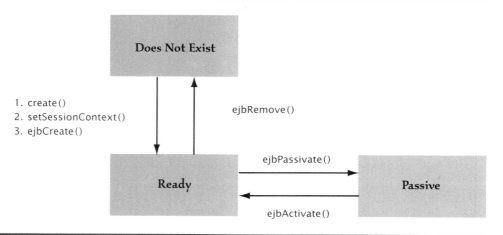

Now that we've seen the state transition diagram, we'll look at how to code the interfaces and implementation classes for our EJB.

Coding the Remote Interface

We'll start with the BenefitEnroller remote interface. This code contains declarations for methods that are exposed to remote clients. One example of a remote interface for our bean is shown in Listing 8–1.

Listing 8–1: The benefitEnroller Session Bean Remote Interface

```
 1 import java.util.*;
 2 import javax.ejb.EJBObject;
 3 import java.rmi.RemoteException;
 4
 5 /**
 6  * Interface for remote clients.
 7  */
 8 public interface BenefitEnroller extends EJBObject {
 9
10    /**
11     * Add a benefit.
12     */
13    public void selectBenefit(String a_benefitId)
14       throws RemoteException;
15
16    /**
17     * Drop a benefit.
18     */
19    public void deselectBenefit(String a_benefitId)
```

```
20         throws RemoteException;
21
22    /**
23     * List all benefits chosen during this session.
24     */
25    public ArrayList getBenefitList()
26         throws RemoteException;
27
28    /**
29     * Confirm current list of benefits.
30     */
31    public boolean confirmElections()
32         throws RemoteException;
33 }
```

Using an interface to represent available functionality in a remote object is a common technique in distributed object technologies. For example, in CORBA applications the Interface Definition Language (IDL) describes platform-independent application objects. IDL code is then used as the basis for generating client and server stubs in the desired language.

A remote EJB interface serves the same purpose as an IDL file for clients. It simply represents remote functionality without forcing the client to know where that functionality might be located and how it's accessed. Instead, it just indicates that it's available, which simplifies the job of accessing and using it, especially from the client's point of view. Behind the scenes, J2EE services manage the availability and scalability of an object and its methods. Conceivably, J2EE can enable highly trafficked functionality to be scalably deployed by creating EJB instances as necessary. In practice, the exact details vary per J2EE implementation.

Coding the Home Interface

As we discussed earlier, the home interface of an EJB provides factory-like methods for a session bean. Thus, it merely includes create() methods that, as we will see, correspond to ejbCreate()methods in the bean class. For the benefits enrollment home interface, we simply need the code shown in Listing 8–2.

Listing 8–2: The BenefitEnroller Session Bean Home Interface

```
1 import java.io.Serializable;
2 import java.rmi.RemoteException;
3 import javax.ejb.CreateException;
4 import javax.ejb.EJBHome;
5
6 /**
7  * BenefitEnrollerHome is the home interface for our
8  * simple benefits processing and registration system.
```

```
 9  */
10
11  public interface BenefitEnrollerHome extends EJBHome
12  {
13    /**
14     * Creates a registration session for a student.
15     */
16    BenefitEnroller create(String a_memberId)
17       throws RemoteException, CreateException;
18  }
```

Calling the create() method eventually results in creation of a corresponding BenefitEnrollerBean instance. Recall that this is a stateful session bean, so there's one per client session. If we hadn't needed to maintain state, we could have chosen to implement BenefitEnrollerBean as stateless. The process of bean instantiation follows the life-cycle contract defined earlier for stateful session beans. The create(), setSessionContext(), and ejbCreate() methods will be called—in that order—by the container. These methods can be implemented by the developer when she codes the bean instance class, which is the topic of the next subsection.

Coding the Bean Class

Listing 8-3 shows one way that a stateful session bean called BenefitEnrollerBean can be written.

Listing 8–3: The BenefitEnroller Session Bean Class

```
 1  import java.util.*;
 2  import javax.ejb.*;
 3  import javax.naming.*;
 4  import javax.rmi.PortableRemoteObject;
 5
 6  /**
 7   * The BenefitEnrollerBean includes the core business logic and
 8   * required SessionBean methods for our school registration system.
 9   */
10  public class BenefitEnrollerBean implements SessionBean
11  {
12    String m_memberId;
13    ArrayList m_elections;
14
15    public BenefitEnrollerBean() { }
16
17    /**
18     * Creates a benefits enrollment session for specified member.
19     */
20    public void ejbCreate(String a_memberId)
21    {
```

```
22       m_memberId = a_memberId;
23       m_elections = new ArrayList();
24    }
25
26    public void ejbRemove() {}
27    public void ejbActivate() {}
28    public void ejbPassivate() {}
29
30    public void setSessionContext(SessionContext sc) {}
31
32    /**
33     * Adds a course to current class list.
34     */
35    public void selectBenefit(String a_benefitId)
36    {
37       m_elections.add(a_benefitId);
38    }
39
40    /**
41     * Removes a course from current class list.
42     */
43    public void deselectBenefit(String a_benefitId)
44    {
45       int idx = -1;
46       String cur;
47
48       for (int i=0; i<m_elections.size(); i++) {
49         cur = (String)m_elections.get(i);
50         if (cur.equals(a_benefitId)) {
51            m_elections.remove(i);
52            break;
53         }
54       }
55    }
56
57    /**
58     * Returns the list of benefit elections, in the current order.
59     */
60    public ArrayList getBenefitList()
61    {
62       return m_elections;
63    }
64
65    /**
66     * Confirms an enrollment, returns a confirmation code.
67     */
68    public ArrayList confirmElections()
69    {
70       if (m_elections.size() == 0)
71          return null;
72
73       ArrayList bList = new ArrayList();
```

```
74
75      try
76      {
77          Context initial = new InitialContext();
78
79          Object objref = initial.lookup(
80              "java:comp/env/ejb/MemberBenefit");
81
82          MemberBenefitHome mbh = (MemberBenefitHome)
83              PortableRemoteObject.narrow(objref,
84                  MemberBenefitHome.class);
85
86          MemberBenefit curMb;
87
88          for (int i=0; i<m_elections.size(); i++)
89          {
90            curMb = mbh.create(
91                m_memberId,
92                m_elections.get(i).toString(),
93                Calendar.getInstance().getTime());
94
95            bList.add(curMb);
96          }
97
98      } catch (Exception ex) {
99          throw new EJBException("ERROR: "+ex.getMessage());
100     }
101
102     return bList;
103 }
```

In summarizing the organization and contents of this code, it's important to note the following:

- `ejbCreate()` methods are required for every manner in which we want our bean to be instantiated. Since this is a stateful session bean, the instantiation information can be recorded in bean instance variables. Lines 22 and 23, for example, show how the member ID is set and how the benefit election list is initialized.

- The other EJB life-cycle methods, such as `ejbRemove()`, are required by the life-cycle contract, but don't need to be implemented. For special session beans, particularly those that also interact with the database or deal with some other external resource, implementation of these methods might be required.

- The methods shown in lines 35 through 63 are the implementations of the business methods exposed by the `BenefitEnrollerRemote` object shown earlier in Listing 8–1. Notice that they simply query and manipulate instance member variables, which are associated with a logical client session.

■ The confirmEnrollment() method is interesting because it shows how a session bean can communicate with another EJB, in this case an entity bean. The purpose here is to use BenefitEnroller to coordinate the creation of a set of elections, just as a shopping cart for an online store might be filled. When the member is done and has confirmed elections, the session bean can coordinate its persistence with other application entity beans. It achieves this persistence by repetitively using the MemberBenefitHome object as a factory to create new MemberBenefit instances.

Entity Beans

Recall that an entity bean corresponds to a persistent object, not a business task. In our benefits processing example, one likely persistent object is Benefit. A benefit in our example is something like a medical or dental plan—any item that an employee can choose as part of his or her benefit package.

The list of benefits, just like the list of employees and the list of benefits chosen by employees, falls into the category of a persistent object. Conceptually, J2EE assumes that the method of persistence is a relational database. Given that such a database is the underlying storage method, we can imagine wanting to persist benefit data in a table consistent with the following SQL statement:

```
CREATE TABLE benefit (
  name CHAR (30),
  type CHAR (15),
  provider CHAR (40),
  cur_participants NUMBER,
  max_participants NUMBER
);
```

In working with this table, we need to be able to create, locate, and possibly delete benefit records. Creation and deletion might happen in an administrative client, while other activities (such as finding a particular benefit) would occur in other clients and by way of other session or message-driven EJBs. Having a benefit record represented as an entity bean is thus reasonable.

Writing entity beans, like session beans, requires defining home and remote interfaces in addition to the bean methods. However, when coding these beans there are some important differences in the responsibilities (or contracts) developers have. Furthermore, there's the big decision on how to handle persistence: specifically whether it should be container managed or bean managed. In fact, if we decide to deploy an entity bean using container-managed persistence, the recent EJB 2.0 specification gives us even more options, making development of an entity bean very different from that of other kinds of beans.

Let's take a more detailed look at entity bean development by first reviewing the interfaces and classes that an entity bean designer must develop:

- *The remote interface*: methods exposed to remote clients, mostly accessor-like methods. The EJB 2.0 specification allows entity beans to have local interfaces, which enables finer granularity without compromising performance.
- *The home interface*: methods that allow entity beans to be created (i.e., factory-like methods) and located. Locator methods are also known as "finder" methods. EJB 2.0 has "select" methods as well.
- *The bean class*: a combination of accessor-like methods for interrogating object attributes and methods for managing database integration and object identification. Depending on how bean persistence is handled, there may be many private methods related to database access.

Notice that these classes are similar to those for the session beans shown earlier. However, there are a few minor differences, most of which relate to a single benefit record being similar to a row in a table of benefit records. In general, the methods found in an entity bean fall into these categories:

- Attribute accessor methods
- Business methods
- Methods that distinguish a particular entity bean from other entity beans
- Database integration methods

Entity Beans and EJB 2.0

In this section, as in others, our discussion will be framed by the new EJB 2.0 specification. EJB 2.0 presents many changes to entity beans, particularly those that employ container-managed persistence. Rather than compare 2.0 and 1.1 specs, we're simply going to focus on what 2.0 provides. As always with J2EE, it's important to know your vendor and understand which levels of the J2EE spec it supports.

The Entity Bean Life Cycle

The life cycle of an entity bean with respect to a container is shown in Figure 8–7. Like the session bean, an entity bean contains a set of callback methods that enable its container to effectively manage it. It's up to the developer to ensure that these methods are properly coded in the bean implementation class, which generally means writing JDBC code and the actual SQL necessary to load, store, remove, and update the underlying persistent representation of the entity as necessary. As we'll see, this can cause the number of lines in even an average bean to explode. On the other hand, with container-managed persistence, coding these methods becomes significantly easier. Plus, your J2EE vendor ensures that all database integration will be automatic.

As with session beans, the entity bean container invokes well-known bean instance methods between activation modes, as shown in Figure 8–7. However, we see a new state value for entity beans: "Pooled."

Unlike stateful session beans, which correspond to sessions between a unique client and the server, entity beans not only maintain state but are frequently shared by multiple clients. To enable scalability and high performance when using entity beans, the EJB specification allows them to be pooled prior to actual use. This negates the effects of runtime object instantiation penalties. Keep in mind that there can easily be many more entity beans than session beans in a given application. This makes sense: An application typically has more business data than it does concurrent clients.

Figure 8–7
Entity bean life cycle

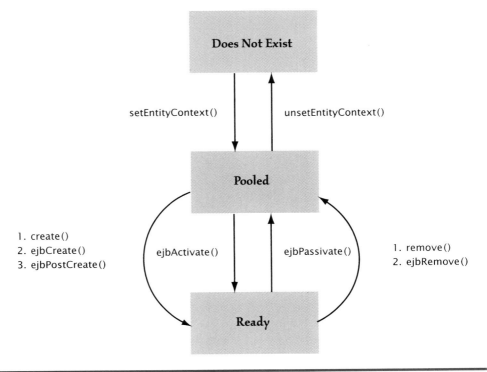

Coding the Remote Interface

The remote interface of an entity bean typically exposes attribute accessors and potentially "single-row" business methods. The need for the attribute accessors is obvious—we have to be able to get and set the individual column values for a given row. Each row in the underlying database table corresponds directly to a bean instance.

The business methods, if they exist, can be directed at computing something based on the attributes of the bean instance. Thus, since they pertain to a per-instance computation, they're considered **single-row functions**. For example, although our BENEFIT table keeps track of both the maximum and the current number of participants in that benefit, a useful business method here is one that returns the number of open member slots left.[*]

Listing 8–4 is an interface that supports attribute accessors and this example method.

Listing 8–4: The BenefitEntity Bean Remote Interface

```
 1 import javax.ejb.EJBObject;
 2 import java.rmi.RemoteException;
 3 import java.util.*;
 4
 5 public interface Benefit extends EJBObject
 6 {
 7    /**
 8     * Name of the benefit (i.e., "MetLife HMO Plan")
 9     */
10    public String getName()
11       throws RemoteException;
12
13    /**
14     * Rename the benefit.
15     */
16    public void setName(String a_name)
17       throws RemoteException;
18
19    /**
20     * Type of benefit (i.e., "Medical")
```

---

[*]For the sake of simplicity in our example, we've performed a deliberate denormalization. Depending on the size of your database and your application, the current number of members selecting that benefit can be calculated by counting the number of records in a cross-reference table that keeps track of benefit elections.

```
21     */
22     public String getType()
23         throws RemoteException;
24
25     /**
26      * Number of open slots for enrollment
27      */
28     public int getRemainingSlots()
29         throws RemoteException;
30 }
```

Does this interface code differ between container-managed and bean-managed persistence schemes? No. As with the home interface, the code is merely an API that guarantees that corresponding functionality exists somewhere in the bean implementation class. The real difference in code between container-managed and bean-managed persistence will become obvious shortly.

Note that the code in Listing 8–4 supports getting and setting attribute values. Also, there's one business method—getRemainingSlots()—that computes the room left for a particular benefit (employers sometimes limit a benefit to a certain fixed number of employees). No attribute in the underlying table stores the number of remaining slots, but this is something that's easily computed using the existing cur_participants and max_participants attributes.

Single-row business methods like getRemainingSlots() have a direct analogue in the database world: **single-row** functions. In SQL, you can apply single-row functions to every row returned by a query. For example, to return the uppercase form of names in your employee table, you can simply write

```
SELECT UPPER(name) FROM employee;

UPPER(NAME)
-----------
MADELINE
ELLIS
GARY
HILDA
```

The uppercasing of each name is independent of the uppercasing of the others. Similarly, the business methods of an entity bean that are coded in the remote interface are instance specific and typically based on the values in other persistent attributes of an instance.

Keep in mind that a single-row SQL function like UPPER() differs from an aggregate function, which returns a value based on a computation that spans multiple rows. For example, SQL allows you to return the maximum salary in your employee table via this statement:

```
SELECT MAX(salary) FROM employee;

MAX(salary)
------------
78200
```

EJB entity beans also support aggregate or **multirow functions**. However, these are coded in the home interface part of the bean because they apply to a set of bean instances. We'll discuss an example of a home interface business method in the following subsection.

Coding the Home Interface

The home interface for an entity bean needs to provide factory-like instance creation methods, just like the home interface for a session bean. However, in addition to these methods, are two others are unique to entity beans—the so-called finder methods and the home-interface business methods.

As for creating an entity bean via the home interface `create()` API call, keep in mind that this action implies something different than it does for session beans. Instead of creating a running instance of a bean, an entity bean instantiation directly corresponds to inserting a row into a database. This makes sense: Entity beans are persistent, so creating them should mean that they'll persist until they're deleted.

The **finder methods** provided by the home interface of an entity bean distinguish a subset of instances (or just one instance) from all the others. You can add any finder methods that you want for your entity bean, but at least one is required, `findByPrimaryKey()`, which takes the object corresponding to the primary key as its parameter and returns a unique bean instance. Finder methods that return more than one instance typically do so by returning a `java.util.Collection` (enumerations are also supported).

With bean-managed persistence, it's obviously up to the developer to write the JDBC and SQL to find subsets of instances. This is coded in the bean implementation class, as we'll see shortly.

With container-managed persistence, however, the container actually does all the work. The only requirement is that the deployment metadata include enough information on how to build the WHERE clause of the underlying query. With EJB 2.0, it's now possible for deployers to use the new J2EE EJB query language, EJB-QL, to accomplish this task.

The details of EJB-QL are beyond the scope of this book. Rather, our aim here is to understand that container-managed persistence provides enough underlying support so that *no* database code is required of the developer. If the method signature and some deployment metadata is provided, all of the necessary database integration can be accomplished automatically by the container.

Listing 8–5 is the code for the home interface of our example `Benefit` bean. As with the remote interface, this code is applicable to both bean-managed and container-managed deployment scenarios. The distinction between the two will become clearer when we look at the code for the bean implementation.

Listing 8–5: The `BenefitEntity` Bean Home Interface

```
 1 import java.util.*;
 2 import java.rmi.RemoteException;
 3 import javax.ejb.*;
 4
 5 public interface BenefitHome extends EJBHome
 6 {
 7     public Benefit create(String a_benefitId, String a_name,
 8         String a_type)
 9             throws RemoteException, CreateException;
10
11     public Benefit findByPrimaryKey(String a_benefitId)
12         throws FinderException, RemoteException;
13 }
```

The obvious things to note are

- The factory `create()` method, which creates benefits and persists them (inserts rows into the database)
- The finder `findByPrimaryKey()`method, which returns a unique benefit that corresponds to the ID requested

Coding the Bean

Coding the entity bean class is similar to coding the session bean class, except that we need to write the code as if we are writing code for an individual row in a table of rows. Also, there's a big difference between container-managed and bean-managed persistence requirements in terms of development.

Before we start, note that there are two types of methods we will see:

- EJB callback methods, like `ejbLoad()`
- Attribute accessors and remote and/or home interface business methods, like `getRemainingSlots()`

Now let's look at Listing 8–6, to see how BenefitBean can be coded when using container-managed persistence.

Listing 8–6: The Benefit Enroller Entity Bean Class, using CMP

```
1  import javax.ejb.*;
2  import javax.naming.*;
3  import javax.rmi.PortableRemoteObject;
4
5  public abstract class BenefitBean implements EntityBean
6  {
7      public abstract String getBenefitId();
8      public abstract void setBenefitId(String a_id);
9
10     public abstract String getName();
11     public abstract void setName(String a_name);
12
13     public abstract String getType();
14     public abstract void setType(String a_type);
15
16     public abstract int getMaxParticipants();
17     public abstract void setMaxParticipants(int a_max);
18
19     public abstract int getCurParticipants();
20     public abstract void setCurParticipants(int a_cur);
21
22     public int getRemainingSlots()
23     {
24         return getMaxParticipants()-getCurParticipants();
25     }
26
27     public String ejbCreate(String a_benefitId, String a_name,
28         String a_type, int a_max)
29            throws CreateException
30     {
31         setBenefitId(a_benefitId);
32         setName(a_name);
33         setType(a_type);
34         setMaxParticipants(a_max);
35         setCurParticipants(0);
36
37         return getBenefitId();
38     }
39
40     public void ejbPostCreate(String a_benefitId, String name,
41          String a_type, int a_maxParticipants) { }
42
43     public void ejbActivate() { }
44     public void ejbPassivate() { }
45     public void ejbLoad()  { }
```

```
46     public void ejbStore()  {  }
47
48 }
```

Notice the following:

- The class and all of the accessors are declared abstract. Internally, the EJB container creates a class that extends this abstract class, based on the information contained in the deployment descriptor. It also implements these abstract accessor methods so that the database integration part is filled in. Remember, container-managed persistence isn't magic—there still needs to be code somewhere (written by the developer or generated) that does all of the dirty work. One of the reasons that container-managed persistence is a part of the EJB entity bean specification is that people who developed application objects like EJBs in the past realized how much of nearly the same code existed in their objects. Container-managed persistence reduces the clutter, lowers the chances of developer error, and makes database access patterns consistent and manageable.

- The home interface business method `getRemainingSlots()` isn't abstract. Since we don't have this attribute declared in the deployment descriptor for this bean (i.e., there's no column in our table for this easily computable value), we need to code it explicitly here.

- Although `ejbCreate()` is written, no other code is required for any of the other life-cycle methods. This is often the case for CMP-based beans.

Listing 8–7 shows the same bean implemented with bean-managed persistence.

Listing 8–7: The `BeanEnroller` Entity Class Using BMP

```
 1 import java.sql.*;
 2 import javax.sql.*;
 3 import java.util.*;
 4 import javax.ejb.*;
 5 import javax.naming.*;
 6 import javax.rmi.PortableRemoteObject;
 7
 8 public class BenefitBean implements EntityBean
 9 {
10     private String m_benefitId;
11     private String m_name;
12     private String m_type;
13     private int m_maxParticipants;
```

```
14      private int m_curParticipants;
15
16      private Connection m_conn;
17      private EntityContext m_context;
18
19      public String getBenefitId() { return m_benefitId; }
20      public void setBenefitId(String a_benId) { m_benefitId = a_benId; }
21
22      public String getName() { return m_name; }
23      public void setName(String a_name) { m_name = a_name; }
24
25      public String getType() { return m_type; }
26      public void setType(String a_type) { m_type = a_type; }
27
28      public int getMaxParticipants() { return m_maxParticipants; }
29      public void setMaxParticipants(int a_max) {
                                        m_maxParticipants = a_max; }
30
31      public int getCurParticipants() { return m_curParticipants; }
32      public void setCurParticipants(int a_cur) {
                                        m_curParticipants = a_cur; }
33
34      public int getRemainingSlots()
35      {
36         return m_maxParticipants - m_curParticipants;
37      }
38
39      public String ejbCreate(String a_benefitId, String a_name,
40         String a_type, int a_maxParticipants)
41            throws CreateException
42      {
43         setBenefitId(a_benefitId);
44         setName(a_name);
45         setType(a_type);
46         setMaxParticipants(a_maxParticipants);
47         setCurParticipants(0);
48
49         try {
50           String insertStatement =
51             "INSERT INTO benefit VALUES (?, ?, ?, ?, ?)";
52           PreparedStatement pStmt =
53             m_conn.prepareStatement(insertStatement);
54
55           pStmt.setString(1, getBenefitId());
56           pStmt.setString(2, getName());
57           pStmt.setString(3, getType());
58           pStmt.setInt(4, getMaxParticipants());
59           pStmt.setInt(5, getCurParticipants());
60
61           pStmt.executeUpdate();
62
63           pStmt.close();
```

```
64          }
65        catch (Exception ex) {
66          throw new EJBException("ejbCreate: " + ex.getMessage());
67        }
68
69        return a_benefitId;
70    }
71
72    public void ejbPostCreate(String a_benefitId, String a_name,
73       String a_type, int a_maxParticipants) throws CreateException { }
74
75    public String ejbFindByPrimaryKey(String a_benefitId)
76       throws FinderException
77    {
78       boolean found;
79
80       try {
81          found = selectByPrimaryKey(a_benefitId);
82       }
83       catch (Exception ex) {
84          throw new EJBException("ERROR: " + ex.getMessage());
85       }
86
87       if (found) {
88          return a_benefitId;
89       }
90       else {
91          throw new ObjectNotFoundException
92             ("Row for id " + a_benefitId + " not found.");
93       }
94    }
95
96    public void ejbRemove()
97    {
98       try {
99          String deleteStatement =
100            "DELETE FROM benefit WHERE id = ?";
101          PreparedStatement pStmt =
102              m_conn.prepareStatement(deleteStatement);
103
104         pStmt.setString(1, getBenefitId());
105         pStmt.executeUpdate();
106
107         pStmt.close();
108      }
109      catch (Exception ex) {
110         throw new EJBException("ERROR: " + ex.getMessage());
111      }
112    }
113
114    public void setEntityContext(EntityContext a_context)
115    {
```

```
116        m_context = a_context;
117
118        try {
119          InitialContext ic = new InitialContext();
120          DataSource ds = (DataSource) ic.lookup(
121            "java:comp/env/jdbc/BenefitDB");
122          m_conn =  ds.getConnection();
123        }
124        catch (Exception ex) {
125          throw new EJBException("Unable to connect to database. " +
126            ex.getMessage());
127        }
128     }
129
130     public void unsetEntityContext() {
131
132        try {
133           m_conn.close();
134        } catch (SQLException ex) {
135            throw new EJBException("unsetEntityContext: "+
136                ex.getMessage());
137        }
138     }
139
140     public void ejbActivate()
141     {
142        m_benefitId = (String)m_context.getPrimaryKey();
143     }
144
145     public void ejbPassivate()
146     {
147        m_benefitId = null;
148     }
149
150     public void ejbLoad()
151     {
152        try {
153          String sqlStmt =
154            "SELECT name, type, max_participants, cur_participants "+
155            "FROM benefit WHERE id = ? ";
156          PreparedStatement pStmt =
157            m_conn.prepareStatement(sqlStmt);
158
159          pStmt.setString(1, m_benefitId);
160
161          ResultSet rs = pStmt.executeQuery();
162
163          if (rs.next()) {
164             m_name = rs.getString(1);
165             m_type = rs.getString(2);
166             m_maxParticipants = rs.getInt(3);
```

```
167               m_curParticipants = rs.getInt(4);
168
169               pStmt.close();
170           }
171         else {
172             pStmt.close();
173             throw new NoSuchEntityException("Row for benefitId "
174                 + m_benefitId + " not found in database.");
175         }
176       }
177     catch (Exception ex) {
178         throw new EJBException("ejbLoad: " + ex.getMessage());
179     }
180   }
181
182   public void ejbStore()
183   {
184     try {
185       String sqlStmt =
186           "UPDATE benefit SET name = ?, type = ?, max_participants
                  = ?, "+
187           "cur_participants = ? WHERE id = ?";
188       PreparedStatement pStmt =
189         m_conn.prepareStatement(sqlStmt);
190
191       pStmt.setString(1, m_name);
192       pStmt.setString(2, m_benefitId);
193       pStmt.setString(3, m_type);
194       pStmt.setInt(4, m_maxParticipants);
195       pStmt.setInt(5, m_curParticipants);
196
197       int rowCount = pStmt.executeUpdate();
198
199       pStmt.close();
200
201       if (rowCount == 0) {
202         throw new EJBException("Storing row for benefitId " +
203           m_benefitId + " failed.");
204       }
205     }
206   catch (Exception ex) {
207         throw new EJBException("ejbStore: " + ex.getMessage());
208     }
209   }
210
211   private boolean selectByPrimaryKey(String a_benefitId)
212       throws SQLException
213   {
214     String sqlStmt =
215         "SELECT id FROM benefit WHERE id = ? ";
216     PreparedStatement pStmt =
```

```
217                m_conn.prepareStatement(sqlStmt);
218        pStmt.setString(1, a_benefitId);
219
220        ResultSet rs = pStmt.executeQuery();
221        boolean result = rs.next();
222        pStmt.close();
223        return result;
224    }
225 }
```

This listing leads to a number of observations:

- The code required is four to five times greater than that for the same bean implemented with container-managed persistence, but of course we knew that going in. In fact, most of it falls into two categories: that related to JDBC and that related to manipulation of member variables such as `m_benefitId`.

- Implementation of the life-cycle methods reveals tight database integration. For example, when `ejbStore()` is called by the container, lines 182 through 209 show that data in the database is indeed changed to match the values represented in the bean member variables. Thus, just as the life-cycle methods correspond to the state of the bean, they also directly affect the state of the underlying data.

- An explicit connection to the data source must be made, as shown in lines 114 through 128. Notice also that a connection to the database is fetched by locating it via JNDI. We could have obtained this connection directly by declaring our driver and using the normal JDBC calls, but that would have negated the pooling of connections that JNDI is already providing us as well as the abstraction of locating a remote database.

Message-Driven Beans

Message-driven beans are very much like session beans in terms of their life cycle as well as their development responsibilities. The main thing to remember about message-driven beans is that they're asynchronous and thus don't return data to the caller. They're always invoked the same way, via a message sent to them. Message-driven beans are stateless by nature—since one logical client session is encapsulated per message, each message stands on its own and doesn't require the back and forth of normal interactive sessions.

Unlike other beans, message-driven beans don't have remote or home interfaces—there's no place for such interfaces in the asynchronous scheme of things. From the client's point of view, there's no creation of message-bean instances or calling of bean-specific methods interactively.

Figure 8–8
Message-driven bean life cycle

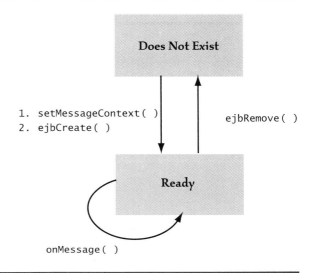

1. setMessageContext( )
2. ejbCreate( )

ejbRemove( )

onMessage( )

The only requirement is that the bean act like a listener to a topic or queue and process messages as they arrive. Thus, developing a message bean only requires a class that implements the standard message-driven bean interface. However, this class must also implement a message-listening interface (javax.jms.MessageListener) so that it can listen for and respond to messages sent to it.

In our example, we'll be exploring how to write a BatchBenefitEnroller bean. Its purpose is the same as the BenefitEnroller bean's—to enroll employees in benefits—but it will perform that task in bulk.

Message–Driven Bean Life Cycle

The state diagram for a stateless session bean, is given in Figure 8–8. As shown, the creation and destruction of a message-driven bean is identical to that of a stateless session bean. The only difference is the addition of the JMS-style onMessage( ) method, which the container can assume exists in every message bean implementation. This method corresponds directly to the javax.jms.MessageListener.onMessage() method.

Coding the Bean Class

We want our message-driven bean to be capable of receiving batches of enrollment records and then processing them one by one. To simplify things, we'll use the java.util.ArrayList class as our vehicle for batching and the data structure shown in Listing 8–8 for an enrollment record.

Listing 8–8: The Enrollment Class

```
1  import java.util.Date;
2
3  public class Enrollment
4    implements java.io.Serializable
5  {
6    private String m_empName;
7    private String m_benName;
8    private Date m_effDate;
9
10   public Enrollment(String a_empName, String a_benName,
                         Date a_effDate)
11   {
12     setEmpName(a_empName);
13     setBenName(a_benName);
14     setEffDate(a_effDate);
15   }
16
17   public String getEmpName() { return m_empName; }
18   public void setEmpName(String a_name) { m_empName = a_name; }
19
20   public String getBenName() { return m_benName; }
21   public void setBenName(String a_name) { m_benName = a_name; }
22
23   public Date getEffDate() { return m_effDate; }
24   public void setEffDate(Date a_date) { m_effDate = a_date; }
25 }
```

Notice that the enrollment record implements java.util.Serializable and
assumes that a client on the other end is capable of building up an array list of enrollment records and then sending them over the wire to our message-driven bean on a
periodic basis. You can imagine this kind of bean being relevant for companies composed of multiple divisions and/or offices that process enrollment information, but
don't all have live access to the benefits system. Those that don't must periodically
report benefit enrollment data in batches.

With Listing 8–8 in mind, Listing 8–9 shows one way that a message-driven
BatchBenefitEnrollerBean could be written.

Listing 8–9: The BatchBenefitEnroller Message-Driven Bean

```
1  import java.io.Serializable;
2  import java.rmi.RemoteException;
3  import javax.ejb.*;
4  import javax.naming.*;
5  import javax.jms.*;
6  import java.util.ArrayList;
```

```
 7 import java.text.SimpleDateFormat;
 8 import javax.rmi.PortableRemoteObject;
 9
10 public class BatchBenefitEnrollerBean
11   implements MessageDrivenBean, MessageListener
12 {
13   private transient MessageDrivenContext m_ctx = null;
14
15   public BatchBenefitEnrollerBean() { }
16
17   public void ejbCreate() { }
18   public void ejbRemove() { }
19
20   public void setMessageDrivenContext(MessageDrivenContext a_ctx)
21   {
22     m_ctx = a_ctx;
23   }
24
25   /**
26    * Messages should be of type MapMessage and conceptually
27    * represent a collection of name/value pairs, for example:
28    *
29    * employee_name = "Seong Rim Nam"
30    * benefit_name = "LIFO Health Plan"
31    * enroll_date = "09/21/1998"
32    *
33    */
34   public void onMessage(Message a_msg)
35   {
36     Object[] objs = null;
37
38     try {
39       if (a_msg instanceof ObjectMessage) {
40
41         ObjectMessage om = (ObjectMessage)a_msg;
42
43         objs = ((ArrayList)om.getObject()).toArray();
44
45         if (objs != null) {
46           Context initial = new InitialContext();
47
48           Object objref = initial.lookup(
49             "java:comp/env/ejb/MemberBenefit");
50
51           MemberBenefitHome mbh = (MemberBenefitHome)
52             PortableRemoteObject.narrow(objref,
53               MemberBenefitHome.class);
54
55           Enrollment cur = null;
56
57           for (int i=0; i<objs.length; i++) {
58             cur = (Enrollment)objs[i];
```

```
59              mbh.create(cur.getEmpName(),
60                      cur.getBenName(),
61                      cur.getEffDate());
62          }
63        }
64      }
65      else {
66        System.err.println("Got message of unexpected type: "
67          + a_msg.getClass().getName());
68      }
69    }
70    catch (Throwable tex) {
71      tex.printStackTrace();
72    }
73  }
74 }
```

There are three important points to make about this code:

- It's obviously less than what's required for even a stateless session bean. Clearly, for tasks that don't require an interactive session, message-driven beans can be much faster to develop.
- The only real implementation required involves the onMessage() method. As we can see in lines 41 through 43 and line 58, there's a need to convert the incoming message to types suitable for their use (in this case, communication of types to the MemberBenefits entity bean).
- Just as in our stateless session bean example, the code shows our message-driven bean communicating with another entity bean (lines 48 through 58). There's actually no real reason to do this other than to make the example easier to understand and relate message-driven beans to our earlier session bean. However, if there were other business logic in MemberBenefit, we would need to create beans as we do in order to enforce it. Otherwise, it would be more efficient to talk directly to the database and process the records as a bulk insert.

Client/EJB Integration

Now that we've explained the differences between the various bean types and have seen how they're developed, we can look at how clients actually interact with EJBs. Per the J2EE architecture, a client can be one of the following:

- An applet
- A servlet

- Another EJB
- A Java Message Service (JMS) provider (depending on the bean)

Generally, a client uses the home interface and either the remote or the local interfaces of an EJB in order to communicate with it. Choosing remote or local is, for the most part, only applicable if the client resides on the same machine as its target.

We've seen how one EJB can communicate with another in our example BenefitEnrollerBean (Listing 8–7, lines 90 through 95). Now let's take a look at another type of client—a simple Java application that processes benefits enrollment for a single member, "Larry Thomas." Conceptually, to accomplish this a client locates a BenefitEnroller bean and then uses the available business methods to select benefits as necessary. In particular, the client in our example needs to

- Connect to a BenefitEnrollerHome object
- Instantiate a new BenefitEnroller object by specifying the member ID associated with the enrollment and calling the create() method on the object
- Using the newly instantiated manager, call selectBenefit() and deselectBenefit() to manipulate the benefits "shopping cart"
- Call confirmEnrollment() to persist the contents of the current benefits shopping cart

One implementation that meets each of the above goals is shown in Listing 8–10.

Listing 8–10: The BenefitEnrollerClient Class

```
1 import javax.naming.Context;
2 import javax.naming.InitialContext;
3 import javax.rmi.PortableRemoteObject;
4 import java.util.*;
5
6 import BenefitEnroller;
7 import BenefitEnrollerHome;
8
9 public class BenefitEnrollerClient
10 {
11     public static void main(String[] args)
12     {
13         try
14         {
15             /* Handle to the context */
16             Context initial = new InitialContext();
17
18             /* Locate a benefit manager factory */
19             Object objref = initial.lookup(
```

```
19                 "java:comp/env/ejb/BenefitEnrollerEJB");
20
21         BenefitEnrollerHome benMgrHome = (BenefitEnrollerHome)
22            PortableRemoteObject.narrow(objref,
23               BenefitEnrollerHome.class);
24
25         /* Use factory to create benefit manager for processnig */
26         BenefitEnroller benefitEnroller =
27            benMgrHome.create("Larry Thomas");
28
29         /* Choose benefits we want benefit manager to process */
30         benefitEnroller.selectBenefit("HealthPlus - HMO Lite");
31         benefitEnroller.selectBenefit("Gamma Dental - Standard");
32
33         /* Display the list of chosen benefits */
34         System.out.println("Benefit list contains: ");
35         ArrayList benefits = benefitManager.getBenefitList();
36         Iterator i = benefits.iterator();
37         while (i.hasNext()) {
38            String benefitName = (String)i.next();
39            System.out.println(benefitName);
40         }
41         System.out.println();
42
43         /* Confirm enrollment */
44         benefitManager.confirmElections();
45
46      }
47      catch (Exception e) {
48         System.err.println("Exception during processing.");
49         e.printStackTrace();
50      }
51      }
52      }
```

The following are the key points in the code, as the comments indicate:

- In lines 22 through 27, locating the `BenefitEnrollerHome` object so that we can create a benefits management session—thus, a `BenefitsManager` object
- In lines 32 through 39, creating the `BenefitEnroller` and using its methods to assign benefits
- In line 56, confirming our elections

Client/EJB Communication behind the Scenes

In the client communication in Listing 8–1, as well as in the interaction with the `MemberBenefit` object shown in lines 90 through 95 of the `BenefitEnroller` bean, communication between clients and EJBs is simple and appears to be local. After we get a handle to a remote object, all we see is a bunch of what look like regular function calls, as shown in lines 32 through 33, 38 and 39, and 56.

There's no evidence of network communication (or so it appears), something that would seem inevitable when dealing with "distributed" objects. Instead, everything seems to occur in the same address space. Of course, this isn't really the case: Behind the scenes, there's a lot more going on.

As with other distributed object technologies, such as CORBA, remote functionality is accessed via stubs and skeletons. For the most part, this type of design has existed since the early days of object-oriented RPC-based communication and has been particularly popularized by CORBA implementations. The general idea is to use two additional proxy-like classes, a stub and a skeleton, to hide the messy details of connectivity required by remote invocation. Obviously, we can't just send regular Java objects down the wire—some sort of conversion to a serial bit stream is necessary at some point in client/server communication.

Here's the process in a nutshell. The local stub object contains the same method signatures as in the remote object. However, instead of processing the parameters given to it by the client, a stub method

- Converts them to a type suitable for network communication (i.e., converts every object into its Java serialized form)
- Communicates this information to a remote skeleton class on the server side
- Waits for a reply in order to send back a return value to the caller

The server-side skeleton receives the communication from the stub and does the following:

- Recasts the serialized form of the objects into real Java objects
- Invokes the destination object method with these objects
- Communicates any return values back to the stub

The complete scheme is illustrated by Figure 8–9.

The process of converting objects to their serialized forms is known as **marshalling**. The reverse process, converting serial data into objects, is known as **demarshalling**. To enable marshalling and demarshalling, all objects to be communicated back and forth must implement the `java.io.Serializable` class. Both processes are generally considered costly because of the bit stream parsing and dynamic object creation per method call required of the stub.

Marshalling and the raw network latency involved are the two major aspects of remote object communication that penalize performance. There are design strategies for reducing this penalty as well as the potential for using "smart stubs" that do

Figure 8–9
Stub/
skeleton-
based remote
invocation

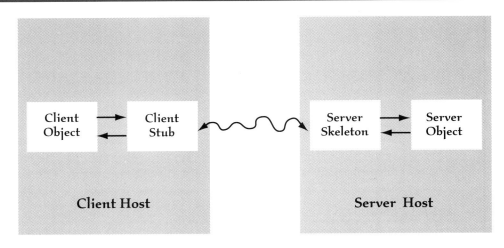

caching and pool objects that would otherwise need to be created. Nevertheless, it remains true: There's generally more expense involved in remote object communication than in local communication under this model.

But what is alternative? To have all of our EJBs on one machine? Not only is this alarming from a fault-tolerance perspective, but we know well enough by now that heavy site traffic quickly forces us to exhaust local resources, particularly by memory and CPU. While the overhead of distributed object solutions like EJB seems like a performance killer from the standpoint of a small site, it's absolutely essential for both performance and scalability for larger sites. We're better off tackling the problem of minimizing and optimizing the calls between objects where possible.

Scalability and Performance Hints

Having completed our whirlwind tour of EJB design and development, it's time to discuss a few scalability and performance hints. Notice that most of these have to do with EJB design, not implementation. Thus, many aspects of efficiency with respect to EJBs can be effected at the very early stages of product development.

Prefer Message–Driven Beans over Session Beans

Messaging is a highly underrated, yet very efficient, method of remote communication. As I'll describe in more detail in Chapter 9, it enables a higher degree of parallelism because it prevents the caller from stalling while the callee is busy processing a request. In turn, a higher degree of parallelism results in a more strategic use of resources between distributed machines and thus typically ensures a faster overall application.

Admittedly, messaging can frequently be impractical when clients have to query (i.e., read from) the remote resource and obviously require an answer. This is perhaps most often true when dealing with interactive clients, where visual confirmation of an application action is essential. Nevertheless, there are many cases where not all of the work needs to be confirmed immediately and can be processed using a messaging-based approach.

Consider an intranet application deployed by an multinational company that allows employees to order new computer equipment or office supplies. When users request new equipment, an order is created and routed to the internal purchasing department, but it's held up until the employee's manager approves the order. Thus, the application action of requesting new equipment consists of two steps:

1. Creating an internal purchasing order and setting its state as *pending approval*
2. Notifying the manager of the employee that the order exists, who replies with an approval message, thus updating the status of the order to *order approved*

Figures 8–10 and 8–11 illustrate the type of application being suggested. Figure 8–10 shows an HTML form that the employee fills out specifying the equipment to be ordered. Figure 8-11 shows confirmation that the order has been placed and is pending.

Figure 8–10
Sample order form

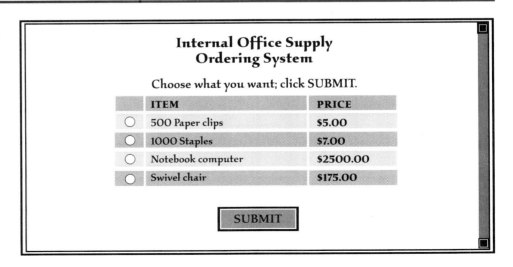

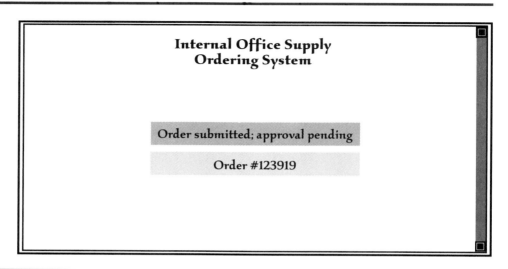

Let's reconsider the second step: notifying the manager. It might turn out that this is actually a complicated, time-consuming process—perhaps several database calls have to be made to find the employee's ID and his corresponding department and then to find the manager of that department. Notification is something that must be handled, but it's expensive to execute and doesn't return any useful result to the end user.

This makes it exactly the kind of task that's perfect for messaging. The end user can be notified much quicker if the creation of the order is synchronous but the approval handling is asynchronous.

Many of these behind-the-scenes tasks, like workflow processing, can be efficiently executed under a messaging scheme. In addition, many B2B-style processing tasks are perfect for messaging, such as batch processing of data from one company to another and supply chain management. Often, businesses establish partnerships to share information without incorporating each other into the actual live transactions of their own services, so the need for an immediate reply from the client is typically unnecessary.

If You Use Session Beans, Use Stateless Session Beans

Certainly, asynchronous solutions don't apply to every application scenario. In fact, unless a lot of care is taken during the design phase, they'll likely be the exception and not the rule. It's inevitable, then, that you'll need session beans in your EJB-based applications. When you develop a session bean, you have two choices: stateful or stateless.

The suggestion here is that you use stateless beans where possible. Stateful session beans provide a quick and dirty solution to the problem of maintaining state during a session, but they can quickly cause very-large-scale applications to buckle under resource constraints. Stateless session beans, on the other hand, can be efficiently pooled and deployed by the container so that the true parallelism demands can be met.

Recall that stateful session beans are allocated per client. That is, once a client starts a session, its bean exists until the session ends. Which means that, even during times of end-user inactivity, the bean instance exists. Of course, in looking back at the state transition diagram for a stateful session bean (Figure 8–6), we see that it can enter a passive state. Having many stateful session beans active at once can thus be alleviated to some degree by keeping some of them passive. However, the decision about when to do this is left up to the J2EE vendor, not the developer. Furthermore, although it has been made passive, the bean instance still exists and consumes memory. Even worse, it's very tempting for developers to take advantage of state management features to such a degree that a container call to `ejbPassivate()` and/or `ejbActivate()` becomes time-consuming in itself because of the necessary cleanup/setup required for the increasing amount of state managed.

With stateless session beans, rather than have one bean assigned per active session, a small pool of beans can sufficiently serve many concurrent sessions. The idea is simple: End users typically require much more think time than request processing time. Even though there may be hundreds of active sessions, most are in "think mode" and only a few actually require service.

So, instead of keeping state in the bean, consider one of the following alternatives:

- HTTP cookies and an external state management server (like a cache)
- URL rewriting
- Hidden form fields
- Servlet-based or HTTP session management

Suppose we use cookies and a state manager. This manager can be another small server on the application side accessible via RMI (or IIOP) that maps cookie values to state information. If it's designed right, it can even be an entity bean with a local interface so that there are no marshalling costs involved and a lookup evaluates to a local function call. Then a single cookie—the session ID—can be stored on the client-side cookie and its value can be used as the key to state information for that client.

Although the downside of this approach is that we have to design our own state manager or code another local entity bean, but we get back a lot more flexibility. We can potentially share state among clients by using an external cache. If the cache isn't designed as an entity bean, we can make it multithreaded and thus able to service many stateless session beans concurrently.

Think of the space efficiency advantages. Suppose we have 100 active sessions (100 clients) with our deployed application but at any one time only 10 are active. Also, suppose each of these sessions requires 1 K of pure state and that each stateful or stateless bean instance requires 1 K (in addition to the state it stores). Using a stateful session beans approach, we need

$$100 \cdot (1 \text{ K} + 1 \text{ K}) = 100 \cdot 2 \text{ K}$$
$$= 200 \text{ K}.$$

Even though only 10 sessions are active at once, we have to store bean instance metadata for the 90 inactive sessions. However, with a stateless session bean approach, suppose we deploy 10 stateless session beans plus a state management server (which requires x Kb of memory). Then we need only:

$$(100 \cdot 1 \text{ K}) + x = 100 \text{ K} + x.$$

This likely will result in memory savings of around 40 to 50 percent depending on the size of the state management server. If we use a URL rewriting approach, the gain is even more—at least 50 percent. In almost all cases, a less lazy approach to state management will improve resource efficiency and lead to more scalable deployments.

Strive for Coarse-Grained EJB Methods

As the designer of an application, you have the ability to control which methods are exposed and which aren't. In addition, you have the ability to choose how coarse or fine your exposed methods are. To understand what I mean by coarse versus fine, consider the following example.

One of the features of a simple banking application is that it supports the transfer of funds between two accounts (e.g., checking and savings) owned by the same member. There are at least two ways to expose this functionality to clients. One way is a **fine-grained approach**, which requires that the client remotely manage all of the details involved in the task. Listing 8–11 shows the methods the remote interface of a BankSession session bean might include.

Listing 8–11: The BankSession Session Bean Remote Interface (Fine-Grained)

```
1 import java.util.*;
2 import javax.ejb.EJBObject;
3 import java.rmi.RemoteException;
4
5 /**
6  * Conduct simple bank transactions.
7  */
```

```
 8 public interface BankSession extends EJBObject
 9 {
10    /**
11     * Withdraw money
12     */
13    public void withdraw(String a_accountId, int a_amount)
14       throws RemoteException;
15
16    /**
17     * Deposit money
18     */
19    public void deposit(String a_accountId, int a_amount)
20       throws RemoteException;
21
22    /**
23     * Check balances
24     */
25    public int getBalance(String a_accountId)
26       throws RemoteException;
27
28 }
```

To transfer money, a client has to make at least two remote calls: one to withdraw money from the source account and one to deposit money in the destination account. However, as many as four method calls can be required if the client also needs to check the balances to make sure that they don't fall below a certain level.

The second way to do this is by using a **coarse-grained** approach, as shown in Listing 8–12.

Listing 8–12: The `BankingSession` Session Bean Remote Interface (Coarse-Grained)

```
 1 import java.util.*;
 2 import javax.ejb.EJBObject;
 3 import java.rmi.RemoteException;
 4
 5 /**
 6  * Conduct simple bank transactions.
 7  */
 8 public interface BankSession extends EJBObject
 9 {
10    /**
11     * Transfer funds
12     */
13    public void transfer(String a_fromAcct, String a_toAcct, int
                           a_amount)
14       throws RemoteException;
15
16 }
```

Here, only one method call is required to achieve what two (or four) accomplished in the fine-grained interface. A `transfer()` method allows clients to require only one network roundtrip. It also reduces the need to marshal data—once from the client and once in reply from the server. Finally, it eliminates the need for the client to execute any transaction management code. The result of all this? *Better execution performance.*

Writing coarse-grained methods doesn't always mean collapsing several simpler calls into a single, more complex call. It can mean designing methods that are capable of doing things in batch rather than one at a time. For example, in our benefit enrollment example, instead of the original remote method:

```
public void selectBenefit(String a_benefitId)
    throws RemoteException;
```

we could have coded a method that takes a list of benefits from the client:

```
public void selectMultipleBenefits(String[] a_benefitId)
    throws RemoteException;
```

Notice that instead of calling `selectBenefit()` for each benefit the employee wants (and incurring the per-call latency and marshalling penalties I described earlier), only one call is required. In our benefit application, this sort of method would probably make logical sense—employees tend to select a set of benefits when they enroll.

Use BMP Well or Don't Use It at All

There has been considerable debate on whether to use CMP when designing entity beans. Some people argue that BMP is the only way you can be sure that the most efficient thing is being done. Others say that, depending on the J2EE vendor, BMP not only is a waste of time, but can lead to less efficient applications because some developers just don't write JDBC or SQL as efficiently as it can be written. This group is quick to point to the fact that features like data caching simply don't exist by default in the BMP case.

The best approach may be to use BMP *well* or not at all. With the arrival of the EJB 2.0 spec and its detailed design for CMP, it isn't unreasonable to assume that vendors will turn out fairly efficient CMP solutions. Since CMP is such a huge development win (in terms of rapid application development), customers will likely push vendors to deliver good implementations. However, for complex data models, for developers who have a decent understanding of JDBC and SQL, and for developers who have enough time, the BMP route is probably the best way to guarantee efficiency.

First, let's agree that, theoretically, CMP can never be more efficient than souped-up BMP. Pretty much every major performance-enhancing feature of CMP can be emulated by skilled BMP designers. Take data caching, for example. Many pro-CMP folks point to the opportunity J2EE vendors have to enable their containers to cache persistent data so that database calls can be avoided where necessary. There's no reason that BMP implementations can't make use of a similar custom caching solution.

BMP implementations can also easily incorporate basic persistence tricks, such as one that processes a SQL update only when data has truly been changed. There may be cases where the container can call `ejbStore()` and force BMP implementations to update data even though it hasn't actually changed. Careful BMP implementation can detect true changes and process SQL updates only when absolutely necessary.

Also, there are cases where BMP is not only just as efficient (or more so) but is necessary. If your entity is spread across multiple tables, or if some of your entities attributes are computed—not stored—in the underlying tables, you may be forced to use BMP. Again, CMP isn't magic—there is only so much that the EJB specification can address.

After all this, you're probably a bit confused. Should you trust CMP or be paranoid and use BMP? I strongly suggest putting your vendor to the test and making sure that a given CMP bean is managed just as efficiently as a BMP bean. Set up an environment where entity bean relationships can be stressed. The results from such a test may make the decision for you.

However, assuming that you've chosen a reasonable J2EE vendor, a good CMP versus BMP algorithm is probably this:

- Design your application using CMP. This will allow you to deploy something quickly that works.
- Identify bottlenecks in your application. It may be that you have much more important things to worry about than BMP versus CMP.
- If you find that database access is truly a bottleneck, try to identify which beans seem affected and then experiment with BMP solutions for them.

The really nice part of the CMP–BMP war is that CMP enables developers to code applications rapidly and to choose a BMP route easily if their vendor's CMP implementation just isn't up to snuff. The winner of the increased coverage and efficiency in the EJB 2.0 CMP spec is clearly the developer.

Know Your Vendor

Finally, as I've hinted throughout this chapter, it really pays to understand how your J2EE vendor implements the various value-added features, such as container-managed persistence. The profit gained by applying any of the techniques and strategies here, such as avoiding stateful session beans and using bean-managed persistence, is directly related to how efficient or inefficient your vendor is in terms of EJB support. When choosing a vendor, ask these questions:

- How do they implement container-managed persistence?
- What is their algorithm for bean passivation?
- Are they fully compliant with EJB 2.0? That is, do they support message-driven beans and EJB 2.0–style CMP?

Understanding what your vendor does well can help you prioritize which aspects of EJB development and deployment you want to leave to your vendor and which you want to take into your own hands.

Summary

This chapter focused on the need for application severs in any multitier Web application architecture. Application servers contain business logic functionality that's at the heart of your application's purpose. Engineers have found that flexibility and scalability can be gained by building these servers as sets of distributed application objects.

The J2EE solution for this is Enterprise JavaBeans. EJBs offer designers a multitude of options to easily model synchronous and asynchronous client sessions and provide an object-oriented "live" representation of the underlying data persisted by the application.

In the context of application servers and EJBs, we covered

- Why serving application logic is necessary
- How EJBs provide the opportunity to implement that logic in a simple, scalable, and object-oriented manner
- The details of client-to-EJB communication
- The types of EJBs: **session**, **entity**, and **message driven** and the details of each type and which parts of an application are suited to it
- The key issues and tasks associated with EJB design and development, along with examples of how each EJB type is developed

With this understanding of EJBs, it's now time for us to investigate an application request processing alternative, specifically to explore the efficiency benefits that messaging can provide to your application.

CHAPTER 9

Messaging for Efficient Enterprise Application Integration

As we discussed in Chapter 8, many applications or parts of applications have the opportunity to solve their problems asynchronously. Application integration models that are broadcast based or where there's a natural one-way dataflow between applications are just two examples of when an asynchronous solution can be appropriate. Although we've spent a lot of time discussing performance and scalability for interactive Web applications, it's also important to understand how these measures apply to asynchronous systems. In this chapter, then, we'll focus exclusively on building solutions the J2EE way, that is, asynchronous with the Java Message Service.

A B2B-style Working Example

Our example for this chapter will focus on the simple task of building a system that communicates product price updates to several resellers or divisional units. As our example company, we'll use Red Planet Electronics, which produces thousands of electronic parts that are priced individually. All products and prices are kept in a corporate database, and Red Planet needs to update the prices to several resellers located throughout the country. These updates are done per item, whenever the Red Planet manufacturing price changes. The flow of data between Red Planet and its resellers is shown in Figure 9–1.

Resellers process the updates in two steps. First they use the Red Planet *product ID* to look up their own *internal product ID*, which may or may not be the same as the Red Planet product ID (keep in mind that resellers often deal with many manufacturers), as well as the markup associated with that product. Then they update their internal price list accordingly, using their internal product IDs. The basic flow of these processes is diagrammed in Figure 9–2.

Figure 9–1   Relationships of Red Planet and its resellers

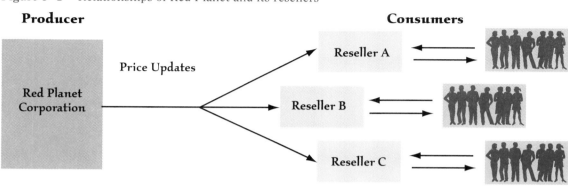

Red Planet is interested in designing a solution that makes this data transfer process efficient. Notice that the nature of the problem is such that data flows in one direction, from one source to many destinations. Also notice that there is no need for Red Planet to process any reply from the recipients of these price updates. All the company wants is the assurance that the updates eventually reach each reseller, so acknowledgment can happen later (if at all). Finally, there's no live end user involved in this data transfer; unlike interactive Web applications, human beings don't transfer these price updates between systems. Instead, the whole process is carried out by communication between a *producing application* (Red Planet's price update application) and downstream *consuming applications*. The solution thus involves two applications talking to each other without any interactive users. This is exactly the kind of problem that messaging is designed to address.

Throughout this chapter, remember that performance and scalability are only two arguments for considering an asynchronous application solution. There are many others, one of the most prominent being ease of enterprise application integration. An intermediate messaging service between two applications frequently

Figure 9–2
Reseller price
update
flowchart

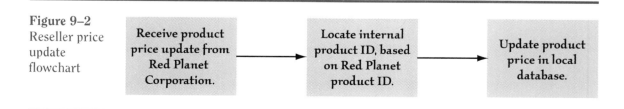

speeds up the integration process because it allows data to be transferred easily between the two systems using a well-known API. What's more important, it prevents integration engineers from spending countless hours arguing about application API modifications, middleware technologies, and other such issues.

With an example problem and a general idea about what the solution looks like, we can move forward. Still, before we get too deep into the details of a suggested implementation, we need to introduce the basic concepts of the Java Message Service and the options it gives us.

The Java Message Service

The Java Message Service (JMS) provides a platform-independent API for building messaging solutions. Like other parts of the J2EE standard, it doesn't represent a complete solution—it's just a reference API that messaging software manufacturers and users can employ as a well-known point of integration—one that ensures both flexibility and interoperability. JMS is Java based, and J2EE 1.3+ includes a reference implementation that acts as a basic messaging provider.

For organizations that already have a messaging system, JMS represents a way to increase system flexibility. Instead of being forced to rely on a proprietary messaging API from a specific vendor, they can use JMS as a wrapper to any vendor that adheres to its API. Many vendors are now following this standard, so there's increased flexibility in choosing and possibly replacing your underlying vendor while incurring the minimum overhead.

For the programmer, JMS offers a very simple, abstract, platform-independent API for messaging. It supports asynchronous and reliable message delivery that ensures that messages are not just received but received only once. JMS also supports two abstract messaging models: point-to-point and publish/subscribe, and it enables messaging deployments to be configured for performance, reliability, or aspects of both. Finally, JMS offers opportunities for integration with existing J2EE technologies, including Enterprise JavaBeans and the Java Transaction API. For example, it's possible to construct a distributed asynchronous transaction system using JMS technologies.

JMS Concepts

Four key abstractions are fundamental to JMS programming models:

- Providers
- Clients
- Messages
- Administered objects

Figure 9–3
General
relationships of
the JMS API,
providers,
clients, and
messages

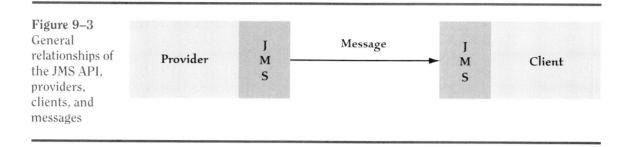

Figure 9–3 shows the relationship between the first three. Because administered objects describe a set of objects, we'll look at them in more detail separately.

Although non-JMS-proprietary client APIs don't necessarily contain these same abstractions, they may still interact with other JMS clients that do, via messaging providers that offer JMS compliance in addition to their own API. For JMS client programmers, this is a point that can be largely ignored; as long as the provider supports a JMS interface, a JMS client can exchange messages with non-JMS clients transparently.

Providers

A **JMS provider** is a messaging system that implements the JMS API and enables the administrative and control features specified by J2EE. Conceptually, the provider manages the messaging queue and coordinates the loose coupling of clients, for example, ensuring that one message is delivered to multiple clients (if desired). It can also guarantee that clients receive messages, and it provides a way for clients to receive messages that were distributed before they joined the distribution list. The provider also supports the ability to persistently store messages for robustness during system failures and for archival purposes.

Clients

A **JMS client** can produce or consume messages using the JMS API. Clients obtain handles to objects controlled by the provider, such as a message queue, and use them to distribute or gain access to messages. Since messaging is a peer-to-peer concept, there are no real servers—just clients. In our Red Planet example, both the system at headquarters and each of the downstream consumers (resellers) are clients.

Messages

A **JMS message** is the fundamental data structure passed between producer and consumer. JMS messages consist of a **header**, **properties** (optional), and a **body** (optional).

The JMS message header, like an HTTP message header, includes metadata about the message contents. Table 9–1 describes the header fields defined by the JMS 1.0.2 specification. It raises two important points:

- As shown, messages can be sent by either provider or client. Although we're primarily considering the headquarters-to-reseller path, messaging does allow for bidirectional communication. Be careful not to confuse bidirectional with synchronous. The former indicates the path between entities; the latter indicates the type of handshake they use.

- Many values are actually set by the method in which the message is sent. This "send method" refers to the exact paradigm that providers use to communicate to clients. If necessary, administrators can override some of these values (JMSDeliveryMode, JMSPriority, and JMSExpiration) if necessary.

Message properties are an optional means for extending the basic information in the header. They're useful when you want to extend the message headers listed in Table 9–1 to include other information (i.e., application or infrastructure specific).

Finally, the body of a message contains the actual business information of value. JMS defines five basic types of message bodies, as shown in Table 9–2.

Table 9–1: JMS Message Headers

Field	*Set By*	*Indicates*
JMSDestination	Send method	Destination of the message
JMSDeliveryMode	Send method	Persistent or nonpersistent
JMSExpiration	Send method	Calculated time before the message expires
JMSPriority	Send method	Urgency of message (0–9). Levels 0–4 generally mean normal; levels 5–9: expedite
JMSMessageID	Send method	Uniquely identifies each message (per provider)
JMSTimestamp	Send method	Time provider was given message to be sent
JMSCorrelationId	Client	Associates one message with another; e.g., client can indicate a response to a particular request.
JMSReplyTo	Client	Where provider reply should be sent
JMSType	Client	References a definition in a message provider's repository (JMS doesn't provide a default repository)
JMSRedelivered	Provider	Provider is resending an earlier message not acknowledged by client

Table 9–2: JMS Body Types and Content

Body Type	Body Content
StreamMessage	A stream of values associated with primitive Java types
ObjectMessage	Any Java object that implements java.io.Serializable
TextMessage	A single Java String
MapMessage	A set of name/value pairs, where names are Java String objects and values are any primitive Java type
BytesMessage	A stream of uninterpreted bytes

In our Red Planet example, the body contains a product ID and the new price. Thus, it arguably falls into the MapMessage category (name = product ID, value = new price). However, to simplify our example we'll use the TextMessage type. The point here is that it's up to the provider how to package the data it sends, as long as it falls into one of the categories listed in Table 9–2. One reason that serializable types are emphasized has to do with the notion of a persistent delivery mode. We'll discuss that mode, in addition to the contrasting nonpersistent delivery mode, later on.

Note that the message body is optional. For example, some messages with empty bodies are simply sent as control messages to indicate acknowledgment.

Administrative Objects

Last but not least, JMS **administrative objects** are important abstractions that form the backbone of communication between clients. They encompass two important subobjects: connection factories and destinations. **Connection factories** are used as a means for JMS clients to create connections to the provider. **Destinations** are the virtual targets for message producers and the source for message consumers.

Suitable destinations can be either **queues** or **topics**, both of which we'll discuss in greater detail later on in this chapter. Communication with these destinations is achieved through the use of **connections**, which are distributed by connection factories. Once a virtual connection has been established between JMS consumer and provider, a **session** can be created in which to produce or consume messages. Specifically, a session enables a **message producer** and a **message consumer** to be instantiated. Sessions also provide a transactional context for communication.

JMS Programming Models

To understand the applicability of queues and topics, we first need to introduce the two basic programming models that JMS supports: **point-to-point** (PTP) and **publish/subscribe** (pub/sub). Although we'll refer to these strictly as messaging

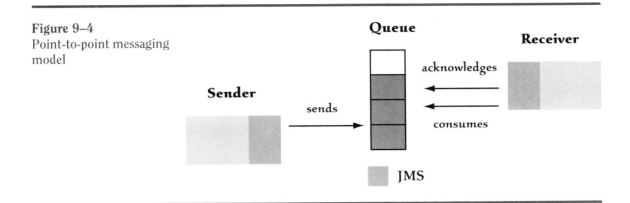

Figure 9–4
Point-to-point messaging model

models, they're also known as *domains* or *messaging styles*. The JMS specification uses these terms interchangeably.

The PTP model is designed for use between a single producer and a single consumer. Messages are added to a queue, to be retrieved by the consumer. In short, only two parties are involved in PTP communication.

In contrast, the pub/sub model is based on the notion of a topic. **Publishers** create topics and send out messages corresponding to them. Consumers are one or more **subscribers** to a particular topic. Subscribers can receive messages synchronously or asynchronously, the latter via a message listener mechanism.

Figures 9–4 and 9–5 show the conceptual distinction between PTP and pub/sub messaging models.

Model-Specific Administrative Object Interfaces

Recall that JMS—like the rest of J2EE—is an API, not an implementation. The set of interfaces it defines can be divided into two subsets: those that are independent of the programming model (PTP versus pub/sub) and those that are dependent. Generally, the latter extend the former in a way suitable for their programming model. This mapping is shown in Table 9–3.

The Synchrony of Message Consumption

An important yet subtle feature of JMS has to do with the synchrony of the client. In particular, the *delivery* of the message to the client may be synchronous or asynchronous.

Think about it this way: While the transfer of data from producer to consumer is asynchronous, it's only necessarily asynchronous from the standpoint of the

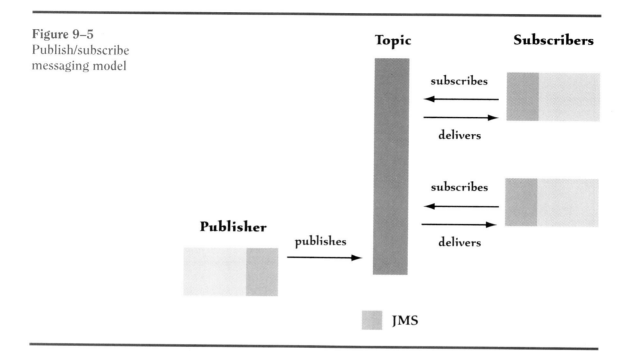

Figure 9–5
Publish/subscribe
messaging model

Table 9–3: Mapping JMS Concepts to Model-Specific Interfaces

Model-Independent Interface	PTP Interface	Pub/Sub Interface
ConnectionFactory	QueueConnectionFactory	TopicConnectionFactory
Connection	QueueConnection	TopicConnection
Destination	Queue	Topic
Session	QueueSession	TopicSession
MessageProducer	QueueSender	TopicPublisher
MessageConsumer	QueueReceiver	TopicSubscriber
	QueueBrowser	

producer—that is, the producer decides when to send data and has no dependency on the consumer. However, the consumer—although conceptually agreeable to receiving the message from a queue—maintains a dependency on the producer *for the message to actually be produced*. Specifically, it can't consume what hasn't been produced and must decide how to discover new messages generated by the provider.

The JMS API allows message consumers to execute in either of two modes:

- Blocking mode, its main thread waiting until a new message arrives
- Nonblocking mode, its main thread continuing with execution while the provider thread executes a message listener method when a new object arrives

JMS Reliability versus Performance

There are several ways to configure a JMS messaging scheme based on the level of reliability desired. The chosen configuration directly affects system performance.

In general, trading reliability for performance is one way to improve system throughput. But make no mistake: It's a dangerous game to play when the messages are important. If the nature of your application is such that consumption of every message is critical, there's no avoiding the reliability controls that JMS provides.

There are two major controls in the reliability versus performance debate: client acknowledgment and message persistence.

Client Acknowledgment

When JMS messages are sent, they can be part of a transaction or not, that is, *non-transacted*. Transactions are very important because they allow a series of messages to be treated as an atomic unit of work: Just like database transactions, either all will succeed or none will succeed.

Depending on your application, transactions may or may not be necessary. For example, consider a banking application that sends two messages to indicate an internal transfer of funds from one account to another. If user Joe is transferring $100 between accounts A001 and A002, these messages can be pseudo-coded as

```
Withdraw(A001, 100)
Deposit(A002, 100)
```

In this case, it's important that both the withdrawal and the deposit are processed or neither is. Otherwise, if a system failure occurs after the withdrawal is processed, the bank client will suddenly lose $100. In this scenario, transactions are necessary. In our Red Planet example, however, price updates are atomic: They don't need to be wrapped in a parent transaction.

If transactions are required, acknowledgment in JMS is automatic. This is because a transaction can't be committed until all actions have been verified complete. The committing of the transaction is thus implicit acknowledgment.

However, if the message is nontransacted, there are three JMS acknowledgment schemes to choose from:

- AUTO_ACKNOWLEDGE: If the client receives the message synchronously, the session automatically acknowledges receipt after the API call to receive the message returns. If the client receives the message asynchronously, the session automatically acknowledges receipt after the call to the message listener handler returns.

- CLIENT_ACKNOWLEDGE: The burden is on the client to explicitly acknowledge a message by calling a function on the message object itself. The client can periodically issue acknowledgments using this scheme. Suppose the client receives (in order) messages A, B, and C, but acknowledges only B. The result is that the first two messages (A and B) are considered acknowledged but C isn't.

- DUPS_OK_ACKNOWLEDGE: This is a lazy scheme for acknowledgment that can result in duplicate message deliveries under certain failure scenarios.

Message Persistence

JMS offers two options related to message persistence. **Persistent messages** are logged (in a file or database) when the provider receives them from the message producer. Thus, if the provider fails at some point before the messages have been consumed, the messages won't be lost and will become available once the provider system comes back online. **Nonpersistent messages** aren't logged upon production, so those not consumed at the time of provider failure will be lost.

Persistence can also be specified per message. This gives a producer the flexibility of a heterogeneous reliability scheme where the majority of messages are nonpersistent and periodic summaries are persistent. For example, in the Red Planet case all individual price changes can be communicated as nonpersistent; only a monthly or weekly update summary is persistent. This scheme guarantees periodic consistency at the expense of a slightly more complicated producer and consumer.

It's very important to note that, by default, *all messages sent are persistent*; the programmer has to explicitly specify that a message is nonpersistent. This has important performance implications, as the two JMS message delivery options allow the programmer to choose sides in the reliability–performance debate. Nonpersistent message delivery results in a faster system—no doubt about it. A provider that doesn't log data as it's sent (in particular, commit the data to a database) will have better throughput because its availability is better.

But before you choose a nonpersistent mode of delivery, remember that this choice sacrifices reliability for performance. And any performance gain is obviously meaningless if the messages are important and the provider fails. Once again, this tradeoff reminds us that, though our focus is on building fast and scalable apps, achieving this goal is unimportant if the basic application requirements must be sacrificed.

What's more, you shouldn't be under the impression that a missed message in a nonpersistent scheme happens once in a blue moon. In fact, it can be quite the opposite! It depends on your publishing model (PTP or pub/sub), where your publishers and subscribers are located, and what kind of resource contentions they face.

Timing Dependencies and JMS Publishing Models

The two JMS distribution models have different affects on the reliability of message consumption. PTP messaging enqueues new messages as they're produced and only dequeues each message once (no matter how many consumers there are). Thus, a producer can be assured that a consumer has the opportunity to receive all messages. However, to ensure that multiple clients receive that message it has to create a destination for each client.

In contrast, pub/sub messaging allows a producer to broadcast a message to multiple clients, but normally ensures only that a client has the opportunity to receive these messages during periods when the subscription is active. Under the default scheme, any messages sent before the subscription is created or during client downtime aren't received. Often this makes sense when old messages aren't useful and new messages aren't critical. For example, if you're broadcasting noncritical stock quotes (for general use, not day-trading), a pub/sub model can be a natural fit.

However, many times it's desirable to have reliable message delivery to multiple consumers. To achieve this, JMS offers *durable subscriptions*. These are subscriptions where the provider assures the producer that a consumer will receive all of the messages for a given subscription until either the messages expire or the subscription is unsubscribed. Each subscription is associated with a single subscriber. To ensure that messages created before the subscription starts can be consumed, the delivery mode should be persistent.

A Sample JMS Pub/Sub Application

In this section, we'll get a better feel for the details involved in writing a messaging application. Instead of discussing how to do this under the different models (PTP or pub/sub) and reliability configurations (persistent delivery, nonpersistent delivery, durable subscriptions, and nondurable subscriptions), we will stick to our Red Planet example, which involves distributing price updates to resellers. This means that we'll commit to specific set of JMS deployment options. Coding under an alternative messaging model with alternative reliability configurations is very similar to what will be presented here.

In thinking about our specific Red Planet example, a few immediate observations and corresponding decisions can be made. Clearly, the role of message producer is played by the main pricing application at headquarters and the consumer roles are played by the applications used by the resellers. Since this means that price updates are being distributed in a one-to-many fashion, the natural delivery model for Red Planet is JMS publish/subscribe.

We should note that reseller applications may crash or be unavailable for reasons that Red Planet can't control. Price updates are not tangential to business—they *are* the business—so failure to receive a message can impact a reseller (it will be charging the wrong price!). To avoid this, we'll design our application using durable subscriptions. Also, since the host running the JMS provider may itself occasionally crash, message persistence is necessary.

Let's examine the code required to build the publisher and reseller subscribers.

Developing the Message Publisher

To publish messages under a pub/sub model, it's necessary to do the following:

1. Create the topic (programmatically or with J2EE tools).
2. Get the initial context (JNDI lookup).
3. Obtain a connection factory from the messaging provider.
4. Obtain a connection using the factory.
5. Create a topic session using the connection.
6. Locate the topic.
7. Create a publisher object for the topic session.
8. Publish the message.

Creating the Topic

The first step is to create a topic on the provider side (the provider owns the queue in this example). We can do this either through the JMS API or with tools that are commonly provided by the J2EE vendor. To simplify our example, we'll choose the latter approach. Specifically, we'll consider how a topic is created using the tools provided by Sun's J2EE reference implementation.

Sun provides a tool called j2eeadmin, which can be used to manage JMS queues and topics. Here's an example of how we can use that tool to create a topic:

```
% j2eeadmin –addJmsDestination PriceUpdatesTopic topic
```

Next, we can use this tool to ensure that the topic has been created by listing available topics and queues:

```
% j2eeadmin -listJmsDestinations

JmsDestination
_____
< JMS Destination : jms/Queue , javax.jms.Queue >
< JMS Destination : jms/Topic , javax.jms.Topic >
< JMS Destination : PriceUpdatesTopic , javax.jms.Topic >
```

With the topic created, we can code the producer so that it publishes messages for that topic.

Coding the Message Producer

In order to obtain a connection to the messaging provider, we need a connection factory. However, before we can get this factory we need to locate provider resources (since connection factories are administered objects). We can do this using JNDI and JMS API calls:

```
Context ctx = new InitialContext();

TopicConnectionFactory tConnectionFactory = (TopicConnectionFactory)
    ctx.lookup("TopicConnectionFactory");

TopicConnection tConnection =
    ConnectionFactory.createTopicConnection();
```

The context created is based on the contents of a JNDI properties file. It helps the producer locate connection factories and destinations (topics and queues).

We can also use the context to locate the particular topic that we'll publish messages about (i.e., the JMS destination):

```
Topic priceUpdatesTopic = ctx.lookup("PriceUpdatesTopic");
```

Note that, if the destination hasn't been created yet, as was done initially, we'll get an error at runtime.

Once we have a TopicConnection, we can use it to create a session context for message transmission:

```
TopicSession tSession = tConnection.createTopicSession(false,
    Session.AUTO_ACKNOWLEDGE);
```

Thus, in this example our `TopicSession` indicates that acknowledgment in this nontransacted scheme will be automatic (when the provider calls the subscriber `receive` method).

Finally, we can create a `TopicPublisher` object:

```
TopicPublisher tPublisher =
    tSession.createPublisher(priceUpdatesTopic);
```

Having connected to our newly created topic, we can start sending messages:

```
TextMessage mesg = tSession.createTextMessage();

/* Describe the manufacturers price of product ID CXL43550 as $10.95 */
mesg.setText("CXL43550:10.95")
tPublisher.publishMessage(mesg);
```

In the subsection on JMS messages, I mentioned that we can use a `MapMessage` or a `TextMessage` body type. Another choice is to use the generic `ObjectMessage` type and remove the need for client parsing. However, this is a tradeoff: If we use `ObjectMessage`, all clients need the corresponding serializable Java class file in order to work with its methods and data structures. And, as that class file evolves, a remote maintenance and support problem ensues.

Developing the Message Subscriber

Creating a subscriber is a lot like creating a publisher. Generally, we need to accomplish the following tasks:

1. Get the initial context (possibly a remote JNDI lookup).
2. Obtain a connection factory from the messaging provider.
3. Obtain a connection using the factory.
4. Create a topic session using the connection.
5. Locate the topic.
6. Choose to be a durable subscriber or a nondurable subscriber.
7. Choose synchronous or asynchronous message processing.
8. Announce that we're ready to consume messages.

As with publishers, it's first necessary to bootstrap subscribers by having them locate an initial context, obtain a connection, and create a session for message consumption. Note that getting an initial context may involve connecting to the remote publisher's machine and name server (or else the topic can't be located). How you do this depends on the location of the physical queue and the underlying transport used for messaging.

For example, the initial code for a remote client may be something like Listing 9–1.

Listing 9–1: Sample Remote JMS Client

```
 1    /* Define remote context information. */
 2    Properties env = new Properties();
 3    env.setProperty(Context.INITIAL_CONTEXT_FACTORY,
 4      "com.sun.enterprise.naming.SerialInitContextFactory" );
 5    env.setProperty(Context.PROVIDER_URL,
 6      "rmi://publisher.somehost.com:1050" );
 7
 8    /* Get the initial context */
 9    try {
10      jndiContext = new InitialContext(env);
11    }
12    catch (NamingException e) {
13      System.out.println("Could not create JNDI " +
14        "context: " + e.toString());
15      System.exit(1);
16    }
17
18    /* Lookup a topic using a connection factory */
19    try {
20      tConnectionFactory = (TopicConnectionFactory)
21        jndiContext.lookup("TopicConnectionFactory");
22      topic = (Topic) jndiContext.lookup(topicName);
23    }
24    catch (NamingException e) {
25      System.out.println("Error during context lookup: " +
         e.toString());
26      System.exit(1);
27    }
28
29    /* Create the connection and session */
30    try {
31      tConnection = tConnectionFactory.createTopicConnection();
32      tSession = tConnection.createTopicSession(false,
33        Session.AUTO_ACKNOWLEDGE);
34    }
35    catch (Exception e) {
36      System.err.println(Error during connection/session creation);
37      e.printStackTrace();
38      System.exit(1);
39    }
```

Once a session has been created, we can locate a topic and subscribers can sub-scribe to it:

```
TopicSubscriber tSubscriber =
    tSession.createSubscriber(priceUpdatesTopic);
```

Creating a subscriber in this manner gets us a client with a nondurable subscription. If we want to improve reliability (on the client side), we can create a durable sub-scription, which is exactly what we want in our Red Planet example. To do that, we make a slightly different API call and specify a client ID:

```
TopicSubscriber tSubscriber =
    tSession.createDurableSubscriber(priceUpdatesTopic, "updatesSub");
```

We need to specify a client ID because durable subscriptions can only be associated with a single subscriber. If we want multiple clients to have durable subscriptions, we need to create a topic for each of them. When using a durable subscription, we also need to make sure that the client ID is properly associated with `TopicConnection`. One way to do this is to make the relevant `TopicConnection` API call:

```
tConnection.setClientID("updatesSub");
```

Since the subscription is durable, the subscriber application can crash all it wants and still be assured that messages missed during the crash will be available for retrieval when the subscriber returns to listening.

Asynchronous Message Processing

As we discussed earlier, we need to decide how messages will be delivered to the client: synchronously or asynchronously. In our example, we choose the latter, and to accomplish this we need to develop a JMS `MessageListener` object and register it with the `TopicSubscriber` object. This listener will be invoked as necessary when messages arrive. The requirements for developing a listener are to have it implement the `MessageListener` interface and, in particular, the `onMessage()` method.

For example, the listener can be defined as shown in Listing 9–2.

Listing 9–2: A Listener for Red Planet Price Updates

```
1 /**
2  * PriceUpdateListener can be used by a subscriber to the
   PriceUpdatesTopic
3  * to process messages asynchronously.
```

```
 4   */
 5  import javax.jms.*;
 6
 7  public class PriceUpdateListener
 8    implements MessageListener
 9  {
10    public void onMessage(Message a_mesg)
11    {
12      try {
13        if (message instanceof TextMessage) {
14
15              /* Process price update */
16
17        }
18        else {
19
20              /* Report unexpected message type */
21
22        }
23      }
24      catch (JMSException jex) {
25
26          /* Handle JMS exceptions */
27
28      }
29      catch (Throwable tex) {
30
31          /* Handle misc exceptions */
32
33      }
34    }
35  }
```

We can then register our handler with the TopicSubscriber object:

```
updListener = new PriceUpdateListener;
topicSub.setMessageListener(updListener);
```

Synchronous Subscription Processing

One of the benefits of the pub/sub model is that we can use either a synchronous or an asynchronous approach to message consumption. In the PTP model, there's no choice—queue consumers are always synchronous with respect to the message queue. To make a subscriber in the pub/sub model synchronous with message availability, we simply block, waiting for the next message via the receive() method on the subscriber:

```
Message m = topicSub.receive();
```

The `receive()` method also accepts a parameter that allows it to time-out after a specified number of milliseconds. With no parameters, as in the preceding example, the subscriber simply blocks until the next message arrives.

Toward Deployment

As you might have inferred, the subscriber listener is where the real asynchronous client postprocessing is done. For example, in the listener code we can either process the update directly via JDBC or connect to an existing client application that performs this same update. Similarly, for the producer we can have another application interface with the message-publishing code or simply integrate this code into that application. Clearly, the messaging code isn't lengthy, yet it provides a simple means for application integration.

To deploy our Red Planet pub/sub application, then, all we need to do is

- Start running all subscriber applications (or add more over time as necessary) so that they can begin listening for new messages
- Start running our publisher application

That's it. Once it's set up, messages can be published as necessary.

Scalability and Performance Hints

As we've seen, messaging is a simple but flexible technology for achieving high-performance asynchronous communication. In this section, we consider a few scalability and performance suggestions related to when and how to use it in your own applications.

Use Messaging

The biggest hurdle with messaging is getting people to realize how it can help make applications efficient. Part of the problem is that many of us are used to thinking of Web applications from the interactive end-user perspective. We see a user action and we expect a corresponding server reaction. By nature, we tend to think serially and synchronously for certain online tasks because we imagine that we're interacting with a virtual person on the server side.

However, not all real-life tasks are serially executed. Consider cooking. Timing is important in cooking, and so you plan out your meal by starting from the goal point—having all dishes ready at the same time. This forces you to schedule certain activities in parallel. For example, since a typical dinner involves multiple independent dishes, you frequently prepare part B of your meal while part A is simmering. The independence of these dishes is what allows this parallelism to be safe.

The point I'm making here is a simple one: Think carefully about your application flow in terms of its true potential for parallelism. Does every request really require a meaningful reply? In many B2B-style application integration scenarios, information sharing among companies often means simply dumping data from one repository to another. Such scenarios are perfect candidates for messaging solutions.

Explore Messaging Opportunities Within

Opportunities can also exist within the guts of an application system. Although an interactive session may require a synchronous reply from the back-end application, some aspects of task execution may be asynchronous.

Consider logging. Complicated application systems frequently contain logging facilities for auditing as well as debugging. However, many logging messages are purely informational and noncritical to execution. With careful thought, an application architect can construct asynchronous logging by using JMS. The result: If the logger normally writes its messages to the filesystem or to a database, the I/O cost involved can be saved by the application components that communicate with the logger.

To flesh out this example a bit, consider this pseudo-code for a server-side method called `transferFunds()`. It's implemented as part of an `AccountProcessing` object, which can easily be an EJB session bean.

```
/**
 * Psuedo-code for AccountProcessing object
 */
public class AccountProcessing
{
  /**
   * Logs message to some well-known file.
   */
  public static void log(String a_mesg){
    appendFile("logfile", a_mesg);
  }

  /**
   * Withdraws money from one account and deposits
   * it into destination account
   */
  public static void transferFunds(int a_fromAcctNum, int
      a_toAccountNum, double a_amt) {

    /* Log attempted action */
    log("Transferring <"+a_amt+"> from <"+a_fromAcctNum+
      "> to <"+a_toAcctNum+">");
```

```
  /* Withdraw funds from source */
  double newBalance = withdrawFunds(a_fromAcctNum, a_amt);
  log("New balance in <"+a_fromAcctNum+"> is <"+newBalance+">");

  /* Deposit funds into destination */
  newBalance = depositFunds(a_toAcctNum, a_amt);
  log("New balance in <"+a_toAcctNum+'> is <"+newBalance+">");
  }
}
```

Figures 9–6 and 9–7 show the benefit of decoupling the logging process from such an application system. Figure 9–6 shows the initial execution flow: As the server-side `transferFunds()` method executes, several logging statements that involve writing messages to the filesystem are executed. However, they don't return any immediately useful information and the application is unfairly bogged down waiting on I/O latencies.

In Figure 9–7, the logger has been decoupled from the `AccountProcessing` object and the two communicate via JMS. In this case, the same logging calls exist; however, they're now executed asynchronously. The result is faster execution of the `transferFunds()` method call.

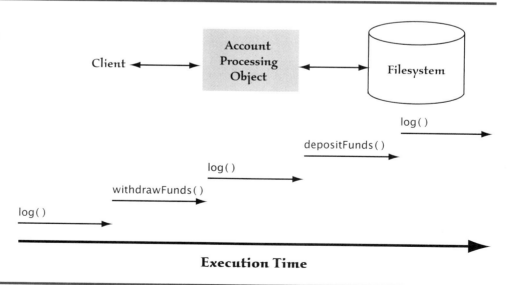

Figure 9–6
Synchronous
I/O-bound
execution
that results
in poor
performance

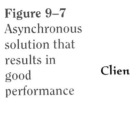

Figure 9–7
Asynchronous
solution that
results in
good
performance

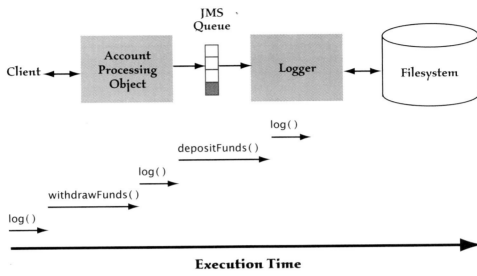

Granularity is important here. As you make choices about how to modularize and distribute parts of your application, give careful consideration to the data dependencies that exist within. Lack of a dependency, as is the case in this logging example, may indicate an opportunity to decouple and parallelize execution.

Understand the JMS Efficiency–Reliability Tradeoff

Now that you've seen the full range of options you have when developing a producer and consumer, it should be clear that JMS messaging affords application designers a number of options in terms of implementing a messaging solution. To review, recall that there are two models to choose from:

- *Point-to-point*: one publisher, one consumer
- *Publish/subscribe*: one publisher, multiple consumers

There are also two message delivery reliability options:

- *Nonpersistent*: Published messages are not logged in a persistent store.
- *Persistent* (*default*): Published messages are logged in a persistent store.

Although the PTP model enforces synchronous message consumption, this is optional for the pub/sub model. Specifically, pub/sub has the following subscription options:

- *Nondurable* (*default*): Messages transmitted during client downtime are lost.
- *Durable*: Messages transmitted during client downtime are potentially saved.

In general, we can make the following conclusions about the performance–reliability tradeoffs implied by these options:

- PTP and pub/sub are roughly equal in terms of scalability for a single producer and a single consumer.
- PTP isn't as scalable as pub/sub for one producer and many consumers. If your reliability model allows it, pub/sub offers a number of options for improving performance (e.g., nonpersistent delivery or nondurable subscriptions). Also, the producer doesn't need to manage multiple queues, as is necessary in a PTP deployment for multiple consumers.
- Nonpersistent delivery leads to *better producer performance* because it avoids synchronous logging of a message to a persistent store. However, it's less reliable if the producer side of the integration encounters a problem.
- Nondurable subscriptions lead to *better consumer performance* because they avoid the need for the client to acknowledge every message received. However, it too is less reliable: Messages transmitted during client downtime can be lost.

The overall rule of thumb for both safety and performance is *choose safety first*. Once you've identified the minimum reliability you need for your application, choose the best performing producer/consumer scheme.

Summary

In this chapter, we explored messaging as a strategy for asynchronous request processing. The J2EE technology for messaging, JMS, can be an efficient solution when integrating enterprise applications across network boundaries or within the components of an application system itself.

We saw that JMS provides two basic models of messaging that allow messages to be sent to one or more clients simultaneously. While both enable information to be sent from producer to consumer asynchronously, the consumer can choose to have the message delivered to it synchronously. In addition, we identified how options for persistence and client acknowledgment can affect both reliability and performance.

When designed and deployed correctly, JMS-based solutions enable applications to realize a higher degree of parallelism during execution. Unless you're doing a lot of scientific processing (i.e., long-running number-crunching routines), there's likely significant I/O during the execution of your application because of communication with the filesystem, the database, or another application. These I/O-bound actions can represent opportunities for parallelism and thus for optimal CPU usage. By decoupling appropriate parts of your application and bridging them via JMS, you can often leverage these opportunities and find that the result leads to a highly efficient application system.

CHAPTER 10

Effective Database Design

How important is the database when considering the performance and scalability of your application? I would argue that it usually represents about *one-third* of the overall challenge. Think that sounds like a lot? It's really not—in fact, for many applications this is a conservative estimate. Remember that an application consists of three things: an interface, business logic, and persistent data. Thus, if we don't consider database integration and the scalability and performance issues involved, we're tackling only two-thirds of the overall problem.

Nevertheless, there are times when tuning your database system may not be critical. Realize that modern commercial database systems are built for speed and scalability. In fact, if you buy a database, set it up, and stick a bunch of JDBC calls in your application code to access it, you may get decent performance. And, again, based on the nature of your application, that may be good enough.

Still, for most large and complex applications, database design and optimization are important. Part of the reason has to do with application-oriented demands.

For example, many large applications require the modeling of complex data relationships. If answering database queries frequently requires navigating those relationships, overall throughput can be dramatically affected by choices made as a result of the modeling. Complex applications also rely on the database to enforce business processes (such as business rules). In this sense, built-in database features such as stored procedures and triggers may be used more heavily than in a simpler application that merely requires a few JDBC simple queries.

Another example of where database optimization makes sense involves the latency caused by I/O during database query execution. Outside Internet-based communication between client and server, stalls during database I/O are likely the most wasteful activity in application execution. This is especially true for very large databases, where the database system cache is constantly in flux and the cost of scanning large tables is high. A key challenge when designing your database is to reduce this I/O as much as possible. This can mean tuning the cache, building efficient data structures (e.g., indexes) in the database, modeling your data more strategically, optimizing the placement of your data, or some combination thereof.

Still another, more system-oriented reason that database design and optimization can be important has to do with the database acting as a *logical point of centralization* in an otherwise distributed system. Many large Web applications have multiple clients, internal and external, both Web based and non-Web based. Even though highly scalable application servers, distributed over multiple server machines, may exist to process client requests, they might all be dependent on a common database to complete their processing. If this database is distributed replication must still guarantee data consistency. There is no way to avoid its cost. Distributed though your application logic might be, access to the underlying data generally must often be serialized. One trick in optimizing application performance and scalability is to realize that not all data needs to be centralized and that there are ways to reduce the time that access must be serialized.

One final system-oriented motivation for optimizing the database has to do with the waste/redundancy that can be associated with servicing multiple client interfaces. In general, the more interfaces to an application, the more likely redundant data retrievals. When different clients use these interfaces, they force the database to do something it has done before and that could have been reused.

Consider a site that sells products to registered users. In addition to pages that display the products and allow the user to order when desired, the site is likely to contain a set of account management pages that are used to make changes to user vital statistics (e.g., password, address, etc.). Even though these are very different from interfaces that access the database, they both deal with user information and—depending on the data model—they may need to read and update data in the same tables. So, even if the interfaces are connected to different Java servlets running on different machines, they're both going to direct their queries to the same logical database. This will often result in redundant data access and application logic.

We approach this chapter with all of these examples in mind. Regardless of the complexity of your data model or the underlying data you store, one thing is certain: If you're persisting data, it's in your best interest to consider optimizing the process. To accomplish this it's helpful to understand database technology as well as selective details of your particular system. Thus, we begin our journey of optimizing database integration by first considering effective database design and how the relational model works.

Database Technology and the Relational Model

Given that not everyone is a database engineer, it's worthwhile to review the important aspects of database systems. Discussions later in this book assume this knowledge, so let's make sure that we're comfortable with the concepts and terminology.

First of all, remember that database systems are commonly known as **database management systems (DBMS)**. This implies two things: that they do more than query data (they manage it) and that their implementation is like that of a "system." In fact, it's more like that of a distributed system: Most commercial databases are composed (at runtime) of a collection of processes and threads on one or more machines that work together efficiently to deliver high performance and scalability. For example, the Oracle 8i database architecture consists of *instances* that act as proxies to the data. In this case, the instance is the part of the DBMS that users and applications interact with—it's composed of a collection of processes (on UNIX) or threads (Windows) that manage the underlying data on disk.

Relational Databases

Over the years, many types of database have been designed and implemented for various purposes. The three most popular designs are the **hierarchical model**, the **network model**, and the **relational model**. While all three are based on the notion of data being stored as records, they differ in many ways, such as the redundancy of the data and how data is located during query processing. Our focus will be on relational databases, easily the most popular model for Web-based applications.

The relational model, first proposed by E. F. Codd in the early 1970s, has passed the test of time. It's based on the simple notion that although data can be classified into distinct entities (such as employees and departments), its underlying attributes are often related (employees work in a particular department). In particular, the relational model is distinguished by the following features:

- It's based on the creation and manipulation of relational data structures (**tables**), which are defined by a list of attributes (**columns**) and contain zero or more items of data (**tuples** or rows).
- It supports a flexible, declarative query and update language. This declarative nature implies that although queries may be specified in a higher-level language, they can be compiled (and potentially optimized) in a lower-level language for execution.
- It supports integrity **constraints**, such as those that ensure uniqueness within a relation and those that guarantee consistency across relations.

Earlier I said that we would be concerned with object/relational as well as relational databases. At some point, you'll have to choose whether to work with your database in terms of objects (not just at the application level but at the database level). Truth be told, while object orientation has become a well-publicized feature of many heretofore relational databases, not many people who use these systems embrace a 100 percent object strategy. Instead, it's probably safe to say that most enterprise deployments still work with the underlying relational tables of these databases while embracing an object-oriented point of view in one tier of the application system. For example, EJBs are object oriented, but they're most commonly integrated with relational databases.

Also, keep in mind that object/relational databases are not the same as object-oriented databases (OODBMS). Although there are many differences between an OODBMS and a relational database system (RBMS), most practical object/relational systems are relational at their core.

Logical Database Design

There are two phases of database design: logical and physical. Just as top-down design is important for standard programming practice, it's also important to start with a logical database design before moving on to the physical design. Throughout **logical database design**, an engineer is concerned with how application requirements map into database requirements. For example, if a business needs to keep track of employees and departments in its database, we need to develop a logical design that meets that goal.

A key process during logical database design is **data modeling**, or deciding how your application requirements translate into database structures, and then relating those structures. The resulting data model represents a set of relationships among tables via attributes, thus illustrating how your data will be logically organized. Surprisingly, even though the data model is a logical representation, choices made during the modeling phase have an impact on database performance. Thus, the data model for an application is not to be taken lightly.

Throughout this section and the next, we'll be demonstrating database concepts in the context of a simple sample database that stores information about both company employees and departments. For each employee, we want to store his or her name, date of hire, salary, and department. For each department, we want to store its name and location on the company campus (e.g., Building 5, Floor 6).

Let's start by attempting to translate these simple requirements into a real data model.

Entities, Attributes, and Relationships

Data modeling consists of defining entities and their attributes, and then relating those entities to each other. An **entity** corresponds to a logical concept or object and contains **attributes** that distinguish each instance. In the example at hand, it seems reasonable to have an EMPLOYEE entity and a DEPARTMENT entity. The attributes for the EMPLOYEE entity are NAME, HIRE_DATE, SALARY, and DEPT_NAME (shorthand for "department name"). The attributes for the DEPARTMENT entity are NAME, BUILDING, and FLOOR.

These two entities and their attributes are diagrammed in Figure 10–1.

One of our example's requirements is that an employee works for a department. More specifically, we'll suppose that every employee works in only one department and that each department has at least one employee. The way to write this model using standard entity-relationship (E-R) notation is shown in Figure 10–2, which we read as

- Each employee works in one department.
- Each department has one or more employees working in it.

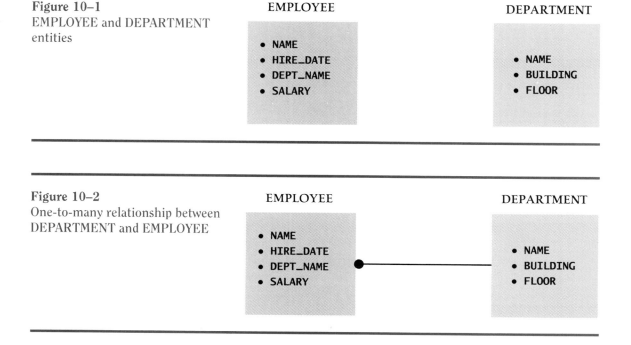

Figure 10–1
EMPLOYEE and DEPARTMENT entities

EMPLOYEE

- NAME
- HIRE_DATE
- DEPT_NAME
- SALARY

DEPARTMENT

- NAME
- BUILDING
- FLOOR

Figure 10–2
One-to-many relationship between DEPARTMENT and EMPLOYEE

EMPLOYEE

- NAME
- HIRE_DATE
- DEPT_NAME
- SALARY

DEPARTMENT

- NAME
- BUILDING
- FLOOR

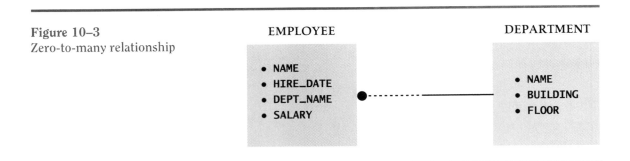

Figure 10–3
Zero-to-many relationship

If our example is changed to say that a department may have zero or more employees, our E-R modeling will contain notation to indicate this, as shown in Figure 10–3.

So, we've shown how our simple example can be modeled. The nature of the relationship between entities (one-to-many, zero-to-many, many-to-many) is also known as **cardinality**. There are some other symbols and paradigms of E-R modeling, but Figure 10–3 captures the basic spirit of phrasing data organization in terms of entities and relationships, the latter qualified by cardinality.

Now that we've briefly discussed how a database is logically designed, our focus shifts to how a database is physically designed. The logical/physical approach is a recurring theme in database systems. As it turns out, strategies at both levels can have a significant impact on database scalability and performance.

Physical Database Design

Once a logical design for the database has been completed, **physical database design** can begin. This phase is the process of turning a specification and its logical model into an implementation. For example, once we know that we need employee and department entities in our database, we can then choose to implement two tables physically. That sounds easy—of course entities correspond to tables! But there are more to databases than tables. Not all of the database requirements for an application can be captured by data modeling. For example, other types of objects, such as views and indexes, can be instrumental in simplifying access and encouraging efficient execution.

In this section, we'll review tables as well as several other key database objects that can help fill out a database specification and complement a good logical data model.

Tables and Rows

As you know, the physical equivalent to an entity is a *table* (formally called a *relation*). A table consists of a *name*, a list of *attributes*, and zero or more rows. For example, a table might be called EMPLOYEE and consist of the attributes NAME, HIRE_DATE, DEPT_NAME, and SALARY, and contain three rows.

Each attribute, such as NAME, corresponds to a specific datatype. Modern databases support a number of built-in datatypes (in addition to a method for extending them)—far too many to cover here. Generally speaking, however, these types can be categorized as character based, numeric (both integer and floating point, with adjustable levels of precision and scale), date based, and binary.

To make our discussion more practical, let's assume that the following two tables exist, filled with the data shown:

EMPLOYEE:

NAME (character)	HIRE_DATE (date)	DEPT_NAME (character)	SALARY (number)
Hannah Smith	12-Oct-1997	Research	46,000
Dan Dessens	6-Jun-1980	Research	71,500
Jill Arroyo	1-Apr-1992	Development	63,200

DEPARTMENT:

NAME (character)	BUILDING (number)	FLOOR (number)
Research	5	8
Development	6	2
Sales	1	2

Notice that each table consists of an unordered set of zero or more records, or **rows** (formally called tuples). Each row contains either a proper value for an attribute or NULL. The NULL designation doesn't mean that a value is zero or empty—it simply means that it's unknown and that no conclusions can be drawn from its existence. For example, suppose the employee table also has this row:

NAME	HIRE_DATE	DEPT_NAME	SALARY
Gary Jones	4-Aug-1989	NULL	NULL

The NULL value for Gary Jones's DEPT_NAME and SALARY doesn't mean that he doesn't work in a particular department or earn a salary. It just means that this information is not known. The fact that NULL doesn't imply anything about the data for that attribute is an important realization and can affect the way you query and populate a database.

Constraints

Constraints are used to implement integrity in the database. They are one of the distinguishing features of the relational model, and they also play a role in the data-modeling process. Generally speaking, there are three types of constraints supported by relational databases:

- *Entity integrity* ensures that all rows in an entity (a table) are unique. Recall that tables normally consist of an unordered set of rows. There's no guarantee that two rows won't contain the same values for each attribute, making them identical. However, this may not make sense semantically. Consider the EMPLOYEE table above: It's possible that two employees named Jill Arroyo are hired on the same day and issued the same salary. From the record-keeping point of view, it makes sense that there are two employees with duplicate values for name, salary, and hiring date. However, in real life it makes no sense—we know they're two distinct people. In relational databases, a **primary key** is the mechanism that implements entity integrity and distinguishes rows from each other.

- *Referential integrity* ensures that row values that refer to values in another table are consistent. This is necessary in order to obey real-world constraints, and it can be an important technique for reducing data duplication throughout the database. For example, if we have a table called EXECUTIVE, we might use the same names as in the EMPLOYEE tables. In this sense, NAME is the attribute that underlies the relationship between EMPLOYEE and EXECUTIVE. Rather than copy the name of each employee who is an executive into the EXECUTIVE table, we can simply point to that entry from the EXECUTIVE table. In addition to saving space, this has another important benefit: It forces us to deal with the case where an employee—who is also an executive—is deleted from the EMPLOYEE table. Either that operation should fail or the corresponding row in the EXECUTIVE table should also be deleted. In relational databases, a **foreign key** is used to implement referential integrity.

- *Semantic integrity* ensures that row values obey some other kind of semantic or application-level constraint. For example, it may make sense to prevent anyone from entering an employee salary that is below zero. This makes sense in the real world, but the database doesn't know what a "salary" is and would normally not force all salary entries to be zero or above. To enforce this property, we implement a semantic integrity constraint, which is also frequently referred to as a **check constraint**.

Querying a Database

Let's take a quick break to discuss how a database can be queried. In this section, we'll cover basic SQL as well as what's involved in single-table and multitable querying. This will not only make the next section easier to understand, but it will help categorize the queries that we'll refer to later.

Querying Data

Clients interact with DBMSs by issuing queries. To **query** means *to inquire*, so, it's no surprise that *queries* is the database term used to refer to the retrieval of data. However, when talking about databases, *query* also applies to the inserting, updating, and deleting of data as well as to the creation, alteration, and destruction of database objects (such as tables). To issue a query to a database means to express it in a **query language**. The standard relational query language, defined by ANSI and supported by all major database vendors, is **Structured Query Language** (**SQL**).

The SQL standard is long and complex, with recent versions specifying more advanced notions such as stored procedures. Unless otherwise specified, we'll be concerned with the SQL-92 standard and focus mostly on two categories of SQL statement: those that manage data structures (**database definition language**, or **DDL**) and those that manipulate data (**database manipulation language**, or **DML**). DDL and DML statements are by far the most common type of SQL, and so we'll focus our discussion on them.

The easiest way to distinguish DDL from DML is that the former always involves the creation, alteration, or destruction of database objects (including tables). In contrast, DML statements simply manipulate data in a table. Here's an example of a DDL query that creates a database table:

```
CREATE TABLE employee (
    name VARCHAR2(50),
    hire_date DATE,
    dept_name VARCHAR2(20),
    salary NUMBER);
```

DML statements insert and retrieve data. Here's an INSERT statement that inserts rows into a table:

```
INSERT INTO employee VALUES ('Hannah Smith', '12-Oct-1997', 12, 46000);
```

Retrieving this data can be accomplished through the SELECT statement:

```
SELECT name FROM employee;
```

It might return

```
NAME
-----------------------------------
Hannah Smith
Dan Dessens
Jill Arroyo
```

The basic DDL and DML commands and their purposes are summarized in Tables 10–1 and 10–2.

DML statements can be *conditional* in the sense that they filter data or are applied to some subset of data. Conditions are phrased using a simple Boolean logic

Table 10–1: DDL Commands

Command	*Purpose*
CREATE	Creates database objects such as tables, views, stored procedures, indexes, etc.
ALTER	Changes the structure or various properties of an object
DROP	Removes the object from the database

Table 10–2: Basic SQL DML Commands

Command	Purpose
SELECT	Retrieves rows from one or more tables
INSERT	Inserts rows into a table
UPDATE	Changes rows in a table
DELETE	Removes rows in a table

that enables complicated conjunctive or disjunctive expressions to be built using operators like AND, OR, and NOT. For example, if we want to retrieve only those employees hired before January 1993, we can write

```
SELECT name
  FROM employee
 WHERE hire_date < '01-Jan-1993';
```

Conditional queries can also be composed of nested Boolean logic, such as

```
SELECT name
  FROM employee
 WHERE hire_date < '01-Jan-1993'
    OR (salary > 50000 AND dept_name = 'Research');
```

As the preceding examples show, the WHERE clause in SELECT queries is used to filter data. It can also be used in DELETE and UPDATE statements. In all cases, the WHERE clause Boolean expression logic is built from relational operators (<, <=, >, >=, =, !=), some additional SQL-specific operators (such as IN and BETWEEN), and the Boolean logic operators AND, OR, and NOT.

Similar to the WHERE clause, the HAVING clause of a SQL SELECT statement can be used to filter groups of data identified via the GROUP BY part of a SQL query. However, to keep things simple in our discussion, we'll stick to examples that involve the WHERE clause.

Nested Queries

There are two special types of query we're interested in because of their impact on performance. One is the **nested query**. The general concept here is that a query might depend on conditions that are the result of another query. For example, if we want to find out which employees work in Building 5. We can issue the following nested query:

```
SELECT name
  FROM employee
 WHERE dept_name IN (SELECT name
                       FROM department
                      WHERE location = 'Building 5');
```

As you would expect, the nested part of the query (getting NAME from DEPART-MENT) is executed first. Then this result—in this example "Research"—is used in the parent query, which is executed (automatically) as

```
SELECT name
  FROM employees
 WHERE dept_name IN ('Research');
```

Join Queries

The other special query of interest to us is the **join query**. Whereas nested queries combine data in the sense that they dynamically build parent queries from the execution results of child queries, join queries combine related data from a series of static or dynamic tables. Combining tables is fundamental in working with a relational database. Entities in data models rarely exist in isolation—most of the time, they're associated with one or more other entities. For examples, employees work in departments, departments are associated with companies, and so forth. This linkage goes back to the nature of the relational model—the idea of normalization—and the desire to reduce redundancy in the database.

Let's look at an example of join queries. Consider a query that allows us to view employees and their respective department, building, and floor locations. What we want is some way to combine the EMPLOYEE and DEPARTMENT tables. Since the EMPLOYEE table has a foreign key called DEPT_NAME that points to the DEPART-MENT table attribute NAME, it seems possible to combine the data in a reasonable way.

In fact, we can see that what's required is to combine rows from EMPLOYEE with rows from DEPARTMENT where the DEPT_NAME attribute of EMPLOYEE (more succinctly written as EMPLOYEE.DEPT_NAME) is equal to the NAME attribute of DEPARTMENT (i.e., DEPARTMENT.NAME). This matching criterion is also known as the **join condition**. Generally speaking, the join condition is the logic of relating attributes in multiple relations to each other so that some meaningful combination of the relations can occur. In nearly all useful cases, the attributes involved in each join condition are linked via a foreign key—otherwise, there would be no meaningful reason to equate them.

Back to our example, we find that we can write our desired query using a join condition as follows:

```
SELECT employee.name, department.building, department.floor
  FROM employee, department
 WHERE employee.dept_name = department.name;
```

The result of executing this query is shown here:

NAME	BUILDING	FLOOR
Hannah Smith	5	8
Dan Dessens	5	8
Jill Arroyo	6	2

As I mentioned earlier, we can also write join queries that involve more than two tables and those that involve dynamically created tables. The latter is typically generated from a nested query, demonstrating that it's often useful to compose both join and nested queries.

For example, suppose another table in our schema, BUILDING, contains building numbers and addresses:

BUILDING_INFO:

BUILDING_NUM	STREET_ADDRESS
5	100 Main St.
6	105 Main St.

We can write the following query to find employee names, building addresses, and floors:

```
SELECT name, street_address, floor
  FROM building_info, (
    SELECT employee.name, department.building, department.floor
```

```
      FROM employee, department
    WHERE employee.dept_name = department.name )
 WHERE building_info.building_num = id;
```

which results in the following:

NAME	STREET_ADDRESS	FLOOR
Hannah Smith	100 Main St.	8
Dan Dessens	100 Main St.	8
Jill Arroyo	105 Main St.	2

Like nested queries, join queries have serious implications for performance. This makes sense—as we've already seen, joining tables requires reading data from multiple tables (and thus possibly very different parts of the disk) and then doing a lot of comparison and matching to determine which rows should be joined.

Other Important Database Objects

There's actually much more to physical database design than tables, rows, and constraints. However, it was necessary to discuss queries in some detail before we introduced other important database objects. I call them "important" because they can play a role in tuning an application for performance and scalability. We'll discuss the "how" part later. For now, let's review what these objects are.

Views

A **view** is a "pseudo-table" derived from a legal query. For example, consider the query

```
SELECT emp_name FROM employee;
```

which returns the following data:

```
Hannah Smith
Dan Dessens
Jill Arroyo
```

We can create a view EMPLOYEE_V for this query with the following SQL:

```
CREATE VIEW employee_v AS
  SELECT emp_name FROM employee;
```

We can then query this view as we would a table:

```
SELECT name FROM employee_v
```

Note that the following query will result in an error:

```
SELECT emp_name, hire_date FROM employee_v;
```

Since views are built from queries, they can represent combinations or subsets of data in one or more tables. More specifically, this means that they can be used in place of more complex queries that perform selections and/or joins. For example, it's possible to construct a view that shows a subset of data in the combination of the EMPLOYEE and DEPARTMENT tables:

```
CREATE VIEW research_and_dev_v AS
  SELECT emp_name, hire_date
    FROM employee e, department d
  WHERE e.dept_name = d.name
    AND d.name in ('Development', 'Research');
```

Views are useful because they *enable more access control options, simplify querying*, and *provide greater data modeling flexibility*. In terms of access control, database designers can associate security privileges with a view instead of associating them with a table.

Suppose we want only engineers and researchers to be able to query information about other engineers and researchers. We can grant read-only access to both groups on RESEARCH_AND_DEV_V. This limits access to information *vertically* (only engineers and researchers are visible from this view) and *horizontally* (salary information is not included). Thus, views allow you to seperate data modeling from access control, resulting in table designs that are more natural and access control that is more precise.

Views also simplify querying. If a query is complex to specify but required often by different users, you can create a view that makes querying the resulting data easy. For example, it's much easier to find each engineer's or researcher's name and location by issuing this:

```
SELECT emp_name, location
  FROM research_and_dev_v;
```

as compared to this:

```
SELECT e.emp_name, d.location
 FROM employee e, department d
 WHERE e.dept_name = d.name
   AND d.name in ('Development', 'Research');
```

Later, we'll discuss how query simplification encourages better performance and scalability in your applications.

Finally, views provide greater data modeling flexibility. By using views as an interface to table data, you can alter and reorganize your underlying data model as necessary without breaking any code that assumes an earlier version of the model. For example, we can alter our EMPLOYEE and DEPARTMENT tables whenever and however we want while retaining a consistent interface to data about researchers and developers via the RESEARCH_AND_DEV_V view.

Stored Procedures

Modern RDBMSs allow you to store and execute functions and procedures in the database. Since they often execute in the address space of the database process, they can be faster than querying the database from an external API. The ANSI SQL Persistent Stored Modules (PSM), or SQL/PSM, standard exists as a specification for stored procedure support. However, while some databases (such as IBM DB2 version 7) follow this specification, other vendors use their own proprietary language. For example, Oracle's Procedural Language (PL/SQL) is roughly consistent with the PSM standard with the addition of some features. The same is true with Sybase's Transact-SQL (T-SQL).

Confusing matters somewhat is the fact that all major database vendors support mechanisms that allow you to call/load external procedures during query processing. Although some vendors feel that such modules are best referred to as "external" and not "stored," not all agree. For example, IBM DB2 calls these external routines "stored procedures." In this book, we'll refer to all SQL/PSM-like languages as *stored procedures* because they're actually stored in the database. We'll refer to other functions or libraries that are loaded from the filesystem as external, mainly because they're stored in the filesystem, not the database.

To see what a stored procedure language actually looks like, consider Oracle's PL/SQL. Suppose that we want to use PL/SQL to write a procedure called ISSUE_BONUS that calculates the bonuses of employees in the EMPLOYEE table based on current salary multiplied with a "bonus percentage." If the salary is below some amount, the procedure issues a standard fixed bonus. In both cases, the bonus is inserted into another table (called BONUS_HIST) that keeps a record of bonus history for all employees.

Now, as may be obvious to you, we could meet our goal by writing a query (though it would be a bit bulky and obscure). For purposes of example, however, let's just consider what would be involved in implementing this functionality as a stored procedure. Without understanding much about the details of PL/SQL, we can survey some of its key features by looking at Listing 10–1.

Listing 10–1: A Stored Procedure for Calculating Employees' Bonuses

```
 1: PROCEDURE issue_bonus (a_emp_id NUMBER,
 2:                        a_bonus_pct NUMBER,
 3:                        a_min NUMBER,
 4:                        a_min_amt  NUMBER)
 5: IS
 6:   emp_sal NUMBER;
 7:   bonus NUMBER;
 8: BEGIN
 9:   SELECT salary INTO emp_sal FROM employee
10:     WHERE id = a_emp_id;
11:   IF ((emp_sal < a_min) OR (emp_sal IS NULL)) THEN
12:     bonus := a_min_amt;
13:   ELSE
14:     bonus := emp_sal * a_bonus_pct;
15:   END IF;
16:   INSERT INTO bonus_hist (emp_id, date_issued, amount)
17:       VALUES (a_emp_id, SYSDATE, bonus);
18: EXCEPTION
19:   WHEN NO_DATA_FOUND
20:   THEN
21:     DBMS_OUTPUT.put_line('Error');
22: END issue_bonus;
```

Here are the listing's high points:

- Line 1 shows that procedures can be named and accept input arguments (just like regular functions in other languages).
- Lines 9 and 16 show that it's very simple to issue SQL statements, and integrate their results with local variables (`emp_sal`, in this case).
- Lines 11 through 15 show that we can write conditional statements. In fact, languages like PL/SQL typically support standard control flow constructs like `IF..THEN..ELSE` and various looping constructs like `FOR` and `WHILE`.
- Lines 18 through 21 show that exception handling is supported.

The point here is not to teach you PL/SQL but to highlight a few key features of the language of stored procedures so that you can weigh your application design options carefully. Choosing where to write your business logic is a big decision. If you primarily write this logic in Java or C, you might be surprised to find that languages like PL/SQL contain many of the same features.

More important, if you never knew that databases supported such languages, you might have rushed into the decision that all business logic should be coded in EJBs. This isn't necessarily a bad choice, but it can result in suboptimal performance for some applications. In particular, database languages may end up suiting your performance needs better because they're tightly integrated with the database. Later, we'll discuss more details related to performance and productivity tradeoffs in choosing the language in which to write your business logic.

Triggers

Triggers are a way to automate tasks that are necessary whenever certain database events occur. They're the primary mechanism for event-driven execution in the database and thus make the database an active mechanism. When you create a trigger, you define the table and event it corresponds to and the body of code that should be executed upon that event. For example, you can use a trigger to specify that tables B and C will be updated whenever a row is inserted, updated, or deleted in table A. You can also enforce constraints that logically involve two or more attributes. Suppose we wanted to allow attribute A1 to be NULL only if attribute A2 equaled some value; a semantic constraint on either attribute wouldn't be possible. Instead, a trigger is necessary.

To see what triggers look like, let's return to our EMPLOYEE and DEPARTMENT example. Suppose our DEPARTMENT table had an additional column called NUM_EMPLOYEES that kept track of how many employees were in that department. Thus, our table should look like this one.

DEPARTMENT:

NAME (chararcter)	BUILDING (number)	FLOOR (number)	NUM_EMPLOYEES (number)
Research	5	8	8
Developement	6	2	15
Sales	1	2	10

It's important to keep this new attribute consistent with changes to the EMPLOYEE table. One way to do this is by writing a trigger. This means that we need to respond to any new or changed data (INSERTs or UPDATEs) related to the

EMPLOYEE table so that we can process the corresponding change to the DEPART-MENT table. In Oracle PL/SQL, we define a trigger very similarly to a stored procedure, as shown in Listing 10–2.

Listing 10–2: A Trigger That Maintains an Account of Department Employees

```
 1: CREATE OR REPLACE TRIGGER MONITOR_NUM_EMPLOYEES
 2:   BEFORE DELETE OR INSERT OR UPDATE ON EMPLOYEE
 3:   FOR EACH ROW
 4: BEGIN
 5:   IF (:old.dept_name != :new.dept_name) THEN
 6:     UPDATE DEPARTMENT SET NUM_EMPLOYEES=NUM_EMPLOYEES - 1
 7:       WHERE NAME=:old.dept_name;
 8:     UPDATE DEPARTMENT SET NUM_EMPLOYEES=NUM_EMPLOYEES + 1
 9:       WHERE NAME=:new.dept_name;
10:   END IF;
11: END;
```

Some things about this code are relevant to triggers in general:

- Line 1 shows that, like other database objects, triggers are named.
- Line 2 shows how you specify triggers with respect to the events that can occur. As you can see, triggers can be associated with various SQL statements that can be applied to a table.
- Line 3 shows that the trigger can be configured to fire for each row that is inserted, updated, or deleted. This is important in our example because each change to the EMPLOYEE table means that we have to increment or decrement in the DEPARTMENT table as appropriate.
- Line 5 shows that we have the ability to look at the previous (old) data as well as the to-be-committed (new) data before the commit on the EMPLOYEE table completes.

In short, triggers enable stored procedures to be executed automatically in an event-driven fashion. This style of reactive execution is *implicit* and distinct from the *explicit* style of executing stored procedures manually.

Indexes

Remember the way we used to find books? No, I'm not talking about earlier versions of Amazon.com. I'm talking about going to your local library, searching for the book, and then checking it out. To locate the book, you used a card catalog, which was convenient because it allowed you to search quickly for what you were looking for. Once you found it, the catalog entry pointed you to its location in the library.

In general, database indexes work just like the card catalog at the library. As data structures inside the database, indexes simply allow information to be looked up quickly. For example, suppose you have a table of employees that's a million rows long. If you want to search for an employee named Wally Westman, the only real choice is to scan the entire table. Although computers are faster than humans at doing this, the cost of such operations adds up—especially if other querying must be done or other users are waiting. For very large tables, this type of scanning represents a very noticeable delay.

However, if you create an index for your employee table based on the name attribute, you'll be able to search that table very quickly. Creating an index is simple. With Oracle, for example, you do it like this:

```
CREATE INDEX name_idx ON employee(name)
```

As the command shows, creating an index means denoting which attribute of which table you want indexed. The database then creates a new data structure that allows that attribute to be efficiently searched during execution. We'll see an example of how this affects query processing later in this chapter.

Creating an index doesn't mean that access to the entire EMPLOYEE table is faster. It just means that when employee names need to be searched, it can be done efficiently. Thus, an index doesn't help when we're locating employees by hire date— for example, those hired on January 10, 1999.

It's important to realize that creating and using an index means that this data structure must be stored. So, indexes do take up disk space and, in this sense, represent a space–performance tradeoff. Still, they're a useful feature of database systems because they're so easy to create and manage. Not only do they speed up explicit filtering operations (such as that specified by the user), but they speed up implicit filtering that occurs during the intermediate stages of query processing.

Sequences

Some databases, such as Oracle, support objects called **sequences**. When these objects are queried, they return a value based on their current value and a step value, which is defined during creation. It's probably easiest to look at an example of creating and using a sequence in order to understand it:

```
SQL> CREATE SEQUENCE order_seq START WITH 1 INCREMENT BY 1;
Sequence created.
```

```
SQL> SELECT order_seq.nextval FROM dual;

   NEXTVAL
----------
         1

SQL> SELECT order_seq.nextval FROM dual;

   NEXTVAL
----------
         2
```

Ignore the DUAL table for now—it's a detail here. The point is that we can create a database object that, given a start value and an increment setting, can be queried so that it produces the next logical value. Sequences are primarily useful because of the frequent need to generate values for columns in various tables that act as primary keys—especially when we don't care about the value of the key but just that it's unique.

Consider the ORDERS table, created like this:

```
CREATE TABLE orders (order_id NUMBER PRIMARY KEY,
                     customer_id NUMBER,
                     order_date DATE);
```

It can be populated by the following statement:

```
INSERT INTO orders VALUES (order_seq.nextval, 100, SYSDATE);
```

Thus, the value of sequences is that they allow application developers to obey entity integrity easily and safely. Note that you don't have to use them. An application-level sequence generator can return unique identifiers whenever it's queried by application-level clients. In fact, this may even be a necessary component, especially if your key isn't something as simple as an integer.

Other Objects

Many other kinds of object are common to database systems. For example, most database systems allow administrators to create and alter users, roles, privileges, and synonyms. However, unlike the objects I described in detail previously, these objects are much less likely (if ever) to play a role in improving performance or scalability. Thus, we will limit our discussion and exclude them here.

Query Processing

Although I've reviewed the basics of SQL, I haven't yet addressed how the database interprets SQL and how results are gathered. The overall process for resolving a SQL query is known as **query processing**. It's a topic that has been and continues to be a major focus of database research because of its impact on performance.

As I mentioned earlier, SQL is declarative. Although it provides a language for questions to be asked, it doesn't specify how those questions should be answered. There's no standard. Instead, each vendor has its own strategy. Understanding the details of query processing can provide you with great leverage in tuning database performance. In this section, I provide a simple overview along with an example to give you the basic idea. I want you to understand generally what query processing is and that there are strategies for improving it that you, as a database administrator, can implement.

Let's start at the beginning. When a query in the form of a SQL string is received by the database, there are three basic phases that must be completed in order for a corresponding answer to be generated:

- *Query parsing:* Syntax-checking of the string-based SQL query to ensure that it's legal SQL.

- *Query plan generation and optimization:* Conversion of the SQL string into an optimized query plan, which is represented as a "dataflow graph" of interconnected operators. This graph represents the low-level database operations to be performed. During this phase a query optimizer attempts to identify the most efficient plan to generate.

- *Plan execution:* Execution of the operators in the generated graph.

These phases are diagrammed in Figure 10–4.

I introduced a few terms in the preceding list, so let us take a moment to define them more. First, a **dataflow graph** is simply a graph that describes the flow of data between a set of operators. Each **operator** is a state machine that corresponds to a low-level data access method. That's all pretty abstract, so let's consider something more tangible.

Suppose we want to process a query that finds all employees hired before 1990. The SQL version of this query commonly results in a graph consisting of two operators: SCAN and SELECT. The SCAN operator reads data from a table. As it reads this data, it sends it downstream to the SELECT operator. SELECT filters data based on a condition, so it filters out those tuples where the hire_date is greater than or equal to

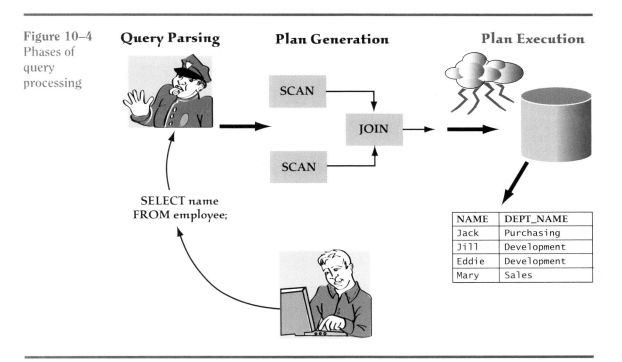

Figure 10–4
Phases of
query
processing

Jan-01-1990 and outputs the resulting stream to the user. The point of this example is simply to show how a simple SQL query maps into a graph of lower-level operators.

Query dataflow graphs are described as *partially ordered* in the sense that parallel flows, conceptually, can be executed concurrently. To understand parallel flows, let's consider a more complex example.

Here is a relatively simple join query that combines employee and department information for those employees not working in the Research department:

```
SELECT employee.name, employee.hire_date, department.name
  FROM employee, department
 WHERE employee.dept_name = department.name
   AND department.name <> 'Research';
```

Because we know the basics of join queries, we know that it's necessary to read data from both EMPLOYEE and DEPARTMENT and then combine them based on meeting two conditions: that the department IDs are the same and that the department is not Research. One possible abstract plan for this is shown in Figure 10–5.

Figure 10–5
Abstract query
plan
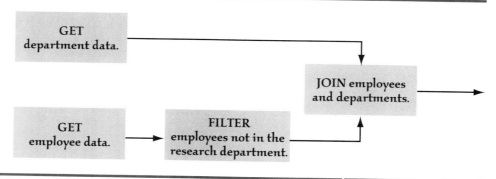

As the figure shows, the flow of data drives execution. For example, when the plan starts to execute, the only two operations that can execute are both GET operations. The other operations (FILTER and JOIN) are waiting for input before they can execute. After the GET of employee data finishes, the tuples containing employees working in the Research department can be filtered out. Finally, after receiving data from its respective tables, the JOIN operation can match employees and departments together based on the join condition. Again, the graph in Figure 10–5 is partially ordered in the sense that getting employee data and getting department data are independent operations and, conceptually, can be executed in parallel.

To illustrate better how this abstract example relates to an actual query plan, consider the real graph generated by the Oracle query optimizer:

```
Execution Plan
----------------------------------------------------------
   0      SELECT STATEMENT Optimizer=CHOOSE
   1    0   MERGE JOIN
   2    1     SORT (JOIN)
   3    2       TABLE ACCESS (FULL) OF 'DEPARTMENT'
   4    1     SORT (JOIN)
   5    4       TABLE ACCESS (FULL) OF 'EMPLOYEE'
```

This graph contains three columns:

- The first column indicates the index of the operator.
- The second column indicates which operator is the target of the current operator.
- The third column indicates the name and options of the chosen operator.

As Figure 10–6 shows, the plan results in a graph very similar to the one for our abstract plan. The only real differences between the two are that the Oracle query plan

Figure 10–6
Oracle query
plan dataflow
graph

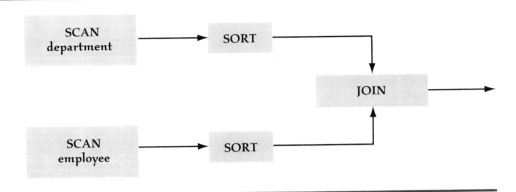

performs a sort prior to the JOIN, which is part of the query optimization phase, and that the additional filtering of non-Research employees is lumped into the JOIN phase.

The process of optimizing SQL queries involves analyzing these plans, determining where the bottlenecks are, and implementing solutions. For example, if both of these tables are extremely large, we can create an index on one of them to speed up the JOIN operation. In fact, this can even change the type of join used by the optimizer. For example, in Oracle, if we create an index on the DEPARTMENT ID column:

```
CREATE INDEX dep_idx ON department(id);
```

and then analyze the plan generated, we see that it consists of the following:

```
Execution Plan
-----------------------------------------------------------
   0        SELECT STATEMENT Optimizer=CHOOSE
   1    0     NESTED LOOPS
   2    1       TABLE ACCESS (FULL) OF 'EMPLOYEE'
   3    1       TABLE ACCESS (BY INDEX ROWID) OF 'DEPARTMENT'
   4    3         INDEX (RANGE SCAN) OF 'DEP_IDX' (NON-UNIQUE)
```

which corresponds to the graph in Figure 10–7.

Obviously, a few things have changed. Instead of performing a SORT on the full scan of both tables, the optimizer chooses to use the index DEP_IDX and changes its join strategy to use the nested loops algorithm. (The details of how a nested loop join differs from a hash join or a merge join is beyond the scope of this text.)

Figure 10–7
Query plan
using index

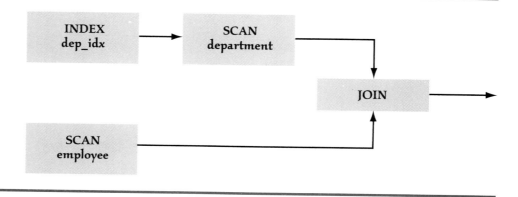

The point here is to demonstrate that the processing of SQL queries involves an important optimization phase that can be analyzed in detail to identify bottlenecks. Based on this analysis, you can find out which SQL queries are the most costly and why.

 Scalability and Performance Hints

We now look at various stategies for designing efficient databases. Note that none of these has to do with JDBC or SQL—we will get to that in Chapter 11. Instead, our present focus is on higher-level issues, such as effective data modeling and the use of stored procedures and triggers.

Understand How to Use the Database

As a software product, a database is complex. If you've ever installed something like Oracle or DB2, you know that there are many, many related subproducts and installation options from which to choose. Some of the subproducts are targeted at reporting or mobile data management. As for installation, one of the choices you may be given is whether to install parallel or cluster-based options. Understanding what these products and options do and how they can be useful can help make your overall system more efficient. For example, depending on the type of hardware configuration you have, installing cluster-related options may make no sense at all. In fact, you will have made your situation more complex by installing subproducts or choosing options that aren't relevant to your deployment. As I mentioned in earlier chapters, keeping your database system as simple as possible will make your optimization challenge much less difficult.

Most modern databases are called database management systems (DBMSs) because they're in fact distributed systems, consisting of a number of concurrently running processes or threads or various machines that work together in an efficient way to deliver fast and scalable data management. In tackling performance and scalability challenges, it's important to understand some of the system details and thus how the various parts work and the roles they play in transaction processing. For example, most databases have a data buffer cache to improve access times to data and functions in the database. Sizing the buffer cache can play a significant role in improving performance.

Finally, a database is very general. Obviously, its basic purpose is to store, manage, and enable access to data. This means that it can be used in various scenarios, for a myriad of purposes. For example, company A might want to store millions of images in a single database table. Company B might not need to store a million of anything in a single table but requires data to be littered among hundreds of related tables.

These two companies have different data models and likely very different needs in terms of query efficiency. In what ways can the database be tuned for the needs of each? What scenario does a particular database handle well by default? Database vendors don't know anything about your deployment. They target their software to the most common cases. Becoming competent at tuning the database to the needs of your application becomes increasingly important as your data management needs increase and performance and scalability concerns become a high priority.

Understand When to Use the Database

Some people consider any kind of application data a candidate for storage in a database. While this might seem like a reasonable default strategy, it may not turn out to be the most prudent choice for all cases in terms of performance or scalability. There are in fact many issues to consider when deciding which data belongs in the database. Keep in mind that, although generally fast and scalable, the database represents a point of centralization in your system. As with any resource in high demand, it's best to use it only when necessary. Again, you can make your optimization problem less complex by keeping your system simple.

Consider the following example. A mythical online art company wants to develop a Web application for selling reprints of famous paintings. It continually updates its inventories, adding new paintings that have reprints as well as removing paintings that no longer have reprints or that didn't sell well. At a minimum, it seems, the company needs to store customer, order, and inventory information. It plans to keep the JPEG thumbnail and high-resolution reprint images in the database as well. However, this last choice may turn out to be a mistake.

There's obvious benefit in storing customer, order, and inventory information in a database. Not only is this information **structured** (i.e., composed of well-known attribute types), but it's highly volatile from multiple interfaces (orders and customer data change constantly). Moreover, many types of query can be posed that combine this information in various ways (e.g., since June of 2001, how many customers have placed orders of $100 or more?).

In contrast, there's little benefit to storing images in the database, even if the database does support mechanisms to query or compare them. One reason—the reprints being sold change frequently, so it's not necessary to remove the JPEG images associated with them. In fact, this might cause more work later if the reprint is reissued and its JPEG image has to be regenerated. A better way might be to change the database so that the online catalog doesn't permit users to see or order such reprints. Another reason that storing the JPEG data in the database is unnecessary has to do with JPEG itself. An image is **unstructured**; it's just a collection of zeroes and ones that are meaningless without special software to decode and present it. The key information from an image (i.e., the objects in it) isn't easily identified automatically. Also, although our database might support operations that compare images efficiently, this is a totally useless feature for our needs. Instead, keyword search (which would be useful) can be done by simply associating the keyword data with the catalog information, not the JPEG data.

By now, we realize that storing images in the database for our online art company doesn't result in many (if any) *usability* benefits over, say, storing them in the filesystem. We can still locate images by storing metadata about and pointers to the JPEG files in the database. The performance benefits (or lack of them) are even more convincing. Since we don't relate the actual image data to anything else in the database, keeping this data there offers no theoretical performance improvement. In fact, the opposite is more likely, since structured database information will be competing with the image data for buffer cache and disk space.

Throughout this example, I've demonstrated that a database is appropriate for some kinds of data, but it's not necessarily the best solution for all data management—even if the data to be managed is dynamic. Here are some basic questions to ask when considering which data to put in the database:

- *Do I often combine this data with other data*? For example, product and customer data is typically intertwined: We often ask questions like "How many California customers ordered my red wine?" But some data (like JPEG images) is rarely (or never) combined with other data.

- *Will this data be updated*? If so, how frequently? Using what methods? If the data won't be updated, the database is simply providing fast access and the ability to query existing data. And if you won't be combining your data, then only fast access is being provided—can you provide more lightweight (but just as effective) functionality to achieve this?

- *What's the performance impact of turning over management of this data to the database*? Can you do a better job than the database of managing this data? Perhaps you're using the database to store all of your information, even some static information that never changes. Do you really require the transaction processing and other capabilities that databases provide to manage it? Would creating, say, a hardcoded data structure in your application logic reduce the demand your applications place on the database?

Understand How Your Data Will Be Accessed

There are many ways to access your data, but there are at least two issues related to access that we have yet to address:

- How will you manage data?
- What type of interface will you use for access?

Let's tackle these issues one at a time.

When thinking about how you'll manage your data, the key questions have to do with the manner and frequency of your SQL use. For example, your application may provide only read-only data and merely need to retrieve it from various tables, perform an occasional join, or access a prebuilt view. There may be no real business logic in such an application; for that reason, simply using SQL might be enough. In another situation, you might be building an application that will store credit card orders and likely involve transactions and security. Having credit card numbers or passwords communicated in cleartext could be an issue. Also, if much of your data is dynamic, you may be hitting the database quite a bit. As you can see, it depends on your scenario.

Some of the key things to identify when classifying how you will use your database are the following:

- Will you be reading and writing to your database? If you'll be writing, transactions will be necessary to guarantee serializability.
- Will most application actions involve database connectivity? Will you use the database only when orders are processed, or is the majority of your application driven from the database?
- Can you encode any of your business logic as a stored procedure?

In terms of interfacing to the database, you'll need to choose the API you'll use. Different APIs have different tradeoffs associated with them, and a lot depends on how your application is deployed. Certainly, if parts of your application are in C or C++, you'll need to choose whether you'll use ODBC, the native API of the database, or perhaps your own homegrown API (that wraps either ODBC or the native APIs).

We're concerned primarily with the choices you have in Java, which means using a Java Database Connectivity (JDBC) driver. As it turns out, more than one JDBC driver can be used for a database. In fact, different drivers are created for different purposes. For example, Oracle supports at least four JDBC drivers: a thin driver suitable for network-level access, an OCI (Oracle Call Interface) driver, and two types of server-side drivers (designed for integration with Enterprise JavaBeans and CORBA). All vendors may not have multiple JDBC drivers, but it's still worthwhile to do your research. It's likely that flexibility and/or resources will be traded for performance when multiple drivers exist.

The message here: Once again, do your homework. Understand your application before you make important development choices.

Normalize Your Data Model

Regardless of how we access data, it's always in our best interest to have it organized in a fashion that enables its access to be fast and scalable. It's probably obvious to you that physical layout matters—for example, optimizing how your disk accesses the underlying persistent bits of information is obviously a plus. However, it may surprise you that there's plenty that can be done at the logical level, for example, during data modeling. And that's where we'll start.

As you know (or can guess), there are many possibilities when it comes to designing the data model. In fact, the database will pretty much let you organize your tables however you want as long as you obey the constraints of your own design. Even so, there are rules for modeling your data. These rules are the so-called **normal forms** of data modeling. In 1972, Codd introduced three normal forms: first, second, and third (also known as the Boyce-Codd normal form). By obeying them, you ensure correctness as well as efficiency.

First Normal Form

A table is in **first normal form (1NF)** if it has no multivalued columns. In other words, for each row we want all column values to be atomic. It helps to visualize this through an example.

Suppose we extend the DEPARTMENT table to keep track of projects per department:

NAME (PK)	EMPLOYEES	LOCATION	PROJECTS
Research	25	Building 5	Kraft, Citibank
Development	85	Building 6	Kraft, NY Times
Sales	10	Building 1	Kraft, Citibank

This is a mistake. There are no rules to govern the order or format in which we list the projects, that is, there's no structure to the data for this attribute. Thus, it's quite possible that this design choice will lead to incorrect query results.

The way to fix this problem is to convert the table into 1NF, which means that we need to break up multivalued attributes like PROJECTS. Specifically, we should

- Promote the multivalued attribute into its own table; assign a primary key
- Alter the primary key of the original table to be a composite key that consists of the original key plus the attribute that corresponds to the key of the newly created table

We can accomplish the first task by creating a new table called PROJECTS that contains only the project name:

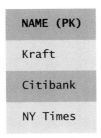

NAME (PK)
Kraft
Citibank
NY Times

Since each name is unique, we choose that as our primary key. Then we can change the DEPARTMENT table so that it contains a composite primary key made up of the original primary key (NAME) plus a foreign key (PROJECT), resulting in a new primary key (NAME, PROJECT):

DEPT_NAME (PK)	PROJECT (PK, FK)	BUILDING	FLOOR
Research	Kraft	A	1
Research	Citibank	A	1
Development	Kraft	C	2
Development	NY Times	C	2
Sales	Kraft	B	1
Sales	Citibank	B	1

You may have noticed that, while this technique is necessary for normalization, it actually leads to more data storage and so seems less efficient. This is true—for now. As we make other changes to the data model, you'll see that the opposite is actually the case!

Second Normal Form

A table is in **second normal form (2NF)** if it's in 1NF and every nonkey column is functionally dependent on the primary key. In plain terms, columns that contain values not related to primary key values should be moved to another table. Usually, these columns will seem more independent than other columns in a table. For example, suppose our PROJECT table is modified to contain the priority of a project and a description of that priority:

NAME (PK)	PRIORITY	PRIORITY_DESC
Kraft	2	High
Citibank	1	Urgent
NY Times	2	High
Clorox	2	High
USA Today	1	Urgent
Champion	2	High

Notice that, although both PRIORITY and PRIORITY_DESC are included in the same table, their dependencies are different. Priority is based on the name of the project (the primary key), whereas priority description depends on the priority.

To solve this problem, we can change our model to obey 2NF for this table. To do that, we need to

- Remove from a table any columns not dependent on the primary key of that table
- Create new tables as necessary, with primary keys based on formerly related values that remain in the original table

By applying 2NF to the PROJECT table, we come up with a new version:

NAME (PK)	PRIORITY
Kraft	2
Citibank	1
NY Times	2
Clorox	2
USA Today	1
Champion	2

as well as a new table called PRIORITY_LEVEL:

LEVEL (PK)	DESC
1	Urgent
2	High

In addition to simplifying our design, we've reduced our storage needs. The old PROJECT table required

6 (rows) x 3 (columns) = 18 value cells.

The new PROJECT and PRIORITY_LEVEL tables combine for

$$(6 \times 2) + (2 \times 2) = 12 + 4 = 16 \text{ cells.}$$

Again, although this seems like a small reduction, these numbers add up. For example, if 1,000 projects were evenly split in terms of priority (half urgent, half high), our original scheme would require 3,000 cells and our new scheme would require only 2,004—a savings of more than 33 percent. Converting to 2NF, then, is not only "more correct" because much of the redundancy of independent information has been eliminated, it also yields more efficient databases.

Third Normal Form

A table is in **third normal form (3NF)** if it's in 2NF and all of its nonkey columns are independent. This is a situation where a so-called **transitive dependency** can exist in the sense that the column values of one table are duplicated in another table (instead of the other table simply containing a key to the first table).

For example, suppose we have a table called LOCATION that contains a composite primary key (BUILDING, FLOOR).

BUILDING (PK)	FLOOR (PK)
A	1
B	1
C	2

Looking back at the DEPARTMENT table, we see that this information is needlessly duplicated. Building and floor are always mentioned together in DEPARTMENT, even though neither FLOOR nor BUILDING is functionally dependent on the primary key of DEPARTMENT.

We can make our design more efficient by converting the DEPARTMENT table to 3NF. To do so, we need to

- Update the "foreign key table" (LOCATION, in this case) to have a single-attribute primary key
- Replace the composite information in the "host table" (DEPARTMENT, in this case) with the proper foreign key values

Thus, we first change LOCATION as follows:

ID (PK)	BUILDING	FLOOR
1	A	1
2	B	1
3	C	2

and DEPARTMENT then becomes

DEPT_NAME (PK)	PROJECT (PK)	LOCATION_ID
Research	Kraft	1
Research	Citibank	1
Development	Kraft	3
Development	NY Times	3
Sales	Kraft	2
Sales	Citibank	2

Again, the amount of data we need to store is less (this time saving three cells), and it obviously improves as the tables get bigger. We've also made the data easier to manage. If a department changes to a different building and floor, we need to update only one row instead of many.

As we saw in the preceding examples, data normalization not only is space efficient (leading to better scalability of server-side resources such as disk), but it helps ensure the correctness and consistency of our data.

Selectively Denormalize Your Model

Now I'm going to criticize my own advice: Although data normalization is important because it ensures correctness and reduces storage demands, it turns out that it can affect performance adversely.

For example, with our new DEPARTMENT and LOCATION tables, if we want to find out what building and floor each department is on, we need to write a join query. Before, such a query merely required a scan of one table. Now, it has to scan two. The more scanning (especially dependent scanning), the worse our performance.

The general problem here is that normalization forces queries to become more complicated in the sense that they have to navigate through more intermediate data to get at the data of real interest. In turn, this can cause multiple queries, join queries, and/or nested queries where single-table queries were all that was previously required. In certain cases, it can be okay to denormalize the data model—to violate one of the forms of normalization—usually for the purpose of improving performance.

Denormalizing a data model typically involves techniques such as

- Replicating data "as is" by maintaining two copies
- Storing a calculation of remote data in a local table

Let's consider a more detailed example of the second technique. Suppose we have three tables, ORDERS, ORDER_ITEMS, and PRICE_HISTORY:

ORDERS

ORDER_ID	ORDER_DATE
1	1-Mar-2001
2	1-Mar-2001
3	1-Mar-2001

ORDER_ITEMS

ORDER_ID	PRODUCT_ID	QTY
1	544	3
2	2218	1
2	4782	2

PRICE_HISTORY

PRODUCT_ID	VALID_FROM	VALID_TO	PRICE
544	1-Jan-2001	1-Jun-2001	23.50
544	2-Jun-2001	1-Apr-2002	27.50

PRICE_HISTORY is necessary because it contains information on the price of a given product at any point in time. This type of normalization is common: To avoid replicating pricing information everywhere, it's consolidated in one table.

To calculate the total amount of an order, the following is required:

- Identifying all line items for that order, each of which indicates the product ID and the quantity of that product being ordered
- For each product ID ordered, using the ORDER_DATE from the ORDERS table to locate the price for that product at the time the order was made
- Summing these calculated prices

This is a lot of work just to calculate the price of an order. Every time a customer logs on to see information about her order, three tables have to be navigated. Thus, the data model itself has caused a problem that will affect performance and scalability.

One solution here is to denormalize the model by storing the calculated subtotal for every order in the ORDERS table. For example:

ORDER_ID	ORDER_DATE	SUBTOTAL
1	1-Mar-1999	70.50
2	1-Mar-1999	63.95
3	2-Mar-1999	35.00

Although this is a replication of data, it's a value-added replication in the sense that it's a calculation on data in other tables. The good news is that finding the order subtotal is much easier. The bad news is that any changes to that order will cause the SUBTOTAL column to be updated. However, this isn't that bad: Most orders are submitted and never changed. Only the few that are updated require a recalculation, so the overhead is minimal.

When discussing denormalization, it's good to weigh performance against the risks of replicating data. In terms of our priorities, there's no contest: It's obviously more important to be correct than fast. From a performance standpoint, however, we want to reduce this effect. For efficiency, it's generally acceptable to denormalize your model as necessary. Note the key phrase "as necessary." I strongly advise you to first normalize and then denormalize. This ensures that your model will be as space efficient as possible, with the exception of a few patches where you've traded space efficiency for performance.

Performance aside, there's no reason to denormalize, so we want to limit such changes. As with many other things we've discussed, simpler is better, so we'll denormalize only when we really must. Many designers denormalize their models after deployment, when working on a more optimized version of the server side of the application. It's sometimes very difficult to know what data should be located with other data until the applications are written and an initial deployment phase has occurred.

In summary, denormalization can be a performance-useful and even reasonable technique if it's done correctly. Here are some specific tips about denormalization, from a purely performance standpoint:

- Consider denormalization only if you're sure that application bottlenecks are being caused by excessive navigation of the data model at runtime.

- Where possible, *limit your denormalization to attributes that either don't change or change rarely*. Replicating frequently updated data can make maintenance a nightmare: You may spend more time replicating data (to manually enforce consistency) than you save by denormalizing in the first place.

- If simplicity and consistency of queries are the only concern, *consider creating views or stored procedures*. A view enables you to retain your normalized model but hide the complexity involved in locating data. A stored procedure does the same and has an added performance benefit. The only negative is that more development is required and the stored procedure is less portable (between databases).

- If you denormalize, *identify value-added denormalizations*, such as those where you can precompute something that would normally have to be computed at runtime. This is particularly useful when it comes to applications that mine or otherwise analyze old data. Without denormalization, each user who wants to analyze this data will force the computation (potentially very expensive) to be redone even though the underlying data hasn't changed.

Use Stored Procedures

Stored procedures are one of the most underrated methods for achieving high-performance Web applications. Used properly, they can dramatically increase performance, especially if the data model is large and the business logic is normally distributed among objects on multiple machines. They also make integration with the database simpler; requiring less code at the EJB or servlet level and hiding the complexities of the data model.

In terms of raw performance, step back and consider how servlets, EJBs, or other application objects typically use the database. For a given application action, they can execute one or more database queries Consider the ORDERS, ORDER_ITEMS, and PRICE_HISTORY tables in the previous section. Suppose we had denormalized our data model, as described, so that ORDERS had a new SUBTOTAL column. Now suppose that a new order item was appended to an existing order.

The application would have to do the following:

- Submit the new line item (INSERT into the ORDER_ITEMS table).
- Look up the ORDER_DATE for that order (SELECT from the ORDERS table).
- Calculate the price of the new item (SELECT from the PRICE_HISTORY table).
- Update the SUBTOTAL of the existing order (UPDATE the ORDERS table).

At least three queries are required. Incidentally, even if we hadn't denormalized, these same queries would likely be required because an end user would want to see this total calculated as part of the application response. Notice that these three queries need to execute in the order shown, independent of each other.

To process the queries, a servlet, EJB, or any other client would need to execute something similar to the kind of JDBC code contained in the function shown in Listing 10–3.

Listing 10–3: Appending an Order Using JDBC (Multiple Queries)

```
appendOrder():
  public void appendOrder() throws Exception
  {
    Connection conn = DriverManager.getConnection(...)

    /* Manually create our order data - for the sake of example */

    int orderId = 1;
    int productId = 544;
    int qty = 3;

    String orderDate;
```

```
      double lineItemPrice;
      double fetchedPrice;

      Statement stmt = conn.createStatement ();
      ResultSet rset;

      /* QUERY 1: Append order items */

      stmt.executeUpdate("INSERT INTO order_items (order_id, "+
        "product_id, qty) VALUES ("+orderId+", "+productId+", "+qty+")");


      /* QUERY 2: Fetch the order date */

      rset = stmt.executeQuery(
        "SELECT order_date FROM orders WHERE order_id = "+orderId);
      rset.next();

      String orderDate = rset.getString(1);


      /* QUERY 3: Fetch the prices so we can calculate the subtotal */

      rset = stmt.executeQuery(
        "SELECT price FROM price_history WHERE product_id = "+
        productId+" and '"+orderDate+
        "' BETWEEN valid_from AND valid_to");
      rset.next();

      fetchedPrice = rset.getDouble(1);
      lineItemPrice = qty * fetchedPrice;


      /* QUERY 4: Update the order */

      stmt.executeUpdate(
        "UPDATE orders SET subtotal = subtotal + "+lineItemPrice+
        " WHERE order_id = "+orderId);
  }
```

Contrast this with appendOrderStored() of Listing 10–4, which calls a stored procedure to do the same work.

Listing 10–4: Appending an Order Using JDBC (Stored Procedure)

```
      public void appendOrderStored() throws Exception
      {
        Connection conn = DriverManager.getConnection(...);
```

```
/* Manually create our order data - for the sake of example */

int orderId = 1;
int productId = 544;
int qty = 3;

CallableStatement cstmt = conn.prepareCall(
  "{ CALL appendOrder("+orderId+", "+productId+", "+qty+") } ");

cstmt.execute();
}
```

Here's the corresponding stored procedure, coded in Oracle PL/SQL as an example:

```
CREATE OR REPLACE PROCEDURE appendOrder(
  a_orderId IN NUMBER,
  a_itemId IN NUMBER,
  a_qty IN NUMBER)
IS
  item_price NUMBER;
  ord_date DATE;
BEGIN

  INSERT INTO order_items (order_id, product_id, qty)
    VALUES (a_orderId, a_itemId, a_qty);

  SELECT order_date
    INTO ord_date
    FROM orders
   WHERE order_id = a_orderId;

  SELECT price
    INTO item_price
    FROM price_history
  WHERE product_id = item_id
    AND ord_date BETWEEN valid_from AND valid_to;

  item_price := item_price * a_qty;

  UPDATE orders
     SET subtotal = subtotal + item_price
   WHERE order_id = a_orderId;

END;
```

Figure 10–8 compares these two approaches in terms of performance. To sim-plify things and take network latency out of the equation, both Java functions were

Figure 10–8
Appending 1,000 items to an order

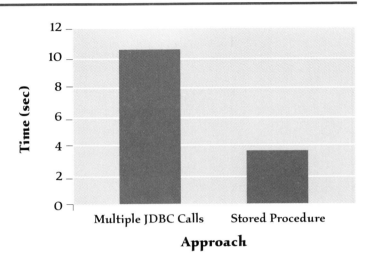

executed on the machine where the database was located, and both were executed 1,000 times to demonstrate the difference clearly. Note that performance would have been much worse if there had been network latency (i.e., client was not on the same machine as the database).

As the figure shows, coding several JDBCs is predictably slower than making a single call to a stored procedure. Specifically, the first approach averages about 10.4 seconds and the second approach averages about 3.6 seconds on the machines tested. Thus, the speedup achieved by using a stored procedures approach is 2.89—a significant improvement.

A few final notes about the stored procedure approach:

- No application-level transaction management is required.
- The code is smaller (even when combined with PL/SQL) and much cleaner, simplifying development. Also, consolidating the code in the database prevents code replication at the application level, which is very common in large projects,

Avoid Triggers and Other Implicit Execution

Triggers are an unquestionably important tool in any large database. They make complex data validation possible and enable designers to enforce elaborate constraints. Also, they're the only event-driven mechanism in the database, which allows designers to implement all kinds of "active" database features (e.g., automatic report generation).

However, triggers can also be the source of many a bottleneck. Since a trigger is executed when certain events occur, it's a reactive mechanism and implicitly executed. Generally, implicit execution is bad: Someone who is invoking that implicit execution may not know he's invoking it. The result: Queries start taking much longer than anticipated, for no apparent reason. The reason should be obvious. In addition to the time required by the explicitly requested operation itself, there's the time required for the implicit trigger execution.

Know Your Vendor

The database is the part of your server-side system that you're least likely to design or extend. Sure, you'll write your own application logic. You may even implement your own distributed application object system or EJB framework. And you might customize the Web server or servlet container to meet your deployment or performance/scalability needs. But the database is very often treated like a black box—data is shoved in and extracted – without much concern or appreciation for how it works or how to tune it.

All too often, it's assumed that integrating a database into your application requires only buying the product and adding JDBC calls to your code. The reality is, however, that such a simplistic approach won't cut it for large-scale Web applications. Your knowledge of the database and judicious use of design techniques to maximize your bang for the buck will play a significant role in improving overall application performance.

Summary

In this chapter, we briefly visited several basic yet important database concepts. We distinguished between logical and physical database design, keeping in mind that both influence how well the database performs and scales. We also surveyed several database objects, not just relational tables. Later, we'll see that understanding how to use these structures can be important during the deployment phase. Finally, we looked at query processing and how some of the database objects we described (such as indexes) play a role at runtime.

Although many engineers are familiar with building and querying databases, they're less familiar with the details of how databases work. This is like driving a race car and not understanding its engine. Instead of treating the database like a black box, it pays to understand what's going on inside and why. Such understanding is absolutely critical when pursuing overall high performance and scalability for your Web applications.

CHAPTER

11

Using JDBC and SQL to Query Databases Efficiently

As you already know, relational databases are at the heart of any serious Web application. And, as we saw in Chapter 10, databases are queried via SQL. The question then becomes, how can we use Java to send SQL to the database and then use it again to parse the results (if any) returned?

The answer, of course, is through the Java Database Connectivity (JDBC) API, a key part of any J2EE infrastructure.

How JDBC Fits In

JDBC offers two key features: *simplicity* and *database independence*. It's considered simple because, with only a few statements, a developer can programmatically query a database. He can easily combine his own local application data with a template for a SQL query and execute the resulting dynamic query. In terms of database independence, JDBC allows engineers to stop worrying about differences in vendor-specific database connection instructions. Instead, it puts the burden on database companies to produce JDBC drivers and build their proprietary connection management codes beneath a common Java API.

JDBC is arguably the most mature of the J2EE technologies we've discussed throughout this book. This is for two reasons. One, even before J2EE had any legs, JDBC was in demand and was used frequently by developers as a way for their Java applications to talk to relational databases. Two, JDBC owes a lot to the spirit and design of ODBC, the original standard API for querying a data source independent of vendor.

JDBC Concepts and Objects

When developers use JDBC, they construct SQL statements that can then be executed. These statements are dynamic in the sense that a template-like query string, such as

```
SELECT name FROM employee WHERE id = ?
```

can be combined with local data structures so that regular Java objects can be mapped to the bindings in the string (denoted ?). For example, a `java.lang.Integer` object with the value of 3 can be combined with the template to dynamically form

```
SELECT name FROM employee WHERE id = 3
```

The results of execution, if any, are contained in a set returned to the caller. For example, the query may return the following results:

```
NAME
------
Angela
Andrew
Anthony
```

We can browse this result set as necessary. This gives us the ability to, say, extract the first 10 rows* from a table—something that is normally nontrivial through SQL itself.

Relevant JDBC Objects and Their Relationships

The important JDBC objects to know include

- `Connection`, which represents a logical connection to a database.
- `DriverManager`, which handles the dirty work associated with setting up a generic JDBC connection for a given database. Database vendors provide their own drivers, and developers use a `DriverManager` to get a connection to a particular database through an available driver.

---

*By "first 10 rows," I just mean *the first 10 rows that happen to be returned*. I'm not implying that relations have any order. In fact, just as is the case with sets, they don't unless a SQL ORDER BY clause is used.

Figure 11–1   JDBC class hierarchy

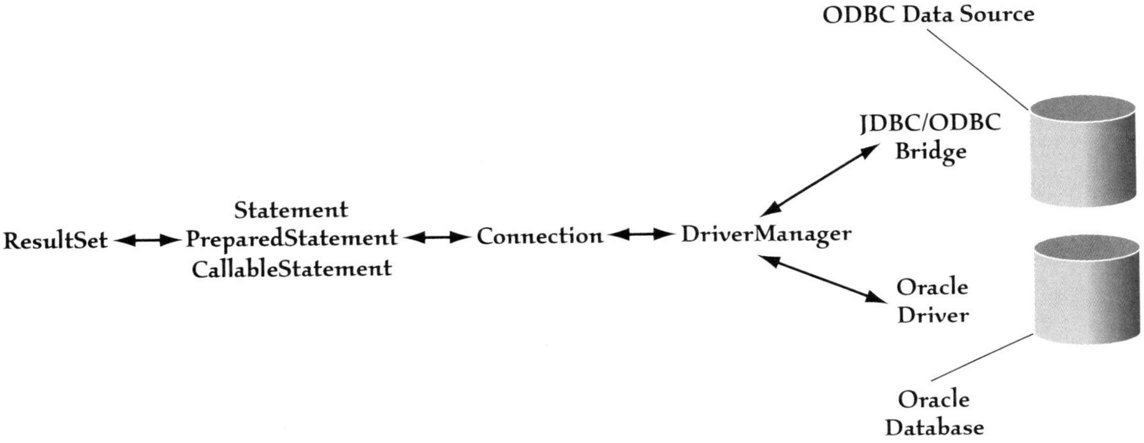

- `Statement`, which contains the SQL statement and bindings to it. Although database administrators frequently use the word *query* for any DDL or DML statement, JDBC and ODBC make a distinction between queries (reading data) and updates (changing data), and consider them both statements. `PreparedStatement` objects allow SQL statements to be compiled before execution. `CallableStatement` objects are used for accessing stored procedures.
- `ResultSet`, which contains the results of an executed statement, if any. A result set is conceptually equivalent to a cursor in stored procedure languages like Oracle's PL/SQL.

The relationship between these objects is shown in Figure 11–1.

Connecting to a Database

One of the slightly trickier parts of getting started with JDBC is making sure that you not only get the right driver but also understand how to reference it. As mentioned, vendors are responsible for providing the JDBC driver. Also, they typically provide a template for what's called the **database URL**, which, although similar in spirit, isn't the same thing as a regular HTTP URL in practice.

A JDBC database URL looks like this:

```
jdbc:odbc:MyDb
```

It's composed of two parts: the `jdbc:` prefix and a suffix that's dependent on the driver you're using. If you want to use the JDBC/ODBC bridge that Sun supplies with JDBC, the first part of this suffix is `odbc:` followed by the name of your ODBC data source. Thus, in the preceding example the database URL refers to connecting to an ODBC data source called `MyDb`.

If you don't use the JDBC/ODBC bridge and instead use, say, the Oracle 8i "thin" JDBC driver, your database URL might look something like

```
jdbc:oracle:thin:@MyOracleDb
```

The suffix is therefore very specific to a given database system, so you should check with your vendor to see how to construct this part of the database URL.

You can establish a connection to the database by instantiating the driver and then using the URL to make a connection. An example is

```
Class.forName("oracle.jdbc.driver.OracleDriver");
Connection conn = DriverManager.getConnection(
  "jdbc:oracle:thin:@MyOracleDb", "scott", "tiger");
```

Notice that getting a connection requires that we also supply the username and password for that database (`"scott"` and `"tiger"`, respectively). Once we have a connection to a database, we can begin executing SQL queries and processing their results.

Writing JDBC Queries

Building and executing JDBC queries is straightforward. The general process is to construct a Java `Statement` object (either statically or dynamically), execute it, and then iterate through the query results.

These are the only aspects of building queries that require a bit of thought:

- Choosing the right kind of statement to construct
- Distinguishing retrievals of data from updates to data

We'll see more detail about both of these issues shortly.

Processing a Statement

To construct a JDBC statement, we simply need to obtain a `Statement` object from a `Connection` object and then execute that statement using a valid SQL query. Say we want to query the first and last names of all employees in our database. For the sake of example, suppose our table contains the following data:

ID	FIRST_NAME	LAST_NAME	HIRE_DATE	SALARY	MGR_ID
1	Jane	Lippert	01-JAN-00	66100	1
2	Allen	Fez	05-MAR-97	62000	1
3	Bill	Cartwright	29-JUN-00	68000	1
4	Les	Thomas	11-JUN-95	56000	2
5	Julia	Grayson	10-OCT-81	56300	1
6	Kendra	Smith	11-JAN-83	59000	2
7	Diane	Lu	08-OCT-86	43000	1
8	Elmer	Bittner	04-APR-98	32500	1
9	Jason	Chen	22-MAY-94	30000	1
10	Eddie	Greenwald	03-APR-99	26000	1
11	Cora	Roberts	23-DEC-92	19300	5

The following code shows how to get the first and last names of these employees:

```
Class.forName("oracle.jdbc.driver.OracleDriver");

Connection conn = DriverManager.getConnection(
  "jdbc:oracle:thin:@MyOracleDb", "scott", "tiger");

Statement stmt = conn.createStatement ();

ResultSet rset = stmt.executeQuery(
  "SELECT first_name, last_name FROM employee");
```

Incidentally, notice that Statement.executeQuery() is called—later we will see that updates require a different API call. Also notice that the SQL is specified at the same time that we request query execution. This is different from the

PreparedStatement and CallableStatement approaches, where the SQL must be declared up front, when the statement is created. Later we'll look at more examples that distinguish the two cases.

Iterating through Results

The preceding code shows that, once the query executes, results are returned. Iterating through the results, like querying, is very straightforward:

```
while (rset.next())
  System.out.println("NAME = "+
    rset.getString(1)+" "+rset.getString(2));
```

This produces the following predictable set of results:

```
NAME = Jane Lippert
NAME = Allen Fez
NAME = Bill Cartwright
NAME = Les Thomas
NAME = Julia Grayson
NAME = Kendra Smith
NAME = Diane Lu
NAME = Elmer Bittner
NAME = Jason Chen
NAME = Eddie Greenwald
NAME = Cora Roberts
```

There are two things to note:

- Results are indexed by position (based on the SQL that generated them), and the first position starts at 1.
- The ResultSet object allows us to force a cast on data as we see fit. This just means that we need to be careful and cognizant of the underlying table design. If we were to call something like ResultSet.getInt(1) instead of ResultSet.getString(1), we might get undesirable conversions.

So far, so good; as you can see, JDBC enables queries to be made simply and intuitively.

In addition to using the ResultSet object to get the individual row/column values returned, we can use it to get the metadata associated with the results. This metadata, contained in an object called `ResultSetMetadata`, consists of information such as how many columns exist and what their types are. Examining the metadata associated with a result is very useful when the SQL is dynamic, when we execute "star" SELECT queries, or when we simply don't know the underlying DDL that created the table.

Suppose we want to query all columns of the EMPLOYEE table. I haven't provided information on any of the columns besides FIRST_NAME and LAST_NAME, so it's necessary to use the `ResultSetMetadata` object and find out information about the columns returned. Listing 11–1 shows one way to do this.

Listing 11–1: Browsing JDBC Queries

```
Statement stmt = conn.createStatement();
ResultSet rset = stmt.executeQuery(
  "SELECT * FROM employee");

System.out.println("Employee table fields:");
System.out.println("-------------------------------------------");

ResultSetMetaData meta = rset.getMetaData();
int numCols = meta.getColumnCount();

String buf = "";
for (int i=1; i<=numCols; i++)
  buf += (i>1 ? ", " : "") + meta.getColumnName(i);

System.out.println(buf);

System.out.println("\nEmployee data:");
System.out.println("-------------------------------------------");

while (rset.next()) {

  buf = "";

  for (int i=1; i<=numCols; i++) {

    buf += i>1 ? ", " : "";

    /* Handle some of the types, treat the rest as strings */
    if (meta.getColumnType(i)==Types.NUMERIC)
       buf += rset.getInt(i);
    else if (meta.getColumnType(i)==Types.VARCHAR)
       buf += rset.getString(i);
    else if (meta.getColumnType(i)==Types.TIMESTAMP)
       buf += rset.getDate(i);
```

```
    else
        buf += rset.getString(i);
}

    System.out.println(buf);
}
```

This code yields the following results for our sample database:

```
Employee table fields:
-------------------------------------------
ID, FIRST_NAME, LAST_NAME, HIRE_DATE, SALARY, MGR_ID


Employee data:
-------------------------------------------
 1. Jane, Lippert, 2000-01-01, 66100, 1
 2. Allen, Fez, 1997-03-05, 62000, 1
 3. Bill, Cartwright, 2000-06-29, 68000, 1
 4. Les, Thomas, 1995-06-11, 56000, 2
 5. Julia, Grayson, 1981-10-10, 56300, 1
 6. Kendra, Smith, 1983-01-11, 59000, 2
 7. Diane, Lu, 1986-10-08, 43000, 1
 8. Elmer, Bittner, 1998-04-04, 32500, 1
 9. Jason, Chen, 1994-05-22, 30000, 1
10. Eddie, Greenwald, 1999-04-03, 26000, 1
11. Cora, Roberts, 1992-12-23, 19300, 5
```

Executing Single Updates

Of course, you'll be doing more than simply retrieving data from the database. You'll be updating it, inserting new rows, perhaps creating temporary tables, and the like. JDBC makes a distinction between querying and updating, so you'll need to do the right thing or an exception will be returned. To process updates, callers must use the executeUpdate() method on Statement objects.

For example, suppose we want to give all of our employees a 10 percent raise. We can accomplish this via the following code:

```
Statement stmt = conn.createStatement ();
stmt.executeUpdate("UPDATE employee SET salary = 1.10*salary");
```

Notice that executeUpdate() returns no results. This makes sense. Our SQL is updating the database, not retrieving information from it.

Other Kinds of Updates: Creating Tables and Stored Procedures

Creating stored procedures or tables is also considered an update. For example, if we want to create a stored procedure that pretty-prints the first and last names of our employee table, we can do so via

```
Statement stmt = conn.createStatement ();

try {
  stmt.executeUpdate("DROP TABLE nice_names");
}
catch (SQLException sqlEx) {
  /* Ignore - table might have never existed */
}
catch (Exception otherEx) {
    System.err.println("ERROR: "+otherEx.getMessage());
    System.exit(1);
}


stmt.executeUpdate("CREATE OR REPLACE FUNCTION "+
  "pretty_print_names(a_first IN VARCHAR2, a_last IN VARCHAR2) "+
  "RETURN VARCHAR2 AS BEGIN RETURN a_last || ', ' || a_first;
  END;");

stmt.executeUpdate("CREATE TABLE nice_names AS ("+
  "SELECT pretty_print_names(first_name, last_name)
                             name FROM employee)");

ResultSet rset = stmt.executeQuery("SELECT * FROM nice_names");

while (rset.next())
  System.out.println(rset.getString(1));
```

This code does the following:

- Drops a table called NICE_NAMES (assumes it exists, recovers if not)
- Creates (or replaces) a stored procedure that pretty-prints first and last names
- Re-creates the NICE_NAMES table based on a query to the original EMPLOYEE table that uses the new stored procedure
- Prints out all of the data in the new table

The result from running this code, in addition to the new table and the new or replaced stored procedure, is the following output:

```
Lippert, Jane
Fez, Allen
Cartwright, Bill
Thomas, Les
Grayson, Julia
Smith, Kendra
Lu, Diane
Bittner, Elmer
Chen, Jason
Greenwald, Eddie
Roberts, Cora
```

Beyond the Basics

Thus far, we've discussed what is minimally required to query databases via JDBC. However, there are a number of additional JDBC techniques that can have a significant impact on performance and scalability. In this section, we'll discuss each of these advanced methods.

Prepared Statements

Recall from our discussion of database concepts that query processing generally boils down to three phases: query parsing and syntactic checking, query plan generation, and plan execution. The first phase can seem unnecessarily costly, especially if we repeatedly execute the same query (or the same kind of query). We know that the SQL is correct and we hope that the database caches previous parsed queries, but we can't be sure. Database vendors like Oracle do in fact cache SQL statements so that reparsing a query seen earlier occurs as minimally as possible.

Still, the cache that database systems have is full of other objects, and there are competing justifications on what to cache and what not to cache. The bottom line: As a developer, you can't guarantee that this sort of optimization always, let alone ever, happens. Once again, the problem centers around implicit versus explicit control. In many prior discussions, we favored an explicit approach where possible, and this case is no different. Rather than rely on the implicit caching done by our database system, we want to somehow cache parsed queries so that a preparsed form can be presented to the database. Then we can be sure that SQL parsing of a repetitively issued query is kept to a minimum.

JDBC lets us do just that with a `PreparedStatement` object. Unlike the regular `Statement` object, a `PreparedStatement` is compiled ahead of time (i.e.,

precompiled) and can be executed as many times as needed. Contrast that with
the normal JDBC Statement object which, as we've seen, sends a SQL string to
the database each time for parsing.

To use a PreparedStatement, the code we showed needs to be modified so that
the query is specified before the call to executeQuery():

```
PreparedStatement prepStmt =
  conn.prepareStatement("SELECT first_name, last_name FROM
  employee");

ResultSet rset = prepStmt.executeQuery();
```

This might seem like a subtle change, but consider how this type of query can be executed 1,000 times:

```
PreparedStatement prepStmt =
  conn.prepareStatement("SELECT first_name FROM employee");

ResultSet rset;

for (int i=0; i<1000; i++) {

  rset = prepStmt.executeQuery();

  /* ...Do something with results... */

}
```

Now compare that to the old way:

```
Statement stmt = conn.createStatement();

ResultSet rset;

for (int i=0; i<1000; i++) {

  rset = stmt.executeQuery("SELECT first_name FROM employee");

  /* ...Do something with results... */

}
```

Instead of parsing the SQL 1,000 times, as we do in the preceding code, the code
before that parsed it only once.

Dynamic SQL

Admittedly, the last example was unrealistic—how often is a static SQL statement repetitively executed? A more realistic case is that the *same kind* of SQL statement is processed over and over again. By "same kind," I am referring to multiple queries that have a common template. Consider how you might execute five SELECT statements that, although distinct, look very much alike:

```
SELECT * FROM employee WHERE id = 3;
SELECT * FROM employee WHERE id = 7;
SELECT * FROM employee WHERE id = 11;
SELECT * FROM employee WHERE id = 15;
SELECT * FROM employee WHERE id = 21;
```

Repetitively executing such statements is a more realistic example, especially for Web applications that serve hundreds of thousands of users. Imagine a Web page that allows you to see employee information at the click of a button. When you select an employee to view and click Submit, the browser sends a request to the server for that information. Correspondingly, a servlet or EJB located somewhere on the server side, given an employee ID, retrieves employee information and returns it to the end user. During the process, it uses JBDC to execute a SQL query that looks like

```
SELECT * FROM employee WHERE id = ?
```

Here, the ? represents a wildcard token or, more precisely, a value binding to be made later. Since we'll always be executing the same kind of query but binding different values to the ? token, it will be very useful if we can precompile the template and then change the bindings as requests arrive. Per request, then, the only work that needs to be done is to bind the incoming value to the SQL statement and execute the corresponding query. No recompilation of the query is necessary.

This is exactly what PreparedStatement objects allow us to do. The following code shows how to iteratively query employees with IDs that range from 1 to 5.

```
PreparedStatement prepStmt =
  conn.prepareStatement("SELECT first_name, last_name FROM
                          employee "+
    "WHERE id = ?");

for (int i=1; i<5; i++) {

  prepStmt.setInt(1, i);
  ResultSet rset = prepStmt.executeQuery();
```

```
    while (rset.next ())
      System.out.println (rset.getString(1)+" "+rset.getString(2));
  }
```

Notice that, similar to the way `getInt()` is used with an index when browsing a result set, `setInt()` is used to identify the value for a binding at a particular index. If we use `PreparedStatement` in the way just shown, the result is more efficient querying.

Of course, in the servlet/EJB example we probably want to precompile the SQL statement upon initialization and cache the resulting `PreparedStatement`. Then we can reuse that object upon request but with different request-dependent values bound to it.

Transaction Management

So far, we haven't talked about transactions at all, yet they're one of the key features of any database system.

The basic idea of transaction processing is to allow end users to execute a series of operations as a single logical unit. Thus, if you want ensure safety during the transfer of funds from one account to another (e.g., at the same bank), your transaction conceptually must consist of the following operations:

```
START_TRANSACTION;

withdraw(from_account, amount);
deposit(to_account, amount);

COMMIT_TRANSACTION;
```

Use of the word *commit* here indicates confirmation of the validity of the transaction. It means that we've executed all of the individual operations that comprise the transaction and now we want to verify that no significant error occurred in the process.

If an error occurs, we usually want to *roll back* the transaction as a means of canceling it. More precisely, a rollback is a way of undoing all of the individual operations in a transaction. As an example, to protect ourselves against an error during a money transfer (e.g., if a `to_account` doesn't exist), we can write something along the lines of

```
START_TRANSACTION;

TRY {
   withdraw(from_account, amount);
   deposit(to_account, amount);
```

```
    COMMIT_TRANSACTION;
}
CATCH (EXCEPTION e) {
    ROLLBACK_TRANSACTION;
}
```

Realize that updates to data are the only operations where a transaction rollback has an effect. It doesn't matter if we roll back a data retrieval because no side effects occurred as a result. Also, most databases don't allow you to roll back any DDL processing, such as when tables are created, just DML statements.

By default, JDBC commits each update to data when you call `executeUpdate()`. For example, the following code results in three transaction commits:

```
stmt.executeUpdate("UPDATE employee set salary =
               1.10*salary WHERE id=1");
stmt.executeUpdate("UPDATE employee set salary =
               1.10*salary WHERE    id=5");
stmt.executeUpdate("UPDATE employee set salary =
               1.10*salary WHERE    id=6");
```

Committing after each `executeUpdate()` can be suboptimal in terms of performance. It can also be downright dangerous if you're performing a series of operations that should logically be bundled in a single transaction, such as the account transfer example mentioned earlier.

To change the default transaction-processing style, developers simply need to set an attribute of the connection:

```
Class.forName("oracle.jdbc.driver.OracleDriver");

Connection conn = DriverManager.getConnection(
  "jdbc:oracle:thin:@MyOracleDb", "scott", "tiger");

/* Do not commit each update immediately */
conn.setAutoCommit(false);
```

Once we have the connection set properly, we can go about the business of creating and managing transactions. Suppose we want to accomplish something like the balance transfer we described. To transfer $100 from savings (account 101) to checking (account 102), the following JDBC code will do the trick:

```
conn.setAutoCommit(false);

Statement stmt = conn.createStatement ();
```

```
stmt.executeUpdate("UPDATE ACCOUNTS SET bal=bal-100 WHERE id=101");
stmt.executeUpdate("UPDATE ACCOUNTS SET bal=bal+100 WHERE id=102");

conn.commit();
```

Notice that it's not necessary to start a transaction explicitly; we actually do that implicitly by the call to `Connection.setAutoCommit()`. However, we do need to commit a transaction with the `Connection.commit()` call. And, if we want to write safer code, we can include a rollback, as shown in the following code:

```
conn.setAutoCommit(false);

Statement stmt = conn.createStatement ();

try {
  stmt.executeUpdate("UPDATE ACCOUNTS SET bal=bal-100
                      WHERE id=101");
  stmt.executeUpdate("UPDATE ACCOUNTS SET bal=bal+100
                      WHERE id=102");
  conn.commit();
}
catch (Exception e) {
  conn.rollback();
}
```

Note that nested transactions are currently unsupported by JDBC.

Bidirectional Results Iteration

JDBC 2.0 has some new features related to result management. First, with the new API results can be scrolled bidirectionally. Instead of iterating over a set of results from start to finish, it's possible to jump around the results set, effectively navigating back and forth within the cursor.

For example, the new API allows us to retrieve a set of results, immediately go past the last result using the `ResultsSet.afterLast()` method, and iterate backward using the `ResultSet.previous()` method, as shown here:

```
Statement stmt = conn.createStatement(
    ResultSet.TYPE_SCROLL_SENSITIVE, ResultSet.CONCUR_READ_ONLY);

ResultSet rset = stmt.executeQuery("SELECT first_name FROM
                                    employee");
```

```
rset.afterLast();

while (rset.previous())
  System.out.println(rset.getString(1));
```

Notice that to work with this kind of a result set—called a scrollable result set—we need to feed some extra parameters to the `Connection.createStatement()` call made earlier. With this code, we get the same results but in reverse order:

```
Cora
Eddie
Jason
Elmer
Diane
Kendra
Julia
Les
Bill
Allen
Jane
```

Updateable Results

Another new feature of the JDBC 2.0 API is the ability to update a results set. The idea is simple: With the `ResultsSet` object that you get back from a query, you can update, delete, or insert rows into the corresponding table.

For example, if we want to change the name of Cora Roberts to Nora Roberts, we do the following:

```
ResultSet rset = stmt.executeQuery("SELECT first_name FROM
                                    employee");

rset.last();
rset.updateString("FIRST_NAME", "Nora");
rset.updateRow();
```

The idea is to update the data via calls like `updateString()` (operations on any native type are permitted by the `ResultsSet` API) and then call `updateRow()`. If we navigate through the results set further before we call `updateRow()`, our change will be lost.

Executing Batch Updates

Even though JDBC transactions allow us to enforce an all-or-nothing style of execution when we update data, each `executeUpdate()` can result in a call to the database.

As we saw in previous chapters, this can lead to very inefficient execution, particularly if the database is remote and substantial network latency exists. Still, there are many times when batch updates are relevant.

Consider a B2B application that integrates two applications through a messaging-based design. One application periodically shovels new product orders to the second application so that they can be added to the company-wide database. If the first application sends 1,000 orders, this normally requires 1,000 `executeUpdate()` calls.

In JDBC 2.0, however, there's a simple solution for this problem: the JDBC batch updates feature. The concept is simple:

- Create a statement.
- Batch the statements as necessary.
- Perform a single `executeBatch()`.

Here's an example of how to process orders in batch:

```
/* Customer orders - local data structure */
CustOrder[] custOrder = ...

Statement stmt = conn.createStatement();

for (int i=0; i<custOrder.length; i++)
  stmt.addBatch("INSERT INTO CUST_ORDER (id, order_date)" +
    "VALUES("+custOrder[i].getId()+
    ", "+custOrder[i].getOrderDate());

int[] batchResults = stmt.executeBatch();
```

Scalability and Performance Hints

Our survey of advanced JDBC techniques has already given us an idea of some of the scalability and performance strategies we can employ. In this section, I review the most important ones and suggest some additional strategies for improving efficiency and throughput.

Use PreparedStatement When Possible

Not surprisingly, precompiling statements can make a big difference in performance. To quantify this a bit, consider how it improves querying 1,000 rows as well as updating 10,000 rows. As I described earlier, a given servlet or EJB instance on a busy site may do this tens of thousands of times over the course of a week.

As for performance with respect to querying, try running the following code, which queries a single employee 10,000 times using both approaches:

```
ResultSet rset;

/* Using a Statement */

long elapsed = System.currentTimeMillis();
Statement stmt = conn.createStatement();
for (int i=0; i<10000; i++)
  rset = stmt.executeQuery(
    "SELECT first_name, last_name FROM employee WHERE id=1");
elapsed = System.currentTimeMillis() - elapsed;

System.out.println("Statement approach took "+elapsed+" ms");


/* Using a PreparedStatement */

elapsed = System.currentTimeMillis();
PreparedStatement prepStmt = conn.prepareStatement(
  "SELECT first_name, last_name FROM employee WHERE id=1");
for (int i=0; i<10000; i++)
  rset = prepStmt.executeQuery();
elapsed = System.currentTimeMillis() - elapsed;

System.out.println("PreparedStatement approach took
                    "+elapsed+" ms");
```

Here are the results:

```
Statement approach took 17275 ms
PreparedStatement approach took 7881 ms
```

Thus, the overhead required for parsing a SQL statement leads to performance that is more than twice as slow as when a PreparedStatement approach is used. Specifically, the speedup with PreparedStatement is

$$17,275 / 7,881 = 2.19.$$

Now, that was a simple query. Suppose we replace the SQL with something more complex to parse, such as

```
SELECT e.first_name, e.last_name, os.num, st.name
  FROM employee e, session_type st,
```

```
        (SELECT employee_id, count(*) num, type_id
            FROM order_session
        GROUP BY employee_id, type_id) os
WHERE e.id = os.employee_id
  AND os.type_id = st.id
  AND e.id = 1
```

The results turn out to be

```
Statement approach took 99954 ms
PreparedStatement approach took 87856 ms
```

What happened? The speedup has been whittled down to a mere 1.14. Why is PreparedStatement not as effective here? The answer is that the bulk of the time isn't spent in query parsing but in execution. The preceding query joins three tables and performs a nested query in addition to a grouping. It reminds us that query parsing is indeed only one of three phases involved in query processing.

```java
/* Using a Statement */

long elapsed = System.currentTimeMillis();
Statement stmt = conn.createStatement();
for (int i=0; i<10000; i++)
  stmt.executeUpdate("INSERT INTO my_numbers
                      VALUES ("+i+")");
elapsed = System.currentTimeMillis() - elapsed;

System.out.println("Statement approach took
                    "+elapsed+" ms");


/* Using a PreparedStatement */

elapsed = System.currentTimeMillis();
PreparedStatement prepStmt = conn.prepareStatement(
  "INSERT INTO my_numbers VALUES (?)");
for (int i=0; i<10000; i++) {
  prepStmt.setInt(1, i);
  prepStmt.executeUpdate();
}
elapsed = System.currentTimeMillis() - elapsed;

System.out.println("PreparedStatement approach took
                    "+elapsed+" ms");
```

Figure 11–2
Comparison of
query types and
approaches

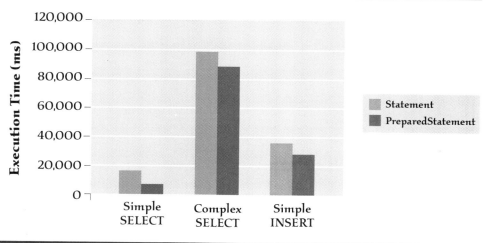

The preceding code results in

```
Statement approach took 36263 ms
PreparedStatement approach took 27930 ms
```

Thus, the speedup is 1.30. We see again that the act of inserting data itself is expensive and dwarfs the impact of using precompiled queries. We can visualize these comparisons better when all three tests are graphed, as in Figure 11–2.

Use Batch Updates with a Remote Database

Like prepared statements, batch updates can result in more efficient SQL execution. However, the added value of batch updates comes from the decreased network latency and fewer roundtrips between client and server.

Hypothetically, we need to insert 10,000 rows in a remote database. As we saw from the earlier test, the time to execute one INSERT using a PreparedStatement is

$$29,730 \text{ ms} / 10,000 = 2.97 \text{ ms per INSERT}.$$

Suppose, however, that our database wasn't local and instead required an average roundtrip time of 50 ms (which is pretty quick, by the way). Then, instead of a 30-second total insert, we would require

$$(2.97 + 50) \cdot 10,000 = 529,700 \text{ ms} = \text{about } 8.83 \text{ minutes!}$$

Contrast that with a batch update approach, which would require the same database processing but only one network roundtrip:

$$(2.97 \cdot 10{,}000) + 50 = 29{,}780 \text{ ms.}$$

Obviously this is almost indistinguishable from the performance with a local DBMS.

One caveat with batch updates is that without that network latency, they can actually be slower than `PreparedStatement` calls. The reason is obvious: With a batched `Statement`, the query isn't precompiled. Therefore, the resulting execution time with zero network latency is on par with the execution time for a normal `Statement.executeUpdate()` call.

Don't Overcommit

Filed under the heading of "don't use it if you don't need it" is the concept of making all commits explicit. As we discussed, the `executeUpdate()` call does an implicit commit for each call unless a `Connection.setAutoCommit(false)` is made. Does committing every update affect performance? You bet it does.

Consider a variation on the `INSERT` code we saw earlier. In this case, two types of `PreparedStatement` bulk inserts are done (see Listing 11–2). The first test implicitly commits after each `executeUpdate()`; the second test turns off the auto-commit feature and commits the transaction only after the final insert.

Listing 11–2: Impact of COMMIT on Performance

```
long elapsed;

/* Using a PreparedStatement */

elapsed = System.currentTimeMillis();
PreparedStatement prepStmt = conn.prepareStatement(
  "INSERT INTO my_numbers VALUES (?)");
for (int i=0; i<10000; i++) {
  prepStmt.setInt(1, i);
  prepStmt.executeUpdate();
}
elapsed = System.currentTimeMillis() - elapsed;

System.out.println("Always-commit approach took "+elapsed+" ms");

conn.setAutoCommit(false);

elapsed = System.currentTimeMillis();
prepStmt = conn.prepareStatement(
```

```
    "INSERT INTO my_numbers VALUES (?)");
for (int i=0; i<10000; i++) {
  prepStmt.setInt(1, i);
  prepStmt.executeUpdate();
}
elapsed = System.currentTimeMillis() - elapsed;

conn.commit();
System.out.println("Single-commit approach took "+elapsed+" ms");
```

Here are the results:

```
Always-commit approach took 28761 ms
Single-commit approach took 9905 ms
```

Once again, we see that explicit control is preferable. Sure, it means more code, but is the payoff worth it? In this case, it is: a speedup of 2.9.

Not only is it more efficient to explicitly commit a transaction, but it may often be the safest thing to do. For example, if you're inserting 1,000 rows of customer credit card activity into your database, do you want some of the inserts to succeed if others fail? Most likely not. When you perform a single logical task, such as "updating client account activity" or "processing all phone-based orders for today," it's more natural to process it as a single transaction—all or nothing. Anything in between isn't really meaningful—in fact, it's often worse that not inserting at all!

Use Multithreading to Query in Parallel

Keep in mind that querying a database is an I/O-bound process, especially if the database is remote. If you have to execute several independent queries it's sometimes not very efficient to do them one after another. Instead, it's wiser to make use of idle CPU cycles that are available and have these queries execute in parallel. The easiest way to do this in Java is by using multiple threads.

Let's return to our hypothetical example of a remote database with 50 ms of network roundtrip time. Those 50 ms are lost on the client machine unless concurrent computation is going to be performed. Similarly, the database server machine is idle from the time it replies until the time the next query arrives. But by using multiple threads, you can request both in parallel and decrease the overall execution time for the two statements by up to half.*

Once again we're trading simplicity and flexibility for performance. There will be more code and more time spent creating it, but as a result our throughput may be

---

* Speedup of 2 in this case is the maximum per Amdahl's law.

much better. Which is more important? I can't say; it's something each application designer should to take into account when building a Web application, or any application at all.

Summary

In this chapter, we looked at the basic and the not-so-basic strategies for querying a database using JDBC. As described, JDBC allows you to use some simple classes and methods to perform all of the basic types of queries you'll need to do. However, by understanding some of the more advanced features of JDBC, such as connection pooling and the ability to precompile SQL statements, you'll be able to write high-performance queries.

One of the challenges of JDBC, and SQL in particular, is simplicity. Complex data models can often demand multiline, cryptic queries that are incomprehensible to all but the person who wrote the code. Instead, try to identify those queries and make use of views and stored procedures as necessary, so that the SQL written is minimal and optimized. On a large development project, with many engineers trying to query a common database, there's the problem of consistency among SQL queries that have the same purpose. Midway through the project, people realize that everyone has his or her own way of navigating to a common piece of data. So the SQL being executed is not only complex but inconsistent across the group. Changes to the data model, which are inevitable, threaten to unleash chaos. The solution is to identify query needs and make it easy and intuitive for engineers to get at the data they want.

Web Services: The Future of Web Applications

Throughout this book, our discussion has remained focused on technologies for building high-performance, scalable Web applications. However, most of these technologies and concepts have assumed an interactive-client/single-server model of application use. In the back of our minds, we've been envisioning how an application at a *single site* can be made fast and able to accommodate Internet-size growth in a reasonable way. Also, with the exception of messaging technology, we've assumed that the main beneficiary of our efforts will be the *human end user*, not another application.

But the Internet is changing. What started as a wonder of connectivity experienced visually is quickly evolving into a high-speed *autobahn* of "service endpoints" and sensor data producers that stream raw data instead of embedding it in visual metadata (i.e., HTML). Also, the consumers of these information streams are no longer just people; they're now applications as well. This is the future envisioned by true B2B processing.

Whether B2B companies will survive these rocky economic times is open for debate. In fashion or not, one thing is for sure: The automated production and consumption of Web data via Internet protocols such as HTTP is here to stay. Within this movement, some key trends are beginning to emerge:

- *The need for self-describing data*: The Internet has been full of data for some time and it's growing by leaps and bounds even as you read this. However, what's missing is metadata and structure—Web data isn't typed, labeled, or related.
- *The publication of remote Web functions* calls for the ability to call functions in a remote Web application, much as RMI allows you to access functions in

remote Java applications. This essentially means extending the distributed object model of system building to the Web, but in a nonproprietary manner.

- *Abstraction and integration of distributed Web functionality* consists of repackaging and reusing more fine-grained functionality, which might exist at multiple remote locations, and collapsing it into one remote abstract function.

Web services technology has become the moniker for this movement. This term refers to the collection of standards and technologies that enables Web applications to be stitched together in a more flexible and powerful way than previously attempted. Specifically, the goal of Web services technology is to allow Internet applications to be queried programmatically, thus enabling application data access to be as easy as making a function call. From the consumer's standpoint, Web services exist as a set of remote objects that can be located and queried in a platform-independent manner, via HTTP. From the provider's standpoint, Web services enable the application to be queried easily by other programs and agents. A key advantage of Web services is the separation between interface and implementation. Providers can continue to implement and deploy their applications however they like—they just need to follow some additional integration steps for parts of their application that they want to make available as a Web service.

It's a lot like one big distributed object system, except that the technology used for deploying the objects at any one site is flexible. One company can deploy its objects via CORBA; another can deploy its objects as EJBs—it doesn't matter. Once they publish these objects as Web services, remote clients can access them without worrying about how they're implemented and deployed on the server side. The end result will allow new applications to seamlessly and dynamically combine functionality from all over the Web, turning the Web into a truly practical, service-oriented distributed system.

Practical Use of Web Services

Thus far, I've given you a set of abstract reasons why Web services are an attractive idea. But unless you've designed many Web applications or struggled with application integration issues, these reasons may not strike a chord. Let me provide a more practical motivation.

At various points in the different projects, you may have found yourself wanting to incorporate data from another Web site directly into your Web application. Assuming there are no ethical problems (i.e., you're not stealing someone else's copyrighted content), the process is pretty simple. It doesn't take more than a few lines of Java in your EJB or servlet to download a remote Web page and repackage selected parts of it for distribution to your clients. This process of downloading and data extraction is known colloquially as "screen scraping." It allows you to use another Web site as if it were a remote database.

The problem with screen scraping is that although it is easy programmatically to download HTML from a remote Web site, it is not easy to pluck out the embedded nuggets of useful information. That is, it is difficult to reliably separate substance (the data you want) from style (the rest of the HTML). In addition, this process also suffers from the fact that the data you pluck isn't typed (i.e., identified as date, number, or character) or self-describing. In short, it's unstructured. You have to classify each piece of data manually and decide how it should be extracted from the accompanying HTML.

What most people really want is to be able to make a function call on the remote site that gives them the data they want. Unlike the unreliable and messy process of screen scraping, calling a remote function is simple and allows the resulting data to be returned in a structured and typed form. Thus, for the consumer, life is good.

Such potential is also attractive to providers (i.e., owners of the Web applications being scraped). A provider who is in partnership or has an information-sharing agreement with another organization may have a keen interest in making sure that its Web data is programmatically accessible. In addition, having remote clients call functions instead of screen scraping enables providers to focus on returning only what is requested. Instead of what may be a costly process of dynamically generating beautiful HTML (that will never be seen by the automated client), a provider's server can focus only on what is needed—delivering the underlying data in demand.

What Exactly Is a Web Service?

The definition I provided earlier for *Web services* essentially describes the technology swirl that surrounds them. However, I haven't really explained what a single Web service is or how it's implemented.

At its core, a single **Web service** is a *remote component containing functionality that can be invoked using Internet protocols*, most notably HTTP. The data communicated to and from it is contained in self-describing XML documents. The functionality of a given service can be implemented in any language (Java, C++, C+, Visual Basic) with any object deployment technology. The only requirement is that it be accessible via Internet protocols such as HTTP. The client doesn't have to worry about how the service is implemented.

Thus, we can think of a Web service as functionality accessible to the client that is

- *Language neutral*: The language used to implement the client does not have to match the language used to implement the service.
- *Platform neutral*: HTTP is the great platform equalizer.

- *Object-technology neutral*: The client doesn't know or care how the object is deployed or managed.

Because access to Web services is accomplished via Internet protocols such as HTTP, a Web service automatically benefits from the following:

- *Firewall and proxy compliance*: One of the ongoing problems with integrating applications over the Internet is that the network infrastructure between two or more companies prevents the use of proprietary protocols and network ports in remote object invocation and thus application integration. Specifically, firewalls and proxies tend to get in the way because many are designed to ensure that only port 80 (HTTP) traffic passes through their membranes. Having services accessible via HTTP affords these services that same entry and doesn't require upgrading of your network hardware.
- *Automatic HTTP authentication*: Since this feature is part of the HTTP protocol, any HTTP-based communication can benefit from it.
- *Encrypted communication via SSL*: The combination of SSL and HTTP is a proven solution for secure transmission of data across the Internet; as deployed over Internet protocols, Web services get this option free.
- *HTTP 1.1 persistent connections*: This is an automatic performance enhancement to HTTP-based communication that is part of the protocol and requires nothing of Web service providers or consumers.

As a component technology, Web services enjoy the benefits of

- *Loose coupling*: There's no need for the client to be tightly integrated with the server or its component technology. Communication is simple, founded on XML-style messaging over a network.
- *Programmatic access*: Right now, it's possible to use Web browsers to execute remote functions, such as checking weather temperatures, stock prices, and loan rates. However, we normally access this information visually. It's difficult, if not impossible, to write code that programmatically accesses that functionality—in particular, the data returned (i.e., an HTML Web page) must be reliably parsed and the embedded data manually typed. However, intelligent agents and other

computer programs want an easy way to access remote functionality programmatically, and Web services provide that.

Nearly all the features suggested by the points just listed are summarized in Figure 12–1, which shows how a remote function that generates price quotes can be remotely accessed. More specifically, clients both human and automated can invoke remote object functionality via Internet protocols such as HTTP, making requests and receiving responses. All they need to know is where the functionality they want is located. Communication of input and output is accomplished in a platform-independent manner (SOAP) and its content is encoded using a self-describing markup language (XML).

Figure 12–1   Web service features

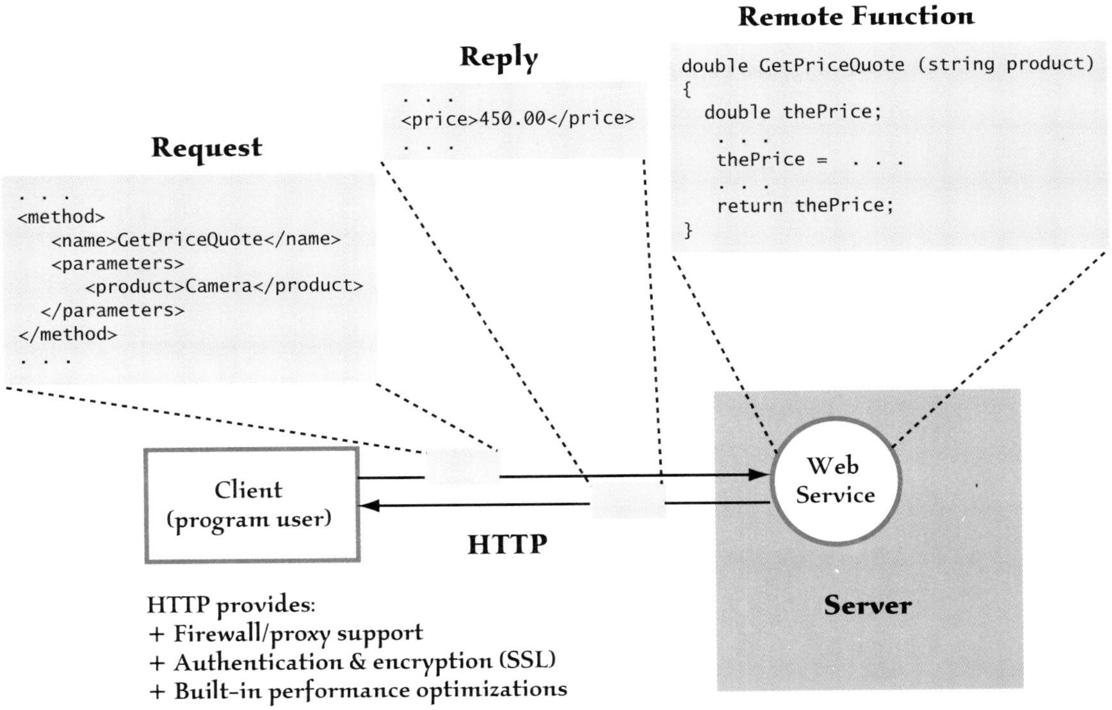

Reply

```
. . .
<price>450.00</price>
. . .
```

Remote Function

```
double GetPriceQuote (string product)
{
   double thePrice;
   . . .
   thePrice = . . .
   . . .
   return thePrice;
}
```

Request

```
. . .
<method>
   <name>GetPriceQuote</name>
   <parameters>
      <product>Camera</product>
   </parameters>
</method>
. . .
```

Client (program user)

HTTP

Web Service

Server

HTTP provides:
+ Firewall/proxy support
+ Authentication & encryption (SSL)
+ Built-in performance optimizations

Now that we have a rough idea of what a Web service is and how it's accessed, let's survey some of the technologies that are essential to its publication and use.

Web Services Technologies

Web services technology isn't being pushed by any one company. Instead it's a common vision communicated by participants from a number of companies—from rivals like Microsoft and Sun to relative unknowns like UserLand and young upstarts like Ariba. This vision has been translated into a set of continually evolving standards, much like the evolving standard of HTML. Standardization is coordinated by the World Wide Web Consortium (W3C). However, those actually implementing Web service technologies based on W3C standards vary from very small open-source groups to very large corporations.

A Quick Tour

The purpose of this section is to survey the Web services landscape. Specifically, a brief definition of the individual technologies is provided so that you can see what they're all about and how they fit together. In the following sections, I provide more detail about each technology.

XML

The Extensible Markup Language (XML) happens to be the de facto language of Web service technology. However, it also has the more general purpose, within the confines of Internet technology, of simply *making data portable*. Like HTML, XML is a markup language that has its roots in SGML; thus, it's a specification for "tagging" documents in a meaningful way. Unlike HTML, which provides only a means for visualizing data, XML allows data to be self-describing and structured and so is meant primarily for the interchange of data, not for its visualization (although that's supported too). XML is human legible (i.e., it looks very similar to HTML and can be read by anyone) and is the language by which Web service requests are issued and corresponding responses are delivered.

SOAP

The Simple Object Access Protocol (SOAP) describes how to invoke a Web service and process its response. It's thus very similar to distributed object technologies, such as CORBA and EJB, but consists of a text-based protocol, which makes it an interoperability abstraction above them. With SOAP, communication between caller and callee involves an exchange of SOAP envelopes, which contain XML-based parameters of the request, how to process it, and rules for how to transform data within the envelope. XML-based SOAP can be transported via HTTP and RPC.

WSDL

The Web Services Description Language (WSDL) describes a Web service. Thus, it functions similarly to IDL in CORBA or an interface in Java in that it represents a declaration (or guarantee) of functionality that is unrelated to its implementation. WSDL is generally considered a more flexible approach to the IDL or Java style of publishing interfaces because it adds a layer of indirection that gives designers more options when it comes to implementation.

UDDI

The Universal Description, Discovery, and Integration (UDDI) effort facilitates the registration and lookup of Web services. More specifically, it makes it easy for providers to publish available functionality and for consumers/users to locate remote functionality. Thus, UDDI operates somewhat like a registry or a name server for a distributed object system—it eliminates the need for clients to worry about where a service is and instead provides yellow-page-like lookup services. In conjunction with other technologies, it extends the traditional notion of a name server by including metadata about each service, thus encouraging the "discovery" of services.

Putting It All Together

The so-called Web services "technology stack" is shown in Figure 12–2. As you can see, each part of the stack has a different role. HTTP and other transport mechanisms allow data to be communicated. SOAP is a platform-independent means for the invocation of a remote service. WSDL provides for the flexible declaration of services. Finally, UDDI allows services to be registered and looked up.

Figure 12–2
The Web services technology stack

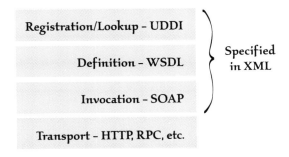

Figure 12–3
Using Web
services
technologies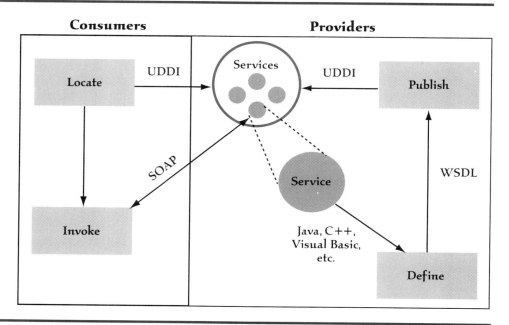

Figure 12–3 represents another way to understand the Web services, this time in terms of each technology's purpose and the interaction of the different parts of the technology stack. As the figure shows, providers first code their service using languages such as Java, C++, and Visual Basic. Then they define interfaces to these services using WSDL. Once defined, the service can be published via UDDI APIs.

Consumers first locate or discover a service that they want via UDDI. They can then interact with that service directly by sending SOAP requests, which are answered by SOAP replies. Not shown in the figure is the language in which each technology is accomplished: As we've already discussed, that language is XML.

XML: Self-Describing Data

The Extensible Markup Language is a flexible language that allows data to be self-describing. It's a subset of the Standard Generalized Markup Language, as is HTML. XML is distinct from SGML in that it's a simple solution for enabling data to be typed and visually represented. SGML is a more general (but complicated) meta-language for marking up documents in a device-independent and system-independent way. XML is also distinct from HTML in that it's extensible and its focus is on the *structural* representation of data. In contrast, HTML has a limited tag set and focuses on the *visual* representation of data.

Listing 12–1 shows a sample XML document. It contains information about a set of old arcade-style video games for sale, including data about available models and current prices.

Listing 12–1: A Sample XML Document

```
<?xml version="1.0"?>
<gamelist>
        <game>
                <name>Gorf</name>
                <model>stand-up</model>
                <price>500.50</price>
        </game>
        <game>
                <name>Galaga</name>
                <model>cocktail</model>
                <price>1199.99</price>
        </game>
</gamelist>
```

From this example, we notice the following:

- *Structure*: For example, the name, model, and price are child elements of the game element.
- *Extensibility*: The tags aren't part of a standard set—they correspond to our own application schema.

Listing 12–1 is considered well formed because it meets the formatting requirements of the XML standard. However, it's unclear if it's valid. To ensure validity, we need to check that the tags and their relationships are legal within the relevant schema. For that, we need another kind of document—a DTD.

DTDs and Schema Languages

Like SGML, an XML document is typically associated with another document, called a **schema definition**. The general purpose of a schema definition is to ensure validity of the documents that reference them, in terms of allowable entities (descriptors of data) and the relationships between them. The **Document Type Description (DTD)** is the most popular schema language used to generate schema definitions.

Listing 12–2 contains an example of a DTD that *describes* each element in the earlier XML document on arcade games (Listing 12–1). Specifically, this DTD introduces each element, types each element, and relates elements to each other.

Listing 12–2: A Sample DTD

```
<!ELEMENT gamelist (game)+>
<!ELEMENT game (name, model, price)>
<!ELEMENT name (#PCDATA)>
<!ELEMENT model (#PCDATA)>
<!ELEMENT price (#PCDATA)>
```

For example, Listing 12–2 communicates the following information:

- Each `gamelist` element can have one or more child `game` elements. The plus sign indicates one or more.
- Each game element consists of `name`, `model`, and `price` child elements.
- Each `name`, `model`, and `price` element contains character data (i.e., characters related not to any schema element but to application data).

A DTD can be encoded in a separate file or embedded in an XML document. In the former case, Listing 12–1 can be augmented as shown in Listing 12–3. In the case where the DTD is embedded, our document would simply include the entire DTD shown in Listing 12–2.

Listing 12–3: An XML Document That References a DTD

```
<?xml version="1.0"?>
<!DOCTYPE gamelist SYSTEM "gamelist.dtd">
<gamelist>
        <game>
                <name>Gorf</name>
                <model>stand-up</model>
                <price>500.50</price>
        </game>
        <game>
                <name>Galaga</name>
                <model> Cocktail</model>
                <price>1199.99</price>
        </game>
</gamelist>
```

Listing 12–4: An XML Document with an Embedded DTD

```
<?xml version="1.0"?>
<!DOCTYPE gameListDoc [
        <!ELEMENT gameList (game)+>
```

```
            <!ELEMENT game (name, model, price)>
            <!ELEMENT name (#PCDATA)>
            <!ELEMENT model (#PCDATA)>
            <!ELEMENT price (#PCDATA)>
   ]>
   <gameList>
            <game>
                    <name>Gorf</name>
                    <model>stand-up</model>
                    <price>500.50</price>
            </game>
            <game>
                    <name>Galaga</name>
                    <model>cocktail</model>
                    <price>1199.99</price>
            </game>
   </gameList>
```

Parsing XML

There already exist several specifications and Java APIs for parsing XML. Arguably, the two most important XML parsing technologies are the Document Object Model and the Simple API for XML Parsing (SAX). Both are programmatic ways to access XML documents—they differ primarily in that the former is a standard pushed by the W3C and the latter has become (implicitly) the de facto standard interface for event-driven parsing, evolving from a collective effort by participants of the XML-DEV W3C mailing list.

DOM

The Document Object Model (DOM) is a W3C-coordinated effort to define a set of platform- and language-neutral programmatic interfaces to document data. In W3C lingo, a "document" is a very general concept; HTML and XML documents are considered subclasses.

The DOM Working Group of the W3C publishes DOM specifications in terms of levels. There are currently three levels of specifications: DOM Levels 1, 2, and 3. DOM Level 2 is the current specification, and DOM Level 3 is under development. More comprehensive information about the status of W3C work on DOM can be found at `http://www.w3.org/DOM/Activity.html`.

The DOM represents documents as trees; a top-level node has children, each of which can have children, and so on. For example, Figure 12–4 shows the DOM representation of the XML in Listing 12–4. Notice that elements are represented with boxes and data values are represented with circles.

The purpose of representing a document as a tree is to enable easier programmatic access to the document and to separate useful application-oriented data from any

Figure 12–4
DOM
representation
of an XML
document

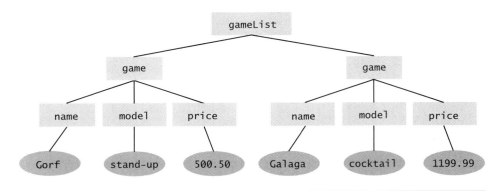

accompanying metadata. Once you have parsed an XML document as a DOM tree, you can use whatever language-specific DOM binding you choose to access and update that document. The W3C publishes abstract DOM interfaces as well as specific bindings for Java and C++.

One key thing to remember about DOM-based XML parsing/processing, as shown by Figure 12–4, is that *a tree must be created before access to the document is possible*. Thus, an XML document can be accessed only in a nonstreaming fashion, and enough local resources (i.e., memory) must exist in order to represent and process large documents.

SAX

The Simple API for XML Parsing is an event-driven parser interface for XML. You use the SAX API to build a set of "callback functions" that are triggered as the document is being parsed. Thus, in contrast to the DOM style of parsing, you don't have to wait for a tree to be built before you access document data. Instead, you have access to document elements and their data during the parsing process. This is an important advantage when extracting data from very large XML documents or when you want to process XML documents in a streaming fashion (i.e., as the document is retrieved gradually from a remote source).

A positive side effect of not having a DOM tree is that you do not have to devote memory to storing the complete tree for documents that you will access only partially. Instead, since data streams in and out of a SAX parser, memory demands are relatively consistent. This consistency and resource demand can again be a major advantage when querying/parsing very large documents that may exceed available memory.

A disadvantage to the SAX style of parsing is that you do not have access to a structure like the DOM tree at the end of the parsing process. You see the elements once—as they are parsed—and that's it. Unless you build the tree yourself (or reparse using DOM), you won't be able to query one. Thus, many people believe that SAX parsing is well suited for processing one-time queries and DOM is better suited for processing multiple queries.

Note that SAX is a public domain API. It is currently at version level 2. As of this writing, it continues to be available at `http://www.megginson.com/SAX/index.html`.

XML Parsing with Apache Xerces 2.0

One example of an XML processor is Apache Xerces 2.0, which supports both DOM and SAX APIs. Xerces 2.0 is the latest in a series of parsers supported by the Apache project. (See `http://www.apache.org/xml` for more information.)

Listing 12–5 shows how we can use Xerces to parse the XML in Listing 12–4 under a DOM parsing methodology.

Listing 12–5: Parsing Using the DOM Approach

```
 1 import org.apache.xerces.parsers.DOMParser;
 2 import org.w3c.dom.Document;
 3 import org.w3c.dom.Node;
 4 import org.w3c.dom.Element;
 5 import org.w3c.dom.NodeList;
 6 import org.xml.sax.SAXException;
 7
 8 import java.io.IOException;
 9
10 public class SimpleDom
11 {
12   private Document m_doc;
13
14   public SimpleDom (String a_fileName)
15   {
16     /* Create the parser */
17     DOMParser dparser = new DOMParser();
18
19     /* Parse the document */
20     try {
21       dparser.parse(a_fileName);
22       m_doc = dparser.getDocument();
23     }
24     catch (SAXException e) {
25       System.err.println(e);
26       System.exit(-1);
27     }
28     catch (IOException e) {
29       System.err.println(e);
```

```
30        System.exit(-1);
31    }
32  }
33
34  private Document getDocument () { return m_doc; }
35
36  /* Recursively print out element nodes */
37  private void printNodeAndTraverse (Node node)
38  {
39    /* Print only element nodes */
40    if (node.getNodeType() == Node.ELEMENT_NODE)
41      System.out.println("NODE = "+node.getNodeName());
42
43    /* Call recursively for each child */
44    NodeList childList  = node.getChildNodes();
45    if (childList != null) {
46      for (int i=0; i< childList.getLength(); i++)
47        printNodeAndTraverse(childList.item(i));
48    }
49  }
50
51  public static void main (String[] args)
52  {
53    /* Create the DOM */
54    SimpleDom d = new SimpleDom(args[0]);
55
56    /* Traverse all children and print out the names of the nodes */
57    d.printNodeAndTraverse(d.getDocument());
58  }
59 }
```

The main things to notice here are

- Line 17, where the parser is created
- Line 21, where the entire document is first parsed into a tree data structure
- Lines 37 through 49, where the document is recursively walked with the element nodes being output in the process.

If we compile and run this code via

```
% java SimpleDom games.xml
```

its execution results in

```
NODE = gameList
NODE = game
NODE = name
```

```
NODE = model
NODE = price
NODE = game
NODE = name
NODE = model
NODE = price
```

To parse the same XML document using SAX, the implementation in Listing 12–6 is required.

Listing 12–6: Parsing Using the SAX Approach

```
 1 import org.apache.xerces.parsers.SAXParser;
 2 import org.xml.sax.Attributes;
 3 import org.xml.sax.helpers.DefaultHandler;
 4 import org.xml.sax.SAXParseException;
 5 import org.xml.sax.SAXException;
 6 import java.io.IOException;
 7
 8 public class SimpleSax
 9   extends DefaultHandler
10 {
11   public SimpleSax(String a_file)
12   {
13     /* Create the parser */
14     SAXParser sparser = new SAXParser();
15
16     /* Set the content handler */
17     sparser.setContentHandler(this);
18
19     /* Parse */
20     try {
21       sparser.parse(a_file);
22     }
23     catch (SAXException e) {
24       System.err.println(e);
25     }
26     catch (IOException e) {
27       System.err.println(e);
28     }
29   }
30
31   public void startElement (String a_uri, String a_localName,
32     String a_qName, Attributes a_attributes)
33   {
34     System.out.println("NODE = "+a_localName);
35   }
36
37   public static void main (String[] args)
38   {
```

```
39      new SimpleSax(args[0]);
40   }
41 }
```

The key parts of this code are

- Lines 8 and 9, where our `SimpleSax` class extends the SAX `DefaultHandler` class
- Line 14, where the parser is created
- Line 17, where we let the parser know what the handler (our class) will be
- Line 21, where we start to parse the file (not completed immediately)
- Lines 31 through 35, the callback function, which is invoked per XML document element, here during the execution of the `parse()` call made in line 21

In a comparison, we notice that DOM appears very straightforward and simple, although it's a bit longer than SAX. However, at least we can easily envision the process of execution. In contrast, SAX forces us to extend a handler and possibly implement some of its methods (i.e., `startElement()`). Also, our processing needs are possibly complicated by SAX's event-driven basis. In particular, SAX often requires data structures that keep state information. For example, if the goal of our XML parsing is to count if there are at least two games in the document, we have to keep a global counter that increments every time the SAX callback is called. This example is admittedly simple, but it should make it clear that SAX-based processing, while sometimes more efficient, is inherently more complex than DOM-based processing.

XML–Related Technologies

I'm only touching the tip of the iceberg of XML in the summary given here, but it's enough for the discussion later in this chapter. What should be minimally clear is that XML

- Enables data to be *portable*: Using a DTD, an XML document can be interpreted by any processor, on any platform.
- Provides *structure*, such as hierarchical information.
- Is "*human legible*": Unlike other binary-encoded documents, we can easily see and make sense of what's contained in an XML document.
- Is *extensible*: You can define and use whatever schemas make sense for your needs.
- Is simply an open *standard* and is not owned by one company.

These five basic points make XML an exciting language for data interchange between enterprises. XML provides the structure and extensibility that HTML lacks, and it separates data from presentation. It's also easy to debug, unlike more cryptic data interchange technologies like Electronic Data Interchange (EDI).

Communication to and from Web services, as well as the advertisement of those services, is phrased in XML. Thus, it's important that we not only understand XML, but also consider issues related to its efficiency.

Developing Web Services

There's nothing magical about developing a Web service. You code one as you would the implementation of a distributed object, like a CORBA object or an EJB bean class. In fact, CORBA objects and EJB components can be registered as Web services. The magic comes in during deployment. By using other technologies in the Web services technology stack, you can make the functionality of your service locatable and accessible in a platform-independent manner.

In this and the following sections, we'll explore a single example: Suppose we want to implement our price-quoting function. To keep things simple, suppose that products are uniquely identified as strings. We'll use Java as the language for implementing our service and have the core application logic of our price quote component include code to the effect of:

```
public double GetPriceQuote(String a_product) {
  double thePrice;
  ...
  thePrice = ...            // lookup price
  ...
  return thePrice;
}
```

Now that we've defined what this remote functionality does, let's examine how to describe it as a Web service.

Describing Web Services with WSDL

We can think of WSDL as an XML-based means for expressing the interface to a given Web service. Describing a service using WSDL boils down to abstractly defining service functionality and then binding it to a physical protocol.

The W3C report on WSDL, online at `http://www.w3c.org/TR/wsdl.html`, is even more general than this, stating that a Web service is the process of *specifying a set of network endpoints operating on messages that contain either document- or procedure-oriented information.* That's a mouthful, and before it can make any sense, we need to discuss endpoints and illuminate the distinction between logical and physical representations of a service.

First, as the text obviously implies, we need to get used to the notion of an "endpoint." An **endpoint**, as far as the WSDL standard goes, identifies a single piece of functionality—for example, the price-quoting mechanism we discussed earlier. The W3C report states that a **service** is a collection of these endpoints, which essentially means that a single Web service can actually be composed of more than one piece of functionality (i.e., method).

The report also makes a distinction between "concrete" network endpoints and "abstract" endpoints. Concrete endpoints are real (physical) pieces of service functionality; abstract endpoints are logical descriptions of functionality. The difference between the two is similar to the difference between tables and views, the latter (like abstract endpoints) being at higher level of abstraction.

Now that we understand something about how WSDL views a Web service, let's consider what kind of service information it allows us to specify. To do this, we need to think of a Web service description as *a set of definitions*.

Definitions

Each definition in a WSDL document is one of the following:

- *Message*: the abstract definition of data being communicated to a service; each of its embedded parts is associated with a specific WSDL type. For example, two messages related to our price-quoting service might be `ProductPriceRequest` and `ProductPriceResponse`.

- *Type*: the named data structures that are typically message specific and map to a valid type system (such as the W3C XML schema recommendation found at `http://www.w3.org/TR/xmlschema-2`). More simply, you can define your own types, such as `Price`, that map to existing types, such as `xsd:float`.

- *Operation*: the abstract description of the action provided by the Web service in terms of its input and output messages. The notion of an operation is important because it describes a specific action and allows various bindings to be mapped to it (see the Binding item below). Two operations for our price-quoting service could be `GetPriceQuote` and `GetBulkDiscountPriceQuote`.

- *Port Type*: a named set of abstract operations. The port type also indicates the nature of the dialog between the caller and the service—for example, *request–response*, or *one-way*.

- *Binding*: the specification of access to operations of an existing port type using a particular protocol. SOAP and HTTP are valid protocols. We can have a `PriceQuoteSoapBinding` that supports price quotes via SOAP. Think of a binding and its operations as an instance (implementation) of a particular port type and its abstract operations.

- *Port*: a named association of a network address with a binding. A caller need know only the port and the binding when making a request of a service.

- *Service*: the combination of related ports. A service comprises one or more endpoints. Like an object that can have many methods, a service can have many ports.

Example

To get a better feel for WSDL, let's look at one sample service—the price-quoting service we hinted at earlier. Suppose that this service consists of a single operation that computes price quotes for a given product. Specifically, given a string that indicates the name of the product, this operation will return a floating-point value that indicates the product's price.

Given this service specification, we'll see how to encode the corresponding service description using WSDL.

Messages and Types

First things first. We need to think about the types and messages being communicated. In terms of types, we know that the client/service interaction will involve the client sending a product name (a string) and receiving a price (a floating point). Thus, we can define two logical types that map to physical types. In particular, let's name the request message `ProductPriceRequest` (a string) and the response message `ProductPriceResponse` (a floating point). Correspondingly, part of our WSDL document will contain information about the types.

```
<types>
    <schema targetNamespace="http://www.example.com/pricequote.xsd"
          xmlns="http://www.w3.org/2000/10/XMLSchema">
        <element name="ProductPriceRequest">
          <complexType>
              <all>
                  <element name="productName" type="string"/>
              </all>
          </complexType>
        </element>
        <element name="ProductPriceResponse">
          <complexType>
              <all>
```

```
                        <element name="price" type="float"/>
                    </all>
                </complexType>
            </element>
        </schema>
    <types>
```

Next, it's a simple matter to associate these types with the logical messages our service operation will send and receive:

```
<message name="PriceQuoteInput">
        <part name="body" element="xsd1:ProductPriceRequest"/>
</message>

<message name="PriceQuoteOutput">
        <part name="body" element="xsd1:ProductPriceResponse"/>
</message>
```

Port Types and Bindings

With types and messages defined, we can move on to describing the operations of our service. To keep things simple, we'll worry about only one logical operation—the ability to get a price quote—which we'll name GetPriceQuote.

First, we need to define a logical port—a port type—that receives one message as input and one as output.

```
<portType name="PriceQuotePortType">
      <operation name="GetPriceQuote">
            <input message="tns:PriceQuoteInput"/>
            <output message="tns:PriceQuoteOutput"/>
      </operation>
</portType>
```

Next, we want to define at least one physical binding to that logical port—an actual mechanism for accomplishing the abstract operation defined by it. The following definition demonstrates how to create a SOAP binding (more about SOAP shortly) for our service that maps to the GetPriceQuote operation we previously defined.

```
<binding name="PriceQuoteSoapBinding" type="tns:PriceQuotePortType">
      <soap:binding style="document"
       transport="http://schemas.xmlsoap.org/soap/http"/>
      <operation name="GetPriceQuote">
            <soap:operation
             soapAction="http://www.example.com/GetPriceQuote"/>
            <input>
```

```
                              <soap:body use="literal"/>
                    </input>
                    <output>
                              <soap:body use="literal"/>
                    </output>
              </operation>
      </binding>
```

Ports and Services

Finally, it's time to define and name the service itself. As part of that definition, we want to create a series of physical ports that correspond to service functionality. Defining each physical port requires that we associate it with a physical binding:

```
<service name="PriceQuoteService">
    <documentation>The Price Quote Service</documentation>
    <port name="PriceQuotePort" binding="tns:PriceQuoteBinding">
          <soap:address location="http://www.example.com/pricequote"/>
     </port>
</service>
```

Invoking Web Services with SOAP

At this point, we have a rough idea of what the language for communicating with a Web service will be like. A service is associated with a binding, and clients who use the binding communicate with the service by sending named, text-based messages. The service parses these messages as requests and returns replies, also in named, text-based messages. Now it's time to find out more about one particularly important binding—SOAP—and understand some of the details involved in using it.

You can think of SOAP simply as the distributed object communication protocol for the Internet. The general idea is to allow programmatic access to remote, Internet-based functionality via HTTP. Although our discussion will focus on SOAP as it's deployed over HTTP, SOAP is indeed a higher-application-level protocol and makes sense as deployed over other communication substrates, such as RPC.

The W3C acknowledgment of SOAP (`http://www.w3.org/TR/soap`) breaks the protocol into three basic parts:

- *The SOAP envelope*, which defines an overall framework for expressing what's in a message, who should deal with it, and whether it's optional or mandatory
- *The SOAP encoding rules*, which define a serialization mechanism that can be used to exchange instances of application-defined data types
- *The SOAP RPC representation*, which defines a convention that can be used to represent remote procedure calls and responses

Our focus will be exclusively on the first part—the envelope—since our goal is to understand the general nature of the protocol. Books devoted to SOAP can provide more information (see Suggested Reading) about SOAP rules and RPC representation.

How SOAP Works

Figure 12–5 shows how SOAP works in the context of our price-quoting example. As the figure shows, clients post SOAP request messages to servers. These messages contain information about the remote method being invoked and any input data to that method (in serialized format). Servers reply with SOAP messages that contain the output values framed in a method response. In the figure, a client is requesting prices for a camera and the corresponding server is responding.

SOAP messages are contained in XML documents that serve as envelopes. Each envelope consists of an optional **header** and a required **body**. A SOAP header typically contains metadata about the exchange (e.g., a transaction identifier). It's also a

Figure 12–5
Basic SOAP-based
communication

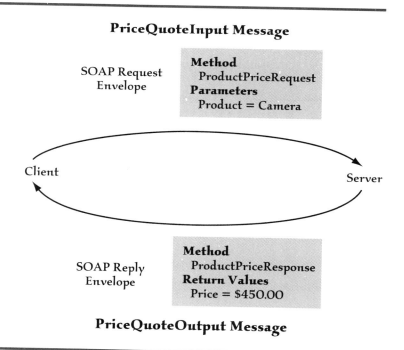

PriceQuoteInput Message

SOAP Request
Envelope

Method
    ProductPriceRequest
Parameters
    Product = Camera

Client   Server

Method
    ProductPriceResponse
Return Values
    Price = $450.00

SOAP Reply
Envelope

PriceQuoteOutput Message

means for extending the protocol, but in a decentralized manner. The body focuses on the data itself, namely:

- The remote method name (or response name)
- The request (or reply) parameters
- The serialized data

Figure 12–6 is essentially a detailed version of Figure 12–5. Notice that the communication is phrased in XML and that the data is self-describing and serialized. Also notice how the server side processes the request: Using a SOAP *translator* to comprehend the request, it rephrases it into server-side calls (some of which may access a database). The circles in the figure indicate instances of objects—for example, CORBA or EJB instances—that are used during request processing.

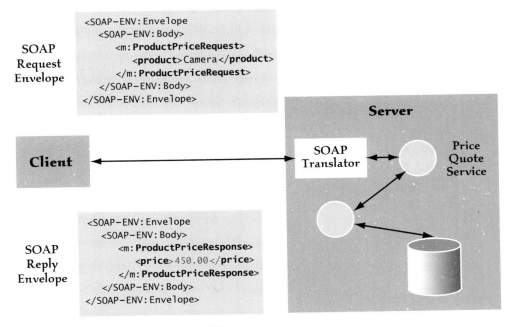

Figure 12–6
Details of
SOAP-based
communi-
cation

PriceQuoteInput Message

```
<SOAP-ENV:Envelope
  <SOAP-ENV:Body>
    <m:ProductPriceRequest>
      <product>Camera</product>
    </m:ProductPriceRequest>
  </SOAP-ENV:Body>
</SOAP-ENV:Envelope>
```

SOAP
Request
Envelope

Client

Server

SOAP
Translator

Price
Quote
Service

SOAP
Reply
Envelope

```
<SOAP-ENV:Envelope
  <SOAP-ENV:Body>
    <m:ProductPriceResponse>
      <price>450.00</price>
    </m:ProductPriceResponse>
  </SOAP-ENV:Body>
</SOAP-ENV:Envelope>
```

PriceQuoteOutput Message

Although Figure 12–6 only shows the simple marshalling of strings and floating-point types between client and server, SOAP supports more complex (compound) data types, such as arrays.

Using SOAP over HTTP

SOAP over HTTP solves a number of problems with prior attempts to unify the Internet's collection of distributed objects:

- *Nonproprietary, committee-based standard*: Unlike proprietary remote communication technologies such as RMI and DCOM, SOAP is open and managed by a number of cooperating corporations and organizations.

- *Simple and easy to debug*: In contrast to binary-based protocols (e.g., IIOP), SOAP communication involves text-based messages. This makes communication errors easy to debug on both client and server sides. In contrast, older interchange protocols such as EDI not only are cryptic to debug, but often require special (proprietary) client software to process. Thus, the simplicity of SOAP makes it easy to deploy and maintain.

- *Deployment over HTTP leverages efficiency, security, and ease of integration*: As you already know, the most recent version of HTTP contains a number of built-in performance optimizations (e.g., persistent connections) to make up for some of its inefficiencies. It also contains mechanisms for authentication and encryption. By deploying SOAP over HTTP, we can leverage all of these existing features. Furthermore, there's an important advantage in ease of integration. One of the difficulties in connecting applications is getting around firewalls. In particular, use of a TCP port other than 80 (the default HTTP port) can cause integration headaches. By using SOAP over HTTP, we avoid the problem altogether in addition to retaining the security and efficiency challenges of the protocol.

To convince you that SOAP is very simple and straightforward to use and debug over HTTP, let's briefly look at it in action. In particular, consider the exchange shown in Figure 12–6 between client and server.

Using HTTP, the client simply requests a product price quote via

```
POST /GetPriceQuote HTTP/1.1
Host: www.example.com
Content-Type: text/xml; charset="utf-8"
SOAPAction: "http://www.example.com/GetPriceQuote"

<SOAP-ENV:Envelope
  xmlns:SOAP-ENV="http://schemas.xmlsoap.org/soap/envelope/"
```

```
      SOAP-ENV:encodingStyle="http://schemas.xmlsoap.org/soap/encoding/">
       <SOAP-ENV:Body>
           <m:ProductPriceRequest xmlns:m="http://www.example.com">
               <product>Camera</product>
           </m:ProductPriceRequest>
       </SOAP-ENV:Body>
    </SOAP-ENV:Envelope>
```

The server simply replies with

```
HTTP/1.1 200 OK
Content-Type: text/xml; charset="utf-8"
Content-Length: (whatever)
<?xml version="1.0" ?>
<SOAP-ENV:Envelope
   xmlns:SOAP-ENV="http://schemas.xmlsoap.org/soap/envelope/"
    SOAP-ENV:encodingStyle="http://schemas.xmlsoap.org/soap/encoding/"/>
     <SOAP-ENV:Body>
         <m:ProductPriceResponse xmlns:m="http://www.example.com">
             <Price>450.00</Price>
         </m:ProductPriceResponse>
     </SOAP-ENV:Body>
</SOAP-ENV:Envelope>
```

One additional note about these requests and replies. Notice that both messages contain some metadata prior to the body of the message. The first line

```
xmlns:SOAP-ENV="http://schemas.xmlsoap.org/soap/envelope/"
```

refers to the structure of the envelope itself (again, self-describing data). The second line

```
SOAP-ENV:encodingStyle="http://schemas.xmlsoap.org/soap/encoding/"/>
```

references the types used by the SOAP message. SOAP supports basic types (like integer and floating point) as well as more complex objects and extensibility.

Registering Web Services with UDDI

Earlier, we saw how a Web service can be defined using WSDL. Now we need some way to publish its existence to the rest of the world. Admittedly, this isn't necessary if the people using your service explicitly know that it exists and how to find information about it. However, it has been suggested that in the future such a scenario will be the exception, not the rule.

The big picture—since the early days of distributed object technologies like CORBA—is that it will be possible for clients to discover your service automatically based on their general needs. Imagine that some need functionality to, say, convert grams into pounds and that your service provides that computation logic. These clients will be able to locate your functionality just as they use a search engine to locate documents containing a set of keywords.

This is where UDDI comes in. By using UDDI technologies and protocols, you can publish the availability of your services to the UDDI registry. This registry is widely distributed among many peer registries. However, you need publish your service to only one registry; the replication of its availability information is automatic. Clients can then discover that functionality by querying a local UDDI registry.

Thus far, I've been saying that UDDI essentially provides a database of services. That makes it easy to visualize, but let's get a little more specific. UDDI actually provides an XML schema that supports four information types:

- *Business information*: metadata about the business itself (name, description, etc.)

- *Service information*: a list of the services provided by the business, usually consisting of high-level descriptive information (i.e., the type of functionality being provided)

- *Binding information*: technical details on how to access the service using some Internet method (e.g., SOAP)

- *Specification of services information*: metadata about the binding information, for example, pointers to the specification of that method. (This type of information is also known as the binding mechanism "fingerprint"; it allows a client to identify the origins of the binding technology in order to discover and reason about compatibility with it.)

Figure 12–7 shows how the parts of the schema relate. Notice that business entities offer one or more services, each service has one or more binding methods, and each binding method is associated with a single set of binding metadata (or a template).

The UDDI information types are used to provide phonebook-like capabilities to clients. More specifically, clients can query three groups of information:

- *White pages*: business contact information
- *Yellow pages*: information related to the categorization of businesses and services
- *Green pages*: technical information about available services

Figure 12–7
UDDI
information
types

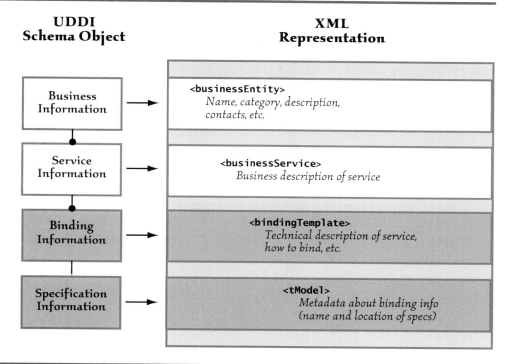

Public UDDI registries are deployed on **operator sites**. Communication with these sites is accomplished via SOAP over HTTP. The spirit of the operator site concept is that simple querying and interaction with a hosted UDDI registry are available to anyone; that is, there should be no charge for basic services. Multiple operator sites can be used to replicate UDDI information so that querying and access are both scalable and reliable.

Standards

UDDI is developed and maintained by several individuals who represent a large group of corporations, including Microsoft, Oracle, and IBM. Together, these companies publish UDDI standards and address issues via a single Web site: www.uddi.org. This site contains a wealth of information on UDDI and is currently the best place to get the latest news on the standard and its associated APIs.

The UDDI APIs

As we discussed earlier, programmatically publishing to and querying from UDDI requires a compatible API. In June 2001, the UDDI 2.0 Programmer's API was published. It consists of two important parts: inquiry and publishing.

Table 12–1: Summary of the UDDI 2.0 Inquiry API

Method	Purpose
find_binding	Locates bindings for a specific business service
find_business	Locates information about one or more businesses
find_relatedBusinesses	Locates businesses related to the business entity specified
find_service	Locates specific services for a business entity
find_tModel	Locates metadata about a particular binding
get_bindingDetail	Gets detailed information about a binding
get_businessDetail	Gets detailed information about a business
get_businessDetailExt	Gets extended details about a business
get_serviceDetail	Gets details about a service
get_tModelDetail	Gets details about metadata for a particular binding

The Inquiry API

This API contains methods for *querying* the four types of information described earlier. To get a sense for the details related to it, take a look at the methods supported by UDDI Version 2.0 in Table 12–1.

Notice that they're broken down into two basic categories:

- find_xx *methods* locate "overviews" about each of the four types of information shown in Figure 12–7.
- get_xx *methods* return full details of the overviews associated with the find_xx methods.

These methods were designed to target the type of querying service consumers are expected to need and to promote efficiency. For example, a client wants to query a business entity for the services it provides without getting back a huge amount of detail. Instead, overviews of the services are returned and the keys associated with them can be used to locate more detail if required. Again, think of the search engine paradigm, where the response you get from a query simply shows the summarized (or in-context) query results. To access any of the details (i.e., the Web page), you have to follow the given link.

The Publishing API

Just as the inquiry API enables UDDI querying, the publishing API enables UDDI *updates*. This class of UDDI API functions is summarized in Table 12–2.

Table 12–2: Summary of the UDDI 2.0 Publishing API

Method	*Purpose*
add_publisherAssertions	Adds information that relates business entities to each other
delete_binding	Deletes a service binding entry
delete_business	Deletes a business entry
delete_publisherAssertions	Deletes information that relates business entities to each other
delete_service	Deletes a service entry
delete_tModel	Deletes metadata about the binding for a service
discard_authToken	Invalidates a previously issued authentication token
get_assertionStatusReport	Gets information on pending assertions
get_authToken	Requests an authentication token
get_publisherAssertions	Gets information about relationships between entities
get_registeredInfo	Gets a synopsis of all registered information managed by a particular individual
save_binding	Updates a service binding entry
save_business	Updates a business entity entry
save_service	Updates a service entry
save_tModel	Updates service binding metadata
set_publisherAssertions	Resets relationship information for a particular publisher

Again, the meanings and purpose of these methods are obvious. In particular, we can identify the two types of methods we expected to see:

- delete_xx *methods* delete entities, services, bindings, and templates.
- save_xx *methods* update entities, services, bindings, and templates.

We also see the following:

- *Assertion-related methods*: *Assertions* are the UDDI mechanism for relating two or more business entities. For example, if company A wants to indicate that it's the parent of company B (i.e., a parent/child relationship), it can use these methods to update and query that information.

- *Authorization token methods*: Since updating and deleting UDDI information for a particular business is a constructive/destructive activity, administrative-style login methods are supported by the UDDI publishing API. Only once an authentication token has been issued can an administrator make use of any UDDI `save_xx` and `delete_xx` methods.

The Big Picture

By now it's obvious that we've jumped into a pretty deep "Web services" lake here, full of perhaps more detail than you wanted to know. Now, it's time to step back and look at the practical use of Web services from the perspectives of both consumer and provider, phrasing this use in terms of the technologies just covered. Following that, we can focus on the efficiency challenges from both perspectives.

The Provider's Perspective

For the provider who wants to embrace the Web service model, here is a rough list of tasks that need to be performed:

- *Identify available functionality using WSDL*: The generation of WSDL definitions can be automated—in fact, providers fully expect Web services development tools to support automatic generation of service definitions. Providers should also consider the kinds of controls or security they want to ensure that their functionality is accessed by a select group of clients (not necessarily the whole world—unless that's what they actually desire).

- *Publish functionality via UDDI*. This means using the UDDI API to communicate with registries deployed at operator sites.

- *Ensure that Web-based request-processing technologies support SOAP requests*. This means handing off HTTP POST requests to a SOAP translator and routing the underlying function calls to the server-side distributed object system.

- *Encode data in XML*. In particular, where does this translation to XML happen? Is data communicated internally in terms of native types and then "translated" (i.e., "stringified") into XML on its way out? Or is it embedded in XML notation all the way down to the database?

The Consumer's Perspective

Consumers have their own tasks to perform to support Web services:

- *Locate remote functions of use.* In the near term, consumers will likely know what functions they want to access and where they are. But one important vision of UDDI is that consumers will be able to query UDDI registries automatically and discover new instances of functionality as they're deployed.
- *Communicate with remote services via SOAP.* This shouldn't be a tremendous change from the way clients normally interact (programmatically) with remote network services.
- *Encode requests in XML.* This is similar to what providers will do, in terms of serializing and "stringifying" their native types for transport.
- *Parse or query XML replies.* Service replies must be parsed and converted to local native types or queried directly using XQuery-like approaches.

Now that we have a reasonable summary of what the provider and the consumer need to do, it's time to consider some likely scalability and performance challenges these responsibilities entail.

Salability and Performance Challenges

Unlike earlier chapters, with their sections on scalability and performance *hints*, this chapter contains a section devoted to scalability and performance *challenges*. The reason behind this is simple: Web services are a new aspect of Internet technology and many of their standards and implementations are in flux. Notwithstanding, we can step back and look at the general process of defining and using a Web service and identify parts of this process that may have scalability and performance implications.

Replicating and Load–Balancing Remote Functions

Just as we were concerned about load-balancing Java servlets, we need to realize that Web services require a way to replicate and load-balance remote functionality. This is definitely one area where embracing a component infrastructure technology such as J2EE can be a tremendous asset.

As we discussed in Chapter 3, J2EE implementations enable new instances of component functionality to be pooled and allocated quickly, with minimal resource demands. The container abstraction in the design of J2EE lets developers worry about function implementation, not function distribution and scaling. Thus, replicating provider functions for J2EE-based deployments is no longer as concern for the application architect and developer. The only real work to be done is to load-balance Web requests across a set of machines running EJB containers that manage the functionality in demand.

In short, the replication and load-balancing demands of Web services are no different from the replication and load-balancing demands on servlets and EJBs. To meet those demands, J2EE is designed from the ground up.

XML Parsing Performance

The key tradeoff with SAX versus DOM parsing is performance against ease of use. DOM is generally considered easier to use but is slower than SAX because it forms an entire DOM tree before enabling access to it. The problems with this approach are exacerbated when the XML being parsed is large—say, gigabytes. In contrast, SAX is a bit harder to use and can require some careful programming, but it's inherently more efficient than DOM.

To understand the efficiency differences, consider the performance of the SAX and DOM code shown earlier. After taking out the System.out.println() statements and instead simply counting the number of elements (and printing this total at the end), the two approaches were compared in how they process XML documents, similar to the games.xml shown earlier, of 1 Kb, 10 Kb, 100 Kb, and 1 Mb in length. Figure 12–8 shows the results.

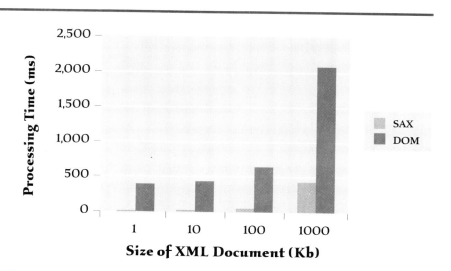

Figure 12–8
Counting nodes in an XML document, SAX versus DOM

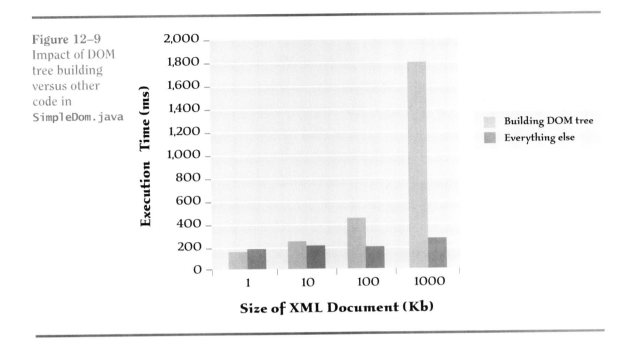

Figure 12–9
Impact of DOM
tree building
versus other
code in
SimpleDom.java

To underscore the impact of building the DOM tree on the entire process (i.e., the recursive counting of nodes isn't to blame), consider Figure 12–9. This figure shows the time required to build the DOM tree—that is, the execution time of `DOMParser.parse()`—for each trial as opposed to "everything else" (i.e., the recursive element counting). Clearly, building the tree is responsible for most of the execution cost.

Parsing versus Querying XML

A more vexing issue once the data is returned by the remote service is what to do with it. One approach is to parse everything and reinstantiate local native types. For example, an XML response containing a price would be parsed and a new local floating-point value corresponding to the XML string-form of that price would be instantiated. An alternative is to use XQuery-like technology to process an XML response into another XML document.

XQuery

XQuery is a proposed standard for querying XML documents directly. It is to XML documents what SQL is to relational databases—a language for querying a specific store of data (relational in the case of SQL, hierarchical in the case of XQuery).

XQuery is actually a stew of prior technologies such as Quilt, Xpath, and XQL. It allows you not only to query a document, but also to simultaneously generate new XML based on the result. The W3C working draft standard of XQuery is available at `http://www.w3.org/TR/xquery/`.

Although we don't want to delve into the details of XQuery here, we can give a quick example of how it's used. Suppose we want to answer the following query about the video games document that was shown in Listing 12–4: *Display all of the names and prices of stand-up model games.* Also suppose we want the answer to this query expressed in XML, for example, given the following XML file:

```
<?xml version="1.0"?>
<!DOCTYPE gameListDoc [
        <!ELEMENT gameList (game)+>
        <!ELEMENT game (name, model, price)>
        <!ELEMENT name (#PCDATA)>
        <!ELEMENT model (#PCDATA)>
        <!ELEMENT price (#PCDATA)>
]>
<gameList>
        <game>
                <name>Gorf</name>
                <model>stand-up</model>
                <price>500.50</price>
        </game>
        <game>
                <name>Galaga</name>
                <model>cocktail</model>
                <price>1199.99</price>
        </game>
</gameList>
```

From the proceding file, we want these results:

```
<myList>
        <myGame>
                <name>Gorf</name>
                <price>500.50</price>
        </myGame>
</myList>
```

Filtering and reformatting XML is a common task of intermediary services that process service requests by calling other services and processing their replies.

Now, if we can somehow express this query in SQL, it will look something like this:

```
SELECT game.name, game.price
FROM game
WHERE game.model = "stand-up";
```

But now we have a relation to deal with and need to reformat the resulting XML. Also, Listing 12–4 is hierarchical and the SQL query doesn't make much sense.

Instead, using XQuery and its path expressions we can write queries that navigate to and return the exact data we want. Furthermore, we can generate results in any XML format. An example of an XQuery that accomplishes our goal is:

```
<myList>
    {
    FOR $g IN document("games.xml")/gameList/game
    WHERE $g/model/text() = "stand-up"
    RETURN
        <myGame>
            { $g/name }
            { $g/price }
        </myGame>
    }
</myList>
```

This code does the following:

- Locates the game element in all gameList elements.
- Returns name and price of the games where the model = "stand-up".

XQuery versus Parsing

The approach you take will likely depend on how you use the data. For example, if your application acts as a middleman that processes XML requests, contacts remotes services to locate data, and replies using XML, it is likely easier and more efficient to use XQuery. Otherwise, you'll have to parse replies from the services your application contacts, reduce their contents to native types, and then end up rephrasing your own application replies using XML.

XQuery is still an emerging standard and it's too early to gauge the efficiency of its implementation. One aspect of XML query processing that seems critical is the ability to rapidly navigate to the path expressed in a query and to return results while an XML document is being retrieved/streamed in from a remote source. Many XML documents of the future (especially XML forms of large relational tables) will be quite big, so the ability to process them as their bytes are being recieved from the network is an important feature.

Summary

Since its inception, the Web has largely been a network of distributed data. With Web services, however, a turning point has been reached. The Web of the future will be a network of distributed functions as well as data. This isn't to say it will eventually consist only of functions, because "functionalizing" truly static data isn't very useful; in fact, it's inefficient. Rather, the Web is evolving into a very large distributed object system comprised of both static data and Web services.

In this chapter, we focused most of our discussion on understanding Web services and how they're used. We saw that there are four important technologies to become familiar with: XML, SOAP, WSDL, and UDDI. XML allows data to be self-describing and thus portable. SOAP is a simple and efficient way to communicate XML-based service requests and replies. WSDL is a way to define services, with several levels of abstraction, so that the location of a particular service and the means to access it are flexible. Finally, UDDI represents a database of provider services defined by WSDL.

At the end, our discussion returned to performance and scalability. The key questions to answer at this point are:

- How do we interpret XML data? Parse it and process embedded values in their native form or use XQuery-like technologies to query XML directly?
- How do we efficiently store hierarchical data in relational databases?
- Is it more efficient to compose an application as a collection of remote distributed services or as as a collection of locally distributed components?
- How do we handle load balancing and scaling remote functions?

The future of application integration and truly distributed Web applications looks bright with Web services technologies. The coming years will bring many exciting new battles to fight in the ongoing war for scalability and performance in Web applications.

Suggested Reading

Alur, Deepak, John Crupi, and Dan Malks. *Core J2EE Patterns: Best Practices and Design Strategies*. Englewood Cliffs, N.J.: Prentice-Hall, 2001.

Birbek, Mark (ed.). *Professional XML (Programmer to Programmer), Second Edition*. Chicago, Ill.: Wrox Press, 2001.

Bulka, Dov. *Server-Side Programming Techniques: Java™ Performance and Scalability, Volume 1*. Boston, Mass.: Addison-Wesley, 2000.

Cormen, Thomas H. (ed.). *Introduction to Algorithms, Second Edition*. Cambridge, Mass.: MIT Press, 2001.

Coulouris, George, Jean Dollimore, and Tim Kindberg. *Distributed Systems: Concepts and Design, Third Edition*. United Kingdom Publisher: Addison-Wesley, 2000.

Elmasri, Ramez, and Shamkant B. Navathe. *Fundamentals of Database Systems, with E-book, Third Edition*. Reading, Mass.: Addison-Wesley, 1999.

Feuerstein, Steven, and Bill Pribyl. *Oracle PL/SQL Programming, Second Edition*. Sebastopol, Calif.: O'Reilly & Associates, 1997.

Genender, Jeff. M. *Enterprise Java™ Servlets*. Boston, Mass.: Addison-Wesley, 2001.

Hunter, Jason. *Java Servlets, Second Edition*. Sebastopol, Calif.: O'Reilly & Associates, 2001.

Internet Engineering Task Force. *HTTP 1.1 Protocol*. IETF RFC 2616. [Online]: http://www.w3.org/Protocols/rfc2616/rfc2616.html.

Java™ API for XML Processing, version 1.1. Palo Alto, Calif.: Sun Microsystems, 2001.

Java™ Servlet Specification, version 2.3. Palo Alto, Calif.: Sun Microsystems, 2001.

Java™ 2 Platform Enterprise Edition Specification, version 1.3. Palo Alto, Calif.: Sun Microsystems, 2001.

Keshav, Srinivsan, *An Engineering Approach to Computer Networking: ATM Newtorks, the Internet, and the Telephone Network*. Reading, Mass.: Addison-Wesley, 1997.

Lea, Doug. *Concurrent Programming in Java: Design Principles and Patterns, Second Edition*. Reading, Mass.: Addison-Wesley, 1999.

McLaughlin, Brett. *Java and XML: Solutions to Real-World Problems, Second Edition*. Sebastopol, Calif.: O'Reilly & Associates, 2001.

Menasce, Daniel A., and Virgilio A. F. Almeida. *Scaling for E-Business: Technologies, Models, Performance, and Capacity Planning.* Englewood Cliffs, N.J.: Prentice-Hall, 2000.

Nielsen, H., J. Gettys, A. Baird-Smith, E. Prud'hommeaux, H. Lie, and C. Lilley. *Network Performance Effects of HTTP/1.1, CSS1, and PNG.* Proceedings of ACM SIGCOMM (pp. 155–166), held in Cannes, France. September 1997.

Patterson, David A., John L. Hennessy, and David Goldberg. *Computer Architecture: A Quantitative Approach, Second Edition.* San Francisco, Calif.: Morgan Kaufmann, 1996.

Sarang, J., et al. (eds.). *Professional EJB.* Chicago, Ill.: Wrox Press, 2001.

Shirazi, Jack. *Java Performance Tuning.* Sebastopol, Calif.: O'Reilly & Associates, 2000.

UDDI Version 2.0 API Specification. UDDI open draft specification, June 2001. [Online]: http://www.uddi.org.

World Wide Web Consortium. *Extensible Markup Language (XML) 1.0, Second Edition.* W3C recommendation, October 2000. [Online]: http://www.w3.org/TR/REC-xml.

World Wide Web Consortium. *Simple Object Access Protocol (SOAP) 1.1.* W3C note, May 2000. [Online]: http://www.w3.org/TR/soap/.

World Wide Web Consortium. *Web Services Description Language (WSDL) 1.1.* W3C note, March 2001. [Online]: http://www.w3.org/TR/wsdl/.

World Wide Web Consortium. *XQuery 1.0: An XML Query Language.* W3C working draft, June 2001. [Online]: http://www.w3.org/TR/xquery/.

Index

Note: Italicized page locators refer to tables and/or figures.

More books from Addison-Wesley

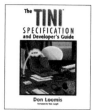

ISBN 0-201-72218-6

ISBN 0-201-70074-3

ISBN 0-201-70244-4

ISBN 0-201-61617-3

ISBN 0-201-70906-6

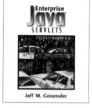

ISBN 0-201-70921-X

ISBN 0-201-72956-3

ISBN 0-201-70043-3

ISBN 0-201-59614-8

ISBN 0-201-72897-4

ISBN 0-201-72588-6

ISBN 0-201-75880-6

ISBN 0-201-75875-X

ISBN 0-201-70916-3

ISBN 0-201-75306-5

ISBN 0-201-61646-7

ISBN 0-201-70252-5

ISBN 0-201-73410-9

ISBN 0-201-73829-5

ISBN 0-201-71962-2

ISBN 0-201-75044-9

http://www.aw.com/cseng

♦ Addison-Wesley

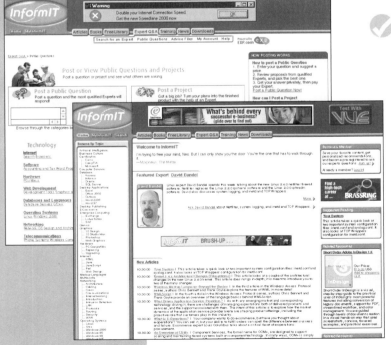

CD-ROM Warranty

Addison-Wesley warrants the enclosed disc to be free of defects in materials and faulty workmanship under normal use for a period of ninety days after purchase. If a defect is discovered in the disc during this warranty period, a replacement disc can be obtained at no charge by sending the defective disc, postage prepaid, with proof of purchase to:

Editorial Department
Addison-Wesley Professional
Pearson Technology Group
75 Arlington Street, Suite 300
Boston, MA 02116
Email: AWPro@aw.com

Addison-Wesley and Greg Barish make no warranty or representation, either expressed or implied, with respect to this software, its quality, performance, merchantability, or fitness for a particular purpose. In no event will Greg Barish or Addison-Wesley, its distributors, or dealers be liable for direct, indirect, special, incidental, or consequential damages arising out of the use or inability to use the software. The exclusion of implied warranties is not permitted in some states. Therefore, the above exclusion may not apply to you. This warranty provides you with specific legal rights. There may be other rights that you may have that vary from state to state. The contents of this CD-ROM are intended for noncommercial use only.

More information and updates are available at:
http://www.aw.com/cseng/titles/0-201-72956-3